D1527260

Romance's Rival

Romance's Rival

Familiar Marriage in Victorian Fiction

TALIA SCHAFFER

OXFORD
UNIVERSITY PRESS

OXFORD
UNIVERSITY PRESS

Oxford University Press is a department of the University of Oxford. It furthers the University's objective of excellence in research, scholarship, and education by publishing worldwide. Oxford is a registered trade mark of Oxford University Press in the UK and in certain other countries.

Published in the United States of America by Oxford University Press
198 Madison Avenue, New York, NY 10016, United States of America.

Library of Congress Cataloging-in-Publication Data
Schaffer, Talia, 1968–
Romance's rival : familiar marriage in Victorian fiction / Talia Schaffer.
pages cm
Includes bibliographical references and index.
ISBN 978–0–19–046509–4 (cloth : alk. paper) — ISBN 978–0–19–046510–0 (ebook (updf))
1. English fiction—19th century—History and criticism. 2. Marriage in literature. 3. Courtship in literature. 4. Love in literature. 5. Domestic fiction, English—History and criticism. I. Title. II. Title: Familiar marriage in Victorian fiction. III. Title: Marriage in Victorian fiction.
PR878.M36S33 2016
823′.8093543—dc23
2015024576

3 5 7 9 8 6 4 2
Printed by Sheridan, USA

To the Musser family, with love and appreciation

Contents

Preface

ROMANCE'S RIVAL BEGAN when I started noticing a pattern in the marriage plot that was so endemic, so widespread, that I only saw it when I encountered a novel in which it had disappeared. In Charlotte M. Yonge's *The Clever Woman of the Family*, I was flummoxed by the wedding scene of Ermine and Colin. The climax of their decades-long love is to sit side by side, in wordless bliss, in a room that is a replica of Ermine's childhood parlor. An infantile regression, an asexual merger, a religious experience—it was all those things, but the one thing it was not was erotically charged. How was I to understand a form of love that paid no attention whatsoever to desire?

I might have ascribed this asexuality to some particular strangeness in *Clever Woman*, but the pattern persisted in all the Yonge novels I read. Proposals were filtered through family members. Young couples insisted on living with elderly relatives. Characters fell in love with people who were severely disabled. In short, marriages seemed designed to consolidate familial structures, not to satisfy desire. Perhaps the problem was in Yonge, who was a lifelong spinster; perhaps she simply did not know about sex, or was especially maladroit in writing about it. Yet that seemed a nastily condescending judgment to make regarding an author who was so observant regarding other aspects of love—suffering, same-sex desire, self-development, self-suppression. Suppose Yonge did know about desire and simply didn't see it as important, I wondered. How might we read her relationships then? How might we understand marriage without desire?

As I continued reading, I realized that we might understand it very well already. To read the nondesiring marriage did not require immersion in the work of a marginalized writer like Yonge, I began to understand, but in fact simply demanded a different sort of attention to the major texts of the tradition. The pattern I had first noticed in Yonge in fact pervaded Austen, the Brontës, Eliot, Dickens, and Trollope. Once I started looking for it, I found it everywhere. The nondesiring relationship pervades nineteenth-century fiction. Of course, the desiring relationship does too. Indeed, I began to see a pattern in which a

Yongian non-erotic lover and a romantic suitor vied for the hand of the heroine. She had to choose between a dangerous erotic man and a man who embodied the virtues I had first noticed in Yonge's novel: security, kindness, safety, care.

As I sorted the familiar lover into various subgenres and began researching them—and above all, as I began to read up on the history of marriage—I realized there was more here than just a narrative pattern; there was an alternative view of love. And this idea of love was based in profoundly different notions of subjectivity than the romantic narrative we had taken for granted. It foregrounded relationships, not individuality; security, not sexuality; communities, not couples.

Our normal idea of marriage was, to the Victorians, a radical irruption. Their normal idea of marriage is, to us, almost unrecognizable. We can only see it through scrims of later constructions, of repudiations and rewritings and rejections. Part of the story of this model of marriage is its history of sinking while modern ideas rose to the surface. The nineteenth century was a long rivalry between competing notions of human identity. The individualist model won the war, but particular battles often went to the relational side, and these battles are novels. In the imagined world of the Victorian marriage plot, this fight could be staged between competing figures embodying different sides, resolved symbolically through the choice of whom to marry. The novel is not the only place we can see the romantic-familiar rivalry, but it is certainly one of the clearest, and one of the most influential.

I came to the marriage plot from a history of writing about what may seem a very different topic: Victorian women's artistic production. Indeed, I was thrilled to work on canonical texts and major movements and to have a wealth of intelligent criticism, biography, and theory to help me after years of trying to dig up any information at all on virtually unknown subjects. Yet in spite of the apparent differences, I soon found, somewhat to my amusement, that *Romance's Rival* was pretty much replicating the structure of my earlier work. My previous book, *Novel Craft*, recuperated an alternative world of aesthetics; this book excavates an alternative world of marriage. In both cases, I take something that was central to Victorian thought (objects, marriage plot) and show that Victorians conceptualized them as multiple, complex possibilities, with the dominant model that we take for granted actually in dialogue with another, older one.

The familiar-marriage plot almost uncannily echoes the amateur domestic handicraft in its trajectory: emerging into popularity around Austen's time, hitting its peak from the 1840s through the 1870s, and then becoming a locus of nostalgic, dissatisfied yearning among more conservative women as the mainstream ideas moved on, and reworked (with more or less success) to try to make it applicable to a more modern framework. Familiar marriage, like amateur domestic handicrafts, carries petrified, fragmented elements of earlier ideas.

Whether this is the typical trajectory for residual ideologies in the nineteenth century, whether it is characteristic of women's culture in particular, or whether it is an artifact of the way I think historically, I do not know. Certainly one thing I have learned through these two books is that what I enjoy doing, and what I specialize in most, is tracking the faint scent of alternative ideologies—residual, oppositional, subversive, or conservative alternatives to the mainstream ways of thought—through the thicket of apparent normativity. But I hope the convergence of these two projects makes a case for a generous attention to the unfashionable, the old, and the outmoded as nonetheless important parts of women's culture in the period. If there is one lesson I learned from both *Novel Craft* and *Romance's Rival*, it is this: the fact that a way of thinking ultimately became unpopular does not make it unimportant.

I ended *Novel Craft* with an epilogue testifying to the continued survival of amateur domestic handicrafts in modern life, and I drafted several versions of a similar epilogue for *Romance's Rival*. After all, the familiar lover, like amateur craft, is still very much around. As I've worked on this project, I've talked to people who have noticed familiar marriage elements in their own lives. Someone mentions a relation who joined a religious organization, choosing an affiliative social network, cemented by a marriage arranged with a spiritually matched individual within the group. Students of mine from China and India recognize the familiar-marriage pattern as the dominant expectation for their own lives. In romantic comedies, a Meg Ryan type often has to choose between a risky romantic suitor, perhaps an actor from Los Angeles who roars up in shades and a red convertible, versus the hometown boy who works at the local garage. Some of the most popular films of the last few decades, from *Bridget Jones's Diary* to *Clueless* to *Frozen*, position a rakish, handsome, dangerous man against the klutzy, decent, kind man at home, the family favorite, whom the heroine overlooks until it is almost too late.

Today the familiar marriage survives as a fantasy about escaping a single life that seems brutal, dangerous, or frightening. But the familiar-marriage cultural fantasies I mentioned above have an important difference from their Victorian originals. Today the rom-com heroine is supposed to feel romantic love for her hometown hero; she is not supposed to "settle" for the emotion that familiar marriage celebrates as the truth of marriage. That meaning is gone. And it is gone, in large part, because of an immeasurable historical advance: today women have a hope of establishing security, perpetuating social and familial relationships, and continuing to do meaningful work, without having to shoehorn these needs into their marital choices. Thankfully, marriage is no longer compulsory, and certainly no longer determinative of everything else. But if familiar marriage emerged because of a fear of romantic marriage, something like it is still needed, an alternative to a high-pressure world of hook-ups, speed dating, objectification, snap judgments, breakups, harassment, and rape culture. A fantasy (and certainly a reality) of loving, egalitarian, socially expansive, and mutually supportive relationships is needed now as much as ever.

Modernity is not all modern. Shards of the past, survivals that have morphed and altered, are embedded in our lives because they serve needs that we still have. I hope with this consideration of familiar marriage to encourage us not only to rethink nineteenth-century fiction's marital expectations but also to recognize how complicated our own ideas of love are today. Through a sympathetic recovery of a different set of values, perhaps we can understand our own culture's deficits, our own culture's dangers. Instead of an epilogue, then, I give this to the reader in the form of a preface: a beginning, not an ending.

Acknowledgments

WRITING THIS BOOK required me to learn a great deal about a lot of fields, and I want to start by thanking everyone who patiently tried to teach me. Many years ago, Martha Stoddard Holmes sat down with me and told me the names of all the disability theorists I should read. Thanks to Kathy Psomiades for a long and helpful phone conversation about Victorian anthropology, and Lauren Goodlad, whose exuberantly generous e-mails helped me to whatever understanding of liberalism I now possess, with substantive further help from Anna Neill and Irene Tucker. I also ransacked my colleagues' expertise; I got guidance on medieval marriage from Glenn Burger and reading advice on early modern marriage from Mario DiGangi, Rich McCoy, Will Fisher, and Tanya Pollard. Needless to say, I have managed to mess up all these fields all by myself, but it wasn't for lack of trying from these eminent scholars. I'm grateful to Deidre Lynch for recommending eighteenth-century women writers to read, listening to my enthusiasm after I'd read them, and being generally an ideal sounding board for whatever crazy idea I had that week. Charlotte Mitchell and George Haggerty were kind enough to send me their unpublished writing on Yonge and Austen, respectively.

More than anything else, my Victorian working group in New York has guided this project from the start. Great gratitude goes out to Tanya Agathocleous, Caroline Reitz, Tim Alborn, Deborah Lutz, Carolyn Berman, and Adrienne Munich, for their personal support, their bracing critiques, and their immense erudition—I am much richer for their friendships, and this project is much richer for their knowledge of cosmopolitanism, colonialism, the Creole, the history of evangelicism, the history of love, Victorian economics and social structures, and Romantic seducers.

When I left New York in 2014–2015 for a year in Cambridge, I was lucky enough to go from one brilliant and sustaining Victorianist community to another. I thank Leah Price for getting me access to Widener Library (among her many other acts of friendship), Deidre for being there with me, and Martha Vicinus for including me in her whip-smart reading group. I had wonderful conversations with Laura Green, Kelly Hager, Anna Henchman, Aeron Hunt, Maia McAleavey, and John Plotz. Between those years, I enjoyed the summer of 2014 at Dickens Universe, where Catherine Robson, Prithi Joshi, George Levine, Sharon Aronofsky Weltman, Susan Zieger, John Bowen, and Helena Michie spent time with me discussing the familiar marriage plot. From New York to Cambridge and Santa Cruz, I had the best interlocutors imaginable. Their conversations clarified, challenged, and celebrated this work.

I've been extremely lucky to have benefited from the kind, energetic scholars in my field. I've mentioned many of them already, but the other people who make me love being a Victorianist include Susan Bernstein, Karen Bourrier, Mary Jean Corbett, Eleanor Courtemanche, Dennis Denisoff, Kate Flint, Elaine Freedgood, Pamela Gilbert, Jonathan Grossman, Nancy Henry, Sharon Marcus, Diana Maltz, Meredith Martin, Elsie Michie, Sally Mitchell, Deborah Denenholz Morse, Catherine Robson, Pamela Thurschwell, Rachel Teukolsky, Tamara Silvia Wagner, and Susan Zieger.

The earliest version of this project was delivered to the Australasian Victorian Studies Association conference in Singapore in 2010. The following year, I spoke at Berkeley, where we had a lively discussion of the persistence of familiar marriage in Meg Ryan's *oeuvre*. I thank British Women Writers, for whom a keynote talk in 2014 gave me the opportunity to put together a narrative of the project as a whole. While I have given talks on every aspect of this book over the past five years, I am particularly grateful for the exceptionally heartening receptions I received at INCS in 2013 and Dickens Universe in 2014. I take the opportunity to thank all these generous listeners.

My colleagues at home also made this book possible. At Queens College, I am grateful above all for Nicole Cooley, my closest friend and my parenting ally, the one person who can sympathize energetically with all sides of my life. Our younger cohort—Seo-Young Chu, Annmarie Drury, Gloria Fisk, Miles Grier, Caroline Hong, Natalie Léger, Bill Orchard, Siân Silyn Roberts, Jason Tougaw, Andrea Walkden, Amy Wan, and Karen Weingarten—are people interested in many of the same things I am, but with a lot more practical knowledge than I have, as well as more youth and energy. It is an honor getting to share a department with you. Special thanks to Glenn Burger for being the world's greatest chair. At the Graduate Center, I have to thank Tanya Agathocleous, Rachel Brownstein, Mario DiGangi, Carrie Hintz, Anne Humpherys, Gerhard Joseph, Richard Kaye, Caroline Reitz, and Nancy Yousef in particular for being such incisive, brilliant, generous, and delightful colleagues. Let me also give a shout-out to my tireless research assistants, Laura Eldridge, Lauren Bailey, and Elissa Myers. Others who have been my advisees include Mia Chen, Christine Choi, Colleen Cusick, Julie Fuller, Aaron Ho, Meechal Hoffman, Miciah Hussey,

Taylor Kennamer, Lindsay Lehman, Rose O'Malley, Jon Rachmani, Zach Samalin, Erin Spampinato, Anastasia Valassis, and Livia Woods. These people are not only superb scholars but also inspirationally supportive, generous, and energetic mentors of one another; it has been a pleasure to see that the field will be in such good hands.

Brendan O'Neill has been the savviest editor a person could want. I'm very grateful to my extremely generous manuscript readers, particularly Mary Jean Corbett, and to Oxford University Press's production manager Molly Morrison, copyeditor Heather Hambleton, and marketing manager Jenny Catchings for their hard work. Material from Chapter 6 appeared in *Victorians Journal of Literature and Culture* (Fall 2015), edited by Deborah Logan and Deborah Denenholz Morse. A section of Chapter 4 appeared in *Queer Victorian Families: Strange Relations in Literature*, edited by Duc Dau and Shale Preston. Material from Chapter 1 also appeared in the introduction I co-wrote with Kelly Hager to our co-edited journal issue, "Extending Families," in *Victorian Review* 39, no. 2 (2013), while a very early version of some of Chapter 1 was published in the *Australasian Journal of Victorian Studies* 15, no. 2 (2010). I appreciate the editors' permission to republish these pieces.

I want to end with more personal thanks. I've loved my friends' caustic humor and feminist fervor in the cause of co-parenting preteens/teens. Thank you, Nicole, LoriJeane Moody, Jane Marcus, Marissa Rothkopf Bates, and Sally Jacobs. Thank you, too, to all the teachers and parents in the Glen Ridge community who let us know we were missed during our year away and welcomed us home when we returned. Thanks also to our equally beloved friends in Cambridge: Reb Pearl, Justin Martinez, Vega and her little brother, Michel DeGraff, Elena, and Nuriel. Tamy Wagner, Ka-Hin, and Amy made all the difference to us in Singapore.

Judy Musser and Eva Szekely; Bret and Eileen Musser; and Aidan, Katherine, and Kieran Musser have anchored us with many a good meal, good conversations, and good times; how great it is when your in-laws are also the people you would choose as your friends. It seems eminently fitting for a book on families and marriage to be dedicated to my family-by-marriage, who have embraced me wholeheartedly from the moment they met me. As for my endlessly supportive parents, Ann and Ben Schaffer, my brilliant and delightful brother, Jonathan Schaffer, and my marvelous nephew, Ezra, I send all my love.

I started this book when Eliana Salka Musser was a cheery, gap-toothed first-grader; I finish it now as she is a confident, poised, generous, kind, and still largely cheery pre-teen. I am so proud of her growth into the kind of person we all want to become.

If you want a great editor, it helps to marry one. George Musser has made every word of this book better, both through his invigorating suggestions and through his modeling of what a marriage can provide. Through the decades we've shared, he has been unfailingly loving, sensitive, supportive, smart, and fun. In working on the tortured versions of marriage dreamed up by my Victorian subjects, I often stopped to think how lucky I am. These fictional figures had to make agonizing choices between meaningful work, rich familial and social lives, and love. But I got it all.

Romance's Rival

I

Theorizing Victorian Marriage

There are different kinds of love, Ferdinand. There is that which a woman gives to a man when she would fain mate with him. It is the sweetest love of all, if it would only last. And there is another love,—which is not given, but which is won, perhaps through long years, by old friends.

ANTHONY TROLLOPE, The Prime Minister

I have a woman's heart, but not where you are concerned; for you I have only a comrade's constancy: a fellow-soldier's frankness, fidelity, fraternity if you like; a neophyte's respect and submission to his hierophant.

CHARLOTTE BRONTË, Jane Eyre

IN *JANE EYRE* (1847), Jane hears a particularly memorable proposal from her cousin St. John Rivers:

> God and nature intended you for a missionary's wife. It is not personal, but mental endowments they have given you: you are formed for labour, not for love. A missionary's wife you must—shall be. You shall be mine: I claim you—not for my pleasure, but for my Sovereign's service.[1]

As we might expect, St. John's "claim" repels Jane. The cousins do agree that they feel familial affection for one another. However, for Jane, this sibling relation means they ought not to wed. "You have hitherto been my adopted brother—I, your adopted sister: let us continue as such: you and I had better not marry," she warns (430). For St. John, however, their adoptive fraternity necessitates marriage. "We *must* be married—I repeat it: there is no other way; and undoubtedly enough of love would follow upon marriage to render the union right even in your eyes" (433). Jane tries to explain that she does not harbor romantic love for St. John. Rather, she feels what she calls "a comrade's constancy: a fellow-soldier's frankness, fidelity, fraternity if you like; a neophyte's respect and submission to his hierophant." Unfortunately, the emotions Jane has listed are exactly what her cousin was hoping for. "'It is what I want,' he said, speaking to himself; 'it is just what I want'"(433). In that exchange, the words that Jane thinks rule out marriage are precisely the terms that St. John is hoping for.

In the clash between Jane's expectations and St. John's assumptions, we find the expression of a major problem in Victorian ideas of marriage. What Jane expects is a declaration of romantic love, which was becoming the dominant rationale for marriage in the nineteenth century, and she is startled and dismayed by St. John's inauthentic performance of such passion. Thus, she says, "I scorn your idea of love . . . I scorn the counterfeit sentiment you offer: yes, St. John, and I scorn you when you offer it" (433).

But in this book, I want to propose that St. John is not offering a counterfeit sentiment. Rather, he is offering a sentiment in a different currency—a currency whose value seemed sterling to many of *Jane Eyre*'s original readers. In the nineteenth century, another version of marriage coexisted with the newly popular notion of romantic marriage. St. John is offering Jane what I call "familiar marriage," and this introductory chapter will explain what familiar marriage was and why it emerged as a crucial literary structure in the Victorian novel, using *Jane Eyre* as the primary example.

Defining Familiar Marriage

Familiar marriage is a Victorian literary convention that developed out of the eighteenth-century ideal of marrying from rational esteem rather than romantic love. Historians often call this "companionate marriage." In the words of A. C. Grayling, "Companionate love does not exclude sexual love, but its premises and aims are very different. It is about the shared project of what is in effect a small business—which is what a home, a household, is—purchasing and budgeting and managing other (usually small) people, and transporting and storing things, saving and spending, and dealing with problems, like illnesses and burst pipes."[2] Grayling's emphasis on a lifetime of management indicates the way the relationship functions as an ongoing negotiation. Thus this kind of marriage takes a chronologically long view, drawing on a past of intimate knowledge ("people who have known each other for a long time") while expecting an extended future of continued emotional development ("it may well develop after marriage"). St. John assures Jane that "undoubtedly enough of love would follow upon marriage to render the union right even in your eyes" (433). What familiar marriage overlooks is the present: it is not particularly interested in the immediate difficulties of two people without romantic love, or even necessarily attraction to one another, suddenly forced to live in the most intimate proximity. Rather, such a marriage stresses trust, comradeship, practical needs, and larger social organization: in Jane's words once again, "a comrade's constancy: a fellow-soldier's frankness, fidelity, fraternity if you like; a neophyte's respect and submission to his hierophant" (433).

The familiar marriage was not exactly the same as the eighteenth-century marriage of rational esteem. It was not a fossil from a past era, but rather a descendant that underwent multiple mutations, responding to the particular pressures of its specifically Victorian environment. For instance, the earlier belief that love would develop after the wedding became unpopular in the Victorian era; familiar marriage needed to be based on some kind of existing affection, not merely esteem. Another alteration concerned the rising status of disability. Largely absent from the eighteenth-century marriage plot (with the exception of *Camilla*), disabled bodies came to occupy a crucial function in nineteenth-century fiction. Moreover, starting in the 1860s, the familiar marriage took on a vocational drive with which it had never been associated in previous centuries, and although marriage to landed gentry had been a popular plot in eighteenth-century fiction, the Victorian version altered the meaning of this kind of squire marriage to express yearnings for organic community and domestic influence. Familiar marriage thus morphed to answer social problems of the period, to provide participants with certain kinds of life choices that the romantic marriage failed to offer.

Moreover, the familiar suitor is a literary device, a stock character, defined according to narrative needs rather than historical verisimilitude. I am not saying it was wholly imaginary—certainly there were plenty of cousin marriages in Victorian Britain, for instance—but rather I want to remind readers that what this book discusses is a fictional structure characterizing novels rather than the lived experience of real individuals. Reading familiar marriage as a literary device in no way renders it less important. It may even be more significant if we regard it as a narrative strategy generated by some way in which the romantic marriage plot failed. Real marriage and its motives vary widely, and historians of the family have disagreed even about its most basic elements.[3] But in the neater case study of the novel, in which marriage is a symbolic resolution to a cultural problem, it is particularly interesting if what modern readers assume to be the ideal solution—marriage for passionate love—seems like a poor choice. If romantic marriage did all it was supposed to do, fiction would not have needed the familiar marriage plot. What, we might ask, were the fears for which this plot had to compensate? Why did Victorians need a different form of marriage? Familiar marriage shines a spotlight onto romantic marriage, revealing its shadows and dark spaces, the gaps that familiar marriage stretched to fill.

The familiar suitor, as the name implies, was someone familiar. Often he was a reliable neighbor, a community fixture to whom a woman could cling as her own household disintegrated. Jane expresses this kind of relief when she leaves her period of desperate homelessness for a stable berth at Moor House. Although she does not get there through marriage, her residence is structurally similar; like any Victorian newlywed wife, she brings in money, redecorates, and cohabits. Often the familiar suitor was a cousin, sometimes a foster sibling. Marrying him reinforced kin ties and strengthened the whole extended family. Jane meets her cousins only as adults, but enjoys this familiar sense of fitness immediately, "the pleasure arising from perfect congeniality of tastes, sentiments, and principles" (376). Sometimes, the woman had no meaningful consanguineal ties, like Jane before she finds her cousins. In this case, novelists could conjure up a new social network by affiliating the orphaned heroine to a disabled man, someone who would necessarily be surrounded by nurses, servants, siblings, parents, and caretakers. Finally, the familiar suitor offered a marriage that gave the woman meaningful work, whether in managing an estate, caring for his disabled body (as in Rochester's case), or assisting with his own career (as in St. John's case), orienting her away from the private conjugal dyad toward a larger public of parishioners, clients, employees, and customers. In novels, these roles frequently overlap; the local squire might be a relation, the disabled suitor offers the woman caretaking work, the person offering meaningful work may be a cousin. However, in this book, I have separated them for analytical convenience, to demonstrate as clearly as possible how each marital structure works and just what aspects it satisfies of the familiar marriage's need for sociality, security, and stability.

In *Jane Eyre*, a bad familiar marriage initially offered to Jane via St. John gets replaced by a better familiar marriage through Rochester's disability. This pattern is not uncommon in nineteenth-century fiction. In *Pride and Prejudice*, Mr. Collins initially offers an undesirable familiar marriage, and he is replaced by a reformed Darcy. In *Our Mutual Friend*, Bradley Headstone is a problematic familiar suitor who must be ejected in favor of a humbled Eugene Wrayburn. The first familiar suitor offers to satisfy a need—Jane Eyre needs an occupation, Lizzie Bennet needs financial stability, Lizzie Hexam needs a safe haven. And although the initial suitor is not suitable himself, he functions to make those needs visible in the novel, until the rival suitor can evolve in such a way as to satisfy that requirement.

The name "familiar" works, I hope, in multiple registers. With its echo of "familial," it reminds us how very often this kind of suitor is a member of the family. With its stress on familiarity, however, it also tells us close knowledge of another is more crucial than biological kin ties. "Familiar" also toggles between a sense of excessively intimate closeness (as in the usage "he was too familiar with her") and pleasurable, casual comfort ("the familiar friends sat together"), capturing, I think, the uneasy way familiar relationships teeter between reassuringly well-known situations and creepily sexualized recastings of existing relations.

In fiction, the familiar suitor's main problem is that he tends to be rather boring. He is often significantly older (John Jarndyce, Colonel Brandon, Mr. Casaubon) or so well known that the woman takes him for granted (Tom Marjoribanks, Johnny Eames, Mr. Knightley). Erotic attraction is not usually one of the benefits of familiar wooing. The familiar lover might well be desirable, but that is not the reason to wed him; it may be a lucky additional point, but not a requirement for the union.

This local worthy generally competes against a romantic stranger. He is a man like Rochester, a mysterious, exciting, potentially threatening lover, who offers the frisson of the unknown and the charisma of sexual adventure. "Romantic passion (or romantic love or infatuation) is defined as any intense attraction involving the idealization of the other within an erotic context," writes William Jankowiak.[4] Often the woman is smitten with him at first glance. He will sweep her away to remote and exciting regions. As Rochester vows, "I shall bear my treasure to regions nearer the sun: to French vineyards and Italian plains; and she shall see whatever is famous in old story and in modern record" (288). He frequently promises a life of leisure in which the couple can enjoy mutual bliss. Deborah Lutz has outlined this figure in *The Dangerous Lover*, describing how the demonic, dark, melancholy, outcast wanderer figure moves from Jacobean tragedy through Gothic tales to contemporary romantic novels.[5] In her analysis of the "dangerous lover," Lutz isolates several characteristics that we can usefully contrast with alternative qualities in his rival, the familiar lover.

First, we might note that the two lovers occupy different chronotopes, to use the Bakhtinian formulation for a dynamic in which time and space organize the narrative events.[6] Time and space, quite simply, work differently in romance than in familiar marriage. The romantic marriage lives in the present moment, collapsing past and future into one intense, immediate contact, devouring time as Marvell recommended in "To His Coy Mistress." Lutz explains: "The insatiable quality of the romantic temporality exposes the romance's addiction to the other. Addiction races through time, finding only the present of importance and eating through it feverishly. Addicted to each other, the lovers must hurry; they must do it all *right now*."[7] Rushing together, frantically maximizing their time, the lovers focus on the intense quality of their mutual experience, not its consequences or repercussions. Romeo and Juliet cannot think of the future, so driven are they by their present urge. By contrast, familiar marriage relies on a shared past and anticipates a long future. It imagines love developing after marriage and it justifies itself by reference to benefits to come: familial advantage, political alliance, property additions. For familiar marriage, the now is immaterial or actually inconvenient, as the familiar lover's rather unexciting immediate presentation must be surmounted through long-term recognition of the man's deeper qualities.

Spatially speaking, quite often the romantic suitor is associated with mobility, first seen (or seen in important scenes) in passing—on horseback; striding down the street; or moving swiftly through a public arena, a ballroom, a marketplace. Examples include Wickham, strolling down the main street at Meryton; Rochester, galloping into the novel on his black horse, Mesrour; and Heathcliff, carried kicking into the Heights. His mobility underlines his status as a stranger to the woman, his appeal and his danger as a modern rootless individual who may be traveling on to other lovers. For the romantic suitor may intend to seduce and abandon the woman. Willoughby, Wickham, Frank Churchill, George Vavasor, Adolphus Crosbie, Stephen Guest, and Rochester are not trustworthy; the women who choose them may well be headed toward disaster. "The Byronic hero, particularly the Giaour and Childe Harold, roams disenchanted and always astray; he has no place in the domesticity of society," writes Lutz.[8] The outcast wanderer or the mobile modern subject, a Cain or a cosmopolitan, the romantic lover contrasts with a familiar suitor whose characteristic is stasis, as we shall see in Chapter 3.

Since this book explores several varieties of familiar marriage that persist in Victorian fiction, one might well object that there are also many forms of romantic marriage, to which I ought to be equally attentive. It is true that I give the romantic side relatively short shrift here, but that is partly because we have assumed for so long that romantic love was all that existed in the Victorian period, making the form much better understood than its rival model. Anyone who wants to read up on desire in the nineteenth century can enjoy a wealth of sources. I also want to note that in this book I tend to use the terms "romantic," "erotic," and "passionate" love interchangeably, not because I think they are precisely synonymous but because they all point equally well to the sexually motivated adoration I am trying to invoke. I endorse Anthony Giddens's distinction between passionate love as a universal emotion (a disruptive, sexually charged ardor) and romantic love as a culturally specific expression thereof. [9] Giddens's point reminds us of the extent to which the emotions we perceive as most essential are in fact constructed. In Chapter 2, I explore the way romantic love has evolved in British history from the twelfth century onwards, stressing its perhaps surprisingly recent, tenuous, and problematic connection with the married state.

I want my use of the term "romantic" to remind readers of the Romantic movement, one of its major historical influences (as we shall see in Chapter 2), but also to conjure up the archaic sense of "romance" as an imaginary tale. Thus

I hope the name helps remind readers that this literary construct has nothing essential or natural about it—that it was in fact built up as an artificial rhetorical convention—and that the uncritical acceptance of these tenets by popular culture, including Hollywood, has functioned to perpetuate fantasies that have very real consequences. Romantic marriage is a rhetorical construct that insists on love as desire-based, immediate, and guaranteeing a glorious—if vague—future. It has nothing to say about other forms of love, about the way feelings can change over time, about other people in the couple's lives, or about the work involved in any relationship, marital or otherwise.

Victorian marriage plots very often stage a rivalry between a familiar and a romantic suitor, something Jean E. Kennard called "the two-suitor plot." As she points out, "the convention of the two suitors exists in some form in almost every novel with a central female character, particularly if the term *suitor* is used loosely."[10] The familiar-romantic rivalry is not just one of many variants that the marriage plot might take; it is by far the most common form of the marriage plot—so frequent that one cannot do it justice by talking about it as a whole but must break it down into subcategories to begin to get a handle on it. Indeed, it is hard to think of a Victorian novel that did not feature this plot in some way. Romantic suitors—those smolderingly charismatic men, their antecedents unknown, their intentions murky—include Wickham, Willoughby, Frank Churchill, Henry Crawford, Rochester, M. Paul Emanuel, Sir Francis Levison, Stephen Guest, Ladislaw, Grandcourt, and Gilbert Osmond. Opposing them are the familiar suitors, those unthreatening and trusted men who offer safe haven: Knightley, Edward Ferrars, Colonel Brandon, Edmund Bertram, St. John, Dr. Graham Bretton, Philip Wakem, Archibald Carlyle, Casaubon, Daniel Deronda, and Ralph Touchett. This list does not even include Trollope's novels of the 1860s, a phase in which he so insistently repeated the two-suitor plot that one reviewer compared him to an artist who annually paints slightly different versions of the same picture of a donkey between two bales of hay.[11]

This particular romantic-familiar structure, I argue, occurs for both an immediate and a deeper reason. The immediate reason is that Victorian subjects were coping with the repercussions of a major historical shift in the idea of marriage. Marriage historians acknowledge that the meaning of marriage changed drastically around 1800, but this fact has not yet influenced most Victorianists' understanding of the marriage plot. Rather, critics often anachronistically project modern understandings of marital love back onto nineteenth-century subjects. In fact, through most of the Victorian era, the older marital model continued to exert strong influence, while the newer romantic ideal felt disruptively thrilling and frightening. The two-suitor plot, with each suitor embodying a different marital ideal, helped Victorians work through different ways of thinking about a subject's future. Wendy Jones explains: "Exploring the implications of marriage for love became the novel's 'repetition compulsion,' as novel after novel attempted to anticipate and resolve the possibilities and problems associated with this new ethic."[12] The Victorian marriage plot—goaded by the "repetition compulsion" of which Jones speaks—constantly replays the problems of marriage and attempts to imagine alternatives.

The deeper reason this plot became ubiquitous is that romantic marriage assumed, and perpetuated, different foundational categories than familiar marriage. Familiar marriage maintained a notion of the self as serving others' needs in a collective, but romantic marriage saw self as an independent agent maximizing its own pleasure. Familiar marriage panned out to show the panorama of the social world, while romantic marriage zeroed in for a tight focus on the couple. Familiar marriage understood life as duration, but romantic marriage intended intense immediacy. Familiar marriage spoke from tradition, while romantic marriage expressed modernity. Familiar marriage promised settled, stable residence; romantic marriage embraced mobility, relocation. They differed about what love meant, what a partner was for, what married life was supposed to do, how to manage the duration of one's life, and what one's attitude toward family ought to be. Working through the choice between these models, or struggling to adjust, compromise, or alter them, was a way of figuring out how one should be in the world.

These remain fundamentally different states today. Elaine Hatfield explains: "Companionate love is defined as '*the affection we feel for those with whom our lives are deeply entwined.*' Companionate love has been described as involving friendship, understanding, and a concern for the welfare of the other," whereas passionate romantic love is "*a state of intense longing for union with another. Reciprocated love (union with the other) is associated with fulfillment and ecstasy. Unrequited love (separation) with emptiness, anxiety, and despair. A state of profound physiological arousal.*"[13] These were not states that necessarily seem compatible, now or then. Cultures that honor one often reject the other.[14]

In fiction, these two marital ideas competed for over a century. It was not a quick switch but a long negotiation, a vexed rivalry, and it was not at all clear that romantic marriage would win. As Raymond Williams has argued, a dominant culture has to incorporate the residue of the past if it is to function; residual elements can speak to those areas that the dominant culture undervalues.[15] Familiar marriage allows us to see what the newly dominant idea of romantic marriage left out, and which of these elements still felt crucial to Victorians.

This book, then, focuses on the non-romantic marriage in nineteenth-century fiction, giving special attention to four of the main formulations of that idea: neighbor marriage, cousin marriage, disabled marriage, and vocational marriage. I am not claiming that these were the only forms of familiar marriage, merely that these particular types of unions were depicted often enough in Victorian fiction to reward in-depth investigation. In each case, the motive for the marriage was not erotic passion or romantic bliss, but a pragmatic advantage: social empowerment, familial benefit, caretaking networks, or career access. In each case, the feeling the woman had for the partner was a companionable affection rather than a passionate desire, and the marriage was a choice that consolidated a useful future in a social nexus rather than a transformative state of private bliss. Oriented toward a wider world, familiar marriage supported the woman's desire to have a useful life.

In this book, I want to take this option seriously, and to do so, we need to explore why familiar marriage has been overlooked until recently. For too long, literary critics have assumed that all relationships are predicated on desire, so that if a character contracted a marriage without obvious sexual attraction, his or her sexual story must be a hidden, problematic one. Thus familiar marriages have been legible only as sexual perversions: incest in the case of cousin marriage, asexuality or masochism in the case of marriage with a disabled person or older neighbor, frigidly self-interested ambition in the case of vocational marriage. A Freudian-based reading popular in the first half of the twentieth century, perhaps most famously represented by Edmund Wilson's speculation about Emma's sexuality in "A Long Talk about Jane Austen" (1944), gave way to the liberated 1960s and 1970s discussions of whether characters had achieved adequate sexual satisfaction, followed in turn by 1980s and 1990s post-Foucaultian queer theory in which desire was seen as endlessly fascinating, complex, and self-masking.

For the better part of a century, then, critics believed that it was erotic desire that guaranteed the depth that novel readers craved. As Foucault writes, "Whenever it is a question of knowing who we are, it is this logic that henceforth serves as our master key." Interrogating desires, seeking subtle clues to a deeper yearning, parsing the body's responses became the way to know someone's truth, and that underlying drive in turn explained everything else. "Sex, the explanation for everything."[16] Thus critics have tended to ignore other motives that might have explained marital decisions. Or they have viewed such motives as mere covers, feeling it their duty—indeed, their pleasure—to reveal a secret desire as the real factor. Jay Clayton points out: "One might expect some theorists, however, to represent desire in other than sexual terms—as cravings for money, power, knowledge, or God—but narrative theorists almost never stray from the sexual paradigm."[17]

In parsing familiar marriage, however, we need to take an alternative perspective. Familiar marriage was opposed to the deep unconscious desire of the romantic plot. Instead, it was a conscious choice based on rational decision-making, influenced by others' advice, widely endorsed, and requiring little explanation on its face. Instead of the "hermeneutics of depth," parsing this very sensible union might require something more like surface reading or Sharon Marcus's "just reading." One of the ways this project is feminist is the extent to which it respects women's agency in their marriage plots, extending them the courtesy of assuming that they made choices that had reasonable rationales for the kinds of lives they were condemned to live, rather than seeing them as helpless victims of deeper unconscious forces.

Because "familiar" and "romantic" marriage are literary structures, these terms need to be flexible enough to accommodate the variation that a range of texts introduces into the convention. In some novels, romantic marriage tips into the seduction narrative or rape plot, in which a dangerous lover carries off a vulnerable woman for nefarious purposes, a type of plot explored by Ros Ballaster and Katherine Binhammer.[18] In some novels, familiar marriage falls into the mercenary marriage plot, in which people who despise each other come together for cold advantage, a convention that Elsie Michie has analyzed.[19] These are the negative extremes of each paradigm. Although main characters in Victorian fiction rarely endure outright rape or cold-bloodedly greedy marriage, these fates offer enough of a threat to propel the marriage plot away from those extremes.[20] The prospect of marriage with men like Jonas Chuzzlewit or George Vavasor is awful enough to push the character—and the reader—toward greater sympathy with the suitor's rival. Most often, the marriage plot ends up on a middle ground, in which romantic lovers get tamed (Rochester, Eugene Wrayburn, and Romney Leigh) or familiar suitors suddenly start looking sexy (Tom Marjoribanks, Roger Hamley, and Mr. Knightley). These variations form part of authors' attempts to work through the two marital paradigms. In creating and playing out extreme versions of each, they can figure out what goes wrong; in crafting a crossover case, they can explore the extent to which elements that seem incompatible may in fact be made to work together. Authors take what is initially framed as a rivalry and rework it into an alliance or a compromise.

Moreover, the marital models could be tweaked according to a wide variation of bodily or consanguineous credentials, living arrangements, or personal histories. Thus familiar marriage can be invoked if anyone with a longstanding familiarity with the main character—including the codger next door, the child of the old family friend, the adoptive sister, or the best friend's brother—becomes a suitor. Similarly, any health condition that requires care can produce this effect; it need not be outright disability according to the modern sense of the term. Recovery from fever, shipwreck, a stroke, or even persistent gout can have the right effect. Sir Michael Audley, Sir Leicester Dedlock, and even Casaubon all suffer illnesses that restrict them to domestic spaces, invoke tenderness in their spouses, and require their wives to care intimately for their recumbent bodies.

Familiar marriage need not even be, technically, marriage. In many disability narratives, the main couple is not married but enjoys a quasi-marital arrangement that may include long-term cohabitation and intimate caring: Phineas Fletcher and John Halifax, Ralph Touchett and Isabel Archer, Thurstan Benson and Ruth Hilton, and arguably even Jane Eyre and St. John. Precisely because it is not in fact a legal marriage, this partnership may provide an alternative model for marital relations. Just as same-sex unions could model egalitarian partnerships, according to Sharon Marcus in *Between Women*, so too could disabled relationships offer a different vision, freed from the lopsided constraints of coverture. As we shall see, disabled partnerships were particularly useful models for same-sex couples.

In many Victorian novels, the man who offers the familiar marriage option is actually a brother. Living with him would provide partnership with a well-known person, often a safer choice than marriage with a stranger. Victorian writers notoriously often patterned marital relationships on sibling ties.[21] However, this connection is not usually intended to make brothers sexual but rather to make courtship brotherly. Valerie Sanders explains:

> Given the ambiguous moral status of any male suitor before he has proposed and made his intentions honourable, the attractions of a brother as "natural protector" are obvious. The brother-as-lover seems a safe alternative to the man who is unrelated to the woman, an unknown quantity, with no common memories and roots. He is above all, morally reliable, and at first, sexually neutral.[22]

Tom Tulliver in *The Mill on the Floss* (1860), Charles Edmonstone in *The Heir of Redclyffe* (1853), and Frederick Lawrence in *The Tenant of Wildfell Hall* (1848) all provide fraternal cohabitation as an alternative to their sisters' marital unions. According to Corbett, affinal bonds "far from being some marked deviation from a nineteenth-century English 'exogamous' norm, themselves constituted a significant norm in their own right."[23]

Indeed, sibling pairings could serve as the ideal model for marriage, as Joseph Allan Boone and Deborah Nord claim: "It is striking how often the apparently chaste, idealized love of *actual* brother and sister is portrayed as being nearly identical to (if not, as in Austen's example [*Mansfield Park*] even more satisfactory than) the 'conjugal tie' of man and wife—taking on, in the process, all the connotations, including that of erotic fulfillment, implicit in wedlock."[24] In their reading, the brother-sister pair comes to provide a model of egalitarian partnership, in which gender difference matters less than familiarity, affection, and resemblance.[25] As we shall see, both Edmund Bertram and Henry Crawford envy Fanny's love for her brother and fantasize about Fanny regarding them with similar warmth. In *North and South,* Thornton's momentary glimpse of Margaret and Frederick Hale's affectionate, trusting clasp teaches him what he should want in marriage. Because Thornton mistakenly sees the siblings as lovers, he can imagine himself in Frederick's place, receiving Margaret's confiding gaze. Similarly, Helen's and her brother's amity enrages Gilbert, but also provides a crucial countermodel to the disproportionate power relation of his parents' marriage. Both cases demonstrate how a potentially tyrannical husband can learn an alternative mode of partnership from witnessing sibling couples.

It is tempting to claim that canonical fiction enshrines romantic marriage, while the lower status of noncanonical fiction is at least partly due to its affinity for familiar marriages, a type of union that is now harder for us to read sympathetically. There is some truth to this hypothesis. Certainly, the unsentimental marriages of Oliphant's novels and the consanguineous unions in Yonge's works may have baffled later readers. Their depictions of familiar marriage may have been read only as ludicrously noncredible attempts to depict romantic marriage. However, it would be incorrect to take this generalization too far. In fact, noncanonical and canonical fiction alike manifest a wide range of marital fates. Ouida's dashing popular fiction is wholly invested in romantic marriage, but Mary Elizabeth Braddon's sensation novels, interestingly, tend toward familiar marriages.[26] In *Sense and Sensibility, Mansfield Park, Miss Marjoribanks, Phoebe Junior, The Tenant of Wildfell Hall, David Copperfield, Pendennis, Aurora Floyd,* and *Can You Forgive Her,* the main character eventually settles down with the safe suitor, growing past the immature and damaging choice of a charismatic lover. However, familiar marriage sometimes fails. In *Bleak House* Esther does not marry her foster father; in *Great Expectations* Pip will not wed Biddy. Sometimes, as we have seen, the author works to make the models converge, taming the romantic adventurer or giving the familiar suitor a makeover. The point is that authors were working through fears about marriage, and that no culturally agreed-upon solution presented itself, as we can see both from the wide range of fictive answers to the question, and from the need to continue reworking the problem in so many Victorian novels.

However, we might ask how our critical judgment has been unconsciously shaped by our own expectations, living as we do in an era when romantic marriage is normative. Modern readers tend to assume romantic unions are pleasurable. Jane ingenuously remarks, "It seemed to me that, were I a gentleman like him, I would take to my bosom only such a wife as I could love; but the very obviousness of the advantages to the husband's own happiness offered by this plan convinced me that there must be arguments against its general adoption of which I was quite ignorant: otherwise I felt sure all the world would act as I wished to act" (216–217). We have a harder time understanding why someone would want a familiar union. After the century of Freud and Foucault, we have to ask: why would women choose a marriage in which sex didn't matter? In other words, what advantages do these other forms (family unions, disabled marriage, vocational marriage) offer that outweigh romantic marriage? What might once have felt *better* than romantic love?

Answering that question requires us to enter the mentality of another era, one in which women had no guaranteed economic agency, legal status, or political representation; one in which women might be entirely at the mercy of someone else in terms of where they lived and with whom they associated; and one in which women had very little capacity to ensure that they could look forward to meaningful work. This radical disempowerment extended across class lines. From the factory worker to the titled aristocrat, nineteenth-century women had dismayingly little capacity to determine their own futures. As Florence Nightingale pointed out in "Cassandra," "women think about marriage much more than men do; it is the only event of their lives. It ought to be a sacred event, but surely not the only event of a woman's life, as it is now."[27] As the sole event of a woman's life, marriage was the portal to all future emotional and professional fulfillment. Joseph Allan Boone explains:

> Because in female variations of the form the climactic event of marriage confers on the heroine her entire personal identity (as wife) as well as her social "vocation" (as mother), the growth of the female protagonist has come to be seen as synonymous with the action of courtship: until very recently the only female bildungsroman has been a love-plot.[28]

However, the very fact that marriage was a woman's only career meant that it might not necessarily be based on heterosexual desire. It could, instead, express community feeling, consanguineal loyalty, social yearnings, or vocational aspirations. Our excessive focus on desire has obscured the extent to which female characters were able to make strategic decisions about their lives through the agency of marriage. Once women could perform these functions outside of marriage, their lives were (obviously) better, but the institution of marriage itself became far more limited.

Thus through much of the nineteenth century, marriage was not necessarily an act of seeking a new, positive pleasure, but rather of guaranteeing, as much as possible, the minimally necessary conditions for a decent life. Romantic marriage is the luxury afforded to women who could earn their own money and decide on their own futures. It gradually grew in popularity throughout the nineteenth century, as women's situations slowly improved. But familiar marriage is the rearguard action of women who were allowed only one major decision in life—that of whom to marry—a decision that would determine all the rest.

It is partly for this reason that *Romance's Rival* focuses on women choosing between male suitors rather than giving equal time to male and female marriage plots. The marriage plot, I argue, was largely driven by women's desperate need to make a viable life for themselves—a need that men could fulfill outside the married state in a way that was precluded for middle-class women.

This is the somber take on familiar marriage, seen retroactively from a modern point of view in which we are used to women having more choices and we find it sad to see them all crammed into the single act of marriage. But if we read from a nineteenth-century perspective, in which women's disempowerment is already a given, familiar marriage looks much happier. For familiar marriage gave women opportunities to guarantee certain aspects of their lives overlooked or even negated by the romantic marriage plot. Familiar marriage acknowledged the continuing importance of kin, for instance, allowing women to contract a marriage that permitted them to live among their extended families. Familiar marriage confirmed that women had practical skills and imagined a work life in which those skills—running a parish, copying manuscripts, teaching children, caring for the infirm—would be useful. It might be said that familiar marriage was healthier in that it saw the woman as a full person in interaction with a varied world over the course of a lifetime, with many of her "familiars," whereas romantic marriage reduced her to an intensely desiring subject in a blissful moment of encounter, a fantasy world: a "romance" in every sense.

The marriage plot is a middle- and upper-class women's plot, by and large, although there is a wide variation within that class, ranging from Jane Eyre's desperately impoverished, barely genteel status to the fabulous wealth of Glencora Palliser. In narratives with characters of the Duke and Duchess of Omnium's rank—aristocracy or even royalty—marriage is constrained by dynastic and property considerations, but there are comparatively few such stories in the Victorian *oeuvre*. Similarly, novels about marriage at the other class extreme, among the working poor, are often inflected by middle-class authors' unconscious assumptions about their subjects' marital aims. In neither case would nineteenth-century fiction be a reliable guide to real marital thought.[29] Historically speaking, working people were often freer to marry for love than their wealthier brethren, since they had no major property whose preservation or transmission was at stake, but their need for pragmatic unions might have been more immediate, since economic survival might have depended on having someone else to help run the shop, till the fields, or care for the ill. As I argue in Chapter 2, romantic love is itself a middle-class construct, and so it is not surprising that in classes above and below the middle, pragmatic marriage arrangements were more common and lasted longer.[30]

It may seem that the heterosexual normativity of a book on marriage goes without saying, but in fact this is one place where attention to the familiar marriage model can change our assumptions. When marriage can be contracted for practical reasons—caring for those in need, running a business, consolidating property—it need not say anything about its participants' desires. In that respect, familiar marriage could well cover (and permit) a range of feeling among its participants beyond a conventional heteronormative orientation. One could achieve proximity to one's real object of desire by marrying his or her relation. Since Eve Sedgwick's *Between Men*, critics have recognized the homoerotic dynamic in which a man marries the sister of the man he wants, but we have a comparable situation among women in a novel like *The History of Sir Richard Calmady*, where a woman marries in order to gain access to her aunt, setting up a quite explicit same-sex female partnership. As we shall see in Chapter 5, disability marriages are particularly liberating in permitting a wide range of partner identities, allowing unconventional people to take on the roles of spouse, parent, or partner.

It is actually romantic marriage that creates the heteronormative assumption. When the only reason for marriage is that one feels love for another person, then that feeling gets intensively policed. Desire must not be too sexual nor too asexual; not exercised within the family but not expended on total strangers; limited to (ideally) one recipient; directed toward an individual of the other gender of the socially approved age, class, and bodily configuration; and returned by the object of one's affections. Ironically, the advent of romantic marriage was not necessarily liberatory at all.

This book addresses the life cycle of the marriage plot novel in Britain from Richardson in the 1740s to Forster in 1910, but it focuses primarily on texts written in the period from the 1850s to the 1870s. Because the marriage plot is intimately enmeshed with particular cultural traditions and legal and political developments, it must be read as a national story and cannot be extended to, say, France or America, which had their own marital histories.[31] In this book I have focused on mid-Victorian Britain, a period of activism that included the Matrimonial Causes Act of 1857 and the Married Women's Property Act of 1870. During this time there was intense public discussion of women's lack of autonomy in marriage and women's vulnerability to exploitative husbands.[32] It is also the period in which two major discourses regarding marriage emerged, the anthropological theory of primitive marriage I discuss in Chapter 4 and the Langham Place feminist rhetoric I address in Chapter 6. In legal, scholarly, and political registers, then, the 1850s to the 1870s marked a period of ferment about what marriage ought to mean, where marriage came from, whether marriage was good for men and women, and how the marriage state ought to be reformed. It is no wonder that novels written during this period canvass these issues with particularly intense interest.

The final note I want to make about the terms in which this book operates has to do with race and colonial reality in Victorian Britain. While few nineteenth-century marriage plots include suitors of explicitly different races, those that do frequently converge on the West Indies and the issue of slavery. The marriage plot of the West Indies requires a little discussion here, since it does not have its own chapter. One of the earliest examples is Maria Edgeworth's *Belinda*, in which Belinda's suitor Mr. Vincent and his servant are both from the West Indies, and Belinda's rival "Virginia" turns out to have a father and a suitor both involved in suppressing a slave revolt there. The most celebrated nineteenth-century examples are, of course, in *Mansfield Park*, where paternal authority and economic viability derive from slave plantations, and *Jane Eyre*, where Rochester's first wife is racially marked and represents an entire plantation history that Britain might well want to lock up, unseen, in its attic. Moreover, in Charlotte Yonge's *Heartsease*, slaveholding profoundly corrupts the workings of a family over three generations, and in Yonge's *The Magnum Bonum*, a family inherits West Indian money along with a West Indian heiress, to disturbing effect. Dinah Mulock Craik's *Olive*, whose disabled main character has a Creole half-sister, creates what is literally a family relationship between racial and disabled bodies. This uneasy connection occurs in *Persuasion* as well: Mrs. Smith's crippled legs parallel her crippled estate, a West Indian plantation whose circulation of money has stopped just as her own mobility as ceased.

Slavery and empire fundamentally shaped the marriage plot, just as they shaped all other aspects of British life. The West Indies was a narrative engine that could drive both extremes of the marriage plot. It enriched main characters. In this sense, slave money could allow for the luxury of marrying for love—or encourage mercenary matches (as in Mr. Osborne's attempt to make George Osborne marry Miss Swartz in *Vanity Fair*). Moreover, the West Indies plot introduced a range of ways of thinking about bodies, a language in which women could both be seen as men's property and be connected to the wild passions thought to mark the Creole.[33]

Jane may be "the antipodes of the Creole" (338), but she is also, of course, intimately identified with Bertha in ways that have been familiar to readers since *The Madwoman in the Attic*. In a comment that ought to give us pause, Rochester remarks, "Hiring a mistress is the next worse thing to buying a slave: both are often by nature, and always by position, inferior: and to live familiarly with inferiors is degrading" (339). This comparison reveals, first, that Rochester himself has bought slaves and, second, that he treats women the same way, as purchased property, whom he then disdains for being purchasable. (As Jane warns herself, if she ever became his mistress, "he would one day regard me with the same feeling" [339].) If British men were taught to view women as objects that they could use for their own pleasure—and if British women were taught that passion marked them as animalistic, people of color—then the forms of love and authority and property available to Victorian characters are already racialized. To embrace the romantic marriage plot too heartily might code them as racially marked. Susan Meyer has explored how the Brontës used the rhetoric of slavery to situate their own heroines' lives.[34] Certainly the rhetorical connection between women and slaves that Meyers analyzes is ubiquitous in nineteenth-century prose, especially in feminist rhetoric (see Chapter 6), which frequently declares that British women under coverture, denied education and employment, are essentially enslaved.

However, adopting the familiar marriage's emphasis on women's points of view might remind us that the West Indies emphasis enabled readers to see male corruption, not just female passion. Problematic men exercise the "absolute power" of Sir Thomas Bertram or the "despotism" of Rochester (302).[35] Because the two-suitor plot usually focuses on two men, it offers an opportunity to ask whether the dehumanizing effects of participation in a slave economy can be overcome, or whether they will corrode all other relationships; whether the public international trade in dark bodies will poison the private domestic agreement; and whether there might be another type of man who is not conditioned to regard humans as property. The West Indies did important work in the marriage plot, not just for constraining white femininity against a racialized swarthy passionate other, but also for vocalizing what was wrong with English men, for locating dehumanizing perspectives in a very specific economic practice.

If the marriage plot had repercussions in space, it also had echoes in time. If the marriage plot included the West Indies as a shadowy other, it also reached back to premodern European community as an ideal. The marriage plot didn't just precipitate people toward modernity; it also acted as a reservoir for older ideas and earlier forms, a way of continuing to knit people into traditional social formations. The marriage plot didn't just underline individuality; it also reinforced relationality. The marriage plot didn't just emphasize desire; it also rewarded companionability. In Chapter 3, we will look at how the Victorian marriage plot helped to invent the notion of organic community in the first place, providing a way to imagine the kind of pastoral social bonds that Victorians both fetishized and mourned as irrevocably past.

In the rest of this book, I look at the marriage plot mainly in terms of women's development and female characters because of its centrality to women's stories, but it is worth noting that the familiar-romantic rivalry was often central to the male Bildungsroman as well. In the most famous works of male development of the nineteenth century, including *David Copperfield* and *Pendennis*, the hero's maturation is proven by his ability to choose (or to merit) a marriage with his relative. In these novels, romantic passion is not the happy ending but "the first mistaken impulse of an undisciplined heart." Impetuous youths have to overcome their infatuations with good-looking, magnetically appealing strangers before they can settle down with the trustworthy companion who was there all along.

Rochester, for instance, bitterly repents his marriage with Bertha: "I was dazzled, stimulated: my senses were excited; and being ignorant, raw, and inexperienced, I thought I loved her," but "I never loved, I never esteemed, I did not even know her. I was not sure of the existence of one virtue in her nature: I had marked neither modesty nor benevolence, nor candour, nor refinement in her mind or manners—and, I married her: gross, grovelling, mole-eyed blockhead that I was! With less sin I might have—but let me remember to whom I am speaking" (332–333). True love means respect and esteem; erotic attraction is not love.

Rochester's belated confirmation of this period belief is in line with other male characters' development. Even St. John, who breathes fast and heavy at the mere thought of the enticing Rosamond Oliver, whom he loves "so wildly—with all the intensity, indeed, of a first passion," characterizes his feeling as "delirium and delusion," reminding himself that "she would not make me a good wife" and that "to twelve months' rapture would succeed a lifetime of regret" (399). In this respect, both St. John and Jane are each other's familiar choices, while both are helplessly drawn toward bewitching outsiders whom they are certain cannot make them happy. Nor is this attraction any secret. St. John reproaches Jane for yearning after Rochester, while St. John actually asks Jane to time him so that he can indulge in an erotic fantasy of Rosamond for exactly fifteen minutes.

Male authors writing about male protagonists also tend toward this pattern of an immature romantic passion followed by a proper familiar choice. In *Pendennis*, Pen outgrows his childish attraction for Emily Fotheringay and Blanche Amory in order, finally, to love his cousin and adoptive sister Laura. Trollope plays out this plot frequently. Harry in *The Claverings* must give up the fascinating Lady Ongar to choose Florence Burton, the good girl and daughter of his employer; Phineas Finn has to turn away from lovely Lady Laura to choose his neighbor, Mary Flood Jones; and Paul Montagu has to relinquish the exotic Mrs. Hurtle to end up with trustworthy Hetta Carbury. These older women are not only beautiful but also attractive through their tragic sexual histories, and may be able to manipulate a callow young man, seriously imperiling his reputation and perhaps his class standing.

In a different model, however, the young man marries a pretty child before he settles down with a reasonable helpmate. We see this plot in *David Copperfield*, in which David first marries the flighty romantic figure Dora before settling down with his adoptive sister Agnes. Similarly, in *The Newcomes*, Clive has to go through marriage to Rosey before he can (presumably) win his cousin Ethel. Pip measures his development by his willingness to marry the familiar Biddy (although this is precluded, he may get a chastened Estella, the romantic suitor reformed).[36]

Finally, as it should be clear by now, "familiar marriage" and "romantic marriage" are my own coinages, umbrella terms that I hope will be useful for us as outsiders trying to understand a Victorian mentality. I do not mean to imply that Victorian writers consciously and deliberately used something called "familiar marriage." Lois Bueler makes a good point: "Just as people living inside an ideology or a language typically do not see it and cannot describe it, for it is what they look through to the world around them, people using a literary structure are unlikely to see it, for it is the naturalized means by which they imitate the human types and actions of their world."[37]

Bueler's argument gives us the insight that to Victorians, no such formulations as "romantic marriage" or "familiar marriage" would have made sense. The very act of isolating and comparing these paradigms was what the literary structures were trying to accomplish, rather than a predecessor to the construction of the paradigms.

Fiction allowed Victorians to play out this transition, its consequences, and its problems. After all, "genres provide a conceptual framework for the mediation (if not the 'solution') of intractable problems, a method for rendering such problems intelligible," writes Michael McKeon.[38] Like McKeon, I read this narrative as "mediation" rather than "solution." The genre of the marriage plot made the problem of marriage "intelligible." It reduced an inchoate mass of changing cultural ideas to a simple binary opposition, a rivalry, in which readers could choose sides, or imaginatively participate in the construction of a compromise formation.

Marriage History and Criticism

Studies of the history of the family in Britain generally begin with Lawrence Stone's flawed but groundbreaking *The Family, Sex and Marriage in England 1500–1800* (1977). Stone argues that the family transitioned from an extended clan of coldly indifferent or actively cruel members to an affectionate, small nuclear family due to the rise of affective individualism in the seventeenth century.[39] Thus, asserts Stone, loving marriages and caring childrearing began with the modern period. However, as historians of premodern periods were quick to point out, familial tenderness and marital love have existed for as long as we have had literary and historical records. Stone argues for his vision of a triumphal progression toward a superior present situation by imposing his own beliefs on a far messier history, selectively choosing sources and ignoring contradictory material.[40]

In spite of its problematic evidence and dubious progressivism, Stone's book set up a grand narrative, a breathtaking sweep of history from the medieval to the modern period, that captured scholars' attention. As Helen Berry and Elizabeth Foyster write, "in his selective use of sources, Stone was less than a model historian, but his hypothesis about the evolution of the modern family has proved to be 'good to think with.'"[41] Today, most historians of the family accept that the premodern family norm was generally some sort of extended kin clan, with marriage arranged by and for the benefit of the group, and that this mode shifted sometime in the early modern era to today's normative pattern of individual conjugal pairs or small, isolated nuclear families, in which marriage is a matter of participants' personal choices. Yet this shift was neither a sudden nor a clean replacement. Consensual marital relationships certainly existed in the premodern world, and the kinship model persisted for a long time into the modern individualist era. The earlier model of family (what Stone terms the "open lineage family", as distinct from the "closed nuclear family") was not obsolete in the nineteenth century but was rather a living residue that we often see in transition in novels like *Wuthering Heights*, in which the Earnshaw household, with its quasi-familial wards and servants, its lack of privacy, and its archaic roots, exists in marked contrast to the modern, closed home that houses the Lintons' nuclear family.

Literary theorists have followed Stone's progressive story, for the most part. Critics have tended to emphasize the novel's strong teleological drive toward the modern individuated subject, an argument made most influentially by Ian Watt in 1957 and by Nancy Armstrong in 1987.

In *The Rise of the Novel*, Watt famously argues that individualism is fundamental to the rise of the novel.[42] By placing Defoe at the start of the novelistic tradition, Watt enshrines the individual self-interest of Robinson Crusoe, Moll Flanders, and Roxana. The novel, Watt explains, is based on "the particularising approach to character" which "resolves itself into the problem of defining the individual person."[43] The growing influences of capitalism and Puritanism produce economic man, most clearly represented in Robinson Crusoe. Watt points out that Crusoe leads an emotionally impoverished life, indifferent to community, family, love, and recreation, with no moral compass. Moreover, Crusoe's belief in his self-made man status is inherently fallacious, since he in fact capitalizes on what other men have made already and benefits from the shipwreck only because his potential competitors have all died.[44] Watt concludes:

> It is appropriate that the tradition of the novel should begin with a work that annihilated the relationships of the traditional social order, and thus drew attention to the opportunity and the need of building up a network of personal relationships on a new and conscious pattern; the terms of the problem of the novel and of modern thought alike were established when the old order of moral and social relationships was shipwrecked, with Robinson Crusoe, by the rising tide of individualism.[45]

The wistful ambivalence of this summation captures Watt's sense of both the inevitability and the regrettability of this historical trajectory.

The problem emerges when Watt tries to fit women into this model. He does so by arguing that *Pamela* and *Clarissa* both outline a new model of conjugal, affectionate, middle-class marriage through—once again—underlining the value of individualism:

> Finally, the rise of individualism is of great importance. By weakening communal and traditional relationships, it fostered not only the kind of private and egocentric mental life we find in Defoe's heroes, but also the later stress on the importance of personal relationships which is so characteristic both of modern society and of the novel—such relationships may be seen as offering the individual a more conscious and selective pattern of social life to replace the more diffuse, and as it were involuntary, social cohesions which individualism had undermined.[46]

The novel, the marriage plot, and "modern society" are entirely in sync in Watt's telling, each fostering individualism and a better, more consciously chosen form of social arrangement.

However, I would argue that the rise of individualism and the emergence of voluntary private relationships forms only one possible plot line in the history of the novel, and not necessarily the one that is most important for women or for the marriage plot. Given that women were traditionally not allowed economic individuality at all—when Roxana or Moll Flanders demonstrate these traits, Watt can only call them honorary men[47]—and given that marriage, for women, traditionally meant joining a family or a community, it seems anachronistic to assume that eighteenth- or nineteenth-century marriage was an assertion of individuality. Watt's position is an inherently teleological one: because individual autonomy triumphed, that must be what the novel points toward. But at the time, the novel did not know what would win. The longstanding idea of marriage, from the medieval period onward, was that it was a merger between two families, an alliance and interlacing of two networks. In the sadly amoral world of Defoe's striving heroes, in Clarissa's terrifying vulnerability when she leaves her family's house, what we might well see is a confirmation that self-interested autonomy is an awful experience and that grounding in a rich social world is utterly necessary for a decent life.

The most influential theorist of the marriage plot for the past generation has been Nancy Armstrong, who builds on Stone's and Watt's assumption that the novel encodes a forwardly propulsive urge toward autonomous, private relationships centered on the modern individual. However, Armstrong argues that "in place of the intricate status system that had long dominated British thinking, these authors began to represent an individual's value in terms of his, but more often in terms of *her*, essential qualities of mind."[48] The modern individual was characterized by intimate emotional depth, private feeling, and moral sensibility. That is why, in her famous pronouncement, "the modern individual was first and foremost a woman."[49] Moreover, Armstrong reads the marriage plot as a way of mobilizing those supposed private qualities into an affective resolution and thereby evading real political activity. "Domestic fiction," Armstrong warns, "unfolded the operations of human desire as if they were independent of political history. And this helped to create the illusion that desire was entirely subjective and therefore essentially different from the politically encodable forms of behavior to which desire gave rise."[50] In other words, the marriage plot translated political stresses into personal desire, in the process stripping it of its real complications.

However, Armstrong's theory rests on two assumptions that may not always be valid. First, while it may be true that the modern individual was "a woman," it does not necessarily follow that women were modern individuals. Many women in eighteenth- and nineteenth-century fiction were actually depicted in a more archaic sense, as profoundly relational subjects with multiple social interactions with a wide range of subjects, as this book aims to show. Second, when Armstrong identifies domestic fiction as driven by universal, subjective "human desire," she is assuming a kind of love that her Victorian subjects might not have recognized. What made people marry in Victorian fiction was not necessarily desire—indeed, Victorians often found "human desire" to be a very bad reason for marriage. We might have more luck looking in the Victorian novel for "nondesire and domestic fiction."

Desire and Domestic Fiction uses "the history of sexuality" to mean "the history of marriage," but these were actually profoundly different fields.[51] Unsticking desire from marriage allows us to see a gap in which different kinds of readings can occur. For instance, Armstrong points out that novels "performed the operations of division and self-containment that turned political information into the discourse of sexuality," offering as her examples *Pamela*, *Jane Eyre*, and *Evelina*.[52]

Yet those are precisely the novels, in the history of the novel, that may be said to work the hardest to keep their heroines out of the discourse of sexuality and insert them instead into the discourse of marriage. Pamela, Evelina, and Jane Eyre can marry because they have successfully resisted almost unimaginable pressures toward sex. Although their marriages will be sexual, the point is that the women have forced the men to revise their predatory pursuits, so that their hard-won marriages can deemphasize sexuality in favor of other issues: companionability, manners, status, carework.[53]

While Watt and Armstrong initiated a powerful, compelling story about the novel's participation in the rise of the modern individual and the modern voluntary, consensual, private bourgeois family, there is another story to be told. As this modern individual formed, what (or whom) got left behind? Might the marriage plot have worked, not just as a mechanism to propel us toward modernity, but also as a reservoir holding older ideas? What would happen, I ask in this book, if we read the history of the novel not as the inevitable triumph of individualism, but as a messy and imperfect, yet heartfelt attempt to retain sociality?

In short, while Watt and Armstrong (echoing Stone) argue that the marriage plot facilitated the development of a modern female subject—a liberal, autonomous, essential, rights-bearing citizen, with unique individuality and deep psychology—I want to add that the marriage plot also served the history of alternative female subjectivity, the notion of selfhood as relational, affective, and networked, governed by feelings and duties instead of rights and reasons. These two ideas of the subject work themselves out via the marriage plot. In fact, the marriage plot dominated nineteenth-century fiction in part because it was where those two drives could compete.

Marriage history and criticism of the past decade have begun to explore alternatives to the progressive individualist story. Ruth Perry's magisterial *Novel Relations* (2004) avoids Stone's sweeping generalizations in favor of meticulous research; it also considers changes in family structure in a literary context and in a much tighter chronological framework than Stone provides (1748–1818, as opposed to 1500–1800). Perry argues that the eighteenth century saw what she calls "the great disinheritance": the economic, legal, and marital disempowerment of women. New laws made women completely financially dependent on their families, who often viewed them as a drain on their resources, and the new ideal of romantic love meant that women were traumatically ripped from those consanguineous families at their weddings. According to Perry, the eighteenth-century novel's fantasies of family reunion compensated for a lived reality that was far more frightening, inasmuch as women had to rely upon potentially resentful or neglectful male relations.[54]

Perry performs crucial work: she takes the myth of the romantic couple and turns it on its head, reading it not as the acquisition of a partner but as the loss of a family and a world. By restoring that older point of view, Perry enables us to see how stressful, upsetting, and dangerous the rise of romantic marriage felt for women. What Stone smugly congratulates us for achieving, Perry reminds us, felt painful at the time.

Historians of eighteenth-century family life, particularly Amanda Vickery, Joanne Bailey, and Naomi Tadmor, have vastly enriched eighteenth-century studies of family dynamics, and recently several Victorianist studies are beginning to do the same for the nineteenth century.[55] Chief among them is Mary Jean Corbett's game-changing *Family Likeness: Sex, Marriage, and Incest from Jane Austen to Virginia Woolf* (2008), which offers a tightly argued case for rethinking love within the family beyond pat assumptions about "incest," providing a more precise sense of Victorian family relations in their evolutionary, economic, and affective registers. Corbett's main argument is that incest itself has a history, specifically, that it emerged as an accusation to serve political ends at particular times.[56] Crucially, she "identifies a cultural tendency toward forging relationships with familial and familiar figures that testifies not only to the perceived perils of intimacy with strangers but also to the ambivalent attractions, for women in particular, of remaining within known or knowable first-family structures that may include sustained and sustaining relations with other women."[57] Perry and Corbett both probe the quality of relations within the consanguineal family, a perspective elided when critics focus exclusively on conjugal relations.

Similarly, Lenore Davidoff's *Thicker Than Water: Siblings and Their Relations, 1780–1920* (2012) provides new insights into the emotional tenor of the consanguineous family. *Thicker Than Water* compellingly describes the difference between that family formation and our own, insisting that in this 140-year period, "as in no other time since, sisters and brothers, often in tandem with their spouses and children, shared material fortunes, social and emotional circles."[58] Davidoff introduces two particularly useful terms: the "long family," a family with at least seven children, and "close marriages," marriages between cousins or marriages in which a pair of siblings married another pair of siblings. The consequences of the long family, in particular, are fascinating. "A family of parents and two children already implies eight possible lines of interaction. With parents and ten children, this reaches a possible 4,093 relationships, almost beyond the imagination of our one-to-three-child contemporary experience."[59] Rachel Ablow's *The Marriage of Minds* (2007) shares Davidoff's emphasis on feeling within the family. Ablow's important book helps diversify our understanding of marriage by affiliating it to the category of sympathy and the act of reading, thereby introducing a crucial alternative emotion as the basis of marital connection.

If Corbett, Davidoff, and Ablow rethink Victorian family feelings, Sharon Marcus and Holly Furneaux generate new understandings of intimate relationships that are not limited to the connubial. Both Marcus and Furneaux build on the foundational work of queer theory to paint an impressively nuanced picture of Victorian homosocial relations. Marcus's *Between Women: Friendship, Desire, and Marriage in Victorian England* (2007) makes the compelling argument that female friendships played a crucial role in nineteenth-century culture and should not be read merely as covers for same-sex relations or as practice for eventual heterosexual marriage. One of Marcus's most original points is that it is the female friend who usually facilitates marriage in Victorian fiction. By carving out space for a meaningful relationship that could be read outside the structure of erotic desire, Marcus also, importantly, argues that same-sex partnerships were voluntary, contractual, egalitarian unions that may well have offered a model for marriage reformers.[60]

In *Queer Dickens: Erotics, Families, Masculinities* (2009), Furneaux "rejects a false logic that places marriage and the biological family as central to thinking about the Victorian and the Dickensian, in favor of an exploration of other forms of intimacy, affinity, and family formation."[61] Furneaux thus extends the notion of family in a way that makes room for "families bonded neither by blood nor marriage." Her focus on "the expandability of Victorian kin in, for example, widespread practices of non-biological adoption, demonstrates that 'families of choice' and 'elective affinities' have a long and emotionally rich history."[62] In this respect Furneaux's theory correlates with Thiel's idea of "the transnormative family."[63] In *The Fantasy of Family: Nineteenth-Century Children's Literature and the Myth of the Domestic Ideal* (2007), Thiel draws our attention to the preponderance of "family units headed by single parents, step-parents, aunts, uncles, grandparents, siblings or the state that exists in opposition to the 'natural' and 'complete' family of husband, wife and children." "These," she argues, "are not merely extended family units. They may incorporate kin, but the transnormative family is identified primarily by the temporary or permanent absence of a natural parent or parents, often by the presence of a surrogate mother or father, who may or may not be related to the child, and, frequently, by the relocation of the child to an environment outside the 'natural' family home."[64]

Three other important recent studies have confirmed that we need to revise our assumptions about Victorian families. Kelly Hager's *Dickens and the Rise of Divorce* (2010) insists that the happy courtship plot coexists with an equally crucial narrative: the story of the bad marriage. Hager writes:

> The novel is just as often (often at the same time as it plots a courtship and ends with a wedding) dedicated to showing how marriage unravels,

> to uncovering the myth of matrimonial bliss, to revealing how many husbands and wives were trying to escape or miserably enduring the wedlock they had so eagerly sought, as it is to plotting courtship. Or to put it another way, we recognize that novels plot marital failure, but we have yet to revise our understanding of the genre with those plots in mind.[65]

One of the major forms of marital failure occurred, oddly enough, when men married rich women. In *The Vulgar Question of Money: Heiresses, Materialism, and the Novel of Manners from Jane Austen to Henry James* (2011), Elsie Michie points out that the rich woman becomes the scapegoat for all the fears associated with money throughout the nineteenth century: bad taste, vulgarity, and cosmopolitan rootlessness. The poverty of the poor woman confirms her virtue and underscores the disinterestedness of the man who marries her. Michie's book reminds us that romantic love was no universal, incandescent truth but rather a difficult ideal that literary plots kept having to reach for, refining away vulgar dross, detaching it from less worthy residues.[66] Finally, Maia MacAleavey's study of bigamy in Victorian fiction breaks us out of the assumption we make that monogamous pair bonding constituted a fictional norm, demonstrating the cross-currents of conjugal experience developed by multiple partners over time.[67]

Familiar Marriage joins these earlier studies but also hopes to provide a larger historical context in which to connect their disparate findings. Sibling cohabitation, cousin marriage, unhappy marriage, sympathetic unions, and mercenary marriage, for instance, though locally different, relate to one another because they share an idea of marriage contracted for reasons other than intense romantic adoration. My book could not have been conceptualized without Perry's parallel evocation of an earlier anti-romantic feeling, or without the varied critiques of marriage in Victorian fiction so ably revealed by Marcus, Hager, Michie, and McAleavey. All these texts converge on the same realization: marriage and family form for multiple reasons, and the result is not always a happy state.

However, readers may wonder why this recognition of non-romantic marriage has occurred so late and so partially, if the familiar-marriage dynamic really is as important as I claim. After all, Lawrence Stone published his book in 1977. But not until 2004 did we start to see the work of Perry, Marcus, Corbett, Hager, Michie, and McAleavey. Why did it take a full generation to start questioning the idea that Victorians married for romantic love?

First, literary critics have taken their cue from historians of marriage, who often tend to see romantic marriage as a minor part of the much bigger story of the shift to marital choice. While Stone, Coontz, Perry, and Jones acknowledge that romantic passion began to dominate in the late eighteenth and nineteenth century, they are mainly interested in the seventeenth-century shift into the great principle of personal choice of prospective spouse, which they see as the moment that establishes modern individualism. Personal marital choice is the issue, then, regardless of whether it was based on esteem or eroticism. These scholars then tacitly treat the shift from esteem to eroticism as a local development subsidiary to the bigger point, perhaps not even worth mentioning. Second, many literary critics remain enamored of Stone's history because of its famous "grand narrative," a sweeping story that is not only appealing in itself but has also been corroborated by central work in the history of the novel. Unaware of the critiques to which Stone's methodology has been subjected, and the subsequent histories that have replaced it, literary critics too often continue to rely on a work that has long since been superseded.

Finally, one big problem is the term "companionate." "Companionate" is so vaguely defined that even the most eminent literary critics use it completely differently. For instance, Sharon Marcus and Wendy Jones use "companionate" to mean an amicable (non-erotic) partnership.[68] But Jennifer Phegley, Mary Lydon Shanley, and Ruth Perry all use the term "companionate" to mean the opposite—they use it to reference *romantic* love.[69] Indeed, Perry critiques Jones for using the term to mean amity.[70] Meanwhile, Nancy Armstrong defines "companionate marriage" differently from everyone else. She uses it to mean a marriage in which women relinquish political control to the male in exchange for control of the private realm, that is, a marriage founded on the notion of separate spheres—a notion that does not speak at all to the quality of feeling between the spouses.[71] If two scholars use "companionate" to mean "amicable," three use the same word to mean "romantic," and one uses the term for an arrangement unrelated to affection, how can a real discussion occur?

This variation among literary critics occurs in part because the histories they read rarely differentiate between types of loving. Often, historians use "companionate" to refer to any kind of affectionate marriage from the seventeenth century onward. After all, the difference does not always seem important to them.[72] This means that when it *is* important to differentiate amicable from romantic unions, we have no vocabulary to do so. Instead, we have a term that counterproductively conflates the two states, or means whatever the author personally thinks it means, muddling the history instead of clarifying it.

Why We Need Familiar Marriage

If we assume marriage is a smooth progress toward a teleologically inevitable affective individualist modernity, we will not see what the marriage plot was really working through. We will not even understand why it should exist, if its triumph was foreordained. Reading the history of marriage as the rise of individualism, without ever noting the perseverance of sociality as a competing paradigm, is like reading the rise of democracy without paying any attention to the persistence of monarchical rule. In both cases, it is impossible to comprehend the core developments of the past three centuries if we erase its main competitor.

For if the familiar marriage plot is, as it were, the dark side of the disk whose brightly lit romantic side we normally see, it should not surprise us that it has terrain that interestingly, even grotesquely, shadows the topography to which we are accustomed. In the topsy-turvy familiar marriage world, we see disabled bodies preferred to vigorous bodies, a life of hard work being more satisfying than a life of pleasures, continued contact with parents and siblings giving more happiness than a private home with one's spouse, and a mutually respectful cameraderie feeling more fulfilling than the lineaments of satisfied desire. Reading from a familiar-marriage viewpoint also unsettles our critical practices. It impels us to pay close attention to St. John, not just Rochester; Hareton, not just Heathcliff; Colonel Brandon, not just Willoughby. It invites us to imagine what the marriage plot might do for women rather than assume women only and always constituted the victims of the marriage plot: disadvantaged in an oppressive legal arrangement, smothered in oppressive domesticity, or passive pawns in powerful dynamics between men. Instead, it sees female characters as active agents making their own choices and insists on respecting their reasons for the choices they made. A woman's choice of suitor may enable her to craft the life story that she wants, regardless of whether we—from our contemporary post-Freudian perspective—want it for her.

Eve Kosofsky Sedgwick's foundational work of queer theory, *Between Men*, shows how marriage to the woman gets endlessly deferred as a way of provoking and sustaining the men's feeling for each other. I want to use one of Sedgwick's justly celebrated examples, her reading of *Our Mutual Friend*, to show what a familiar marriage perspective might add to the dynamic she elucidated. Sedgwick argues that Eugene Wrayburn and Bradley Headstone engage in a fatal rivalry over Lizzie Hexam as a way to keep them engaged with one another. "Imagery of the sphincter, the girdle, the embrace, the 'iron ring' of the male grasp" dominates the Headstone-Wrayburn dyad; it is a story of male violence.[73] In Sedgwick's telling, the woman in this story is mute and victimized.[74]

Yet what happens when we read the triangle from the point of view of Lizzie Hexam? In that case, the marriage plot reveals two facts: first, the terrifying extent of Lizzie's vulnerability and, second, the mechanism by which Lizzie solves this problem. If we read from the woman's point of view, we can parse her not just as the men's passive object of desire but as a person who becomes able to shape her own story.

Lizzie is in a classic familiar-romantic rivalry. Handsome, charismatic, and compelling, Eugene Wrayburn is a man whom few know well and whose intentions toward Lizzie are dubious. Meanwhile, Bradley Headstone is a familial connection who offers a useful future, with work for Lizzie and advantages for her family. As Charley remarks, "Mr. Headstone has always got me on, and he has a good deal in his power, and of course if he was my brother-in-law he wouldn't get me on less, but would get me on more" (394). Sedgwick notes that "Charley's offer of Lizzie to his schoolmaster represents the purest form of the male traffic in women."[75] In this respect, Lizzie's marriage plot is a nightmare situation in which she is stalked by two relentless predatory males, sexually obsessed with her and sadistically fixated on one another. The men who should be protecting her, her father and her brother, only exploit and degrade her, and their circle of friends, the rough watermen with whom they socialize, offer no help.

This dire situation forces Lizzie to develop her own social network, an affiliative group of friends to hide and protect her: Jenny Wren, Riah, and Riah's friends the factory owners. As is typical in a familiar dynamic, a disabled person, Jenny Wren, is at the center of this social world, and one might argue that Lizzie responds to a disempowering marital choice by embracing the nonmarital cohabitation of the disability union, as she lives with Jenny in an emotionally and physically intimate partnership. It is Jenny who teaches Lizzie a new dynamic, one of mutual care, so that once Eugene becomes disabled, Lizzie has already learned a more sustaining, kindly, and loving mode of partnership. Sedgwick mentions Jenny Wren only to remind us that her real name is Fanny Cleaver and that this name reminds us of aggression, rape.[76] This is true, but perhaps it is equally important that Jenny overwrites this given name with a fairy-tale moniker, revising herself not as a person whose name bears witness to male violence but rather as someone with the right to choose what she signifies, and to choose a harmless, lovable creature.[77] In the Ballad of Cock Robin, the sparrow accidentally shoots Cock Robin while aiming for the attacking Cuckoo, but Cock Robin's bride, Jenny Wren, remains unhurt. Turning Fanny Cleaver into Jenny Wren means becoming a creature who stands aside from male violence. The painfully divided body implied by the once-mentioned name Fanny Cleaver is replaced by Jenny's repeated assertion that she is "the person of the house," an assertion of wholeness, importance, and agency.[78]

Just as Jenny Wren shows the capacity to write her own story, so too does Lizzie. For in spite of Sedgwick's claim, the point is that Charley does *not* traffic Lizzie; Lizzie insists on managing her own body. Lizzie puts herself at the disposal not of a dangerously sexualized man but of a loving disabled woman. From Lizzie's point of view, then, this is a novel in which a woman rejects the heterosexual paths available to her, choosing instead to construct an alternative social realm and cohabit with an alternative kind of partner. This familiar union with Jenny can be transposed back on the eventual marriage, reforming and improving it, so that Eugene Wrayburn, disabled in his turn, becomes remodeled on this better predecessor.

Thus if we perform the feminist act of taking the woman's perspective seriously, instead of seeing her merely as a convenient occasion for homoerotic male bonds, we would see the two male suitors as generated by *her* needs to serve *her* emotional, economic, and legal hopes. The resolution would mean that she had come to terms with her marital choices, not (just) that the men had resolved their feelings for one another. In other words, without denying the intensely important work of Sedgwick's "between men," my theory turns that triangle upside down to place the woman at its apex.

Both Sedgwick and Armstrong treat marriage as a cover for something more important, a thin scrim through which we can discern the larger contours of homoerotic relations or political conflict. It is true, of course, that marriage has been used as a cover to normalize homoerotic ties or to reduce political complexities, but that does not therefore mean that marriage must necessarily only be a stand-in for something else. To give an analogy: Jane Eyre's sudden inheritance of a fortune from an unknown uncle in Madeira is obviously a wish-fulfillment fantasy, but we should not let that fact preclude analysis of the colonial, trade, and inheritance networks that made it possible for her to have such a windfall. That an event may transparently serve a character's wishes should not deter us from investigating the texture of the event in itself.

Familiar marriage deemphasizes desire. This does not mean that familiar marriages in fiction were necessarily chaste, nor, for that matter, that they were enthusiastically and frequently consummated. Rather, it simply means that familiar marriage produced other forms of feeling that, to its participants, were more important than erotic desire. In his foundational study of desire, Denis de Rougemont reminds us:

> The West is distinct from other cultures not only by its invention of passionate love in the twelfth century and the secular elaboration of conjugal love, but by its confusions of the notions of eros, agape, sexuality, passion. Classical Greek used at least sixteen different terms to designate love in all its forms: *eros* for physical love, *agape* for altruistic love, *philia* for tender or erotic feelings, etc.[79]

The Victorians differentiated between affective and erotic love in ways modern marriage does not, and it was quite possible for marriage to have one without the other. For instance, cousin marriage in fiction consistently foregrounds familiarity, but treats the sexual component far more erratically. Some cousin marriages are consummated and produce children (*Bleak House, Mansfield Park*), some have a troubled sexual component (*Jude the Obscure*), and some are explicitly chaste (*The History of Sir Richard Calmady*). The variability of desire seems to suggest that it was not a significant part of the model. It could be played with, rejected, or ignored.

To read desire not as central, not as repressed, not as perverse, but simply as relatively unimportant is extraordinarily difficult for modern literary critics. Our post-Freudian, post-Foucaultian working assumption is that all fictional characters feel a powerful, propulsive, erotic drive that must be kept secret if it does not fit heterosexual reproductive norms, but whose intensity makes it seep out into clues that the astute reader can follow. Critics sometimes express indignation about "suspicious readings" that probe beneath the surface of the text, and quite often the dispute centers on sexual imagery, as if the critic is violating the text.[80] The backlash against suspicious reading shows a growing discomfort with the critics' role as exposer of sexual secrets, a discomfort that has perhaps helped generate the recent critical works that emphasize non-erotic elements in cultural formations like incest (Corbett) and female friendships (Marcus).

However, as Honor McKitrick Wallace writes, "narrative desire does not have to be erotic. For the female protagonist, trapped between the stasis of lyric feminine desire and the masculine trajectory of traditional narrative, narrative desire may simply be a desire for agency."[81] My study follows Wallace's suggestion that the real desire expressed by many Victorian middle-class females, fictional and otherwise, was for agency, not for sex; for an ability to determine a meaningful life through the only mechanism afforded to them, the mechanism of marriage. But that "desire" might also have been to continue living near a beloved sister, or to care for someone who needed nursing, or to have friends, or to stay in one's community. That does not, of course, mean that the Victorians were too repressed to enjoy sex. It means that they had something they felt to be more important on their minds. Familiar marriage proponents did not care enough about desire to prohibit or to fetishize it. Rather, such advocates prioritized sociality, not sexuality.

In other words, Victorians did not necessarily feel that familiar marriage harbored a lamentable lack of sexual interest but rather that it positively proffered a delightfully robust companionship. In *Between Women*, Marcus asks us to read female friendship as a category in itself instead of assuming it is a code for a covert lesbian desire. This book performs a parallel project in insisting on familiar marriage as a strong category in itself instead of seeing it in terms of lack, or assuming it redirects us to a "real" desire that must exist somewhere else.

Reader, I Married Him

Jane Eyre offers a chance to rethink desire as we look at Rochester's final trauma. Traditionally read as a castration scene, what if we see his disability not as a loss of sexual potency, but rather as a gain of other opportunities? How might his somatic condition provide Jane with the qualities she wants in marriage—qualities that St. John's failed (but tempting) proposal made visible to us?

One of the functions of the failed first familiar suitor is precisely to make it clear what the woman needs. The rejected suitor is a bad choice, but one who models the reforms that the romantic suitor must undertake. Reading St. John as a model for Rochester is one example of how the familiar marriage model might alter our reading practice, magnifying aspects of the novel that we tend to overlook and putting others in different relation to each other.

Once we conceptualize a character as a representative of the familiar-marriage category, we can see him in terms of cultural attitudes toward that particular type. Just as we now read Bertha as a commentary on Creole characterization, so too St. John becomes a variant of the familiar suitor—a version whose disinterest in sexual connection is chilling, whose emphasis on vocation is dehumanizing. St. John becomes one way that this novel trains its readers to dislike the familiar category. *Jane Eyre* thus powerfully contributes to the growing influence of romantic marriage.

St. John seems to offer a great deal. He gives Jane the chance to travel that she has craved since childhood. He is, Jane comments, "a very good man," and the Rivers in general are "good people; far better than [Rochester]: a hundred times better people" (463, 465). "It seemed I had found a brother: one I could be proud of—one I could love" (411). Marrying this cousin would cement her participation in the Rivers clan, stabilizing a lonely, homeless woman. He has many traits in common with her: self-discipline, capacity for hard work, ambition. At the same time, however, he notes that Jane has "the qualities I seek. Jane, you are docile, diligent, disinterested, faithful, constant, and courageous; very gentle, and very heroic: cease to mistrust yourself—I can trust you unreservedly" (429).

St. John's genuine appreciation of Jane's intellectual and moral qualities contrasts with Rochester, who veers between deriding Jane as "provoking puppet" or "malicious elf" and dressing her "like a doll," an experience she finds profoundly degrading (297, 302).[82] Rochester dehumanizes Jane, making her intelligence into a perverse attitude and her body into a sexual object. Jane's fine moral compass, which St. John recognizes as an attraction, is for Rochester merely (and shockingly) "the hitch in Jane's character" (329). In his first proposal, Rochester had insisted "my equal is here, and my likeness," but he cannot sustain that egalitarian awareness, almost immediately redefining her as a piece of property whose possession must be secured: "I have her, and will hold her" (282, 284). Their troubled courtship constantly threatens to swerve into the seduction that is the nightmare result of the romantic plot, starting with Mrs. Fairfax's warning on the very first morning of their engagement ("believe me, you cannot be too careful . . . distrust yourself as well as him" [294]) and Rochester's infamous comparison between Jane and "the Grand Turk's whole seraglio" (297). His constant sexual predation endangers Jane, who crushes "his hand, which was ever hunting mine, vigorously, and thrust it back to him red with the passionate pressure" (297).

St. John offers Jane a future of meaningful work, whereas Rochester's first proposal is predicated on the end of Jane's teaching career. Throughout their relationship, Rochester ignores her status as his employee, trying to romanticize their connection instead. When Jane reminds him of her position, he irritably exclaims, "What, you are my paid subordinate, are you? Oh, yes, I had forgotten the salary!" (165). When she requires money to visit Gateshead, it turns out that he has in fact quite literally "forgotten the salary," and he tries to renegotiate their financial relationship on the basis of personal obligation instead of legitimate disbursements. When Rochester threatens to send her to Ireland, he employs a sneering parody of professional language in order to goad Jane into a direct confession of her love.[83] Yet Jane is attached to her work. When Rochester demands that she "give up" her "governessing slavery at once," Jane responds firmly, "Indeed, begging your pardon, sir, I shall not. I shall just go on with it as usual" (298). She clings to the prospect of continuing her teaching, even though she has only a month until her marriage. Marriage with powerful, dominant, wealthy Rochester offers no new vocation and indeed threatens the meager, somewhat unsatisfying one that Jane already has.

By contrast, the familiar marriage allows such questions to be discussed without reproach. St. John's proposal largely consists of enumerating Jane's qualifications to run an Indian school. Her teaching skills actually motivate St. John to propose, while Rochester regards Jane's teaching with distaste. In fact, St. John's greatest attraction is that he can offer Jane missionary work, which builds on her current vocation. He courts her by offering an entry-level job in remedial education and advanced language classes, unlike Rochester, whose gifts are jewels and silks. Where Rochester wants to showcase the erotic appeal of Jane's body, St. John wants to test Jane's employability. As he explains: "I have watched you ever since we first met: I have made you my study for ten months. I have proved you in that time by sundry tests: and what have I seen and elicited? In the village school I found you could perform well, punctually, uprightly, labour uncongenial to your habits and inclinations." Observing Jane's money management and her assiduity in studying Hindustani, St. John concludes that she will be ideal as a "conductress of Indian schools" (428–429). St. John's proposal is really a promotion, with marriage a mere formality in order to carry out the job properly.

Since St. John has dutifully quashed his own romantic yearning for Rosamond, he expects Jane to do the same with her own feelings for Rochester. But Jane refuses to accept a wholly familiar proposal without a vestige of romance. "Oh! I will give my heart to God," she retorts, "*You* do not want it" (431). The language of romantic attachment was quite legitimate; the explanation of one's professional requirements was perfectly acceptable. But St. John's pretense of the former is repulsive when his real interest is in the latter. Charles Lindholm explains:

> Any overt or calculated appraisal of the other as a good provider, a useful ally, a potential mate, a vehicle for sexual enjoyment, or even as an avenue to God, is felt to be a sin against the very nature of romantic love, which is defined and experienced as spontaneous, total, and boundless in its devotion to the actual person of the other—to love "for a reason" is not to love at all.[84]

In reality, St. John does not want her heart, but her hands and her head. If it had been a purely comradely proposal, it would have been fine—Jane agrees to go to India if they can go as siblings—but the problem is that St. John mixes in a pretense of romantic love, a combination Jane finds offensive.

In one sense St. John seems like the ideal familiar suitor: a morally admirable man, a cousin, offering a career. Yet Brontë undermines each of these advantages. The career is unsatisfying: as Jane cries, "I am not fit for it: I have no vocation" (428). The cousinship gives them affinity but not safe familiarity, since they are almost strangers. The marriage will not give Jane a home at Moor House, but will condemn her to dangerous traveling in India. The moral strength is intimidatingly mingled with tyranny. Instead of a familiar marriage offering a safe neighborhood haven with a trusted comrade, this union offers a dangerous exile with an icy taskmaster.

In this respect, Brontë trains us to despise St. John's offer and to challenge each element in the familiar marriage plot. Because of the extraordinary popularity and influence of *Jane Eyre*, this novel's certainty that marrying the familiar suitor would be a catastrophic error helped romantic marriage gain appeal. St. John makes non-romantic marriage look bad.

However, *Jane Eyre* does not fully endorse the romantic model either, for it reforms Rochester by disabling him. Rochester's dehumanizing, self-serving, sexualized pursuit of Jane must be turned into a new form of love. Once he becomes disabled, Jane Eyre can initiate contact, soothing and ministering to the man's body. She combs his hair, strokes his eyebrows. Whereas on the trip to the silk warehouse, she crushes his dangerously wandering hand, now "he stretched out his hand to be led. I took that dear hand, held it a moment to my lips, and then let it pass round my shoulder" (473). Instead of the stark choice of either responding to or refusing male sexual overtures, the woman can generate touch herself, in a different way. Disability empowers the woman to be more than a sexual gatekeeper, but to express tenderness, care, and sympathy.

Not only does the disability endow Jane with new capacity for physical response, but it also gives her a vocation: his disability "was that circumstance that drew us so very near—that knit us so very close: for I was then his vision, as I am still his right hand" (476). In a beautiful example of mutual caregiving, he is happy to take the services she is pleased to provide (476). Jane describes the scenery, and although she does not mention it, she presumably does the account-keeping and estate management Rochester is no longer visually capable of overseeing. Helping Rochester is her new career, and it suggests a retrospective reading of Jane's life in which her real vocation has actually always been nursing, not teaching.

We can read the signs of Jane's medical interest if we read with the kind of care we usually reserve for ferreting out covert signs of desire. Jane's lifelong interest in noting and recording physical suffering begins in the first two paragraphs of the novel, and underlies her description of John Reed's attack ("the cut bled, the pain was sharp" [43]) and the scene in the red room ("I suppose I had a species of fit" [50]). It is the nurse-to-be who speaks authoritatively of the way that "semi-starvation and neglected colds had predisposed most of the pupils to receive infection" and enumerates their illnesses (typhus, consumption, fever) (108). Jane's interest in illness, as much as her emotionally stunned state, gets revealed when she "stands so grave and quiet at the mouth of hell" watching Bertha (322). In recording her own starvation, dizziness, and weakness, Jane reveals a steady fascination with the variations of suffering.

A critical example is the scene when she holds Helen Burns on her deathbed. Creeping into Helen's bed obviously invites a queer reading, but it is surely just as relevant to a vocational reading; perhaps what draws her is desire not for Helen's body but for a chance to nurse her? Helen's deathbed scene can be read as a scene of vocational discovery, just as much as Lydgate reading about the chambers of the heart. Jane's sensitivity to Helen's extremity and Jane's ability to provide physical comfort at the end both demonstrate her innate nursing skill. Jane's desire, Jane's vocation, is to manage pain. That opportunity, in fact, is what the marriage with a damaged Rochester gives her, making her marriage with Rochester a vocational as much as a romantic wish-fulfillment.

Thus, by the time they marry, Rochester has been refashioned: a disabled man, who gives Jane a lifetime of meaningful work, he can enter a marriage characterized by something more like the kind of egalitarian mutual respect of the familiar marriage. In the second proposal, Jane, not Rochester, offers the terms via a vocabulary that draws on familiar marriage. She "meant more than friends, but could not tell what other word to employ" (469). So she attempts several others: "I will be your neighbour, your nurse, your housekeeper. I find you lonely: I will be your companion—to read to you, to walk with you, to sit with you, to wait on you, to be eyes and hands to you" (460). The word she does not use is "lover." It is Jane who initiates this new arrangement and who specifies its terms. The romantic marriage with Rochester must be flattened and filed and notched until it resembles the supposedly counterfeit model of marriage that St. John had originally offered.

The profoundly satisfying conclusion of *Jane Eyre*—and *Our Mutual Friend, The Vicar of Bullhampton, Pride and Prejudice, Miss Marjoribanks*, and *Wives and Daughters*, among others—is that the woman gets *both* romantic and familiar marriage. The two models converge; one might say they marry each other. To make a romantic suitor into a safe member of the family was the aim of the Victorian marriage plot, as it was, indeed, the aim of marriage itself. How could one imagine becoming so linked to a stranger as to be his closest kin or, in Jane's words, "absolutely bone of his bone and flesh of his flesh" (476)? The marriage plot used familiar marriage just as much as it used romantic marriage to perform this strange alchemy. Although rivals, they reshape each other. The marriage plot of the nineteenth-century novel could not exist unless both contributed to it. Whether the character starts as a stranger or as a cousin, he must acquire some of the virtues of the other side to become a viable marriage partner. Any account of the marriage plot that neglects the familiar suitor is leaving out half the story. The Victorian marriage plot was not about loving the unfamiliar, but about familiarizing oneself with love.

The Plan of the Book

In order to see how familiar marriage develops as the necessary competitor, corollary, and contributor to romantic marriage, I trace the history of its emergence in the next chapter. I explore the development of marital expectations and practices from the medieval period through the early nineteenth century. Personal consent and social pressures converged in marital decisions through most of British history, but literary critics' notion of the history of marriage fails to account for this kind of complex interrelation. Part of the problem is the ambiguous term "companionate," and part is the post-Lawrence Stone narrative of cataclysmic changes in marriage history. As the consensual aspect of marriage gradually assumed more primacy, anxieties about youthful impetuosity versus parental safeguards appear in texts like *Romeo and Juliet*, where the clash of expectations becomes a tragedy. It is, however, *Clarissa* that develops the problem most centrally for the next century. In Richardson's great novel, romantic attraction is dangerous and parental matches are awful. *Clarissa* demonstrates the need for a third choice: the suitor of rational esteem who would come to dominate eighteenth- and early nineteenth-century fiction and conduct manuals. Affectionate, kindly, and trustworthy, the suitor of rational esteem becomes the ancestor of the Victorian familiar lover, while his rival, the dashing rake, turns into the Victorian romantic lover. I end Chapter 2 by talking about how these figures evolve through the periods of Evangelicism and Romanticism, respectively, and how both get folded into a marriage plot to which the rake had previously been a stranger.

Chapter 3 introduces the familiar-romantic rivalry through the most vanilla of nineteenth-century marriage plots, the one in which a woman is courted by a neighbor, usually an older man who owns an estate. While the woman usually feels little erotic desire for the neighbor, he offers a refuge to a female character experiencing housing precarity, as in *Sense and Sensibility*, in which the Dashwoods are evicted from their home, and *Pride and Prejudice*, in which the Bennets know their exile is inevitable. Marrying the squire allows the woman to participate in a fantasy of her own social empowerment, as she anticipates managing a household and organizing a local community. Since the squire is often a Member of Parliament, his wife may be able to participate in the government of the nation through either running a political salon or ghost-writing his speeches. I juxtapose the promise of social instrumentality with the threatening, disempowering future offered by the romantic lover, who will sweep away the woman to a private retreat; indeed, this chapter requires us to read the romantic lover as worrisome, not welcome. This chapter reads neighbor marriages in the two early Austen novels, in Rhoda Broughton's *Cometh Up as a Flower*, and in Trollope's *The Vicar of Bullhampton*—all of which show the romantic lover refashioning himself in the shape of the squire so as to become acceptable. The chapter ends by discussing *Daniel Deronda* and *Howards End*, two novels that fundamentally challenge the preconceptions of the neighbor plot. The neighbor plot, I conclude, functioned to reinforce Victorian yearning for *Gemeinschaft* (organic community) and Victorian belief in the efficacy of female influence. In other words, it expressed nineteenth-century fantasies about female power, about moving from the margins of a community to its absolute center.

In Chapter 4 I turn to cousin marriage, stressing the fact that the way it functioned in Victorian fiction was actually antithetical to its construction in the emerging discourse of Victorian anthropology. In Victorian anthropological theories of "primitive marriage," men supposedly kidnapped and married women from rival tribes, a mechanism that sets warfare, trade, and alliance into motion. But this theory infamously treats women as passive, mute sexual objects for heterosexual trafficking by men. I point out that the marriage plot offers the opposite view of women: its female characters have agency, choose partners, and engage in social relations with various people. Nowhere is this more true than in cousin marriage. Anthropology sees endogamous marriage as a null set, but the Victorian novel sees a cousin as an ideal partner. Not only do cousins generally enjoy equivalent status and shared history, but marrying within the family strengthens family ties. I explore how cousin marriage works in *Mansfield Park* and *Wuthering Heights*, pointing out that in both cases a second-generation cousin marriage works to repair the familial dissension of the first generation. Then I look at Charlotte Yonge's revision of *Mansfield Park* in *Heartsease* to reveal how fully a world of consanguineal love could be imagined, how the family could repair the ravages of a poorly chosen romantic union. The chapter ends by showing how eugenic and hereditary fears began to cloud the practice of cousin marriage by the fin de siècle.

Cousin marriage knitted one more firmly into the family, but what if one was orphaned or alienated from one's family? In Chapter 5, I discuss how the familiar marriage plot provided social grounding for isolated women by, interestingly, affiliating them with disabled men. A Victorian disabled man would generally be attended by a retinue of carers (nurses, servants, siblings, parents, friends), and a woman who joined that group would have a ready-made social realm. In order to understand the appeal of this sort of community, I utilize ethics of care, a modern feminist theory in which subjectivity is defined not by independence but by interdependence, and mutual care is the fundamental act of community-building. Nowhere is this better attested than in *Portrait of a Lady*, where Ralph Touchett weaves a loving social world around his own deathbed. However, in this chapter we start with *Persuasion*, in which Anne Elliot replaces her unsatisfactory natal family with individuals endeared to her by a history of nursing. Moreover, because the fundamental act of nurturance is caregiving, it is a gender-neutral, role-less act that can be performed by anyone, leading to loving cohabitation among individuals who would normally be debarred from marriage. *John Halifax, Gentleman*—usually seen as a paean to the self-made man—is actually a story of that man's intimate co-dependence on a disabled beloved, Phineas Fletcher. I also read Yonge's *The Clever Woman of the Family* as an homage to *Persuasion* that emphasizes the social power of disability even more than Austen did. I end Chapter 5 with *The Mill on the Floss*, where I see the stirrings of a more modern notion of disability as a medicalized, pathologized case. Philip Wakem cannot give Maggie the social grounding normally associated with the disabled man, and his emotional state is depicted as damaged by his bodily history.

Finally, Chapter 6 discusses the rhetorical structure by which women were affiliated with a fundamental but always doomed urge for meaningful work. Until the 1850s, I argue, vocationalism was an individuated process; some characters sought work, some fled from work, some worked after marriage, some didn't. In *Emma*, for instance, Jane Fairfax's governessing is seen as an appalling prospect, but the narrator also makes fun of the futile leisure of Emma and Harriet, which produces nothing but mischief. Generally, however, familiar suitors offer some form of work to the women to whom they are proposing. Orienting oneself to the social world, dealing with persons outside the nuclear family or marital dyad, is crucial to familiar marriage. This consistent interest in work—and inconsistent forecast of work—changed at mid-century. Starting in 1855, the Langham Place activists popularized the idea that all middle-class women were suffering because the work they urgently needed was consistently denied them. Women's lives had to be rewritten as tragedies, according to what I have dubbed the "suppressive hypothesis." I show how women's fates in *Can You Forgive Her, The Clever Woman of the Family*, and *Middlemarch*—three virtually contemporary novels engaged with the Langham Place cause—closely follow the new narrative of female vocational failure. From 1855 onward, feminism evolved in a way that required a rhetoric of female failure and enforced a vision of marriage as the opposite of work. The emergence of modern liberal feminism in the mid-nineteenth century is usually seen as part of a strongly progressive narrative, but in Chapter 6, I make a case for viewing it (ironically) as the mechanism for popularizing a cultural belief in female incapacity, misery, and decline.

Each of these four final chapters traces a through-line for one particular narrative structure that forms part of the familiar marriage dynamic. In each case, I contrast the familiar-marriage understanding of relationships with the theories that we have traditionally used. For instance, in Chapter 3 I acknowledge that scholars have usually seen gentry marriages as perpetuating a country-house view of England, but I stress the ways that such unions facilitate women's social centrality. Similarly, in Chapter 4 I outline the familiar story of anthropological primitive marriage but emphasize the way women often tended, instead, to regard endogamous marriage as a safe haven. The normative story is not wrong, but it tends to describe the man's perspective on marriage. Edward Ferrars, for instance, inhabits a marriage plot of personal choice, individuality, and mobility, moving toward a nuclear family. Elinor, however, does not. Her marriage plot focuses on familial interests in a static region. A real reading of their union requires equal sensitivity to both sets of interests.

In each chapter, I begin by looking at Austen's formulation of the pattern and move on to mid-Victorian rewritings (both popular and canonical fiction) of the narrative Austen developed. Starting with Austen in each chapter implies her crucially formative status in the history of the Victorian marriage plot, while my highlighting of fiction by Broughton, Craik, and Yonge works, I hope, to show how a reading of the familiar plot invites us to prioritize texts that have not made it into the traditional canon. Moreover, emphasizing familiar marriage means subtly shifting the canonical texts I address. Attention to familiar marriage suggests that we read the second generation of *Wuthering Heights* and the first generation of *Mansfield Park* with more attention than we usually give them. It means reading Philip Wakem and Henleigh Mallinger Grandcourt as divergences from a tradition, rather than as initiatory depictions. This focus also suggests a different grouping of Trollope's works; instead of reading the Barchester or Palliser series lengthwise as a long series written over many years, we can read in a tight chronological framework, noting the primacy of the familiar marriage question in the novels Trollope wrote between about 1865 and 1875.

I have aimed to cover enough novels to make good my claims to representativeness and yet center each chapter on a few major texts I can address in more depth. No doubt that balance has not always worked, but my hope is that I have managed to provide a kind of map of the nineteenth-century novel from the vantage point of familiar marriage, a map that shows both how extensive the familiar marriage plot was, and how usefully different might be the readings it leads us to do. Those of us who love the Victorian novel should find a way to recognize and respect the kind of love the Victorians espoused. If this book helps readers do that, it will have done all I want and more.

2

Historicizing Marriage, Developing the Marriage Plot

> *It seemed to me that, were I a gentleman like him, I would take to my bosom only such a wife as I could love; but the very obviousness of the advantages to the husband's own happiness, offered by this plan, convinced me that there must be arguments against its general adoption of which I was quite ignorant: otherwise I felt sure all the world would act as I wished to act.*
>
> CHARLOTTE BRONTË, Jane Eyre

IN ORDER TO understand who the familiar suitor was, we have to go back in time to see how his different layers built up over the centuries, shaping the figure in a particular way. We also have to see how the romantic suitor developed; he is no more natural a figure than his familiar counterpart. This chapter charts the changing means of marriage during the two centuries preceding the Victorian era, stressing the cultural expectations and legal changes that gradually accumulated into these literary constructs.

I explain how marriage developed in counterpoint to major texts in the evolution of the marriage plot, looking at how *Romeo and Juliet, Clarissa,* and *Northanger Abbey* (among others) built up the key elements of the story that the Victorians would develop, and noting ways in which these earlier texts are crucial as much for what they leave out as for what they establish. In other words, the marriage plot was not just a matter of copying one's predecessors but of noting problems with the current understanding of marriage and trying to recalibrate the married state to improve the situation. Nor was the marriage plot a simple reflection of lived practices. While marriage practices changed profoundly in the centuries I consider here, the marriage plot was an imagined structure, not a documentary record. It commented on reality, often by positing a compensatory fantasy that worked very differently from real practices.

Through the historical record and the literary tradition, however, I aim to show that the familiar suitor emerged not as a new invention but rather as a compendium of older expectations that received a new package, a fresh presentation. The qualities that the familiar suitor offered—trustworthy companionship and practical benefits—had been the normative goals of marriage for several centuries. Familiar benefits could therefore be taken for granted. They got articulated only when familiar marriage faced some kind of competing model. In the seventeenth and eighteenth centuries, the three main rivals were mercenary marriage, marriage based solely on filial obedience, or marriage to a rake. In the eighteenth and early nineteenth century, however, it was the rake that emerged as the main threat, the one that drove writers to develop an alternative. Terrified of the prospect of a headstrong youth forever tied to an unacceptable person for whom she felt overmastering desire, eighteenth-century writers began to imagine a prototype of the familiar suitor, an early figure I call the "suitor of rational esteem." Women had to be retrained to exercise deliberate affective choice and not give in to passion; they had to use reason to learn to prefer a verifiably honorable partner to a speciously thrilling seducer.

This model of rational esteem is what Victorian authors inherited. As this chapter will show, early Victorians reworked the suitor through the cultural iconography of Evangelicism. Similarly, Romantic marriage has a history; the image of the aristocratic rake was softened and rethought through Romantic ideas.

In writing this history, I offer a somewhat undramatic story of slow, complicated, contested change over time, an alternative to the much more dramatic story told by Lawrence Stone and his followers. Stone argues that "arranged marriage" gave way to "consensual marriage" in the late seventeenth century. He and his followers depict consensual marriage as a sudden blast of personal liberation, a clarion call of the right to pursue one's own happiness for the first time, the event that makes modern individuation possible. However, in the words of Helen Berry and Elizabeth Foyster, "Subsequent historical research . . . has provided a much more nuanced and detailed picture of the early modern family than Stone presented, but considerably more confusion over the 'bigger picture.' That there is no immediate alternative to Stone's model (its flaws notwithstanding) for thinking about change over time in the history of the English family is partly" due to new developments in history-writing.[1] In this chapter I draw on recent work, particularly historical research by Shannon McSheffrey in the medieval period, Diane O'Hara in the Tudor and Stuart eras, and Naomi Tadmor and Amanda Vickery in the eighteenth century. Such research has revealed that from the medieval period onward, the individual's personal happiness had to remain in balance with social responsibilities, although over time the dominant side gradually altered. By the eighteenth century, when it had become widely accepted for people to choose their own marital partners, it was not a sudden, liberating revolution. Rather, it was a further development of an aspect of marriage that had been present since the medieval period, and it did not eradicate social or familial pressures but altered the way in which such pressures were articulated and experienced. Moreover, this research has confirmed that marriage does not have its own separate history but rather depends intimately on developments in private property, transportation, and urbanization, while also expressing changing cultural ideals about virtue, desire, individuality, duty, consent, and choice.

In this respect, I am following the fine example of Joseph Allen Boone, whose *Tradition Counter Tradition* remains the definitive book on the marriage plot in British history. Boone also begins with a brief history of changes in marital ideology that have literary resonances, and, like me, he focuses on medieval courtly love, Renaissance love lyrics, Puritan ideas, and eighteenth-century esteem.[2] However, whereas Boone is tracking the emergence of romantic love, my interest lies in the twinned evolution of two disparate notions, the one that would become familiar marriage (companionable, comradely affection) and the one that would become romantic marriage (passionate idealization and erotic attraction). My survey therefore differs from Boone's in three important ways: first, by reading romantic love as one option among others rather than the telos of all marriage; second, by stressing the composite nature of marital decisions; and third, by taking advantage of historical work that postdates Boone and allows me to read marital change in terms of contemporary economic, philosophical, and material developments in a way that was not available to him.

In the earliest periods of Western history, it is hard to determine exactly what kinds of feelings were associated with marriage, but we can be fairly sure it was not something we would recognize as romantic love. R. Howard Bloch explains:

> The notion of romantic fascination that governs what we say about love, what we say to the ones we love, what we expect them to say to us (and to say they say), how we act and expect them to act, how we negotiate our relation to the social—in short, the hygenie [*sic*] that governs our erotic imagination right down to the choice of whom we love or the physical positions we use to express it—did not exist in Judaic, Germanic, Arabic, or Hispanic tradition, in Classical Greece or Rome, or in the early Middle Ages.[3]

This is not to say that medieval subjects did not feel love but rather that their feelings may well have taken different forms and expressions from ours. Most significantly for our purposes, love was not necessarily associated with marriage. Marriage in the medieval era was usually a pragmatic arrangement, an alliance to benefit the larger kin network and to accumulate property and power, or (at a lower class level) to partner with someone who had helpful skills.[4] Because a marriage readjusted relations within a group, the marriage was generally arranged by kin, church, and community, with the prospective bride and groom having little say.[5] It was not incompatible with affection or enjoyment, but that was not its primary goal.

Treating marriage primarily as a community and property arrangement made sense, given that the couple's survival depended on land and family. Frances and Joseph Gies write:

> Though to modern perceptions the economic concerns that preoccupied parties to a marriage in former times seem discordantly mercenary, to families entirely dependent upon land for their livelihood such concerns were inevitable and primary. Modern industrial society provides a multitude of options for young people contemplating marriage, but traditional land-based society did not. Inheritance of land and the contributions of families to marriage were indispensable [*sic*] basics.[6]

While it certainly would be pleasant to feel love for one's spouse rather than indifference or distaste, and while many medieval couples obviously did feel such affectionate bonds, this feeling was expected to develop after the marriage ceremony, not before.[7] In a study of marriage cases in the ecclesiastical courts at York in the fourteenth century, Frederik Pederson found only a single litigant who cited marital affection as an expectation for his union.[8] Martha Howell sums up: "Husband and wife in, say, 1000 or 1200, could be attentive to one another's needs and were by no means indifferent to their spouse's person; occasionally they even spoke of conjugal love. These sentiments were not, however, the principal motivations for marriage, and medieval people did not associate marriage with the deep emotional attachments that would later give the companionate marriage its normative character."[9] Of course, some medieval matches allowed more freedom than others. Males had much more freedom than females, and wealth also affected how much choice an individual could exercise.[10] However, the point is that even when a medieval subject was allowed to choose a spouse freely, that choice was supposed to be determined by practical needs, not love.

If love factored in, it was supposed to be affectionate trust, not romantic passion. In fact, "passionate love was widely condemned as irrational and disruptive," Ralph Houlbrooke writes. "According to Peter Idley, expressing a view already old when he wrote in the mid-fifteenth century, its malign influence set a man on fire and deranged his wits."[11] Excessive love might, in fact, threaten one's other loyalties: to the family, the state, and the church.[12] It was a wildness to be contained, certainly not a basis for a lifelong decision. In medieval and early modern conduct manuals, "love is invoked as a necessary aspect of marriage, but it is almost always dissociated from marital motives per se. In fact, marital motives receive little attention, and the fact that there is no urgency or anxiety about the subject suggests that it was not a significant issue."[13] Shannon McSheffrey points out that the marriage formula, "may you find it in your heart to have me as your husband" indicates a hope for love in the future, but a sense that the love was not yet there.[14] This is hardly surprising, given that the couple might have seen one another only once or twice before the ceremony.[15]

The notion of an idealized romantic love, as opposed to disruptive passion, is generally thought to have emerged with the idea of courtly love in the twelfth century.[16] Courtly love meant an experience of all-consuming suffering as one yearns after an inaccessible beloved; romances in the courtly love tradition, like Tristan and Iseult, Abelard and Heloise, and Romeo and Juliet, inevitably end in tragedy, as its participants can never unite, much less marry. Thus the idea of romantic love developed actually in opposition to marriage; indeed, Denis de Rougemont has called courtly love anti-marriage.[17] As one courtly love commentator remarked in 1180, "I am greatly surprised that you wish to misapply the term 'love' [amor] to that marital affection [affectio maritalis] which husband and wife are expected to feel for each other . . . since everybody knows that love can have no place between husband and wife."[18] Courtly love inculcates a worshipful stance toward an idealized, distant female, a quasi-religious experience which consummation and daily cohabitation would destroy.[19] Courtly love found an ineffable, divine model for romantic love, although its relation to everyday marriage practices remained tenuous at best. By the late Middle Ages, a concept of "marital affection" had developed, but this did not mean romantic love—it meant mutual care for the other's physical and moral well-being, which might take the form of chastisement or obedience.[20] Neither courtly love nor marital affection resembles modern marital feeling.

Although romantic love never became a primary consideration in medieval marriage, other elements of modern marriage were laid in place during the period. Frances and Joseph Gies have tracked the development of marriage into a Church-controlled, monogamous, patriarchal establishment between the ninth and the eleventh centuries. Before that period, the kindred practiced "partible inheritance [dividing inheritances among descendants] and gave equal weight to maternal and paternal forebears. Now the family assumed a vertical dimension, firmly seated on an estate, a patrimony which descended from father to one son and which gave the family its new, unique surname."[21] The development of patrilineal family organization would shape British marriage for the next several centuries. Although patrilineage was entirely taken for granted by the eighteenth and nineteenth centuries, we should remember that a more equitable assignation of property was once the dominant practice.

However, for our purposes, what is most suggestive about medieval marriage is that it already contained a consensual element. It was a multistage process that began with two people pledging to marry each other in the presence of two witnesses. McSheffrey explains:

> A couple could exchange consent anywhere, anytime; all that was needed to prove the marriage in a church court were two witnesses. . . . As Michael Sheehan remarked, this was an "astonishingly individualistic" marriage system, indeed one that in many ways ran counter to the prevailing currents of medieval society that emphasized the importance of the participation of parents, guardians, and (to a lesser extent) priests in the making of a marriage.[22]

McSheffrey's point is that the individualistic nature of this contract was in serious tension with the social and communal responsibilities that a marriage had to fulfill. In the late Middle Ages, this quasi-private personal consent had to be followed by two events meant to bring in the community, the public reading of the banns and the church solemnization of the union. Personal wishes could conflict with the preferences of parents, employers, or neighbors, and their interference in the public components of the wedding could derail the union. Thus marriage featured competing needs, a personal agreement by participants having to coexist with social pressures. Marriage became conceivable as a sacrament, according to Burger, inasmuch as it was "constituted solely by the individual choice of its partners (made real in the utterance of the words of consent in front of witnesses)"; in other words, this moment of a socially ratified personal consent was crucial to the medieval imagination of marriage.[23]

This marital arrangement did lead to national prosperity. Tine de Moor and Jan Luiten van Zanden argue that consensual marriage choice set the British economy on a different track from that of Southern Europe. British men and women had mobility, earned their own money (to be pooled into a shared conjugal fund), and married late, a situation that conduced to more equality, smaller families, and greater wealth than contemporaries in Italy or Spain enjoyed.[24]

In the Tudor period, marriage continued to be a multistage process that involved the community at key points, although there was some murkiness about which processes were in fact legally necessary.[25] The medieval tension between individualism and public approval continued to be an issue, a dynamic deftly described by Diane O'Hara, whose marriage history stresses the way that individual preference always occurred within a social and economic context. O'Hara writes:

> Marriage decisions were conducted against a backdrop of constraints and expectations which did much to determine and shape individual choice. The final choice of partner, while it may indeed often have incorporated personal liking or love, was linked indissolubly to questions of family credit, economic worth and the successful handling of both courtship ritual and the sensitive negotiations that accompanied them.[26]

Due to cultural developments in the sixteenth century, that consensual core of marriage could be oriented more toward personal love than practical choice. Since space forbids anything like a full accounting of these developments, which have been amply addressed elsewhere, I will simply mention a few briefly. The new humanism celebrated human lives, exploring people's motives, conditions, and feelings. Moreover, Petrarch's enormously influential poetry perpetuated and popularized the courtly love tradition in which a suffering lover gazes from afar at his perfect female beloved. And the development of Protestantism, with its emphasis on self-reflection and self-discipline, also strongly encouraged analysis of one's own emotions. In particular, Puritanism fostered affectionate companionate marriage, holding up wedlock as a goal for earthly harmony. Men's and women's souls were equally important, and spouses needed to help each other achieve the proper spiritual state.[27]

Thus in a cultural atmosphere in which personal feelings were of great interest, it is hardly surprising that marital feeling came in for new attention. By the early modern period, affection began to be seen as a necessary preliminary to a marriage, rather than a hopeful subsequent development. According to Carol Thomas Neely, the "loving amity of the couple" became a priority, so that "love, once denounced as a dangerous disrupter of marriage, was now decreed essential to it."[28] Clergy advised aiming for "'friendly' love"—regarding one's spouse as companion, friend, and source of comfort.[29] This still does not seem to have been romantic passion. Rather, early modern subjects were supposed to choose the kind of spousal arrangement that historians would later dub "companionate." Lawrence Stone describes companionate marriage as

> a state of mind and not a passion—which is one of settled and well-tried mutual affection. This develops between two people who have known each other for a long time and have come to trust each other's judgment and have full confidence in each other's loyalty. This condition of caring may or may not be accompanied by exciting sexual bonding, and may or

> may not have begun with falling in love. Indeed, it may well develop after marriage rather than before it.[30]

This kind of confidence in another's judgment would make marriage into a spiritual opportunity, a chance to ally oneself to a trustworthy advisor regarding the state of one's soul, descended from the medieval practice of marital affection.[31]

Economic changes in the early modern period also facilitated this interest in love. Martha Howell argues that in an economy based on land, property fixed social ties and forged relationships between the current occupier and the kin who would inherit it. Although land-based wealth created tensions and resentments, it also guaranteed subsistence in future and stability in social standing.[32] The new idea of portable property encouraged a different social organization. Now someone might generate wealth through personal qualities: craft skills; capacity to manage business clientele; and a skillful choice of investments in ships, raw materials, and resalable property like cattle. Love was necessary for bonding people together to endure the vicissitudes of the new marketplace, argues Howell.[33] But love might also be a name for the feeling one got from identifying and admiring someone's particular personal capacities. Never had an individual's specific qualities been so important for generating future wealth; never had it been so crucial to measure prospective spouses according to that yardstick. If men had a language inherited from Petrarch for admiring female qualities, women were now developing a taxonomy for selecting male traits.

More generally, the early modern market economy was visibly a large organization formed of men cooperating according to their own interests. Once accustomed to market workings, then, one could imagine a universe that operated according to mundane human machinations rather than a supernatural hierarchy.[34] Particularly after it became possible to buy and live off the interest on government stocks in the 1690s, one could see oneself as an individual distinct from land or kin, an individual whose fortunes could rise or fall based on personal decisions.[35] The theories of atomism and universalism facilitated global trade, since individuals everywhere could behave harmoniously as long as they were all following the same rules of rational self-interest.[36] In investments, in trade, and in social interactions, the notion that all men followed rational self-interest provided a shared point of view for otherwise disparate participants, allowing them to pull together and achieve larger changes in governments and markets.[37] Growing interest in individualism, and appreciation of others' skills and motives, fostered success.

Such skills could be learned, taught to others, and consciously followed. We can read the Elizabethan love lyric as part of a larger elaboration of love within the context of a relationship rather than the distant worship of courtly love;

Shakespeare's sonnets expect, and demand, a response from the beloved, and reproach the beloved when that response is inadequate. In satirizing Petrarchan conventions, Shakespeare instead imagined a relationship.

Romeo and Juliet may be a tale indebted to courtly love in its suffering and sacrifice, but it is significant that Romeo actually wants to marry Juliet, not just worship her from afar. It is also significant that Juliet expresses equal passion for Romeo, being indeed unusually forthright about her desires.[38] Certainly *Romeo and Juliet* is one of the most important texts in our culture for elaborating the modern idea of love.[39] Dympna Callaghan writes that "the play's ideological project has become the dominant ideology of desire."[40] Inasmuch as the play depicts desire as a mutual, powerful, anarchic force, it does indeed instantiate the modern sense of this feeling.

Yet desire is not the same as marriage, and if *Romeo and Juliet* helps construct the modern sense of passion as a strong mutual drive, it produces at the same time a marriage plot that would be unrecognizable in later narratives. Juliet is not troubled by agonies about her ability to obey or need to disobey—she simply rejects her father to sneak off with Romeo (as Desdemona does with Othello). Similarly, Juliet has absolutely no doubt, from the instant she first sees him, that Romeo is the man for her. Their marriage is the easiest transaction imaginable, compared to what their fictional descendants will have to endure. Indeed, a reader acclimated to the complicated marital arrangements of the eighteenth- or nineteenth-century novel may be forgiven for missing the marriage of Romeo and Juliet completely, so devoid of the usual protocols is it. They need no parental consent; endure no anxieties about whether their love is the right sort; do no research into the potential partner's moral history; undergo no ritual or legal process of betrothal; require no public announcement, no documentation, no witnesses, no canonical hours or place or celebrant—their marriage is simply a mutual agreement followed by consummation. Perhaps because they never get to the public reading of the banns and the church solemnization, the marriage remains incompletely realized, so it is perfectly possible for Juliet to contract a "second marriage" to Paris, an option the Nurse strongly endorses. No concerns about bigamy, blasphemy, or the illegality of remarriage while the first spouse lives haunt Juliet at all. A wedding, for Romeo and Juliet, is a process rather than an act, and the elements of that process may be manipulated.

This is, of course, a fantasy, and the lovers' tragedy shows the impossibility of its enactment in a real world of princely power, familial allegiance, and patriarchal disposition of daughters. What *Romeo and Juliet* helps institute, as a central tenet of love stories, is a clash in which ardent youths long to run off together while elders try to stop them. There is nothing necessarily natural about representing love stories in terms of generational conflict. Doing so sets up certain assumptions that have shaped later narratives, among which is the important one that love is associated with the self-definition of a passionate teenager, while a prudent match is proclaimed by an often interchangeable roster of elders (the Capulets and the Montagus, in this regard, speak with one voice). Thus prudent marriage becomes a familial, shared, public concern, in which the state has an interest, while passionate marriage becomes associated with individuation and youthful rebellion.

In 1597, however, it is impossible to give the victory to either side. Either the lovers will lose their families (their social standing, their economic basis, their very identity) or the families will lose their youths. From the lovers' perspective—which is largely the audience's—their personal pleasure matters the most. But from the parents' perspective, the lovers' passion is a dangerously uncontrolled feeling that imperils the fundamental structure of social organization in Verona. Nobody can win; it is a tragedy. The youths achieve validation of their feelings, but only at the cost of self-destruction.

Romeo and Juliet shows the growing popularity of the idea of consensual marriage as we move through the early modern period. To Shakespeare's audience, it presumably seemed right that Juliet should pick her own Romeo, instead of having a parental Paris foisted upon her—and yet that marriage cannot be depicted, perhaps cannot even be imagined, and Paris remains an attractive choice nonetheless.

For the seventeenth-century marriage prospect continued to balance personal wishes with social needs, perpetuating the kind of dynamic O'Hara described in Tudor England in which affection was a cultural goal, but only within obedience to parental authority. David Blewett explains:

> Children were, in theory at least, accorded a veto [over their parents' choice of marriage partner], but they were not expected to seek their own mates, even when their parents failed to provide a marriage partner. Mutual affection was often mentioned as something desirable and the possibility of it was sometimes insisted upon as a condition for marrying. But the central point was, as Gouge put it, that children ought to settle their affections "on the party whom their parents have chosen for them." Certainly no seventeenth-century moralist would have maintained that the presence or absence of mutual affection was by itself a reason for marrying or not. Indeed, such reasoning would have appeared to place marriage on a very uncertain and treacherous foundation.[41]

Interestingly, in seventeenth-century practice, consent was required of parents, not of children, who were widely perceived as their parents' possessions. John

Stockwood asserted in 1589 that "children are worthily to be reckoned among the goods and substance of their fathers." Thus "in seeking to betroth themselves at their own pleasure, not regarding to have the good will and leave of their parents, deal as preposterously, and overthwartly, as if the goods should go about to dispose the owner and possessor of the same."[42]

Well into the eighteenth century, it remained the parents' responsibility to choose the individuals whom their children would marry. As one woman summed it up, "I receiv'd the Addresses of my Lord—through the Recommendation of my Parents, and marry'd him with their Consents and my own Inclination."[43] A servant contemplating marriage in the eighteenth century prayed hard to make the right decision. She noted that "my friends approve it, and I think it my duty to pay some regard to their advice; but a business for life, requires deliberate consideration." Finally accepting her suitor, she worried, "I hope I have not been too hasty, the character of the person being so well known, and though I have not been long acquainted with *him*, He has known *me* seventeen years."[44] The writer never mentions, and seems quite unconcerned about, whether she loves the man.

Although by this period the married couple were indeed supposed to feel "love," Ralph Houlbrooke explains that "the word love had a number of meanings, ranging from friendship to passionate mutual absorption. Furthermore, it was widely believed, especially among the upper classes, that mutual affection could easily develop within marriage between well-matched partners. In this view a strong prior attraction between prospective spouses was inessential."[45] What we have from the twelfth through the mid-eighteenth century, then, is a situation in which personal affection is supposed to be accommodated within a marital arrangement determined by parental needs and social approval, but that affection is generally a companionable, trusting comradeship. Passionate erotic love and idealized romantic adoration remain on the margins of marriage, respectively disruptive or tragic, elements of heightened emotional states worthy of poetry or madness but hardly compatible with the ordinary constraints of marital arrangements.

In thinking ahead to the marital norms of the late eighteenth century and the nineteenth century, it is important to remember two facts that derive from this earlier history. The first is that what historical subjects called "love" was not necessarily the kind of passion we recognize as a suitable basis for Western marriage today. The second is that although all marriage was supposed to be consensual at some level, in fact consensual marriage means nothing more or less than the fact that both parties consented to the match. It does not necessarily imply anything about the quality of feeling between those consenting participants. Indeed, consent might say more about the child's obedience to the parent, the employer, or the patron than the child's feeling about the spouse.

Consent was an issue partly because it implies an independent agent voluntarily agreeing to something, a model of subjectivity at odds with the traditional view of the self as bound to obedience to elders and to God. In this respect it is telling that throughout the seventeenth century, the hottest debates about consent did not focus on the partners' wishes but on parental-filial responsibilities. Should parents force daughters to marry men they find abhorrent?[46] Should daughters obey such commands? George Savile, the Marquis of Halifax, gave an unqualified "yes" in 1688, asserting that if the woman's "inward Consent may not entirely go along with" the match, she simply ought to work harder to reconcile herself to the union.[47] However, another writer urgently advised daughters, "Whatever you do be not induced to marry one you have either abhorrency or loathing to; for it is neither affluency of estate, potency of friends, nor highness of discent [sic] can allay the insufferable grief of a loathed bed."[48] This vivid evocation of "a loathed bed" calls up a tradition of marital grieving perhaps most prominently associated with Milton's divorce tracts, in which Milton described an unhappy couple's "unspeakable wearisomnes and despaire [sic] of all sociable delight."[49] Although Milton's insistence on a right to divorce based on personal happiness was extreme—and extremely controversial—in 1644, his position would become normative in the next century. Milton proclaimed that enforced marriage was a "savage inhumanity."[50] By 1744, this would no longer be a minority position.

The revulsion at "a loathed bed," the "unspeakable wearisomnes" of a bad marriage—this kind of rhetoric revealed an expectation of personal happiness and a corresponding outrage when such expectations were denied. Such ideas derived from a crucial way of thinking that emerged in the seventeenth century.

This period is famous for its new idea: the notion that an individual had a right to pursue personal happiness. This classic liberal idea of the self is best known by John Locke's claim that "every man has a *property* in his own *person*: this no body has any right to but himself."[51] Lockean liberal thought enabled seventeenth-century subjects to see themselves as agents with the right to personal happiness and the self-determination to develop that happiness through choices in the marital marketplace. Wendy Jones writes: "It is no accident that the rise of married love and the cultural hegemony of liberal theory coincide, or that consensual married love, with its emphasis on the individual's significance, identity, and right to self-fulfilment, articulates the very characteristics that liberal theory grants to its citizen-subjects."[52] To imagine oneself as an autonomous being meant that one could, and should, determine one's life apart from the needs of one's larger social network. Marriage could become a private decision, not a social alliance. Perry cites William Goode's summation: "The ideology of the conjugal family proclaims the right of the individual to choose his or her own spouse, place to live, and even which kin obligations to accept, as against the acceptance of others' decisions. It asserts the worth of the *individual* as against the inherited elements of wealth or ethnic group."[53]

But not everyone was admitted to this admirable state of freedom. The classic liberal model of individualism required "rationally competent adults who, as Locke says, are, in the state of nature, 'free, equal, and independent.' "[54] Defining individuals this way prompts us to imagine someone who is not rational, not free, not equal, not independent, the kind of shadow persona against whom the liberal agent can be defined. Such shadow subjects may include slaves, the poor, women, and the disabled.[55] "The family and state arose in conjunction with each other and . . . their very structures are interdependent," writes Linda J. Nicholson.[56] Seyla Benhabib notes that in the early modern Enlightenment universe, "the experience of the early modern female has no place. Woman is simply what man is not; namely they are not autonomous, independent, but by the same token, nonaggressive but nurturant, not competitive but giving, not public but private. The world of the female is constituted by a series of negations. She is simply what he happens not to be."[57]

In other words, when the monistic agent emerges, a man in a marketplace, so does its implicit opposite, a woman in a family. Both structures became understood against one another. Locke's idea established the notion of the state as public and the domestic space as private—an opposition that would have been wholly foreign to late medieval subjects. In the fifteenth century, marriage, sex, and family were public interests, formalized by public utterances, regulated by the church, and determined through intermediaries. It was the Enlightenment that created a private-public divide.[58] In Gal Gerson's words: "The private sphere is identified with emotion and the body. It is populated by reproductive women and their offspring. The public sphere is characterised by the symmetrical lines of law and justice. It is populated by mutually unconcerned, freely moving individuals. It is a male sphere."[59] Each sphere depends upon the other; one cannot imagine a purely rational and disembodied realm of the state unless one can relegate need, desire, and the body to the messy world of the family. One buys universality in the public realm at the cost of particularity in the private sphere.[60]

Both public rational man and his counterpart, private emotional woman, were ideals. This does not make them any less powerful. Nancy Yousef has pointed out that the liberal subject is a thought experiment. Hobbes and Locke and their successors knew perfectly well that people were not really independent, but by imagining them that way, it became possible to think of human qualities differently.[61] As plenty of feminist critics have pointed out, the self-sacrificing domestic angel was just as impossible. It functioned as a cultural ideal against which real women might measure themselves. But the development of these opposed categories of thought—regardless of the degree to which they found real-world analogues—meant a fundamental recalibration of people's visions of their world and their selves.

Thus the emergence of liberal theory allowed some people to occupy a new kind of subjectivity in which they could make personal choices for their own betterment, but consigned some to a condition of subordinating their own needs to the needs of others. We can see here the basic attitudes that would eventually come to underlie romantic and familiar marriage. The romantic union produces personal pleasure; the familiar marriage satisfies a larger social organization. In the seventeenth century, these were not yet entirely distinct pathways. Marriage was undertaken for many reasons—companionship, assistance, alliance, improvement, reproduction—and the extent to which one might expect pleasure in this state (or the type of pleasure one might reasonably expect) remained variable. But over time, marriage practice was shifting. By the end of the eighteenth century, it had become normative to be able to expect to choose one's own partner, and to choose that spouse so as to prioritize personal enjoyment.

The case of Mary Granville exemplifies this shift. In 1717, at the age of sixteen, Mary's family forced her to marry someone she found repulsive: an obese, dirty, alcoholic man in his sixties, Alexander Pendarves.[62] Mary's wealthy uncle Lord Lansdown forced her into the match through threats to her parents' financial well-being, guilt trips, and insulting intimations about her sexual virtue.[63] What is significant is not just that Mary was made to marry much against her will in 1717 but also that she was able to write about it as a horrifying tale by 1740.[64] Within Mary's own lifetime, norms changed, and by the time she married her second husband, Patrick Delany, in 1743, she was able to exercise her own preference. In 1717 marriage existed for the betterment of the family; but in 1743, Mary married out of rational esteem, choosing someone she approvingly denoted a "worthy, and sensible friend."[65] Mrs. Delany later became famous for her remarkable botanical paper collages. She became a friend of Samuel Richardson's and may have recognized her experiences with Pendarves in the sordid tale of the Harlowes's pressure on Clarissa to marry the elderly, unattractive Solmes. Her story, like her fictional analogue's, shows that consensual marriage in the early eighteenth century might well amount to enforced, reluctant, horrified consent.[66]

The fact that the woman's consent *was* required (even if extorted) in both Clarissa's and Mary's cases, reveals something important: a development that historians have named "consensual marriage." By the eighteenth century, individuals were largely expected to choose their own partners. We may see it as a development from the medieval period, when one moment of individualistic self-assertion—the mutual verbal contract—stood out in a marital process that was otherwise wholly oriented toward community. Several centuries later, this one utterance had expanded to become the dominant practice governing the marital decision itself. What was once a small intense consensual kernel cushioned by a thick rind of social regulation swelled to a much larger size, with the rind correspondingly shrinking. As individuals' personal choices became a larger part of the marriage arrangement, the question of whom they chose, and why, was less regulated than ever before. This new freedom might be dangerous, as adolescents might well make bad choices. But it also might be liberating, the beginning of modern autonomy and marital ties that were truly based in love.

As we saw in Chapter 1, Lawrence Stone's *The Family, Sex, and Marriage in England, 1500–1800* (1977) argued that the rise of consensual marriage marks the turn to modernity because it reinforced individuality and facilitated affectionate relationships. His thesis has influenced family and marriage history profoundly, although it has also been intensely contested. Family historians in the late 1970s and early 1980s split into two hostile groups. Stone and other historians of the family, including Philippe Ariès, Edward Shorter, and Randolph Trumbach, differed in important ways but all argued that once people could choose their own partners, the nuclear family came to replace the larger extended family, a change that ushered in key elements of the modern world: familial affection, private life, competition, and self-awareness. However, Peter Laslett and other historians, including Ralph Houlbrooke and Alan Macfarlane, argued that there was in fact no significant change, since familial affection and nuclear families could be found even in the medieval period.[67] Consensual marriage, in their view, may have been a longstanding practice, but even if it developed when Stone said it did, it had no larger repercussions. [68] Subsequent historians, including O'Hara and McSheffrey, have developed a more nuanced understanding. The best marriage histories today no longer assume consent and obedience were mutually exclusive but instead explore the complex way in which some element of consent coexisted within a framework of social determinants.

In this study, as I hope is clear by now, I follow the lead of these more recent marriage histories, but I do use some elements of Stone's work. Specifically, I draw on Stone's characterization of "companionate marriage" and his claim that it emerges around the seventeenth century, two relatively uncontested elements in his theory. I do not endorse Stone's assertions that before 1660, family relations were characterized by indifference or cruelty, and that personal affection, kindly parenting, private life, and the nuclear family only emerged after 1660, as these claims are clearly not historically sustainable.[69] I also concur with Laura E. Thomason that "the so-called rise of companionacy was not as smooth as scholars of marriage have previously suggested."[70] Affectionate marriage arrived more slowly and unevenly than Stone suggests.

In the eighteenth century, marriage took multiple forms, from Mary Delany's rational approbation of a partner to mercenary matches enforced by guardians of the kind that Hogarth made famous in his "Marriage à la Mode" series of engravings, to the kind of romantic elopement Clarissa's family believes she has contracted with Lovelace. Stone's narrative of a triumphant, inevitable progress toward the haven of modern affectionate nuclear families was certainly not the full truth, but today we can see that the dynamic Stone described did exist; it just existed in company with older imperatives to obey parents and with composite marital ideals that tried to combine disparate aims. The eighteenth century was, in short, a mess of wildly conflicting marital ideals—so chaotic that it perhaps required the invention of the marriage plot to help work through them.

Overall, the widespread shift to consensual marriage was more like a new fashion than a new law, a trend rather than a sudden, drastic change. Consent blossomed as the assertion of individual right of choice, an expectation of personal happiness with one's own spouse. Consensual marriage meant that people needed to think for themselves about the kind of future they wanted. One might pick a spouse who offered financial guarantees rather than emotional pleasures, or one might pick an alliance with a politically powerful clan rather than a personally attractive suitor, but it was, crucially, an individual decision.

Deciding to choose a partner is only possible when one's culture has developed a notion of what makes a man, or a woman, choice-worthy. Consensual marriage required a literature about marriageability—a discourse teaching individuals how to assess potential partners. As Ian Watt, Nancy Armstrong, and most recently Hilary Schor have argued, the novel provided this information. The modern novel helped limn what an ideal man or woman might look like, imagined what kinds of lives might result from different marital choices, and trained readers to imagine their responses to types of suitors.[71]

Women had to learn not only how to choose a spouse but also how to make themselves into the sort of person someone else would be likely to choose as a spouse. Consensual marriage practice required people to monitor their own (and others') individual personalities, social interests, class and economic status, and religious faith, constantly adjusting, compensating, disciplining, and performing each criterion. This self-awareness, which grew out of Protestant ideas, was a relatively new way of perceiving the self, at odds with the traditional practice of familially determined marriage, which required suppressing one's individual preferences and autonomy for the good of one's kin.[72]

Once it became normative to pick one's own spouse, the question changed. On what basis should one make this choice? Should a person pick someone erotically attractive, someone who seemed likely to be a trustworthy comrade, or someone who offered a beneficial economic and political situation? Ideally, those three factors would coincide. In fiction, they might (witness Fitzwilliam Darcy). But in real life, they often did not. Seventeenth- and eighteenth-century writers expressed particular anxiety at the prospect of inexperienced youths following their hearts. Erotic pleasure was still only tenuously connected to the marriage state. But now that marrying out of erotic desire was even a possibility, it became necessary to articulate an alternative to it. The shaping of sexual feeling in marital discourse generated a powerful need for a riposte.

Sexual desire was presented as a danger, not a pleasure, for most women. Faramerz Dabhoiwala has shown how predatory seventeenth- and eighteenth-century men were encouraged to be, while women were supposed to defend their chastity at all costs. "Everywhere one looks, especially in the private writings and conversations of the period, there can be found the chillingly ruthless, misogynist celebration of gentlemanly sexual conquest—not merely for sensual enjoyment, but as the exercise of power over one's inferiors."[73] The dangers of men's sexual passion were vividly depicted in eighteenth-century seduction narratives and Gothic novels, in which helpless young women were victimized by powerful men bent on ruining them. Katherine Binhammer argues that there is good reason the seduction narrative arises alongside consensual marriage. "Seduction narratives tell the story of a woman's struggle to decode the new semiotics of courtship and love."[74] They reveal ways "in which lovers do not always act in the interests of the community."[75] In such major texts of the British novel tradition as *Pamela, Clarissa*, and *Evelina*; in women-authored eighteenth-century novels like *Belinda, Emmeline*, and *Millenium Hall*; and even in Austen's earliest novels, *Northanger Abbey, Pride and Prejudice*, and *Sense and Sensibility*, we see women assaulted, abused, and abandoned by men. The female victims are helpless against male villains who are far worldlier, physically stronger, richer, and more powerful.

This fear of an anarchic, destructive sexual desire propelled eighteenth-century writers to try to redirect feelings into a new structure, a different kind of suitor. Advice manuals addressed the newly urgent issue of love.[76] In these manuals,

> A new emotion was identified—a new form of emotional consciousness defined and elicited—to govern these choices: a form of sexualized love suitable for marriage. This new emotional consciousness, about which a public discourse mushroomed in journals and sermons as well as novels and poems, was needed to supply the place of earlier kin controls on sexuality; it had to regulate and direct sexual impulses in a way that sustained the values of the society.[77]

These advice manuals and novels created what we might call the suitor of rational esteem. He is Sir Charles Grandison, the later Mr. B, Lord Orville, Fitzwilliam Darcy: a polite, respectful man who safeguarded women instead of threatening them. The manuals stressed that women ought to examine a man's moral rectitude over a sustained period of time and only when certain that they could genuinely esteem his character would they marry. In the suitor of rational esteem, eighteenth-century thinkers codified the kind of companionable trust previously sought in marriage, and imagined the kind of man who might be worth such feeling. The marital affection that might previously have been taken more or less for granted now had to be explicitly articulated and consciously sought, to give an alternative to a dangerous sexual pairing.

The suitor of rational esteem only works if one assumes that women could deliberately direct their love toward a polite man with good moral qualities.[78] Readers had to believe that women were not uncontrollably oversexed. In what Dabhoiwala has dubbed the first sexual revolution, in the late seventeenth and eighteenth century, women were reinvented as sexless, angelic beings who could act as men's moral guardians.[79] This allowed a woman to be conceptualized as someone who was not driven wild with desire but rather was rationally capable of choosing a marital partner. Love in such cases was a calmly settled, well-tested, thoroughly vetted admiration. Ingrid H. Tague reads the eighteenth-century insistence on marrying for this kind of love as a way of reinforcing women's status. A woman had to love enough to voluntarily submit herself to a husband, to choose her own obedience.[80]

Such a rational marriage seemed superior to other alternatives. It was clearly more pleasant than a cold-blooded marriage of interest, in which partners wed for political or economic benefit. Interest might bring together two people who actively disliked one another too much to collude. But it also worked better than passion; romance might create unstable and dangerous emotions, leaving people yoked together who ought not to be connected, and whose union might damage the class interests of the participants and their connections. As one conduct book writer asserted: "Violent love cannot subsist, at least cannot be expressed, for any time together on both sides; otherwise the certain consequence, however concealed, is satiety and disgust."[81] Certainly in fiction of the period, violently passionate lovers endanger themselves and others, as in Charlotte Smith's *Emmeline, or, The Orphan of the Castle*, where Lord Frederic Delamere's obsession with his cousin Emmeline causes him to stalk her, abduct her, and engage in suicidal activities. Laura E. Thomason studied a range of eighteenth-century female subjects who concurred that "passionate love represents a loss of control and judgment, qualities of which women were often deprived and qualities that they believed a companionate marriage should enable, protect, and preserve."

They defined marriage as an egalitarian relation of mutually rational beings. Thomson sums up: "The advancement of this ideal of companionacy—marriage understood as a form of friendship—gave women a means of promoting gender equality in marriage at a time when they considered marriage 'serious and hazardous' but socially and economically necessary."[82]

If rational partnership offered some opportunity for self-determination and egalitarianism for women, no wonder it was more popular than romantic marriage. Indeed, "evidence of hostility to sexual desire as a basis for choice of a marriage partner can be found in every commentator of the seventeenth and eighteenth centuries," Stone asserts.[83] For instance, *The Lady's Monthly Magazine*, in 1799, asked whether the individual was truly marrying "from the tenderest, from the most exalted principles of esteem and affection?" After all, "others, again mistake the transient glow of passion, or the fond delirium of the imagination, for the fervours of a rational attachment, and rush presumptuously into the marriage state without reflection."[84] The pseudonymous compiler of *The Gentlewoman's Companion, or, a Guide to the Female Sex* (1675) put it concisely: "Now the difference betwixt a wife and a wild love is this; the one ever deliberates before it loves, and the other loves before it deliberates."[85] Such a relationship was the safe alternative to the risks of seduction. Women were supposed to choose wisely, whatever men did. John Gregory explained that "a man of taste and delicacy marries a woman because he loves her more than any other. A woman of equal taste and delicacy marries him because she esteems him, and because he gives her that preference."[86] Men might be ruled by passion, but women ought to be governed by esteem.

The suitor chosen out of rational esteem became the dominant cultural ideal by the end of the eighteenth century, a crucial point when we think about the lifespans of Victorian authors. Dickens, Thackeray, Eliot, Gaskell, the Brontës, Yonge—all born in the 1810s and 1820s—had parents who would have met and married in the heyday of the fervor for rational esteem. Presumably this is the model that they would have imparted to their children. As we shall see, in the Victorian fiction these children would grow up to write, elders do usually try to impart the rational esteem model to their heedless offspring. It cannot be overemphasized that the marriage plot at the dawn of the Victorian era is not about triumphant progress toward individual choice but terrified fleeing of dangerous prospects. It is not about embracing passionate love but moderating one's feelings toward a safer kind of fellow. It cannot be overemphasized that the formative marital ideal for the major Victorian authors was the marriage of rational esteem.

In this light, I want to ask what happens if we reconceptualize the rise-of-the-novel story by putting a different text at its center. We might read *Clarissa* (1748) as the initiating text of the modern novel tradition, instead of *Robinson*

Crusoe (as Watt does) or *Pamela* (as Armstrong does). *Robinson Crusoe* is the ur-story of modern individuation; *Pamela* is the original tale of the domesticated marital woman. But *Clarissa* is a different kind of novel. If we read it as the origin of the marriage plot, then we see this tradition beginning with the story of a woman pulled between the worst imaginable romantic and familiar suitors, torn between familial coercion and independent disaster, unable to marry yet unable to have a future without marrying. The impossible situation of Clarissa is the marriage plot in its most implacable form. Clarissa expresses a sense of marriage as a scene of dread, not pleasure:

> Marriage is a very solemn engagement, enough to make a young creature's heart ache, with the *best* prospects, when she thinks seriously of it!—To be given up to a strange man; to be engrafted into a strange family; to give up her very name, as a mark of her becoming his absolute and dependent property: to be obliged to prefer this strange man to father, mother—to everybody: and his humours to all her own—Or to contend, perhaps, in breach of a vowed duty for every innocent instance of free will: to go nowhither: to make acquaintance: to give up acquaintance—to renounce even the strictest friendships perhaps; all at his pleasure, whether she think it reasonable to do so or not. Surely, sir, a young creature ought not to be obliged to make all these sacrifices but for such a man as she can approve. If she *is*, how sad must be the case!—how miserable the life, if to be called *life*![87]

Clarissa's horror of marriage, and her refusal to marry any of her suitors, allows us to read this as a novel that diagnoses a crisis in marital ideology just as vividly as *Romeo and Juliet* did a century and a half before. In both cases, a young woman has no viable future but marriage, and yet she finds the conditions of her culture make marriage impossible. Clarissa's stalemate is symptomatic of a crisis in her era.[88] At the origin of the marriage plot are two stories that show marriage to be impossible, doom suitors to death, and construct courtship as catastrophe.

Most *Clarissa* evidence focuses on the rape, ignoring Richardson's own interest in it as a marriage novel. The novel's full title is *Clarissa: Or, the History of a Young Lady: Comprehending the Most Important Concerns of Private Life, and Particularly Showing the Distresses That May Attend the Misconduct Both of Parents and Children, in Relation to Marriage.* In writing *Clarissa* as a cautionary tale regarding love and marriage, Richardson was continuing to discuss what his biographers identify as his favorite subjects. In the collection of letters he wrote during the time he was penning *Pamela,* almost half of the letters concern this topic, covering popular current debates like a parent's responsibility and a child's duty to obey.[89] Moreover, he was proud that *Clarissa* helped influence marital legislation.[90]

What happens, then, if we take seriously the eponymous idea that *Clarissa* "particularly show[s] the distresses that may attend" marital misconduct? The first thing we will need to do is read *Clarissa* as a study of marriage, not of rape. We will need to see it stressing filial versus parental consent, not sexual consent. We will need to focus on the first third of the book, not the final third. This is the kind of recalibration a familiar-marriage perspective opens up, when the sexual plots on which critics have traditionally focused can recede to allow us to focus anew on the marriage plots we might previously have rejected as uninterestingly conventional.

Moreover, reading *Clarissa* as a marriage novel rather than a rape novel refocuses us on the issue of Clarissa's agency. Because the marriage plot shows women making active choices, the frustration of Clarissa's capacity to choose—even to make the negative choice of saying "no"—becomes newly outrageous; the first third of the novel becomes a litany of Clarissa's energetic proposals, all maddeningly, illogically refused. This ingenious innovator Clarissa is a different kind of character from the passive victim who retreats into inner purity after the rape.[91] Clarissa claims gleefully, "Had they thought me such a championess, they would not have engaged with me." Her uncle admits: "We are all afraid to see you, because we know we shall be made as so many fools" (L45, L60). Indeed, her uncle writes, writes, she is "a bold challenger" and "too artful for me" (L62). Clever, tireless, and determined, the Clarissa of the marriage plot section enacts her period's debates over filial obedience, personal liberty, and abhorrence with great flair. Bonnie Latimer has argued that Richardson constructs a new idea of women as self-controlled rational agents, as opposed to the promiscuous, emotional, irrational, undifferentiated beings depicted in the amatory fiction and anti-female satires of the period.[92] Certainly Clarissa's remarkable rhetorical force makes her the most admirable individual agent of the whole opening section of the novel.

Much *Clarissa* criticism has focused on the question of just how much Clarissa might desire Lovelace and whether she unconsciously facilitates her rape—a critical orientation that is obviously profoundly disturbing.[93] Binhammer points out that "late twentieth—and early twenty-first-century scholars who most often read the truth of Clarissa's heart as a hidden sexual truth" "actually place themselves in the same position as Lovelace, claiming to know more about Clarissa's desire than she does herself."[94] Literary critics performing invasive sexual readings of Clarissa, of all subjects, is too bitter an irony to need elaboration. This goal clearly arises out of our obsession with desire as the truth of the subject and has little to do with any understanding of female subjectivity or marriage in the eighteenth century. Such critiques require us to overlook or second-guess Clarissa's perfectly sensible explanation that while she could have preferred Lovelace to anyone else, his moral deficits make her unwilling to marry him. Indeed, the fact that sexualized readings inevitably end up "proving" that Clarissa desires Lovelace is perhaps as cogent a proof as one could want that excessive emphasis on desire can lead literary criticism into bad paths.

Rather, if we read *Clarissa* with attention to the status of marriage in its own historical period, the issue of Clarissa's desire—unconscious, denied, repressed—ceases to become important. The more significant question, I suggest, is why Richardson does not provide Clarissa with a suitor for whom she can feel rational esteem. As the man who started his career by giving courtship advice to women, and the man who would end his career by writing *Sir Charles Grandison*, Richardson certainly had the notion of the morally estimable man very much at heart. What does the absence of that man do for Clarissa's story?

Clarissa is initially set up as an updated version of *Romeo and Juliet*. Richardson establishes the Lovelace and the Harlowe families as murderous rivals after a scene in which Lovelace and James Harlowe nearly kill each other, like Tybalt and Mercutio. Richardson's reworking of *Romeo and Juliet* is hardly surprising, given his intense interest in Shakespeare.[95] Casting himself as the heir of this narrative of impossible familial/personal collision, he sets up *Clarissa* to work out the same tragedy in a new era. But *Clarissa* makes some key changes. The patriarchal authority vested in both the state and the families in Shakespeare's play is now deeply troubled; the brother has seized control of the Harlowe family, and the uncle and cousin who might control the mayhem are too far away. No principle of mature centralization, no wise Prince Escalus will subdue the anarchy of the feuding youths. Moreover, in lieu of the equally ardent lovers of Shakespeare's play, this Romeo's desire is a toxic brew of pride and violence, while this Juliet is an angelic, nondesiring, nearly disembodied subject. In the dystopic eighteenth-century urban space of Richardson's great novel, Mrs. Sinclair has replaced Friar Laurence and the brothel takes the place of the chapel.[96] In spite of these dire deteriorations, one factor remains absolutely true to Shakespeare: the woman must, once again, embrace her coffin as her final resting place.

The novel is capable of a radically different reading from Ian Watt's account of Clarissa as "the heroic representative of all that is free and positive in the new individualism, and especially of the spiritual independence which was associated with Puritanism."[97] Watt reads *Clarissa* as a novel of private feeling and individualism, a tradition that has most recently been carried on by Latimer, whose "key argument is that Richardson's fictions are instrumental in a cultural shift in which women become imaginable as individuals—that is to say, as stable, autonomous, contained and rational selves."[98] However, "individual" has two meanings, and only one is really true of Clarissa. If it is true that Clarissa is individual in the sense of being a stable, spiritually independent, and rational soul, it does not necessarily follow that she is therefore individual in the sense of being an autonomous agent. In fact, Clarissa is intensely interdependent. Her tragedy occurs when she is ripped away from her social network, torn from her family, deprived of her friend's help, and made utterly vulnerable. Moreover, when forced into a dyad with a man who embodies the most dangerous aspect of the modern individualist, self-seeking, romantic suitor, Clarissa gets destroyed. *Clarissa* can be read as a case study in the dangers of individualism and the necessity of relational enmeshment.

Such a social reading consorts with what we know of Richardson and the composition of the novel. Certainly the man who worked amid a coterie of female correspondents, whom he invited to rewrite, discuss, and critique the manuscript in process, was someone profoundly invested in social networks. Indeed, the very structure of an epistolary novel, with utterances shaped for another consciousness and with voices chiming into a communal account of each activity, itself enacts a multifaceted, not an individualist, sense of experience. In the apt words of Hina Nazar, "epistolarity in *Clarissa* ascribes to virtue a sociable and immanent dynamic."[99] Thus *Clarissa* is susceptible to exactly the opposite of Watt's reading; instead of the narrative of the rise of a heroic individual, it is the cautionary tale of the appalling work done by a single appetitive individual, as he rips someone out of her social circle into a world of danger.

Clarissa vividly shows that, in the dangerous new world of personal choice, it was terrifyingly easy to go wrong. If a man had reason to believe a woman felt erotic passion for him, that could make the woman shockingly vulnerable. It could put her into the power of someone who might well ruin her. Lovelace, like other romantic suitors, makes time converge on a single present moment. "The effect of Lovelace's plotting is to collapse the time of narrative, to see the end in the beginning. For this reason, he thinks consent is retroactive, and that the end of sex will turn Clarissa's 'no' into 'yes,' thus demonstrating his expert knowledge that sexual insatiability is the true nature of women," Binhammer explains. Thus, "once subdued, always subdued. In collapsing the diachronic pattern of events into a single act, the plot of sexual intrigue reduces love to sex."[100] The very fabric of this novel—its immense duration and interpersonal epistolary form—is against him; the narrative itself speaks of a kind of personal time that Lovelace cannot occupy.

If Lovelace is dangerous, so too is Solmes. Consenting to wed someone like Solmes for money meant a lifetime of misery for the wife as the husband exercised his legal mastery. There was great anxiety about mercenary marriage in the early eighteenth century.[101] Imagining marriage with Solmes requires ignoring the present, focusing only on a future in which Clarissa will grow to be contented with him (L32.4). Here again the narrative structure itself belies this vision. Clarissa is in a perpetual now, seeing only this Tuesday, yestermorn, the precise date of that day's letter. For Clarissa, the promises of future stability mean nothing. When she considers the advice, "Marry first and love will come after," she objects: "But 'tis a shocking assertion! A thousand things may happen to make that state but barely tolerable, where it is entered into with mutual affection: what must it then be, where the husband can have no confidence in the love of his wife . . . ?" (L32.1). Caught between dangerous passion with Lovelace and revolting mercenariness with Solmes, where is Clarissa to turn? As she herself puts it, "I see in Lovelace, the rocks on one hand, and in Solmes, the sands on the other; and tremble lest I should split upon the former, or strike upon the latter" (L69).

There is no safe shore on which Clarissa could land. Or rather, there is a harbor, but it is destined for someone else's boat. Charles Hickman is the man of rational esteem, the ancestor of the familiar suitor, the immediate precursor of Grandison. He is not an immediately enticing prospect; it takes Anna the full duration of the novel—during which she mercilessly makes fun of his awkwardness—to consent to marry him. Like the familiar suitors who would follow him, Hickman is endorsed by his beloved's family and notable for his excellent morality (which gets tested repeatedly), but the woman thinks of him more as a paternal or fraternal relation than a romantic prospect (L46, L523). In the end, however, Anna and Hickman form the only happy marriage in the novel, which is otherwise a grim record of male tyranny over females: Mr. Harlowe, the Harlowe uncles, Solmes, James Harlow Jr., and Lovelace.[102] In the brief glimpse we get of their married life, we find that Anna and Hickman have an unusually egalitarian, harmonious partnership, with Anna managing Clarissa's Poor Fund, but "in every other case, there is but *one will* between them; and that is generally his or hers, as either speak first upon any subject, be it what it will" (Conclusion, 1492). Through the figure of Hickman, Richardson was able to imagine the only happy marriage of the novel.

The absence of such a suitor causes Clarissa's tragedy. Both Anna and Clarissa are aware of this fact. Anna half-jokingly offers Hickman to Clarissa, and Clarissa rather more seriously responds: "Although you say I would not like him myself, I do assure you, if Mr. Solmes were such a man as Mr. Hickman, in person, mind and behaviour, my friends and I had never disagreed about him if they would not have permitted me to live single" (L55). Indeed, Terry Eagleton regards this figure as necessary, as the person whom the novel colludes to make us want: "Lovelace is a reactionary throwback, an old-style libertine or Restoration relic who resists a proper 'embourgeoisment'; the future of the English aristocracy lies not with him but with the impeccably middle-class Sir Charles Grandison. The death of Clarissa is the mechanism of his downfall, and in that sense the triumph of bourgeois patriarchy."[103] In other words, the moral bourgeois man triumphs because *Clarissa* shows the desperate need for him, because Clarissa's tragedy swells to fill the negative form of the shape he should have taken. The work of *Clarissa* is to make legions of readers demand a moral, amiable, estimable man. Such a man could have saved Clarissa. Indeed, *Clarissa* quite literally generated an outcry for a good man, as Richardson wrote *Sir Charles Grandison* in response to the demands of his readers to show them what such a man might be.[104]

In a deft evocation of Clarissa's misery, Katherine Binhammer has elucidated how much Clarissa wants a life she does not quite know how to articulate. Clarissa wishes for a story "that does not reduce subjectivity to sexuality."[105] This story, of course, is already in the novel it is Anna and Hickman's relationship. Thus when Binhammer points out that "Clarissa's story of a love that is not reducible to desire, nor desire to love, finds no place within the diegesis of the novel and so the truth of her heart is never externalized, never given an existence in her physical world," she overlooks the fact that a love story without desire is in fact occurring, in Anna's parallel plot.[106] The origins of the moral suitor, the choice of rational esteem, is visible in the gap in Clarissa's life story, the missing man who ought to have been there to mediate between the dangerous erotic lover and familial rapacity.

One important sign of the estimable man's worthiness was his intention. The good man imagined marriage, not seduction or rape, as the long-term resolution of his relationship. In Burney's *Evelina* (1778), Evelina is constantly harassed by dangerous men, but even her most troublesome suitor, Sir Clement Willoughby, though driven half mad by passion, cannot bring himself to propose. Only the rational-esteem choice, Lord Orville, announces his love in the same moment that he begs for her hand. Marriage becomes a guarantor of respectful admiration. Vicious aristocrats aim for rape or seduction instead.

Clarissa's aunt and Anna's mother are aware of this problem. They give similar lectures to the younger women, cautioning them that marriages of love are far riskier than marriages of convenience because the participants are blinded by adoration, and when disenchanted, they resent their spouses all the more (L58, L83). The older generation can see only desire or arrangement, only mutually consensual unions or familially determined matches. It is the younger generation, Clarissa and Anna, who can imagine an emerging alternative, a man who might combine the best of both worlds, a person whom one could safely choose because he already satisfies the requirements of the family. This man would surface in the major marriage plots published in the next century, particularly in the form of Henry Tilney, Fitzwilliam Darcy, Edward Ferrars, and Colonel Brandon, who may alienate their own parents in their marital choices, but amply satisfy their bride's guardians.

Clarissa thus sets up a model for the eighteenth-century marriage-plot novel. After Richardson, these stories would tend to feature virtuous women beset by dangerous aristocratic lovers. This man, powerful, wealthy, and devoid of principle, will abduct his victim in order to rape or marry her. On the other side, the woman has the kind of suitor that Clarissa so conspicuously needed: a reliable, honorable man whom she can decide to love. Such plot elements characterize Richardson's next novel, *Sir Charles Grandison*, but also Burney's *Evelina*, Smith's *Emmeline* and *Desmond*, Scott's *Millenium Hall*, Brunton's *Self-Control*, and Sheridan's *Memoirs of Miss Sidney Bidulph*. Richardson may not have invented the opposition between the rapacious rake and the honorable suitor of rational esteem, but in *Clarissa* he offered the most vivid, influential evocation of it.

It is this suitor of rational esteem that we might say, as Nancy Armstrong says of the modern individual, was invented in fiction and emulated by real people. Certainly the extent to which Richardson intended his work to be read as conduct literature and the many readers who testified to their imitation of the fictional characters make it clear that this was a deliberate campaign.[107]

That the suitor of rational esteem was a fictional character, more than a real option, is demonstrated in the most important piece of marital legislation of the eighteenth century, Lord Hardwicke's Marriage Act of 1753. As we have seen, through the medieval and early modern periods, a marriage was ratified if both parties expressed consent, usually (though not necessarily) confirmed through banns, a church service, and consummation. The vagueness of this protocol meant that many people could move about in a state of quasi-marriage, having enacted part of this process but not all, or having gone through a private wedding unrecorded in official records. The situation was problematic in that it encouraged clandestine unions, bigamy, cross-class marriage, and underage unions—although it also meant that absconding men could be hauled back to their responsibilities if the deserted woman could prove that he behaved maritally. But in 1753, the Marriage Act decided what made for a legal marriage: it had to be performed by recognized clergy, during canonical hours, in a particular manner. Most crucially, it required paternal consent for those under the age of twenty-one who wished to wed.

David Lemmings points out that "the Marriage Act seems to represent a uniquely authoritarian assertion of the economic and political interests of parents over their children, rather than the growth and recognition of love and individual rights in the family."[108] It reinforced the idea that children, especially daughters, were pawns to be exchanged in their fathers' commerce; it gave fathers complete power over their children (the bill did not give mothers the same rights and in fact explicitly refused remarried mothers any say over their children's choices).[109] Above all, the Marriage Act ensured that fathers could force their children to marry into their own class, thereby keeping property among the elites instead of letting it circulate throughout society.[110]

The act insisted on a month's pause between the calling of the banns and the performance of the wedding, an attempt to ensure that marriage was what the Earl of Hillsborough called "a sedate and fixed love" rather than a sudden passionate impulse.[111] In other words, it sought to redirect participants into a marriage of calm companionable affection, not romantic passion. And it turned those private declarations of passion, which might sometimes have worked as a kind of private marital contract, into an unregulated state outside marriage. "In the wake of the Marriage Act, 'free love' was also something quite new, something created by the formal legal demarcations of marriage in the Marriage Act as its outlawed, nonbinding, and illicit other," writes Eve Tavor Bannet. "Repositioned in this way, 'free love' came with a devastating price tag for women and . . . continuing to yield upon a promise would only turn more and more of the population into bastards and whores."[112] Erotic passion was affiliated, quasi-officially, to the underworld of abduction, rape, seduction, illegitimacy, and cohabitation. Rational esteem, with parental permission, became the state-sanctioned rationale for good marriage.

Ruling a large array of human relations illegitimate, Lord Hardwicke's Act created a regressive definition of marriage. Dabhoiwala sums up:

> Nowadays we take for granted that romantic attraction and individual choice should be the foundation of marriage: it is one of the distinguishing features of western society. Yet the pre-eminence of this principle is a comparatively recent development. In the eighteenth and early nineteenth centuries its political and legal strength amongst the propertied classes was still very limited. The 1753 Marriage Act directly contradicted it—by trying to make it impossible for the young and infatuated to marry against the wishes of their elders, it ranked individual happiness firmly below the material interest of the patriarchal family.[113]

The Marriage Act reminds us that we must not view the history of marriage as a straightforward progress toward affective individualism. Rather, it would take a century to sort out what marriage should be—erotic obsession, companionable comradeship, pragmatic self-interest, passionate adoration, or some combination of the above. The retrograde politics of the Marriage Act pose a problem for Stone's triumphant history of marital progress toward modern affectionate nuclear families.[114] But from our perspective, Hardwicke's Marriage Act is significant because it shows how widespread was the fear of the romantic lover.

The Victorians would inherit these multiple anxieties. But Victorian writers would rework these figures. They would turn the rake into the romantic suitor and the rational esteem gentleman into the familiar suitor. They would use the marriage plot to work through their culture's continuing confrontations, adjustments, and realignments.

Eighteenth-century marriage plots are obsessed with the questions of consent and obedience. They ask, over and over: Does the child owe the parent the duty to marry whomever the parent selects? How does one balance filial duty with personal happiness? But nineteenth-century marriage plots are consumed with the question of what kind of feeling constitutes an appropriate basis for marriage. Their overriding anxieties are whether one should marry for companionable trust or romantic passion. What sort of love is appropriate for marriage? Ought one to feel it before or after the wedding? Can one love a second time, if one has already been in love? Parsing the extent, legitimacy, and capacity afforded by one's feelings became a very important activity. This was, after all, the era that developed psychology: it was an era profoundly committed to naming, interrogating, and policing the emotions.

The marriage plot was necessary because marriage was unsettled. If it had been clear how to make marital decisions, there would have been no need to work through it in fiction. But what specifically made the marriage plot emerge as a dominant narrative choice was a particular confluence of two events: the emergence of the suitor of rational esteem and the recalibration of the rake as someone bent on marriage rather than seduction. My point is that, in order to have a marriage plot, the sexualized romantic figure has to have a realistic rival, a morally admirable familiar figure. This is true partly because marriage is a social transaction and the familiar suitor embodies this issue of how marriage aligns the woman with her social world. Inasmuch as the romantic suitor is about personal, private fulfillment, it need not have anything to do with marriage.

Indeed, the stories that precede and succeed the Victorian marriage plot demonstrate that a narrative focusing on desire does not need to invoke marriage as part of its story. The seduction plot of the eighteenth-century novel does not deal very prominently with marriage, because this genre is far more interested in the issues of men's erotic power, entitlement, and exploitation, and how a good woman ought to respond to them, than in the social arrangements marriage produces. Women get abducted, raped, and unhappily married, but the novels often explore the virtuous woman's capacity to adapt to conditions over which she has little control, of which marriage is one among many. If the eighteenth-century seduction plot is largely about sexual violence, relationships in the twentieth-century novel focus on erotic satisfaction, charting the forms desire might take and the methods by which desiring subjects might seek to satisfy themselves. Such feeling need not have anything to do with the formal state of marriage; one can explore the innermost psychology of the self in relationships, affairs, divorces, couplings, and renunciations.

In the nineteenth-century novel, however, the characters experience erotic desire *and* a need for social arrangement, and both are supposed to be satisfied solely through the married state. Marriage is the only acceptable portal to one's future, and marriage needs to fulfill two crucial and often incompatible goals: personal romantic pleasure and pragmatic future security. It is the rivalry between these needs that makes the marriage plot necessary, and it is their embodiment in competing male characters that makes the marriage plot happen.

The Victorians, however, changed the marital figures they inherited. By the end of the eighteenth century, the romantic lover was emerging as a dangerous if charismatic figure, a development from the Restoration libertine, the aristocratic rake: a leisured person seeking sexual pleasure, a Lovelace or an Earl of Rochester. At the same time, the suitor of rational esteem was emerging from novelists' and conduct writers' imaginations, not to mention the legal requirements of Lord Hardwicke's Act, modeling middle-class virtue: reliability, duty, trustworthiness. He will develop into the familiar lover.

The romantic lover, although derived originally from the rake, was fundamentally refashioned by Romantic ideals. Romanticism translated erotic passion from the predatory behavior of the seventeenth- and eighteenth-century seducer into a more inward-turning melancholy, a sympathetic rather than a dangerous feeling. Byron provided the popular image of a smolderingly magnetic, irresistible, dangerous, melancholy lover. The Byronic hero profoundly influenced Victorian writers, particularly the Brontës, who patterned Rochester and Heathcliff on this brooding, charismatic, sensual, amoral model.[115] Romanticism also popularized narratives of obsessive, doomed love: young Werther hurling himself to death for love of Charlotte, Coleridge's woman wailing for her demon lover. The reading public thrilled to a depiction of love as suffused with tragic desire. Lord Frederic Delamere in Charlotte Smith's *Emmeline* (1788), for instance, harbors a fanatical passion for his cousin that causes him to flout his parents, immure himself in gloomy retreats, abandon his duties, threaten suicide and murder, go into fits, abduct Emmeline and harass her so intensely that she spends most of the novel trying to escape him. If Smith intended Delamere as a commentary on aristocratic male power, however, he was read quite differently by Romantic readers, who often wished Emmeline would marry him.[116] And it is worthy of note that Delamere only wants to marry Emmeline—in spite of his friends' incredulity, in spite of the abduction in which he has Emmeline in his power for several days and nights, he refuses to rape her, holding out for a legitimate wedding. No wonder that Laura Kipnis can remark, "Our version of romantic love [is] a learned behaviour that became fashionable only in the late eighteenth century."[117] The romantic lover became much more attractive when his violence was turned in upon himself, when he was more willing to die than to rape, and when he was eager to prove his love via marriage.

While the rake was influenced by Romanticism, the familiar lover was also inflected by another early Victorian cultural movement. The Evangelical movement perpetuated and updated the culture of self-assessment that began with Puritanism.[118] Evangelicism's emphasis on moral seriousness, earnestness, good works, productive labor, sense of duty, fear of damnation, and hope for salvation created an ideal of male and female behavior that was fundamentally opposed to the careless hedonism associated with aristocratic life. "Evangelicism was above all else the religion of the home. It idealized and sanctified family life," explains Ian Bradley.[119] In an Evangelical household, the woman stayed home to care for the family; the children were trained by clergy; and everyone regarded the state of their soul with sober, unremitting, and mistrustful attention.

This influence is visible in Mary Brunton's *Self-Control* (1810/1811), which depicts the romantic lover as dangerous indeed. A generation after Smith's *Emmeline*, Brunton, the wife of a Church of Scotland minister, wrote out of an Evangelical consciousness of sin and crime. In *Self-Control*, Laura Montreville must conquer her initial attraction to Colonel Hargrave, who becomes more villainous as he sinks deeper into unrestrained passion, and redirect her love to the virtuous Montague de Courcy. De Courcy is "a Christian from the heart," "industrious in his pursuits, and simple in his pleasures," with domestic habits, strict schedules, and self-denial, while devoted to "the regulation of his passions, the improvement of his mind, and the care of his property."[120] Like Delamere (and like Lovelace before him), Hargrave stalks, harasses, and kidnaps the heroine, ultimately dying as a result of his own violence. In this Evangelical narrative, however, Brunton depicts his behavior as abhorrent, making it almost impossible for the reader to sympathize with him. The dangerous romantic lover, with his powerful erotic fixation and propensity to violence, might seem attractive in a Romantic novel like *Emmeline* but becomes appalling in an Evangelical novel like *Self-Control*.

Charlotte Brontë offers a particularly clear formulation of these early nineteenth-century influences, since in *Jane Eyre*, the broodingly Byronic Rochester competes against an Evangelical clergyman. In comparing Rochester with St. John, we can see that romantic and familiar suitors do not just counterpose two ideas of marriage but also two cultural visions. The familiar/romantic rivalry could be a way of working through alternative cultural ideals of sin, repentance, attractiveness, and even masculinity. One of the major differences is that St. John is able to keep his desires in check—he is characterized by a level of self-control that Jane finds frighteningly cold—whereas Rochester licenses himself to pursue his passions. This is an inheritance from the eighteenth-century novel, where the good man is characterized by his heroic self-discipline.

One other text may help us understand how the marriage plot changed as we turn to the nineteenth century. Jane Austen develops the way the nineteenth-century marriage plot will work—an achievement that the following chapters will explore in detail—but in this historical chapter, I want to end with the novel that most pointedly critiques and rewrites the eighteenth-century tradition we have traced here: *Northanger Abbey* (written 1798–1799, although not published until 1818). In *Northanger Abbey*, Austen scrutinizes the eighteenth-century plot of the rake, the estimable suitor, and the angelic woman they both pursue. Reading this novel gives one what Jill Heydt-Stevenson aptly calls a feeling "like having two tastes on the tongue simultaneously," as Austen conjures up the conventions of eighteenth-century courtship, only to change them into something new.[121]

Although *Northanger Abbey* explicitly satirizes Gothic novels, critics have concurred that, in the words of Mary Waldron, "Charlotte Smith's *Emmeline* is the most obvious target" for *Northanger Abbey*.[122] Austen makes Catherine the mirror image of Emmeline, as Mary Lascelles noted as long ago as 1939.[123] Where Emmeline is beautiful, intelligent, dignified, and a talented artist, Catherine is plain, not very clever, tomboyish, and deficient in drawing. Austen was deeply influenced by Smith, the only contemporary author named in her juvenilia.[124] Indeed, William Magee claims that "Charlotte Smith influenced [Austen] the most frequently and profoundly of any of her predecessors."[125] *Northanger Abbey* rethinks the major character types and the central relationships that formed the core of Smith's earlier text, so that reading the specific connection between Austen's and Smith's novels can help us see the larger issue of how Austen revised the marriage plot she inherited.

Austen, first of all, cheekily displaces the courtship plot onto female friendship. *Northanger Abbey* has a dangerously attractive rake, who fascinates the heroine, engages her completely, and then drops her to move on to another victim: Isabella Thorpe. *Northanger Abbey* also has a person who merits the heroine's rational esteem, a person whose elegant "manners shewed good sense and good breeding," who reads serious books, enjoys nature, and knows landscape theory: Eleanor Tilney.[126] As Catherine moves from her first ingenuous attachment to the volatile Isabella to a genuine appreciation of the worthy Eleanor, she rehearses the behavior of the eighteenth-century heroine. She also experiences the kind of growth that will be necessary for Austen's other heroines as they move from Wickham to Darcy, from Willoughby to Brandon, from Frank Churchill to Mr. Knightley. Discovering the proof of Isabella's flightiness, Catherine has what D. A. Miller identifies in *Jane Austen, or, the Secret of Style* as a useful mortification, the moment of salutary self-abhorrence that signals her entry into maturity. Catherine certainly feels this shame when Henry learns what she suspects about General Tilney, but she also experiences such a moment about her first bosom friend. Catherine becomes "ashamed of Isabella, and ashamed of having ever loved her" (160).

Austen's gender switching extends to the novel's conclusion, where she features a disobedient son instead of a miserably submissive daughter, and a happy result of filial rebellion instead of a disastrous one. Austen ends, "I leave it to be settled by whomsoever it may concern, whether the tendency of this work be altogether to recommend paternal tyranny, or reward filial disobedience" (187), a comic nod at the great anxiety of so many courtship plots in her period, in which women's struggles to accommodate themselves to their parents' wishes cause them a lifetime of grief. In this case, the gender reversal of the disobedient child makes it a comedy, not a tragedy.

Catherine has two suitors, the brothers of her rake and her rational-esteem companion, respectively, who are morally aligned with their sisters. John Thorpe, like Isabella, is a dangerous person to trust, while Henry Tilney is a virtuous man. Yet neither exactly resembles his predecessor. Thorpe is in the tradition of Delamere and Lovelace, but with some important alteration, while Tilney differs, in crucial ways, from the virtuous men of the eighteenth-century novel: Grandison, Faulkner in *The Memoirs of Miss Sidney Bidulph*, or Delamere's rival Godolphin in *Emmeline*.

Consider John Thorpe as the dangerous romantic lover. Nancy Yee calls him "the true villain of *Northanger Abbey*."[127] He resembles earlier abducting seducers, particularly when he grabs Catherine to try to force her into his carriage (72). In this passage, notes Jill Heydt-Stevenson, "Austen makes it impossible to read this kidnapping as anything other than a symbolic double of rape."[128] However, Thorpe is no Lovelace, let alone a Delamere or a Hargrave. Thorpe is driven by greed, not lust; he is stupid, not criminally inventive; he is dully unattractive, not dashingly charismatic; and he only wants to take Catherine on a sightseeing drive, not to rape her. Yet there are ways in which these very qualities heighten, rather than minimize, his threat. Miriam Rheingold Fuller explains:

> Austen makes him seem a laughable villain with his mediocre looks, clumsy manners, and vulgarity, but these qualities add to his menace. . . . His lies, blatant violation of Catherine's wishes, and delight in violating them show him fully capable of coercion and rape. Austen deliberately

> strips her villain of any charm, thus stripping away the veneer of romanticism disguising the sordidness of abduction.[129]

Stripped of the sex appeal of the romantic lover, it is easier to see Thorpe as an example of male entitlement and an enactor of sexual violence. Yet Thorpe also, interestingly, carries elements of the figure of the mercenary lover. Ugly and awkward, with vulgar manners and financial interests, he resembles Solmes and the mercenary figures who followed him: the banker Rochely in *Emmeline* and Mr. Branghton in *Evelina*. In *Northanger Abbey*, Thorpe is "impudent," "a stout young man of middling height, who [had] a plain face and ungraceful form" (29). Combining as he does the unattractiveness of the mercenary lover and the dangerousness of the romantic lover, Thorpe presents a compendium of unmarriageable traits not normally consigned to the same figure.

Henry Tilney is also a kind of composite figure. He is not quite the suitor of rational esteem; Catherine does not consider the evidence of his behavior over time in order to make a rational judgment that he is a moral individual to whom she can trust herself. In fact, he spends much of the novel making fun of Catherine. Caustic, satirical, and often quite nasty, Henry Tilney gives Austen what George Justice calls "the chance to mock aristocratic courtship."[130] His ironic mockery of conventions of which Catherine is ignorant baffles her, however much it might amuse himself or the reader, and his wit also reveals his misogynist contempt for women's feelings, whether he is informing Mrs. Allen that her muslin looks cheap or instilling fears into Catherine about the ebony cabinet at Northanger Abbey. However, by the end of the novel, Catherine's ingenuous admiration of Tilney inspires him to a certain authentic generosity. "Catherine's good nature has defeated the courtly wit of Henry," Justice explains.[131] In other words, by the end of the novel, he becomes an early Victorian gentleman, earnestly following his moral calling. His is a form of virtue appropriate to "the midland counties of England" (147), an unobtrusive but reliable sense of duty. Behaving according to "the sanction of reason and the dictate of conscience" and sustained "by a conviction of . . . justice," Henry acts out of a sense of "honor" as well as affection (183).

These qualities distinguish him from his predecessors, particularly Grandison, Godolphin, Desmond, and Faulkner. The earlier characters revealed their virtues by sternly suppressing their strongest feelings in heroic acts of self-control. But Henry's qualities derive not from mastery over his own powerful emotions but from adherence to a socially shared code of gentlemanly behavior which he maintains even when his own father violates it. Virtue, in *Northanger Abbey*, becomes signaled by participation in a larger imagined community. "Remember the country and the age in which we live. Remember that we are English, that we are Christians," Henry counsels Catherine (145). Because of "education," "laws," and "social and literary intercourse," "where every man is surrounded by a neighbourhood of voluntary spies, and where roads and newspapers lay everything open," Henry belongs to the England signalized by Benedict Anderson, a place whose shared participation in public culture guarantees a certain level of behavior (145).[132] In *Northanger Abbey*, virtue derives not from personal triumph over one's own feeling but from participation in shared language, ethical assumptions, political preferences, and conventional manners.

Thus it is significant that Henry and Catherine marry not as unique specimens of superlative virtue but as ordinary citizens. It is indeed true that "no one who had ever seen Catherine Morland in her infancy, would have supposed her born to be an heroine," what with her normal talents, unremarkable upbringing, and respectable family, while Henry is merely "a very gentlemanlike young man" (5, 14). Perfectly fine specimens of their respective types, Henry and Catherine are hero and heroine not through their unique and extraordinary merits but through their representativeness.

In *Northanger Abbey*, Jane Austen is not just satirizing the high-flown romantic language of earlier fiction. She is also creating an alternative, a sturdily realist counterpart. She is imagining what a marriage plot might look like for "the midland counties of England" in the new century. Such a story will have a heroine remarkable not for her extraordinary virtue and beauty but for her endearing averageness, and a hero admirable not for his feats of remarkable self-control but for his fundamental decency. Such a story will have its good characters live in comfortable modern residences, travel by sensible transportation choices, and behave according to ordinary social conventions. *Northanger Abbey* offers a new definition of virtue for both men and women. It imagines the value in ordinary people. And it advocates a marital feeling based on affection, admiration, and gratitude rather than the dangerous propensities of erotic passion or financial greed. It relocates the marriage plot, in other words, to the middle class.

In making this argument, I do not mean to say that *Northanger Abbey* was the first or only novel to imagine the marriage plot as type of narrative appropriate to ordinary middle-class subjects. Indeed, because this novel was not published until 1818, it appeared at a time when other novels (including other Austen novels) had already moved into a less exalted, less idealized set of characters. But because *Northanger Abbey* was written in the 1790s, in an energetic rush of rebellion, its objections to the eighteenth-century heroine and hero are particularly clearly pointed.

Both a satire and an alternative, *Northanger Abbey* rethinks character, but it does not interrogate marriage itself the way Austen would do in her subsequent fiction. There is virtually no romantic-familiar rivalry, since Thorpe is never a serious contender. More importantly, Catherine sails blithely into a marriage with a man she hardly knows and with whom she shares few interests and little knowledge. At eighteen years old, she appears to feel no anxiety whatsoever about moving seventy miles from her family, dealing with a tyrannical father-in-law and a wastrel brother-in-law who has destroyed her own brother's prospects. Nor does she seem to have given any thought to running a household ("'Catherine would make a sad heedless young housekeeper to be sure,' was her mother's foreboding remark" [184]). Readers of *Northanger Abbey* may be excused for fearing that this will not in fact be a marriage of "perfect felicity," "perfect happiness." With a foolish woman married to a sardonic, clever man, the Tilneys may instead come to resemble the Bennets in *Pride and Prejudice* (185, 186). In *Northanger Abbey*, Austen is interested in creating new types of characters, but she does not seriously interrogate the structure of the marriage plot.

This will not be the case in *Sense and Sensibility* or *Pride and Prejudice*, both of which portray a thoroughly developed romantic-familiar divide and soberly address the female character's readiness for marriage. In Chapter 3, we shall see how these two formative marriage plots help establish the shape that romantic-familiar rivalry would take for the next century. In these novels, the Thorpe-type character offers a real attraction, and ending up with the Tilney-type figure may be painful. Willoughby is an entirely different man from Colonel Brandon, and although Marianne does choose each in turn, her feelings for each choice are as different as night from day—or, to use Catherine Earnshaw's later comparison, foliage from rocks. Both may be legitimate forms of feeling, but only one can be fulfilled in marriage. Chapter 3 will show how the early nineteenth-century novel develops the nascent figure of the familiar suitor. In *Sense and Sensibility* and *Pride and Prejudice*, and later in *Cometh Up as a Flower, The Vicar of Bullhampton, Daniel Deronda*, and *Howards End*, we can see the familiar lover taking a particular time and space: he becomes the squire next door.

3

Neighbor Marriage

LOVING THE SQUIRE

I grieve to leave Thornfield: I love Thornfield: I love it, because I have lived in it a full and delightful life—momentarily at least. . . . I have known you, Mr. Rochester; and it strikes me with terror and anguish to feel I absolutely must be torn from you for ever. I see the necessity of departure; and it is like looking on the necessity of death.

CHARLOTTE BRONTË, Jane Eyre

THIS CHAPTER TRACES the emergence of the nineteenth-century novel's familiar suitor in two ways: by looking at larger structures of economic and social change that shape the familiar lover and by regarding the familiar lover through a particular narrative form, marriage to the kindly neighbor/local squire. Intertwining these two strands makes sense, since the squire marriage works specifically to soothe Victorian anxieties about modernity. Thus by tracing the emerging modern, male-identified, fluid, self-seeking individual, we can understand why Victorians sought as a counterpoint the most grounded, traditional, and community-centered persona available. On the other hand, we can rescue neighbor marriage from its apparent ordinariness, its status as an almost unmarked case, when we see it as a particular reaction to a particular historical moment, offering its own way of thinking about space, time, class, and social organization.

What, I ask, would make a woman want to marry her neighbor? Two important factors are at play: the neighbor's status, predicated on a particular type of communal life, combined with the woman's social and economic precarity. In other words, what the neighbor offers is a fantasy of social centrality that highlights the terrifying uncertainties implicit in romantic love. In the nineteenth-century novel, that neighbor is, more often than not, the local squire. I define "squire," broadly, as a financially stable man living on his own estate, a category that ranges from local gentry who farm their own land, like Roger Carbury, to nationally prominent aristocrats like Plantagenet Palliser. The important factors—the ones that define him as a marital choice—are his social centrality, his economic prosperity, and his geographical stability. Through looking at marriage with the neighboring squire in *Sense and Sensibility, Pride and Prejudice, The Vicar of Bullhampton*, and (more briefly) *Daniel Deronda* and *Howards End*, we can see the way this subject position functioned to facilitate a certain kind of social and class life for the woman—and the way that women continued to adhere to older marital and family norms, while men often pursued modernity. In other words, as the idea of romantic marriage developed in the nineteenth century, male characters' expectations often diverged from those of their female counterparts. Male characters are increasingly identified with a contemporary world of mobility, modernity, travel, and self-invention. Against this romantic stranger, the figure of the familiar neighbor emerges: a reassuringly grounded identity, a formation that allows women to marry into a place. This first case study of a familiar marriage, then, shows how the familiar lover provides the alternative to a worrisome culture of modern individualism.

Inventing Romantic Marriage

Historians of marriage agree that the great innovation of the late eighteenth and early nineteenth century was the rise of romantic marriage. Stephanie Coontz explains:

> By the end of the 1700s personal choice of partners had replaced arranged marriage as a social ideal, and individuals were encouraged to marry for love. For the first time in five thousand years, marriage came to be seen as a private relationship between two individuals rather than one link in a larger system of political and economic alliances.[1]

We need to be aware, however, that being "encouraged to marry for love" did not mean that such a notion was universally celebrated. This was no progressive triumph but an inconclusively gradual and controversial movement, often interrupted by retrograde legal and cultural formations like Lord Hardwicke's Act. In Wendy Jones's words, "nineteenth-century writers . . . shifted the terms of valorization towards passionate love, although they never completely rejected companionship as an acceptable basis for marriage."[2] Indeed, companionship received a fresh impetus from this new competitor.

Eve Sedgwick reminds us that there are "relations enabled by the unrationalized coexistence of different models during the times they do coexist," and we need to "invest attention in those unexpectedly plural, varied, and contradictory historical understandings."[3] Practices that had been around for centuries received new attention; other traditional practices continued but dwindled as they became unfashionable; and the difficult, fraught, complex period of transition is not something to be skipped over but is exactly what this book examines and what the novel worked through. The transitional period, moreover, lasted much longer than we might expect. Coontz explains that romantic marriage took two centuries to become widely accepted in Western culture.

> The new norms of the love-based, intimate marriage did not fall into place all at once but were adopted at different rates in various regions and social groups. In England, the celebration of the love match reached a fever pitch as early as the 1760s and 1770s, while the French were still commenting on the novelty of "marriage by fascination" in the mid-1800s. Many working-class families did not adopt the new norms of marital intimacy until the twentieth century.[4]

Even well into the twentieth century, "mutual affection" was more common than passion when arranging marriage. In 1909 Lady Selborne wrote in a letter to her son: "As the choice of a wife is a very important thing, it ought to be submitted to your *judgement* before you give free reign to your affections. . . . The affection that is inspired by the judgement is a much higher and more lasting affection that that which depends merely on the passions."[5]

As readers of the literature produced during this transitional period, we might ask what kind of difference the innovation of romantic marriage made. What might it have meant to have the madly passionate, dangerous lover actually considered as a realistic marriage prospect? What might we notice if we regarded marrying for love not as our cultural norm but as a strange idea that needed explaining?

We can see the resistance to romantic marriage in nineteenth-century conduct manuals, which typically express great anxiety about the risks of "falling in love." T. S. Arthur advises: "It is mere passion that loves blindly and irrationally; but true love is wise and discriminating, and its devotion more real and lasting."[6] Conduct literature for young men cautioned them to tamp down their passions by subjecting their love to the test of reason rather than letting their feelings run away with their judgment.[7] Mid-century manuals are especially anxious to ensure that readers seek out "mutual esteem" rather than passion. Sarah Stickney Ellis cautions women that a feeling "which originates in mere fancy, without reference to the moral excellence of the object," is unworthy.[8] Similarly, the anonymous author of *The Etiquette of Love, Courtship and Marriage* warned darkly,

"Men are so apt to disguise their real character that it is no easy matter for a lady to scan it."[9]

Anthropologist Charles Lindholm explains how intimately romantic marriage is tied to risk. In societies where people derive a sense of worth from their place in a social network, they do not have to use romantic love to glue together new familial configurations. But when traditional ties are loose or nonexistent, romantic love swells up to create those powerful bonds that are otherwise lacking.[10] Intensely pleasurable affiliations must provoke people to form the connections that in another culture already exist due to location, religion, or kin. No wonder, then, that romantic love is generally taken as "a relatively modern and particularly Western phenomenon; a direct consequence of the evolution of an uncertain 'risk society' which has liberated individuals from the moorings of kinship, social status and religion without offering any alternative points of attachment or security," Lindholm explains. "The appearance of romantic love is also thought to coincide with the advent of a leisure culture, where self-cultivation is possible; it has been linked with the modern 'invention of motherhood,' smaller family size, and a greater emphasis on the emotional tie between husband and wife that occurred in response to the industrial revolution."[11]

Romantic marriage, then, is a relationship of modernity. It is based on a liberal belief in each person's autonomy, self-awareness, and ability to maximize pleasure (the "hedonic calculus" associated with utilitarianism). It is correlated with cultures in which isolated and leisured individuals seek a personal mooring point.

In the nineteenth century, urban growth, relocation, and transportation facilitated this new romantic practice. After all, one can only choose a spouse if one meets different people and is not limited to the few potential mates in one's home village or extended family. Wage labor and the new industrial economy freed young people from dependence upon family property and the need to placate kin, and allowed men to reinvent themselves, selecting helpmates for the lives they invented, not the ones they inherited. Mike Featherstone explains that "in effect, the growing predominance of passionate love had the function of encouraging strangers to meet and converse."[12]

Michael J. Freeman points out that "in 1831, some 44 per cent of the population of England and Wales was urban. By 1911, the figure was at least 80 per cent."[13] To live in a mobile urban milieu, surrounded by strangers, became the norm for the first time in British history in the nineteenth century. One of the symptoms of this change was that weddings began to be solemnized differently. The seventeenth- and eighteenth-century wedding was a communal, rowdy, multiday event, involving neighbors, kin, employers, and friends all publically participating in (and thus sanctioning) the union. By the late eighteenth century, weddings had become private celebrations, partly because so many people had left their villages, but also because weddings were starting to be seen as predominantly personal choices rather than larger familial alliances.[14]

New forms of transportation made this change possible, particularly for wealthier men, who had the independence and financial wherewithal to make travel possible. Much has been written about how railways facilitated new spatial and social organizations, rendering every part of the nation accessible and recentering existing towns around railroad access.[15] Because railways traveled at least three times the speed of a stagecoach, distance seemed to be annihilated; Victorians had to reconfigure their spatial and temporal sense of how places related to one another. And individuals could easily separate from their families of origin and reinvent themselves elsewhere. Strangers could shake up local social patterns, relationships could be broken by one party leaving, and a young couple could get a fresh start in a new place.

This spatial insecurity underlined the emotional vulnerability women, in particular, felt in marriage. Alone with a relative stranger, to whom they had surrendered their identity, their relatives, and their property, they might well mourn for their lost natal families and fear their new vulnerability. Like Clarissa, many writers saw marriage as fearful: "To be given up to a strange man; to be engrafted into a strange family; to give up her very name, as a mark of her becoming his absolute and dependent property: to be obliged to prefer this strange man to father, mother—to everybody."[16] A writer of conduct literature imagined the transition:

> Here you stand upon the threshold of a two-fold existence. This moment you are under the guardianship and protection of your parents, the next you are transferred as a trembling bride into the hands of another. One moment more, and parental control will cease entirely, and you will have to yield obedience, and exercise submission to him who now gently encloses your hand in his. One moment more, and you will exchange the honary [sic] name of Miss, for that of Mrs.; and the surname by which you have been distinguished, for that of the gentleman whose wife you now become. One moment more, and you will be transformed, as by talismanic influence, from a maiden into a wife.[17]

This writer sees marriage as a fundamental transformation of identity, and not always for the better. As Ian Watt reminds us, "greater security and continuity of the woman's lot [was] afforded by more cohesive and extended family systems," not by the privileged dyad of romantic marriage.[18] Indeed, as Ruth Perry remarks, the isolation offered by romantic love was a problem for women: "Romantic love, for example, frequently imagined as the cutting loose from other kin ties in a scenario of elopement followed by isolated bliss, is often opposed to powerful longing for family, place, belonging, and community."[19]

Unfortunately, for women, "family, place, belonging, and community" were all ebbing in the eighteenth and nineteenth centuries, with property increasingly concentrated in a few male hands. Women of this period were traumatized by the stringent enforcement of patrilineal inheritance, the dowry system, and coverture. Perry dubs this "The Great Disinheritance." Increasingly, women were seen as financial drains on the family, whom the male inheritors resented and to whom they often gave as little as possible.[20] As Perry writes,

> Romantic love-in-marriage as an ideal developed in English culture as women were increasingly isolated from their consanguineal kin and the communities of their youth. In the fiction of the day characters wailed their dismay at their vulnerability to the absolute authority of the men they married. . . . The newly privatized marriage—privatized in the sense of private ownership as well as seclusion in domestic space—detached a woman from her family of origin and from her pre-existing friendships and concerns in order to put her at the service of being a companion to her new husband.[21]

Romantic love responded to this vulnerability by stressing the specialness of the home, the sacredness of the nuclear family. In Lindholm's model, it is when the family can no longer be taken for granted that it has to be voluntarily reconstructed through high-flown ideology, as a heavenly haven, an angelic realm, a special and sacred configuration. It was the insecurity of romantic marriage that drove the Victorian idealization of the family. Randolph Trumbach writes that "the new marriage pattern lay at the heart of domesticity—two people married for love, lived constantly thereafter in each other's company, and put great effort into the rearing of a large brood of children."[22] The new romantic marriage pattern made the modern family, the modern home, possible. Anthony Giddens explains:

> The spread of ideals of romantic love was one factor tending to disentangle the marital bond from wider kinship ties and give it an especial significance. Husbands and wives increasingly became seen as collaborators in a joint emotional enterprise, this having primacy even over their obligations towards their children. The "home" came into being as a distinct environment set off from work; and, at least in principle, became a place where individuals could expect emotional support, as contrasted with the instrumental character of the work setting.[23]

Because romantic marriage depends on caretaking (of the self, of relationships, of others), it also requires the kind of time and effort made possible by postindustrial leisure. If one is working flat out for subsistence-level survival, one hardly has the luxury of exploring one's emotional life. But in a new, insecure environment, where personal qualities were what a person could use to earn money, attract love, and found a family, it was understandable that emphasis shifted to whatever it took to maintain those personal qualities. Thus the change to romantic marriage ushered in not only a culture of emotional support but also crucial ideas about the body and the self, what Foucault called "an intensification of the body, a problematization of health and its operational terms," with emphasis on "the body, vigor, longevity, progeniture, and descent of the classes that 'ruled.' "[24]

The rise of romantic marriage had particularly disruptive effects in the laboring classes. The tradition of "spousals" ensured that a marriage would result in children. After a man had gotten a woman pregnant, the family and the village made sure they would marry.[25] However, once marriage was based on personal preference rather than duty, the man might simply decide he no longer liked the woman enough to wed; the spousal could thus be interrupted. Women had to learn what Katherine Binhammer describes as "a new semiotics grounded, not in the traditional practice of spousals in which love, sex and pregnancy always lead to marriage, but in relation to individualized emotion in which lovers do not always act in the interests of the community."[26] Moreover, under the romantic marriage regime, working people tended to get engaged more quickly to people they did not know well, a much riskier situation than the traditional mode of agreeing to marry a well-known local.[27]

If we regard the rise of romantic marriage from the point of view of early nineteenth-century subjects, for whom it is a new phenomenon, we will realize why it was not necessarily embraced as a refreshingly liberatory exercise of personal choice. Rather, the rise of romantic marriage meant a narrowing of acceptable feelings, a valorization of a single type of emotion above other, previously perfectly legitimate, human needs. To make marriage about romantic passion meant *not* making it about caring for the family, the home, and the future. Yet these needs remained urgent. The problem was that one could no longer admit them as real motives for marriage. Indeed, the mere suspicion that one was proposing for political or financial gain could scupper a fictional marriage. For instance, in *The Tenant of Wildfell Hall*, Gilbert Markham feels he cannot propose to Helen once she inherits her husband's estate; in *Can You Forgive Her?*, Glencora Palliser is haunted by the fear that her husband married her only for political advantage. From an eighteenth-century perspective, it is bizarre to see marriages threatened by what had previously been the very qualities that had previously made them seem eligible.

Anthony Trollope was particularly attuned to this trauma. In his novels of the 1860s and early 1870s, Trollope repeatedly emphasized the bittersweet idea that marrying one's true love could require relinquishing a rewarding life. In *Lady Anna* (1871), Anna refuses to marry an earl, a union demanded by her family and one that would guarantee her status and an estate; in *The Vicar of Bullhampton* (1869–1870), Mary rejects a marriage that would make her the lady of the parish. Alice in *Can You Forgive Her?* (1864) ultimately refuses to marry a politician in spite of her own yearning for a political career, while Nora in *He Knew He Was Right* (1869) rejects a marriage that would make her a nobleman's wife. Instead, each of these heroines marries for romantic love alone, accepting impoverished positions as a result. Although the women proclaim that they are glad to have made the right choice, nonetheless it is clear that the familiar marriage tempts them because of its promise of a meaningful, secure role. Trollope records the difficulties of choosing the romantic path, with its uncertain future.

Romantic love might leave one unemployed and in a precarious economic situation, but it might also lead to worse abuses. Victorian fiction offered vivid examples of what might happen if women picked bad romantic prospects.[28] As Kelly Hager points out, the most influential public voices of the nineteenth century, from Queen Victoria to John Stuart Mill to Charles Dickens, viewed marriage with alarm.[29] The Victorian novel, according to Hager's persuasive study, is as obsessed with failed marriage as it is with courtship, if not more so. Novels like *He Knew He Was Right* and *Middlemarch*, of course, focus on marital disaster, but as Hager has shown, even in fiction with celebratory marriage endings we see troubled couples: Edith and Dombey, Betsey Trotwood and her husband, Ralph Nickleby and his wife, Dr. Strong and Annie.

Victorian readers were fascinated with this nightmare scenario of the disastrous romantic marriage. What if one fell in love with an alcoholic scoundrel, like Helen Huntingdon in *Tenant of Wildfell Hall*? What if the object of one's affection had a terrible secret, like Rochester? What if he was unable to support a family, or gambled, like Wickham? What if he used his legal power to abuse and exploit his wife and children, like Heathcliff? What if he went insane and victimized his family, like Louis Trevalyan in *He Knew He Was Right?* What if one misjudged one's feeling and discovered it wasn't really love, like Cosima in *A Writer of Books* (1898) or Evadne in *The Heavenly Twins* (1894), in which case one was essentially prostituting oneself? Moreover, the doctrine of coverture meant that the woman lost all independent legal identity upon marrying, being wholly absorbed into her husband, who held all property, custody, and legal agency in the marriage. Coverture remained in force throughout most of the period this book discusses, for it was not significantly modified until the Married Women's

Property Act of 1870 and not fully repealed until the Married Women's Property Act of 1882.

The earlier idea of parentally vetted marriage at least had the advantage of subjecting the suitor to some kind of scrutiny before the woman relinquished all her identity and property to him.[30] The notion of familiarity meant that women knew whom they were marrying; he was a neighbor or relation, someone who could safely be trusted. But now the woman was being encouraged to bet her entire future on an irrational, fluctuating, purely private feeling rather than a reasoned assessment of the man's qualities. Fiction became the way readers could explore their anxieties about romantic marriage. But fiction also provided space for acknowledging the attractions of romantic marriage, and the most canonical of nineteenth-century novels achieved their popularity partly because they thrashed out ways to make romantic marriage work—ways from which readers could learn.

Fictional descriptions of meetings with strangers helped readers acquire the codes they needed to parse unknown suitors' qualities. Once any "tall, dark, handsome stranger" could be one's mate, one had to learn to assess credentials without any of the social background one would normally share. The idea of romantic love, therefore, helped people want to navigate—and learn how to navigate—a changing social world. However, in the nineteenth century, these elements of modernity—mobility, severing ties with original family, seeking work—appertained mainly to men. Impoverished rural young women might experience mobility via domestic service and agricultural labor, but their middle-class compatriots were trammeled by the demands of gentility, which required access to an expensive coach, horses, and chaperones to move anywhere.

Perhaps it is not surprising, then, that nineteenth-century romantic marriage plots tend to depict male mobility and female stasis. Thus the man is generally a stranger who sweeps the woman away from a stifling, unsatisfactory home, bearing her off to a private paradise elsewhere. Quite often, the romantic lover is a military man, stationed in multiple places. But whether military or civilian, the romantic lover assumes a global network of easy transit, in which one can move about forever, evading pursuers, seeking the right community. As a condition closely tied to modernity, to urbanization and transportation, romantic marriage is all about temporary and distant locales.

It is fitting that the form of familiar marriage plot that developed to answer this romantic challenge reversed its spatial coordinates. Where the romantic lover is a stranger, the familiar lover is a neighbor. Where romantic marriage is about leaving town, neighbor marriage is about consolidating a community. Where romantic marriage imagines travel, neighbor marriage assumes a landscape of settled estates. Where romantic marriage is about temporary stays in random spaces, neighbor marriage imagines residence over generations in a beloved landscape. Where the romantic-marriage pair of Lydia and Wickham, for instance, ends up roaming around the British Isles, Elizabeth Bennet realizes that "to be mistress of Pemberley might be something!"[31]

Neighbor Marriage

Familiar and romantic marriage each have their own chronotope, ways of organizing space and temporality. Familiar marriage is characterized by extension and duration. It thinks of love as something that develops over years of shared work. It justifies marriage according to long-term rewards. In Chapter 2, we looked at the long-term historical development of familiar marriage, a temporally extended treatment of a form that itself implies an extended purview. Correspondingly, this chapter charts familiar marriage's spatial imagination. That sense of space is extensive; it foresees the marriage working on a neighborhood scale, featuring ongoing interaction with local connections. The familiar-marriage home is porous, accommodating passage and space for extended family, servants, apprentices, poor relations, visitors, customers, parishioners. Familiar marriage's forms and scales of spatiality range from the enormous to the intimate, from the global to the national, to the communal, to the domestic. By contrast, romantic marriage's chronotope is one of intense contraction. Temporally, it lives in the passionate and immediate present moment, and spatially, it prioritizes the private space in which lovers can enjoy their exclusive pleasure, or later, the nuclear family can be walled off in a private haven.

Given that familiar marriage is a narrative that engages geographical relations as a quality to be considered in a union, we need to investigate exactly what space means in these plots. Thus we might start with the basic question: What does it mean to see a neighbor as marriageable?

First, it means that one knows one's neighbors and, therefore, that one lives in a fixed community involving long-term relationships. It also implies a particular density of settlement that is characteristic of a village or at most a small town: a community whose inhabitants live near enough to know each other, but one sparsely populated enough that the person next door really matters. Neighbor marriage has little meaning in an urban environment with a mobile population of thousands, and is not really possible in a rural environment in which nobody lives nearby at all. As Jane Austen so famously remarked, "3 or 4 Families in a Country Village is the very thing to work on."[32] Neighbor marriage derives from, and in turn supports, the nineteenth-century novel's preference for the provincial setting, the imagined community.

Second, to marry a man because he is your neighbor means that the man's spatial fixity might well be his most important attribute. His permanence contrasts with the mobility of the romantic lover. As we saw in Chapter 1, the romantic lover is characteristically traveling, bursting in and out of the relatively fixed frame of the woman's perception. In the Romantic era he is often an outcast, a wanderer or an exile; in Victorian fiction, as this chapter shall show, he is very often a military man, his wandering determined by the needs of imperial or military engagement. And in modernist work, his mobility may function more as a sign of his modernity, his rootlessness and cosmopolitan nature.[33] The woman attracted to this romantic traveler is often eager to get away from a stifling home—Lydia Bennet's fictional compatriots include Lady Isabel Carlyle, fleeing an emotionally oppressive household as Sir Francis Levison spirits her away to France, or Edith Dombey, eager to escape her loveless marriage by running to France with James Carker.

The neighbor marriage, however, features a man who not only lives permanently on a particular estate but often feels rooted to that soil, attached to the generations of ancestors who have lived on that land. The neighbor is, surprisingly often, the squire. Such characters are common in Trollope's novels, generally inarticulate worthy middle-aged men: Roger Carbury in *The Way We Live Now*, Christopher Dale in *The Small House at Allington*, Harry Gilmore in *The Vicar of Bullhampton*. If not literally a squire, the man might be the actual owner of the property in which the woman is allowed to reside, a wealthy older man—Archibald Carlyle or John Jarndyce, for example—who asks the temporary resident to become "the mistress of" his house. In this variant, which we might call the "landlord marriage," it is almost impossible to say no, because the suitor could evict the woman who refuses him. Although we are supposed to believe that both Carlyle and Jarndyce are too courteous to contemplate such a raw use of power, that capacity is terrifyingly visible to both the reader and the female character who (more or less reluctantly) concurs with his proposal.

The woman attracted to this sort of man often fears imminent or actual homelessness. Think of Lizzie Bennet and the "Madame Vine" incarnation of Lady Isabel, two women who face a terrifyingly insecure future and who covet, who love, a comfortable estate and the man who embodies it. Think, too, of Gwendolen Harleth in *Daniel Deronda*, who faces eviction from Offendene; or Marianne Dashwood in *Sense and Sensibility*, sorrowfully banished from Norland; or even Margaret Schlegel in *Howards End*, forced to give up her lease without a clue where to move. Facing housing precarity, desperate and afraid, the woman finds a reassuringly permanent stake in her neighborhood through this marriage.

The fact that this neighbor is generally a middle-aged squire is important. His age confirms his reliability and respectability, particularly since he is often of the same age as the woman's parents and therefore likely to be a family friend or at least share their generational values. Well known, thoroughly approved by parents, with a public record of good estate management, the squire is a safe choice indeed. Even if the man is younger, his status as a neighbor offers some guarantees. In the familiar plot, moreover, an aging body affords opportunities of tender care that may itself appeal to a woman, in a different way from the virile appeal of the youthful masculine body, but perhaps just as powerfully.

But even in the cases where the neighbor is a younger man, his presence in the community guarantees his good behavior. In Trollope's *Rachel Ray*, a mother wishes a neighbor would court her daughter, because the neighborhood "would know of all his doings. Such a young man, when he asked a girl to marry him, must mean what he said. If he did not there would be no escape for him from the punishment of his neighbours' eyes and tongues."[34] We see such a punishment in *Middlemarch*, when community pressure works to reform Fred Vincy into a man worthy of marrying Mary Garth. Neighborhood surveillance can guarantee some probity.

Marrying a squire makes the female character into the lady of the manor, a notable advance from her previous existence as a marginal, impoverished, near-homeless individual. Her marriage brings her in from the ragged edges of her society to its absolute center. Distributing coal and flannel, overseeing tenants' repairs, reading to the elderly, teaching in the Sunday school, going district visiting, and inviting guests—the lady of the manor has much to do.[35]

By contrast, the neighbor himself is often a rather minimally sketched character. In *The One vs. the Many*, Alex Woloch argues that minor characters can serve a merely instrumental function, "the flat character who is reduced to a single functional use within the narrative," when "the character is smoothly absorbed as a gear within the narrative machine, at the cost of his or her own free interiority."[36] Although one would expect the husband (or potential husband) to be a protagonist, in many nineteenth-century plots, he is in fact a generic placeholder, who functions primarily to move a woman into a position of importance. It is her story, not his, that matters.

In neighbor marriage plots, it is this status that women covet, rather than everyday domestic labor. In most Victorian novels, women have little interest in the endless household responsibilities of mending, scrubbing, cleaning, sweeping, preserving, shopping, storing, and cooking.[37] Indeed, the most famous advocate of the domestic sphere, Sarah Stickney Ellis, actually despised "domestic drudges" who "employ their whole lives in the constant bustle of providing for mere animal appetite."[38] Rather, women wanted to run a household, a role involving quasi-professional skills of hiring, firing, budgeting, and management.[39] In Isabella Beeton's famously stirring opening line in her *Book of Household Management*, she writes: "As with the commander of an army, or the leader of any enterprise, so is it with the mistress of a house."[40] It was this grand fantasy rather than daily housework that often stirred female characters to marry.

The fantasy of the powerful household manager hearkens back to the feminist inspiration for the domestic sphere in the first place. In the 1790s, activists argued for "women's mission" in the home in order to posit a place where women could have primacy.[41] "The profession of mother, wife, and mistress of a family would be a branch of government" that would be "equal in dignity to the professions of men," explains Eve Tavor Bannet.[42] Advocates could endorse female moral and domestic leadership, contesting the dominant belief that women were simply inferior to men.[43] By the 1830s, this tactic had succeeded, having largely driven the assumption of female inferiority out of serious publications.[44] Barbara Caine explains that "feminists resorted to Victorian domestic ideology" because "it was the only language in the nineteenth century which offered the basis for asserting the sexual differences between men and women, not in terms of women's inadequacy, but rather in terms of their distinctive merits and virtues."[45]

Thus the neighbor marriage is not a fantasy of establishing a cozy little nest, but a dream of centrality to a community. Women in the neighbor plot covet importance. When Oliphant's Lucilla Marjoribanks is going to marry her cousin Tom, the couple decides to purchase the family estate. Becoming a squire's wife satisfies Lucilla: "It gave her the liveliest satisfaction to think of all the disorder and disarray of the Marchbank village. Her fingers itched to be at it—to set all the crooked things straight, and clean away the rubbish, and set everything, as she said, on a sound foundation."[46] The need to reform the village justifies her marriage, she feels.[47] The neighbor marriage imagines the house as a space through which local individuals can circulate, a center for economic distribution, government, and social events. Socialist Marcella, in Mary Ward's novel of 1894, who marries the landowner and Member of Parliament next door, quite literally turns a room in her house into a community center for the town. To establish such an estate has to be read as a political act.

Marrying the squire has obvious political repercussions: it strengthens the gentry class and allows for its perpetuation. In *Romantic Austen*, Clara Tuite argues that the country-house novel functions to naturalize domestic roles and class relations. She reads *Mansfield Park* in particular as producing a narrative of a nostalgic, aristocratic, restorationist green core of England.[48] Such a reading is also applicable to *Emma* and to *Pride and Prejudice*, which end with the reinforcement of the future of Donwell Abbey and Pemberley, respectively. This kind of marriage conservatively reinforces gentry class power during what is otherwise a period of class mobility enabled by industrial and military turmoil.

However, I want to complicate this conservative reading in two ways. First, viewing the squire as a minor character reveals that the *sjuzhet* or narrative structure is working toward a different idea of class than the *fabula* or story. While the *fabula* may be enshrining the squire in the central, most coveted position, the *sjuzhet* meanwhile depicts him as an interchangeable cog, an agent who serves an instrumental need. "The nineteenth-century novel's configuration of *narrative* work," Woloch writes, "creates a formal structure that can imaginatively comprehend the dynamics of alienated labor, and the class structure that underlies this labor. In terms of their essential formal position (the subordinate beings who are delimited in themselves while performing a function for someone else), *minor characters are the proletariat of the novel*."[49] Like factory workers, then, minor characters perform one specialized function—and in that respect, the squire, ironically, looks like alienated labor. In the neighbor plot, the lord of the manor gets formally demoted to a status facilitator serving the woman's needs.[50]

If we then pick up the woman's centrality to this neighbor-marriage plot, we may ask, quite simply: What does this marriage offer her? From the female character's point of view, this marriage is not about reinforcing the continuation of the squirearchy. Female characters rarely see themselves as mere reproductive carriers. Glencora Palliser, for instance, is terribly wounded by the Pallisers' reduction of her to this instrumental function. Glencora certainly does not marry Plantagenet to ensure the Palliser lineage—but why, then, does she consent to it (or, perhaps it would be more accurate to ask how she comes to terms with it)? I want to suggest that Glencora's famous political salon offers us, in some sense, the answer.

We need to recalibrate our idea of the estate and see it not as the locus of class power but the enabler of a social vision. This vision begins at home. As we know, the domestic space of familiar marriage is not a closed private realm. It is a porous public/private space, through which clients, customers, parishioners, and colleagues, as well as servants and apprentices, circulate. This premodern house correlates to the premodern family, an extended complex that could involve poor relations, servants, apprentices, and pupils, as well as elders and friends and patrons.[51] The extended-family network fed into the notion of an organic community. The lady of the manor oversees a harmonious quasi-rural group of neighbors.

However, this premodern notion of community was produced by the Victorians, and among other places, produced in the novels that depicted neighbor marriage. It was the nineteenth century that began to describe and deplore a soulless modern society and to valorize, by contrast, the idea of a timeless, harmonious, unified organic community. The lonely woman wandering through an indifferent town, finally given safe haven in a beloved estate, exemplifies the contrast between the two states that would come to be known as *Gesellschaft* and *Gemeinschaft*.

The term "individualism" was invented in the mid-nineteenth century, and it was invented as a negative word.[52] "The term individualism stood for spiritual rootlessness, destructive rationalism, utilitarianism, hedonism, and exploitation under the disguise of laissez-faire."[53] Indeed, individualism "constituted a serious evil undermining the political and social order of their times," a social disintegration, explains Koenraad W. Swaert.[54] The drive to compete, the relentless focus on gaining profit regardless of others, and the vision of oneself as an independent agent fighting for a place in the market did not promise self-development or self-fulfillment to Victorians but rather "anomie, isolation, and egotism."[55]

One could identify the problems with individualism by imagining a contrasting situation, a world of traditional, mutually nurturing bonds. Anna Vaninskaya writes that Victorians were

> obsessed with setting up contrasts between different types of social organisation. Writers returned again and again to the dichotomous nature of social types: organic vs mechanical, barbarian vs civilised, simple vs complex, traditional community—based on kinship ties and common ownership—vs modern society. Many viewed the history of Western civilisation in terms of a linear progression or decline, a movement from intuitive and organic kinds of association to the rational and instrumental.[56]

This lost haven was thought to have characterized medieval life and to have finally slipped away in the last decades of the eighteenth century.[57] As Raymond Williams so memorably showed, the pastoral age is always gone, vanished during the era that has already ended.[58] But simply locating it in the past already did some political work. "A valuing society, the common condition of a knowable community, belongs ideally in the past," Williams writes. But this distances it from possibilities of current action. "The real step that has been taken is withdrawal from any full response to an existing society. Value is in the past, as a general retrospective condition, and is in the present only as a particular and private sensibility, the individual moral action."[59] If community is the site of a group moral dynamic, and if community is gone, we are left only with the individualist anomie that the Victorians so feared.

The Victorians developed the notion of the "community" in multiple fields at once, including economics, anthropology, legal studies, and history, and in at least two national cultures, German and English scholarship. While a full accounting of the Victorian construct of community is beyond the scope of this chapter, a brief survey will reveal how widespread the yearning was.

Among historians and sages, community allowed for a critique of industrial capitalism. Thomas Carlyle famously hoped that the principles of medieval community could restore some of the depredations of Victorian factory life. He begged industrial magnates to return to feudal care for their employees, imagining mutual loyalty that the modern world ought to recover. The notion of organic community can also be credited to Thomas Macaulay, Karl Marx, and Max Weber, and to Victorian anthropologists and legal and economic historians like Edward Burnett Tylor, Lewis Henry Morgan, Sir Henry Sumner Maine, and Frederic Seebohm (author of *English Village Community* [1883]).[60] Both Seebohm and Jacob Burckhardt saw history as a progression from an archaic communal life to a modern realm of liberty and individualism. Burckhardt's influential study, *The Civilization of the Renaissance in Italy*, published in English in 1878, argued that during the Middle Ages, "man was conscious of himself only as a member of a race, people, party, family, or corporation—only through some general category," whereas in the Renaissance, for the first time, free and full personhood could flourish.[61] These writers posited organic community as a lost period of archaic history, an Anglo-Saxon or feudal past.[62]

Throughout the nineteenth century, British fiction writers urgently tried to imagine how this sense of community must have felt. Katie Trumpener has shown how Romantic-era writers valorized a past vision of an organic national community in Welsh, Irish, and Scottish tales.[63] As we have seen, Austen's country-house novels have been read, by critics from Alistair Duckworth through Clara Tuite, as nostalgic recreations of a pastoral aristocratic England. Sir Walter Scott, importantly, popularized a historical, premodern imagination in his romantic evocation of a doomed Highland society. George Eliot located her communities not sixty years since, as Scott did, but a generation earlier, in the 1830s. The dream of harmonious, organic medieval communities motivated William Morris's socialist and artistic initiatives and undergirded John Ruskin's yearning for economic cooperation in *Unto This Last* (1862), as well as helping inspire utopian communities like those of Fourier and Owens. By the end of the century, Thomas Hardy's earlier novels tapped into a widespread yearning for an irretrievably vanished agricultural England, structured by ancient fairs, festivals, harvests, speech patterns, and customs.

However, perhaps the single most influential developer of the communal thesis was historian Ferdinand Tönnies, who wrote *Gemeinschaft und Gesellschaft* in 1887. Tönnies contrasted *Gemeinschaft* (a traditional community rooted in the land and the family) with *Gesellschaft* (a modern, urban, heterogeneous, industrial society).[64] In the *Gemeinschaft*, Tönnies wrote, "those who love and understand each other remain and dwell together and organize their common life."[65] *Gemeinschaft* relationships consist of mutual service and close bonds facilitated by shared language, customs, and beliefs. But in the *Gesellschaft*,

> everybody is by himself and isolated, and there exists a condition of tension against all others. There spheres of activity and power are sharply separated, so that everybody refuses to everyone else contact with and admittance to his sphere; i.e., intrusions are regarded as hostile acts. . . . Nobody wants to grant and produce anything for another individual, nor will he be inclined to give ungrudgingly to another individual, if it be not in exchange for a gift or labor equivalent that he considers at least equal to what he has given.[66]

The cold, mechanical, competitive individual is reminiscent of the Lockean monad or *Homo economicus*, and he is governed by contract, by personal striving for advantage. Whereas the *Gemeinschaft* realm is that of small rural folkways—the household, guild, or craft—the *Gesellschaft* world is that of modern urban industry, characterized by trade and world markets.[67] Although Tönnies himself does not gender these worlds, they map quite clearly onto female and male spheres.

Of course, this *Gemeinschaft* fantasy had little to do with real medieval or early modern conditions. Late medieval communities had to work out conflicts through bargaining, litigation, and governance.[68] Communities, after all, consist of people who may not have compatible interests or personalities, but who are forced to live together regardless. At least through the sixteenth century, associational forms remained a robust way of organizing social experience.[69] At the same time, there is evidence that this period was also characterized by an ethos of competitive mercantile individualism. Alan Macfarlane goes so far as to assert: "What now seems clear is that England back to the thirteenth century was not based on either 'Community' or 'communities.' It appears to have been an open, mobile, market-oriented and highly centralized nation."[70] While Macfarlane is at an extreme in denying all forms of communal life, his research does make clear how fallacious it is to separate a gauzy premodern *Gemeinschaft* of rustic timeless harmony from a striving modern urban *Gesellschaft*. Just as the medieval and early modern marriage structure combined personal consent with social pressures, medieval and early modern social organization included elements of both relationality and individuation. The nineteenth century taught us to see these forms as opposite, but in historical life they were intimately enmeshed.

What we are seeing in the neighbor plot—as always with familiar marriage—is a fictional construct, not a lived reality. There were never harmonious homogeneous organic communities of happy peasants; equally, there were never urban societies consisting exclusively of self-aggrandizing economically competitive individuals. But Victorian writers set these up and connected them to domestic and to public space as a way of working through what they themselves wanted. What familiar marriage does is posit a lost tradition whose values it can claim to retain. Neighbor marriage is no exception.

Marriage to a squire makes the woman consolidate a *Gemeinschaft*. Any community centered on a single estate—and the social ties and economic management deriving from a single family—must be rural, small, and traditional. Thus the neighbor marriage plot became a venue for imagining, in fiction, the maintenance of an idealized *Gemeinschaft*.

Of course, when the author worked out the details, such a *Gemeinschaft* fantasy proved as nonviable in fiction as it had been in historical reality. As Tony Tanner writes of *Emma*: "There is social contact and contiguity (enforced and suffered, or sought-for and welcomed); there is indeed a community—it would be perverse to withhold the term. But it is a community on the one hand bound together by acknowledged hierarchy, and on the other riddled with potential—if not actual—divisiveness."[71] Not only is the Box Hill group a divided community, but community in general, in Austen, is a highly selective one. It consists, as Raymond Williams has noted, of gentry, with the laboring poor invisible.[72] Similarly, the provincial villages in Eliot's novels retain their homogeneous harmony through cruelty toward anyone who violates communal norms, no matter how innocent or minor their deviations might be. Williams identifies a customary behavior, a traditional cohesion, in Eliot's working people, and this lack of individuation can correlate with a frightening unanimity of rejection.[73]

In fiction by both Austen and Eliot, the neighbor marriages may not establish the woman at the center of community but pull the woman out of the real social world of the novel. Emma's marriage to Mr. Knightley can be read as the defensive retreat of a dwindling population, holding a last doomed redoubt while the robust and prosperous middle class, the Coles and Eltons, thrive in Highbury. Similarly, in *Middlemarch*, Celia's classic neighbor marriage to Sir James Chettam cannot stave off her sister's marital misadventures, her uncle's electoral disasters, or the toxic gossip of the townspeople. In other words, some nineteenth-century novels interrogate the assumption that marrying the squire will reconstruct an idyllic organic community; these novels, aware of the ebbing power of the squirearchy, point out that allying oneself to the landed gentry may actually make it more difficult to participate in the increasingly dominant milieu of middle-class bankers, shopkeepers, and military families.

However, more optimistic neighbor-marriage plots envision it as a source of power, not an exclusion. Such fictions may imagine the woman as the center of a large household and the linchpin of a community, but they may go even further: they might involve the woman in the governing of the nation. Such a case is Glencora Palliser's.

Just as the normative view of squire marriage favors the man's desire to perpetuate the squirearchy, so too, the way we theorize national power tends to assume a male public-sphere perspective. The most influential theorists of the emergence of nationhood, Jürgen Habermas and Benedict Anderson, concur that it is generated by the shared participation of individuals in an intellectual public sphere. As newspaper readers in widely separated geographical regions come to share the same concerns, reading the same materials, they begin to feel that they are part of the same community.[74] Once readers become accustomed to the imagined space projected by the newspaper, they feel rationally empowered to be part of its governance. A robust modern culture of salons, art shows, musical concerts, coffeehouses, and museums allowed for a bourgeois public sphere to develop in the eighteenth century.

We might ask how women could have imagined their own participation in the formation of the modern idea of the nation.[75] Some, like the bluestockings, had access to male-marked forms of intellectual inquiry, but did women see their hard-won private sphere as a different form of access to a national imagination?[76] What might the domestic realm have meant, politically, in the neighbor-marriage plot?

To understand this, we need to relinquish the fundamental qualities of the public-sphere man: his status as an autonomous, self-contained, rational being. The private sphere imagines interaction in an entirely different sort of way. In lieu of rational argument generated by newspaper culture, we see emotional sway generated by affective bonds. In lieu of self-containment, we see permeability, tenuousness, intermingling.

For the neighbor marriage imagines a woman's interaction with a national community, not through an intellectual public sphere but rather through the Victorian concept of "influence," which itself dates back at least to an eighteenth-century practice Helen Thompson has called "ingenuous submission."[77] In Thompson's words, "the free or ingenuous practice of compliance, rather than the entity we presently call the abstract individual, [is] the standard against which the eighteenth-century domestic novel represents women's political difference."[78] In other words, an eighteenth-century woman was defined not as a free individual with agency but a being who would voluntarily obey another. Always showing cheerful acquiescence, the woman not only underlined her own virtue but also perhaps shamed the man into better behavior.

"Influence" picks up the notion of indirect management, and the way in which submission can itself subtly reshape another's will. Influence theorists advised women to learn to speak enthusiastically about subjects their men cared about, whether fox hunting or business, and thereby introduce improving ideas, which men would imbibe without knowing it. These writers argued that women shaped men's minds, and as those men moved into the public sphere, they disseminated the women's ideas. Sarah Lewis exclaims that "it may be objected that [influence] is confined in its operation to the family circle: as if the aggregate of families did not constitute the nation!"[79] Focusing on maternal influence, Lewis insists that the education of sons determines the fate of Britain: "On the maternal character depends the mind, the prejudices, the virtues of nations; in other words the regeneration of mankind."[80] Similarly, Sarah Stickney Ellis celebrated the formative qualities of maternal influence in imperialist expansion, arguing that as Englishmen went out to every corner of the globe, they carried women's teachings with them.[81] Men carried the germs or spores of their women's thought, seeding them everywhere.

Women's influence was both vague and endless. Ellis admitted that "the sphere of their direct personal influence is central, and consequently small; but its extreme operations are as widely extended as the range of human feeling."[82] Influence was "boundless," wrote Lewis, a force "which may pervade the whole of society."[83] This amorphous cloud of feeling, this tenuous miasma of morality, was unconsciously borne about the world by men. By contrast, male citizenship was quantifiable, consisting of a series of discrete acts: votes, elections, purchases, laws. Ellis and Lewis conceptualized this male world not as an enviably direct form of action but rather as exhausting entrapment in a ruthless, endless, vicious sequence of dehumanizing activity, a demoralizing *Gesellschaft*.[84] Lewis notes approvingly that "men frequently resist power, while they yield to influence an unconscious acquiescence."[85] Quite simply, the women's *Gemeinschaft* worked better.

This notion of influence undergirds the neighbor plot's vision of women's civic life. Inasmuch as the local squire was generally a Member of Parliament, the woman would become a parliamentary wife. By influencing his political thought, by shaping his political language, she could change the course of the nation. In neighbor marriages, this influence is often represented when the wife either runs a political salon, like Trollope's Glencora Palliser and Lady Laura Standish, or acts as a parliamentary ghostwriter for her husband's speeches, like Oliphant's Phoebe Junior, Trollope's Alice Vavasor, and Eliot's Dorothea. What the salonniére or ghostwriter role reveals is a vision of public participation that is nonmaterial, linguistic, and formed of rhetoric and social pleasures spreading outward from the hearth, rather than one of rational conviction exercised in a marketplace.

In the neighbor plot, divisions between persons are tenuous. A woman's voice can speak through a man's lips. A woman's ideas can move a man's hands. It is reminiscent of Natalie Zemon Davis's comment on sixteenth-century feeling: "The line drawn around the self was not firmly closed. One could get inside other people and receive other people within oneself, and not just during sexual intercourse or when a child was in the womb. One could be possessed by someone else's soul."[86] Zemon Davis is referencing magicians and witches, but the nineteenth-century version of this idea was influence.[87] Influence offers a sense of the woman as diffuse, disparate, and all-pervasive.

This idea resembles George Eliot's famous notion of sympathy. Sympathy is supposed to enlarge feeling, while influence is supposed to direct a man's political actions, but they share the same idea of a permeable self through which moral imperatives can circulate. We might, then, fairly think of Dorothea, whose two marriages manifest this dynamic; she initially marries an older neighbor who has an estate, and then she becomes a political ghostwriter through her second marriage. Not surprisingly, "her full nature, like that river of which Cyrus broke the strength, spent itself in channels which had no great name on the earth. But the effect of her being on those around her was incalculably diffusive."[88] We might think, too, about Catherine as a ghost who permeates Heathcliff's world. He notes, "What is not connected with her to me? and what does not recall her? I cannot look down to this floor, but her features are shaped on the flags! In every cloud, in every tree—filling the air at night, and caught by glimpses in every object by day, I am surrounded with her image!"[89] Attenuated to nothing—or swollen to everything—the woman's own private persona disappears; she becomes the animating soul of a larger politics, a bigger presence.

Austen's Neighbor Plot: Female Stasis and Male Mobility

By looking at two early versions of the neighbor plot, *Sense and Sensibility* and *Pride and Prejudice*, we can trace how neighbor marriage evolves in response to modernization and how the squirearchy serves women's dreams of centrality. Because both books were written in the 1790s but not published until the 1810s, their composition history spans the most intense period of change in the idea of marriage, the rise of the romantic suitor, associated as he is with new notions of individuation, pleasure, mobility, and self-interest. If *Northanger Abbey* focuses on making the marriage plot the property of the ordinary subject, *Sense and Sensibility* and *Pride and Prejudice* turn their attention to the qualities of marriage itself. These novels interrogate the new romantic figure and imagine the kind of familiar suitor who might respond to him. *Sense and Sensibility* and *Pride and Prejudice* both have neighbor-marriage plots, but I want to use these neighbor marriages not just to show a particular subgenre of familiar marriage but, more importantly, to represent the larger development of the marriage plot we would come to know in the nineteenth century. In this respect, the neighbor marriage plot allows us to trace the growth of familiar-romantic rivalry.

Sense and Sensibility and *Pride and Prejudice* commemorate two decades' worth of new urgency and fresh anxiety about the rise of romantic marriage. Stephanie Coontz writes of the shift from eighteenth-century esteem to nineteenth-century love:

> Love, wrote Benjamin Franklin, "is changeable, transient, and accidental. But Friendship and Esteem are derived from Principles of Reason and Thought." During the nineteenth century, however, young people started to believe that love was far more sublime and far less reasoned than mutual esteem.[90]

In tracing the intersection of "Esteem" and "love," *Sense and Sensibility* more strongly endorses the earlier model, while *Pride and Prejudice*, which Austen revised later, contains remnants of the earlier mode of thinking but participates more willingly in the rise of romantic marriage.

Although Coontz assigns each these ways of thinking to the eighteenth or nineteenth century, they coexist in Austen's two early novels, in the form of two sisters. The young headstrong sister who embraces "the romantic excesses" and the older prudent sister who "warned against" them are really only a few years apart, whether we examine Lydia and Lizzie, or Marianne and Elinor. Lizzie is "disgusted" by Lydia's frank sexual pleasures, while Lydia seems fundamentally indifferent to Lizzie's emotional life (239). Elinor and Marianne are more affectionate but disapprove of each other's emotional styles. When Elinor uses the language of rational esteem to describe her feelings, Marianne fulminates, "Esteem him! Like him! Cold-hearted Elinor! Oh! worse than cold-hearted! Use those words again and I will leave the room this moment."[91] Meanwhile, when Elinor contemplates Marianne's passion, she "wished that it were less openly shewn; and once or twice did venture to suggest the propriety of some self-command to Marianne. But Marianne abhorred all concealment" (54–55). While it is tempting to assign these feelings to different centuries, as Coontz does, *Sense and Sensibility* and *Pride and Prejudice* remind us that they overlapped in the same period, in the same family, and that such conflicting imperatives felt terribly painful.

Marianne has both a romantic and a familiar suitor, a wildly mobile stranger and a reliably settled neighbor. The novel strongly endorses the latter. Colonel Brandon, a reliable neighbor, fits the familiar model perfectly. As is typical of the neighbor plot, he is an older man on a long-established landed estate, and he can save Marianne from a tenuous residence in a cottage that she never wanted and that is only sustained by the generosity of a distant relation. To love Colonel Brandon is to engage a different set of emotions than Marianne had employed on Willoughby's behalf. After all, Marianne was "born to discover the falsehood of her own opinions" about the superiority of romantic love. She has to determine not to fall "a sacrifice to an irresistible passion" but rather, "with no sentiment superior to strong esteem and lively friendship, voluntarily to give her hand to another!" (352). When Marianne marries Colonel Brandon, she learns to love him *after* they are wed, not before: her "whole heart became, *in time*, as much devoted to her husband, as it had once been to Willoughby" (352, my italics).[92] Moreover, Marianne notices Colonel Brandon's "advanced state of life" and associates his body with "infirmity" and "aches, cramps, rheumatisms, and every species of ailment that can afflict the old and the feeble" (37, 39, 40). Insisting on a body that evokes sympathy, Austen invites us to imagine a care relation between Marianne and Brandon. Thus Brandon will win Marianne, not in spite of the fact that he "still sought the constitutional safe-guard of a flannel waistcoat!" (352) but because of it. The tenor of this relation will require kindness and sympathy, a different feeling from the passionate erotic desire that Willoughby's handsome body and physical prowess evokes.

Pride and Prejudice is more sympathetic to romantic union and less interested in forcing its heroines into unmitigated familiar marriage. In Mr. Collins, Austen caricatures the familiar suitor as unbearably pompous, making it impossible to want anyone to marry him, in spite of his flawless credentials as cousin and heir. Freed from any imputation of personal feeling, Mr. Collins simply chooses the daughters of the house in strict chronological order. He feels secure that "my situation in life, my connections with the family of de Bourgh, and my relationship to your own, are circumstances highly in my favour," and he is convinced that "when sanctioned by the express authority of both your excellent parents, my proposals will not fail of being acceptable" (83–84). Collins is not in fact unreasonable in this supposition. Wedded as he is to an older model of aristocratic patronage, he also assumes that the older marital guarantees of familial approval and pragmatic self-interest are still in play. Elizabeth, however, speaks for a new generation, in which personal liking has an importance unimagined by Mr. Collins.

Yet Collins's marital model is not wholly rejected by *Pride and Prejudice*. Charlotte Lucas accepts him, and Austen depicts their union as satisfactory. Like

Marianne, Charlotte marries a man whom she does not love. Yet she feels no sense of sexual disgust, any more than Marianne does. Ruth Perry argues this indicates that sexual disgust was an emotion invented and imputed to women in the eighteenth century, part of the larger reconfiguration of women's sexual behavior in the period.[93] Charlotte is, Perry argues, a "vestigial character, left over from an era of pragmatic rather than romantic matches."[94] We might add Marianne to that vestigial category as well.

At the same time, Lizzie's marriage to Darcy, and Jane's marriage to Bingley, both fit the neighbor marriage model. The Bennet women are at risk—they will lose their home when their father dies, and already, their lack of money and vulgar relations hamper their social status. Marrying stable men on landed estates gives the "two most deserving daughters" new roles (364).

Managerial prowess on a major estate is clearly one of the great attractions of these marriages. It is perhaps no coincidence that *Pride and Prejudice*'s first line of dialogue is the information that Netherfield Hall has been let at last; Bingley is in want of a wife, not just because he is in possession of a large fortune, but also because he is now in possession of a large house. When Lizzie tours Pemberley, what gives her the keenest regret is realizing that "of this place . . . I might have been mistress! With these rooms I might now have been familiarly acquainted! Instead of viewing them as a stranger, I might have rejoiced in them as my own, and welcomed to them as visitors my uncle and aunt" (186). Her interest in the estate does not lie in appreciating its scenery but in running the establishment, being its "mistress," inviting whom she wishes. And, as she tells Jane subsequently, she can date her attraction to Darcy to the moment that she saw Pemberley. Lady Catherine de Bourgh functions to show us the job Lizzie will be taking on. But Lady Catherine's detailed directives regarding other people's linens, meat, and servants is no longer appropriate in an era that respects personal privacy, and Lizzie's resentment of her "impertinence" marks a new style of patronage, conducted more through diplomacy and personal relations (perhaps through influence) than through direct interference (160).

Marianne does not covet an estate the same way Lizzie does, but Austen specifically underlines her role as estate manager. When Marianne marries Colonel Brandon, she finds herself "submitting to new attachments, entering on new duties, placed in a new home, a wife, the mistress of a family, and the patroness of a village" (352). The attachment, the affective part of marriage, only forms one item out of six. All the others have to do with her new job, her new status, and her new responsibilities.[95]

These are happy endings partly because of how very much the Bennet and Dashwood women are geographically vulnerable and economically endangered. The women circulate only when banished from their natal homes or when undertaking slow, stately visits accompanying matrons to the Lake district or Derbyshire or London. The young women cannot determine when or where to travel, depending as they do on others. Distance has a very different meaning for women than for men, with their easier access to horses, roads, and stagecoaches. "What is fifty miles of good road? Little more than half a day's journey. Yes, I call it a *very* easy distance," says Darcy, although Lizzie responds, "I should never have considered the distance as one of the *advantages* of the match . . . I should never have said Mrs. Collins was settled *near* her family" (137). Lizzie's comment reveals the intensity of constricted distance, the sense in which family and neighborhood was fundamentally a geographical settlement rather than a chosen network. As Franco Moretti points out in *Atlas of the European Novel*, in Austen's plots, women are static, and men understand distance as relative.[96]

The Bennetts' and Dashwoods' experience is one of circumscribed, impoverished, and vulnerable living situations dependent on the goodwill of male relatives, in a home from which they may be evicted at any moment regardless of their own wishes. Moretti describes "Austen's novelistic geography" this way: "Her plots take the painful reality of territorial uprooting—when her stories open, the family abode is usually on the verge of being lost—and rewrite it as a seductive journey: prompted by desire, and crowned by happiness."[97]

Sense and Sensibility begins with perhaps the most famous example of Ruth Perry's Great Disinheritance in British fiction. When John Dashwood inherits the family fortune, his wife convinces him to deny his sisters support and redirect the money away from the consanguineous family toward his own conjugal family.[98] As a result, the Dashwood women lose their home and their immediate social circle. The Bennett women's deprivation is still in the future, but the fact that the estate is entailed on a male heir makes it inevitable. Their forthcoming Great Disinheritance shapes all their lives. This economic vulnerability makes a good marriage, in a stable locale, all the more crucial.

The sign of a good marriage in both novels is that the unions restore the women to their place—in every sense. In a neighbor marriage, the woman becomes the center around which the family can be consolidated. "Elinor's marriage divided her as little from her family as could well be contrived . . . for her mother and sisters spent much more than half their time with her" (351). When married, Marianne and Elinor remain neighbors. Bingley "bought an estate in a neighbouring county to Derbyshire, and Jane and Elizabeth, in addition to every other source of happiness, were within thirty miles of each other." Moreover, "Kitty, to her very material advantage, spent the chief of her time with her two elder sisters" (295). Marriage gets the women thoroughly and permanently enmeshed in a social and geographical nexus of consanguineal family. A happy ending in an Austen novel is constituted by sisters' continued proximity, as guaranteed by marriages to sympathetic men.

Interestingly, however, for the men, a happy marriage involves not sustaining but severing their consanguineal ties. In particular, Ferrars and Darcy use the opportunity to cease relations with inconvenient family members. Darcy's marriage becomes possible because he defies his aunt, Lady Catherine de Bourgh, and the marriage creates a profound breach that is later only partially patched up. Ferrars is relieved to separate himself from his problematic mother and siblings. The men flee from overbearing female relations, eagerly embracing the chance to choose a new family.

Thus, instead of consolidating their own kin, each man identifies themselves with his beloved's extended network. Darcy's determination to resolve the Lydia-Wickham affair baffles as much as it impresses the Bennetts. When Elizabeth first gets notice of Darcy's involvement, she feels "utter amazement" (243). Colonel Brandon's voluntary assistance is equally astonishing. When Edward Ferrars's mother disinherits him, nobody can imagine "what is to become of him," his brother-in-law John Dashwood opining that "I cannot conceive a situation more deplorable" (251). However, the men replace their consanguineous family with an affiliative family. The inherited property gets replaced by a new living, due to Ferrar's individual merit rather than his place in the birth order. Colonel Brandon helps Ferrars because, "I have seen Mr. Edward Ferrars two or three times in Harley-street, and am much pleased with him. He is not a young man with whom one can be intimately acquainted in a short time, but I have seen enough of him to wish him well for his own sake, and as a friend of yours, I wish it still more" (264). To assist a deserving stranger instead of one's own kin violates the rules of patrilineal inheritance and the normative circulation of property, and it astounds everyone, including Edward himself, who exclaims, "Can it be possible?" and John Dashwood, who expostulates, "Really!—Well, this is very astonishing!—no relationship!—no connection between them!" (271, 276).

Sense and Sensibility and *Pride and Prejudice* imagine, in fear and fascination, the new state of individuation that its male characters inhabit when Ferrars and Darcy are no longer constrained by their kin ties and responsibilities. This free agency is terrifying, liberating, and devastating all at once. Claudia Johnson writes that in *Sense and Sensibility*, "isolation from the patriarchal family is a precondition for honest liberty." Indeed, "Brandon himself is in a position to offer modest patronage only because his own days of subjugation to a corrupt father and older brother are happily behind him."[99] Brandon's transaction, like Darcy's friendship, is a sign of the future: a world where affiliations are voluntary rather than kinship based, where relations with strangers can be fruitful, where one is judged on the moral merits of one's acts instead of the inherited status of one's birth, and where good men want work rather than inherited wealth. Moretti notes that this is the new world of the city:

> In the village, not only are mothers (or substitute mothers) always present, but every important relationship takes the form of a family tie: early sweethearts are sister figures . . . while early friends are as many older brothers. . . . In the great city, though, the heroes of the *Bildungsroman* change overnight from "sons" into "young men": their affective ties are no longer vertical ones (between successive generations), but horizontal, within the same generation. They are drawn towards those unknown yet congenial faces seen in the gardens, or at the theater; future friends, or rivals, or both.[100]

At the end of *Sense and Sensibility*, neither Brandon nor Ferrars lives anywhere near their families of origin, or even appears to keep up much contact with them. They have begun their new conjugal families on their own accounts. Darcy and Bingley choose one another as their new affiliations, purchasing contiguous estates and creating a newly filtered family structure that includes Georgiana Darcy and Kitty Bennett as quasi-permanent inhabitants, Mr. Bennett and the Gardiners as frequent guests, and occasional visits from Lydia, Miss Bingley, Mrs. Bennett, and Lady Catherine de Bourgh (but not Wickham). Familial networks are being constrained and revamped according to individual preferences. They are being recentered on the women, not the men. Although the men retain their political and economic power, the women are being shown as the centers of a different kind of network, a social, emotional, linguistic power, the power to make careful status distinctions in order to select and filter the community that they generate.

If the men are more willing to break with family, that may be because the male characters also embody a new urban orientation and geographic mobility. Mr. Bennett and Mr. Gardiner visit Epsom, Clapham, and London in pursuit of Wickham; Wickham dashes from Meryton to Brighton to London; Willoughby hides his mistress in the crowded streets of Bath; Colonel Brandon rushes off at a moment's notice to rescue her; Brandon shows up unexpectedly at the Dashwoods' cottage one fine day; and Willoughby posts down from London in a day to explain himself to Elinor. Circulation and transportation determine the emotional life of the novel.[101] Men show up suddenly, disappear suddenly, pounding over a Britain that accommodates the traveler with inns and posting stations. The rapidity of the men's transit staggers Elinor; the men think nothing of riding to (or from) London in a day (65, 297).

This circulation allows them to court women who do not know them. Moretti sees Austen's fiction as innovative in that it imagines a national marriage market, a move away from regional centers toward places where people from all over the country can mingle.[102] But in these early novels, one need not go to Bath for this kind of contact with strangers. Willoughby steps out of nowhere, literally sweeping Marianne off her feet, and their romantic interest in each other encourages the formation of a relationship unsanctioned by traditional introductions or chaperones. Similarly, Wickham arrives as a handsome stranger in a militia temporarily quartered in Meryton, a situation that permits dangerously free mixing without elders' oversight. Each man is a relative stranger, moving among different estates and encampments. The men's story is one of personal choice and personal liberty—a very different tale from the women's.

Because the men are strangers, local advisors know only unhelpful scraps of information; Sir John Dashwood testifies that Willoughby is a good rider who has a fine dog (34), while Miss Bingley offers a confused impression of Wickham's untrustworthiness (72). With no reliable witnesses to his character, family members have to measure the man's worthiness solely by the local clues of his appearance and manners, like Willoughby's "manly beauty and more than common gracefulness" and his due appreciation of poetry (44). Wickham, too, "had all the best part of beauty, a fine countenance, a good figure, and very pleasing address" as well as "a happy readiness of conversation—a readiness at the same time perfectly correct and unassuming" (54).

Unfortunately, beauty, grace, and conversability do not indicate a man's moral qualities. Desperately in debt, a seasoned rake who has ruined (or tried to ruin) at least one helpless teenager, the man turns out to be cynically willing to sell himself for money.[103] Willoughby, as it turns out, is taking advantage of Marianne's adoration, and when he falls in love with her (in spite of himself) he carefully avoids committing himself by a proposal, then lies about their attachment in order to marry a wealthy heiress. Wickham, an even worse case, at first flirts with Lizzie, then callously ruins Lydia and holds the family reputation and finances hostage to buy his acquiescence to a patched-up marriage, having already tried to abduct his benefactor's daughter. Each man's plausible exteriors only enable him to be a greater danger to women. In separating from Willoughby, Marianne has had "an escape from the worst and most irremediable of evils, a connection, for life, with an unprincipled man, as a deliverance the most real, a blessing the most important" (175). Marrying the romantic stranger is a terrifying prospect.

Marianne's attraction to Willoughby is clearly eroticized, as Eve Sedgwick has famously shown in "Jane Austen and the Masturbating Girl."[104] Her blushing, her ecstatic self-absorption, her excitement, and her distraction all signal sexual incitement. But this is not the whole story. Because all along, Marianne is also reacting to a different man, who provokes alternative feelings in her: initial impatience turning to grudging respect, pity, friendship, reliance, and gratitude. *Sense and Sensibility* says that these are better ingredients for marriage, and in so doing, it provides an alternative to Foucault's teleological account of the rise and triumph of sexuality. Marianne must learn to renounce passionate love, choosing instead the affable kindliness she might feel toward a silent, depressed, elderly neighbor. Marianne must learn to renounce the thrill of mobility and instead value the stability of the estate.

Lydia, however, is stuck forever in romantic marriage's perpetual present, a state of passion that Austen implicitly decries as immature and selfish. Lydia is a caricature of Lizzie, as their similar names suggest. Both are characterized by intense private emotional lives, a love of pleasure, and an insistence on choosing their own mates. In a modern story, Lydia's elopement with Wickham would be a Hollywood fantasy of following one's heart, but in 1813, nothing could be more appalling than Lydia's pursuit of individual romance with a stranger who sweeps her away from home.[105] When Lizzie thinks about Lydia's elopement, she has no interest in the question of Lydia's personal happiness but considers only "the humilation, the misery, she was bringing on them all," as she says, reverting to a plural perspective that reestablishes her own status as familial component (210). The liberty of mobility and choice that male characters can take for granted is reprehensible for female characters.

If the erotic passion of Marianne and Lydia needs to be reformed, it is their elder sisters who model good marital feeling, the "rational esteem" we saw in the eighteenth-century ancestor of the familiar model, the proper valuation of the social opportunities of estate management. In Elinor's case, her prospect, Edward Ferrars, was "not recommended to their good opinion by any peculiar graces of person or address. He was not handsome, and his manners required intimacy to make them pleasing" (17). What Elinor and Edward feel for each other is a type of attachment that they denote "partiality" (17). Even in *Pride and Prejudice*, Lizzie's feeling for Darcy is explicitly presented as a companionable approbation rather than passionate desire:

> If gratitude and esteem are good foundations of affection, Elizabeth's change of sentiment will be neither improbable nor faulty. But if otherwise, if the regard springing from such sources is unreasonable or unnatural, in comparison of what is so often described as arising on a first interview with its object, and even before two words have been exchanged, nothing can be said in her defence, except that she had given somewhat of a trial to the latter method, in her partiality for Wickham, and that its ill-success might perhaps authorise her to seek the other less interesting mode of attachment. (211)

"Partiality" here has shifted to mean an unthinking bias, to be combatted by the superior emotions of "gratitude and esteem."

Thus both of Austen's first published novels end up endorsing marriages of rational esteem for the women—but, interestingly, marriages of romantic interest for the men. Elinor, Marianne, Jane, and Lizzie all marry men whose worth is thoroughly tested, and their marriages stabilize their consanguineal families and allow them to live near one another. They are either already neighbors or become neighbors. But the men achieve a different marriage plot. Ferrars, Darcy, and Brandon have unprecedented mobility and affiliative, rather than kinship, ties. Both Darcy and Ferrars reject their parents' choices of wives, insisting instead on their own prospects, even though their elders disapprove.[106] The men are free agents, while the women remain enmeshed in social relations.

Because we read the novels from the women's point of view, the reader's overriding impression is the endorsement of familiar unions. As Mary Evans notes, Austen's "characters are not, in any romantic sense, 'in love.' They may well have acquired, through trial and tribulation, a considerable respect and affection for the other party but that affection has been based on a key component of workable relationships: Socratic conversation and discourse."[107] Rarely does Austen depict a woman's romantic union positively. Rather, she aims to show how "unhappy marriages and ill-matched partners . . . result from those courtships in which the appearance and the expectation of love was allowed to take precedence over rational understanding."[108] Indeed, in Evans's words, Austen is "the most profound, and most articulate, critic of romantic love."[109]

Over Austen's lifetime, however, this certainty changed. By the time she completed her last full novel, Austen had reversed her earlier thinking to allow a woman to experience this new marriage plot. *Persuasion* supports a nineteen-year-old's choice of "a stranger" over the cousin and heir who is endorsed by all her elders.[110] In *Persuasion*, the romantic, charismatic, risky outsider turns out to be the better choice than the decorous familial connection. The man who whisks the heroine away, right off terrestrial ground, is better than the man who might anchor her in a neighborhood. Anne believes—and, astonishingly, we agree with her—that it is better to go to sea with an unrelated man than to live on the Kellynch estate with a cousin. *Persuasion* offers the ship, the antithesis of the estate.[111] Wentworth thus reverses the work of Wickham and Willoughby.

Yet if we look a little more deeply, we find the early novels' male characters are not simply triumphantly modern independent men. Fitzwilliam Darcy, Edward Ferrars, and Colonel Brandon mingle their modern capacities with older qualities. Each man's biography aligns him with the Romantic rake: he has a brooding secret (sexual) mystery, he has mysterious absences and fits of despair, he is a man of monied leisure. Yet his Romantic exterior hides a virtuous proto-Evangelical core identity, which renders him an acceptable husband. Darcy's secret is his beloved sister's near-elopement with Wickham; his moodiness testifies to his good family feeling rather than his personal demons. Similarly, Colonel Brandon's gloom derives from the contemplation of his first beloved's sexual fall. He has never had any romantic trysts, and his big secret is the rather paternal and domestic fact that he is the guardian of his cousin's daughter. Meanwhile, although Edward is haunted by an unfortunate romantic entanglement with a declassé woman, she is his fiancée, not his mistress. These men want nothing more than "domestic comfort and the quiet of private life" (18). They are determined to fulfill the new masculine ideal even if it leads to a permanent rift with their parents and aunts, and their debarment from more remunerative fates. Their Romantic (Byronic) appearance proves only to be a husk, hiding the vital principle of middle-class virtue.

In this respect, *Sense and Sensibility* and *Pride and Prejudice* actually craft compromise formations. Each novel has one already stable, landed squire (Darcy, Brandon), and each novel has one friend of the squire's, an initially aimless, mobile man whose marriage finally makes him settle on an estate (Bingley, Ferrars). Male individualism enables exciting new relationships and careers and possible lives, but the women must marry those for whom they feel companionable affection, and these marriages must stabilize the men within their static social world. The reason is that women's economic precarity renders the continued reliance on family—and on trustworthy partners—necessary, whereas Brandon, Ferrars, and Willoughby can afford (in every sense) to take risks, pursuing attractive individuals regardless of how the unions might affect their prospects. *Sense and Sensibility* acknowledges the attractiveness of the emerging nineteenth-century model: mobile, self-made men and romantic passion. But the novel comes down firmly on the side of eighteenth-century moral virtue, companionable ideals, and social enmeshment.

However, *Pride and Prejudice* creates an amalgamation of old and new, as Darcy has qualities of both the romantic suitor (he is a handsome stranger who sweeps Lizzie away) and the familiar suitor (his moral qualities get vetted at Pemberley, he proves himself willing to work for the Bennetts' interests, and he settles Lizzie near her sisters). It is Darcy's strong familial loyalties—his affection for his sister, his good attitude to his servants and tenants, and his bargaining with Lydia—that confirm his eligibility as a husband. At the same time, Darcy insists that "your *family* owe me nothing. Much as I respect them, I believe, I thought only of *you*" (280).

Brandon versus Willoughby presents an either/or—familiar or romantic, neighbor or stranger—but Darcy offers an improvement, for he can be familiar and romantic at once. He exemplifies both bourgeois moral self-determination and aristocratic privilege, familial loyalty and individualist self-assertion, moral excellence and handsome charisma. Darcy is a fairy-tale prince in that he can fulfill both sets of ideals, and this allowed him to become the cultural model of a perfect man. In *Pride and Prejudice*, we have the comedic ending at last, the happy amalgam of familial acceptability and personal passion achieved against all the odds.

Cometh Up as a Flower: *The Impoverished Marriage Plot of Romantic Love*

Fifty years later, however, Rhoda Broughton would write *Cometh Up as a Flower* (1867) as a very different marriage plot, a critical revision of *Sense and Sensibility*. Although it offers the same plot of the romantic teen taught to abjure her stranger in order to marry the elderly neighbor, this version treats it as a tragedy. The Marianne character continues to believe that a person denied a romantic marriage can only hope to die. But what *Cometh Up* presents is not a rejection of neighbor marriage but a case study of the kind of mind that would reject neighbor marriage and a warning about what kind of damage such an attitude might wreak.

Broughton's debts to *Sense and Sensibility* are clear. In both novels, a tempestuous, impoverished, romantic younger sister flings herself into a passionate affair with a mysterious, handsome soldier who adores her, but whose poverty prevents him from marrying her. Each girl has only one parent, who overidentifies with the younger's madcap passion and thus cannot control her. Instead, the calmer elder sister patiently redirects her sibling toward an amicable match with a perfectly kind, trustworthy older neighbor. This marriage settles the family at last.

And yet with the same plot, the affective import of almost every event gets reversed. Significantly, it is the passionate teenager, not the sedate elder sister, who is named Eleanor (Nell for short), a detail that in itself represents Broughton's topsy-turvy relation to her source.[112] *Sense and Sensibility* is most often focalized through Elinor's point of view, but *Cometh Up* is narrated by a rebellious teenager who has no adult advisor. (Her elders are her father, whose rules of conduct she disregards, and her sister, whom she detests.) Julia Prewitt Brown's description of Marianne's passion applies even better to Nell's: it "is an adolescent passion—dazzling in its very ignorance of the complexity that surrounds it, destructive in its determination to annihilate the forms that restrain it, and devoid of the irony of the adult passion in *Persuasion* or, for that matter, in *Antony and Cleopatra*."[113] We are swept away by it, even while we note its failings of crudity, incomprehension, and violence.

In *Sense and Sensibility*, Marianne is absolutely certain of her culture. Indeed, we first meet her when she is expressing horror at the inadequacy of Edward's taste for Cowper (19, 49). "I could not be happy with a man whose taste did not in every point coincide with my own. He must enter into all my feelings; the same books, the same music must charm us both," she announces (19). But Nell has no such criteria. Indeed, because her education has been so neglected, Nell has no framework within which to understand the events of her own life. In reality, Nell's education is probably no worse than many young women's, but she evinces great frustration about her lack of knowledge. Her literary knowledge derives from the Bible and a smattering of ancient myths, plus the newspaper, Tennyson and Wordsworth poems, slang, and popular ditties.[114] In an early meeting with M'Gregor (the Willoughby figure), when M'Gregor begs her to teach him something, she looks at him incredulously and then says bitterly, "It's a good idea my teaching anybody anything. I'm the greatest dunce in Europe" (89). (This is a sentence one cannot imagine Marianne uttering.) In defending her aristocratic heritage, she sputters out the names of two famous battles and then runs out of references (125). Broughton is stressing Nell's ignorance for a reason: it cues us in that she may not know other cultural formations that are far more relevant to her than Cressy or Agincourt.

Nell has no way of reading her own plot. She does not, for instance, recognize the romantic suitor when she almost literally trips over him. Richard (Dick) M'Gregor is a handsome, sexual, potentially untrustworthy stranger. Nell is overwhelmed by his charm, his enormous strong body, his tawny hair, his strong hands. But instead of inquiring into his character, or ascertaining his family and class situation, she immediately identifies him as her "King Olaf," "my Viking," affiliating him with mythic or romanticized ancient history (55). Nell's and Dick's whole relation vibrates with sexual tension. Nell remembers Dick's "long eager gaze, the remembrance of which still stirred my silly little soul in the newest, queerest, joyfullest fashion" (67). And when contemplating her own death, she even pleads for a sexualized heaven, with bodies and passions, where she can rejoin him.[115]

Dick M'Gregor communicates the menace of the romantic stranger. Sexually aggressive and unreliable, he violates basic protocols—as we see from Nell's father's perspective, when he finds "his favourite daughter sitting in the dusk of the evening with a man, whom, to his certain knowlege, she had seen but twice before in her life, lying at her feet and clasping her hand." Nell's father is furious at the man, but Nell has little respect for her father's code of propriety, which she considers ridiculous, "rigidity's self" (146). However, this is a complicated moment, one that emblematizes the double work of *Cometh Up*, in which Victorian readers recognize cultural norms to which their narrator remains oblivious. Although Nell flouts her father's rules, almost all readers of 1867 would have endorsed a behavioral code which prohibited a teenage girl from secret nighttime assignations with a lover unknown to her family. Broughton could well have made Nell's father a tyrannical General Tilney; that she gives him a reasonable, mild rule certainly complicates our reading of Nell's rebellion against him.

Nell's father's dislike of M'Gregor seems justified. When he objects to this stranger's presence in his garden, M'Gregor immediately produces what Nell, horrified, identifies as "a tissue of fibs!" (71). McGregor is penniless, flirts with other women, and, as Dolly acutely surmises, "likes billiards and Chateau Lâfitte, and actresses" (203). He also disappears, torturing Nell with his silence, although this is later explained away. Like Willoughby, M'Gregor appears when it is too late, on purpose to explain and ameliorate his behavior.

In short, M'Gregor, like Willoughby, is a handsome dangerous stranger, whose military unit gets stationed in a provincial town and who is flattered by finding that the pretty, poor but well-born, ingenuous local teenage girl is clearly besotted with him. He falls in love with her, but realizes that his debts make him unable to marry. Each man has a history of alternately sexually aggressive and neglectful behavior toward his beloved. While M'Gregor seems better than Willoughby in certain local ways (he admits his poverty instead of hiding it; he leaves Nell because Dolly tricks him, not because he prefers to marry an heiress), he is not necessarily a good man at all, let alone a good marital prospect. This is the information the reader has, but Nell lacks.

Where Elinor speaks eloquently in favor of a trusting partnership with a good man, Dolly fights for another form of union: cold-blooded marriage for money and rank. This mercenary marriage is the nightmare version of familiar marriage, just as seduction is the horrifying extreme of romantic marriage. Dolly exclaims, "Is there any old lord between the three seas, so old, so mumbling, so wicked, that I would not joyfully throw myself into his horrid palsied old arms, if he had but money; money! money! money is power; money is a god!" (204). Nell views the familiar marriage as a kind of legalized prostitution, ensuring that we see it as appalling. Nell asks herself, miserably, after marrying Sir Hugh, "Am I not his property? Has he not every right to kiss my face off if he chooses?" (Broughton, 269.) The ideas of violence, ownership, and property mark the first time we see concerns about neighbor marriage—concerns that will surface far more disturbingly by the end of the century.

Broughton complicates Nell's position by creating a perfectly amenable familiar union, a neighbor plot in all the best ways. Like Colonel Brandon, Sir Hugh Lancaster is a well-known older neighbor, who has loved Nell and patiently waited for her for a long time. He and Brandon even share sartorial preferences.[116] Marriage with him helps Nell's family by bringing a local benefactor into their kinship network. Hugh also offers familiar marriage in other recognizable ways: he is kindly and reliable, although not sexually interesting.[117] No melancholy Byronic hero, he is merely a good-natured English squire. He is actually an improved version of Colonel Brandon, jolly where his predecessor was glum, sociable where his predecessor was reserved. Nell explicitly tells us he does not even have Brandon's worrisome sexual secret: "Nobody ever accused him of having ever had his affections blighted" (102).

Hugh is the perfectly generic squire suitor, and as such, we have no interest in his own interior consciousness but rather see him as an instrument to give Nell the powerful managerial role women in this position crave. As her father says, Nell's marrying Hugh gives him pleasure, "to see [her] raised to [her] right level again, and doing something towards bringing the old family back into its right position in the county" (235–236). Neighbor marriage gives Nell real work to do; instead of running free as she did in her father's home, she now has to learn to perform the role of the domestic manager, knitting socks, leading family prayers, and participating in social calls, under the tutelage of Hugh's mother (293, 307).

As in any familiar marriage, cohabitation gradually produces a companionate, affectionate, trusting love. After a year of marriage, Nell admits that she is "growing to love Hugh with all love '—except the love/ Of man and woman, when they love their best/Closest and sweetest'" (319).[118] The machinery of familiar love rolls onward, generating social power, domestic management skills, middle-class feminization, and affectionate interest in one another. As Pamela Gilbert points out, "Hugh Lancaster, with his colonial wealth and adjacent estate, is clearly the perfect match from a practical point of view. Nell's whole family desires the match, and many readers might consider her blind pursuit of what Dolly, in exasperation, calls Nell's 'big wax doll' and considers a 'childish besotment' for a thoroughly unsuitable match, to be selfish."[119] But Nell, who passionately believes that romantic love is the only possible motive to wed, cannot find a way to believe her life is acceptable.

Nell weds in despair, wishing she were dead. Sobbing uncontrollably, heartsick for her lover, Nell does not try to conquer her pain but to convey it. "My misery rose up before me, huge, unnatural, gigantic; terribler 'than ever woman wore'" (291). Fifty years earlier, Marianne nearly kills herself from grief and must be brought to see misery as a dangerous self-indulgence (*Sense*, 322). But Nell wants to experience as much unhappiness as she can. She admires her decay in the glass, with her hollow cheeks and weeping eyes, her untidy hair and drooping body (254). Her romantic decline has nothing to do with any narrative of moral improvement. Instead, it affirms her own sensibility, her own intensity of feeling.

In a perverse way, then, *Cometh Up* testifies to the necessity of the category it is trying to do away with. If she had known the neighbor-marriage structure, Nell would have been able to watch out for M'Gregor as potentially untrustworthy, to make peace with her marriage, and to accept her amity for Hugh. But Nell is denied these consolations. When we read *Cometh Up*, restricted to the mind of an emotionally flamboyant teenager steeped in the literature of romance, we see a kind of nightmare version of the Victorian novel's favorite plot.

For when the familiar marriage disappears—or at least, as in *Cometh Up*, loses its meaning—what we have is a radical narrowing of the world for women. Nell can only be with M'Gregor or die. No other duties, no other loves, no other career, no other function for marriage is possible. Their romantic abandon means bliss or suicide. Paradoxically, Broughton's depiction of a world without any consciousness of the older familiar form of marriage made the strongest possible case for it.

We may think back to Marianne Dashwood, who was, indeed, born to an extraordinary fate. "Instead of falling a sacrifice to an irresistible passion, as once she had fondly flattered herself with expecting," Marianne "found herself at nineteen, submitting to new attachments, entering on new duties, placed in a new home, a wife, the mistress of a family, and the patroness of a village" (352). Marianne "found herself" all these other roles. But Nell, fifty years later, refuses to accept any of them. Her world has shrunk; her options have dwindled. She is determined to "fall a sacrifice to her irresistible passion," and does so, refusing all attempts by her husband, sister, and mother-in-law to help her "find herself" in new roles. *Cometh Up* is a confirmation of the dominance of romantic marriage by the late Victorian period. But it also shows what was lost. Nell rejects neighbor marriage; but then again, Nell dies. It is the character who learns to marry Colonel Brandon who has a viable future.

The Vicar of Bullhampton*: Learning from Familiar Marriage*

Anthony Trollope's *The Vicar of Bullhampton* (1870) perpetuates the painful critique levied by Broughton, the vision of a neighbor plot gone wrong, in which the woman suffers. In *The Vicar of Bullhampton*, however, we see a more mature woman able to take the lessons of the neighbor plot into her eventual romantic union. Trollope's novel endorses this genre's emphasis on female managerial power but finds a way to import it into the rival plot.

The Vicar of Bullhampton focuses on Mary Lowther, a young woman torn between an inappropriate, impecunious, handsome lover and a respectable elderly neighbor. The 500-page duration of her long and hard-fought journey toward romantic marriage, littered with two failed engagements, familial estrangements, and strained friendships, testifies to the enormous difficulty of coming around to romantic marriage, the cost of that transition, and the suffering it produced along the way. In *Vicar*, as in *Cometh Up*, a romantic marriage is the only acceptable fate—and yet the pursuit of that romantic union is nothing but painful, leading to an impoverished life and the destruction of social ties. Like *Cometh Up, Vicar* offers material for a counter-reading in which the neighbor marriage would indeed have been the better fate, if only the woman could have brought herself to pursue it. But what *Vicar* shows is that the mere presence of the familiar suitor fundamentally changes the course of romantic love. Because Mary is more mature than Nell, because we are able to read her story from outside her first-person perspective, and because she gets her romantic marriage in the end, we can see something that was not evident in *Cometh Up*: in order to succeed, a romantic union has to be refashioned to resemble a familiar one.

Mary Lowther's well meaning friend, Janet Fenwick, would like Mary to marry Harry Gilmore, the local squire and kindly neighbor. Gilmore, the generic good man, is "just such a man to look at as a prudent mother would select as one to whom she might entrust her daughter with safety" (84). He is the typically conventional minor character of the neighbor plot. And since Harry is a perfectly fine prospect—a kind, prosperous man who lives near Mary's dearest friends—there seems no reason to refuse. Indeed, Mary "thought ill of herself because she would not [accept Gilmore]. 'I do believe,' she said to herself, 'that I shall never like any man better.'"[120] Eventually Mary allows herself to be talked into accepting Gilmore, envisioning a future of caring for the poor and managing the household, a plan that satisfies everyone in her social network. Foreseeing managerial prowess and political efficacy, Mary intends a neighbor-marriage familiar plot.

But when Mary meets her second cousin, Walter Marrable, she has to rethink this serene fate. Marrable is handsome, but swarthy, defiant, and ferocious—and penniless as well (84, 85). He is a military man, a stranger, rootless and violent—sharing a career with M'Gregor in *Cometh Up*, Wickham in *Pride*, and Willoughby in *Sense*. Marrable has returned home in rage because his father has swindled him out of his fortune, and he is therefore violently at odds with his family and debating what to do next. Although he and Mary fall in love, their union is financially impossible. Moreover, both have familiar unions awaiting them. Marrable's family intends that he should marry another connection, the pleasant and pretty Edith Brownlow, which will facilitate his inheritance of the estate. In a nutshell, "if a marriage could be arranged between Walter and Edith, the family troubles would be in a fair way of settlement. No good could come to anybody from that other marriage. As for Mary Lowther, it was manifestly her duty to become Mrs. Gilmore" (319). In spite of their love for each other, therefore, they break off their engagement, and each acquiesces to the familiar marriage already set up. Mary tells Gilmore, "I esteem you as we esteem our dearest friends. . . . I do love you,—but not as I love him. I shall never again have that feeling" (357). However, a fortuitous death in the Marrable family makes Walter the heir to the family estate, and he is able to marry Mary at last.

The Vicar of Bullhampton vividly commemorates the struggle of one woman between a passionate love for an impecunious man and a choice of rational esteem for a prosperous man. In the end, romantic love wins, and Mary can become Marrable's wife. Thus *Vicar* seems to come down fully on the side of romantic marriage. It would be easy to read it as if the Gilmore plot is merely an older leftover that temporarily tempts our heroine but that she must eventually abjure.

But the reality is a little more complicated. The Gilmore engagement (like the Edith engagement) is a genuinely good plan, endorsed by every character, not an archaic notion that the modern woman should leave behind. Gilmore is a likeable man, as Edith Brownlow is a pleasant woman, and neither of them has any happy resolution once their chosen partners abandon them for a more haphazard and reckless life. They appear to be condemned to perpetual loneliness, rendering the reader uneasy. On the romantic side, we have the uneasy status of sexual entanglements represented by the returning prostitute Carry Brattle, often read as a parallel character to Mary.[121] Carry's life story functions as a vivid reminder of the dangers of following one's heart. If Mary has a "want of capability for passion," Carry has evidently had too much experience of passion (8).

Moreover, the Walter–Mary marriage only becomes possible when Marrable gets remade in the image of Gilmore. Mary does indeed become what she calls "the deputy Squiress" of the parish, but only when the squire is Marrable, not Gilmore (516). Thus the terms of the neighbor marriage prevail, although the identity of the squire changes. Through this inheritance, the violent, gloomy, moody Walter Marrable we met at first, cursing his father and threatening to blow his own brains out, develops into a pleasant, filial, courteous family member, caring for his uncle and cousins and dutifully maintaining the estate. In both situation and personality, Marrable becomes like Gilmore. The romantic marriage becomes possible only when the romantic suitor gets refashioned to resemble the familiar suitor, when the soldier becomes the squire. And the squire's minor character status gets confirmed by this substitution; far from fetishizing the perpetuation of the gentry class, the marriage novel is quite coolly uninterested in the squire, regarding him merely as an interchangeable instrument, a form of disrespect so profound that it in itself means that the squire's days are over.

The Vicar of Bullhampton confirms that even those novels that stage the triumph of the romantic suitor can only do so by borrowing key elements of the familiar plot. It is as if the emergent novel of romantic love has to absorb its residual alternative, to dialectically assume its key qualities, if it is to present a credible portrait of the new kind of marriage. Michael McKeon describes an analogous structure: "The traditional categories do not really 'persist' into the realm of the modern as an alien intrusion from without. Now truly abstracted and constituted *as* categories, they are incorporated within the very process of the emergent genre and are vitally functional in the finely articulated mechanism by which it establishes its own domain."[122] McKeon's explanation may hold good for the way the novel processes historical ideologies. The older idea—in this case, the idea of a marriage of rational esteem, or marrying into the squirearchy—mutates into the Victorian notion of neighbor marriage, thence contributing its DNA to the formation of a new species that is both its rival and its descendant, romantic marriage.

If *Vicar* works its way toward endorsing romantic marriage, it is only via recognizing the appeal of familiar marriage, commemorating the tragedies generated by the rejection of familiar marriage, obliquely warning us about romantic dangers through a parallel character, and finally reconfiguring romantic marriage to resemble familiar marriage. In terms of the plot, there is no inherent reason the Gilmore entanglement should exist. Mary could have met Walter Marrable, fallen in love, broken it off due to pennilessness, and re-engaged herself when he became the heir. Trollope puts Gilmore in this novel to thrash out the question of whether a neighbor marriage is still acceptable—and although the main character and narrator come down firmly in the negative, in fact Walter Marrable's transformation indicates its continuing appeal. One should marry for love, yes—but one should love the kind of estimable squire that one would have rationally chosen. Like Darcy, Marrable is a compromise formation, an empowering match whom one can personally adore.

The End of the Neighbor Plot

It is tempting to believe that the neighbor plot crumbled because the squirearchy died away, because nobody believed anymore in the supreme power of the landed estate, because with increasing mobility people were no longer attached to one beloved spot of ground, or because people no longer knew their neighbors thanks to urbanization and globalization. This is all true, although in fact every one of these factors is operative in the neighbor plot from *Sense and Sensibility* onward.[123] The neighbor plot was designed to produce the effect of a *Gemeinschaft*, though the *Gemeinschaft* cultural fantasy was always implausible enough that a moment's close attention reveals its nonviability, in fiction or in fact.

The real reason the neighbor-marriage plot disappeared is more subtle. We need to recall that neighbor marriage attracted a female character because it offered a fantasy of social centrality and powerful agency—a promise that was enormously attractive to a person who was profoundly disempowered. Neighbor marriage attracted readers because it spoke to (and perpetuated) a vision of England based on small, stable, provincial social organizations, the organic communities for which Victorians were yearning.

However, this plot only worked insofar as it cast the squire as a minor character. The novels do not care very much about exactly why Ferrars, Brandon, Bingley, Lancaster, and Gilmore want to marry the female characters. They function instrumentally. But once endowed with interiority and development, once the marriage plot becomes their story as well, the male character's different sense of the marriage plot looms larger and may override the female character's. Nowhere is this more common than in George Eliot's fiction. As we shall see in this book, once it is not "always Dorothea," once it is Casaubon's, Wakem's, or Grandcourt's story too, the marriage plot changes. Frederic Jameson has argued that Tito in *Romola* is a paradigmatic minor character who gets promoted into a protagonist, his very blandness becoming the source of a new kind of interiority.[124] In this chapter we can see how Grandcourt, similarly, turns the basic colorlessness of the generic squire into a psychological horror.[125]

Grandcourt exemplifies the man whose interiority derives from his landowning status. Since ownership of property is the basis of the squire's identity, it is hardly surprising that he views his wife as an additional piece of property.[126] Examples of such squires include Trollope's autocratic, self-damaging men: Louis Trevalyan in *He Knew He Was Right*, Christopher Dale in *The Small House at Allington*, and Roger Carbury in *The Way We Live Now*. The squire is characterized by entitlement, often reinforced with physical, verbal, and legal violence. In *Daniel Deronda*, Eliot remakes the neighbor plot into a psychological study of the pathological effects of power—the way people behave when they have too much, and the way they feel when they are denied any power at all.

Grandcourt serves as a good example of Eliot's interest in undoing familiar marriage norms. In this chapter we will look at Grandcourt as a bad neighbor, but in Chapter 5 we shall see how Philip Wakem constitutes a problematic kind of disabled subject and in Chapter 6 how Casaubon is an unsatisfactory vocational partner. Gwendolen, Maggie, and Dorothea—unlike Nell—are fully read in what they imagine to be their respective narratives. They know exactly what to expect. The problem is that their author changes the terms on them. The men no longer have the good qualities associated with the women's familiar-marriage prototypes; instead, the men are psychologically complex characters who are shown, by a brilliant technique, to have precisely the opposite of the qualities that the familiar plot habitually ascribes to them. In Eliot's novels, the man is no longer simply the facilitator for opportunities in the woman's life, but has himself been poisoned by the very qualities he is traditionally supposed to provide. For Grandcourt, that issue is power. Instead of providing power for his wife, he becomes a case study in the bad effects of a lifetime of having power oneself. And the male subject's adherence to a dominant narrative—in this case, the frank recognition of the power vested in legal ownership—counteracts the more diffuse and dubious dreams of the female, including her fantasies of household management, community centrality, and influence.

Gwendolen thinks she is entering a conventional neighbor marriage with a nondescript, quiet, polite, older local squire. As she tells her mother, "there is less to dislike about him than about most men. He is quiet and *distingué*. . . . Indeed he has all the qualities that would make a husband tolerable—battlement, veranda, stables, &c."[127] *Daniel Deronda* offers the classic neighbor-marriage plot: a desperately impoverished woman facing imminent homelessness marries the older local squire. Naturally, she expects to achieve what the neighbor marriage offers: social centrality and local/national power. "She was thinking of him, whatever he might be, as a man over whom she was going to have indefinite power; and her loving him having never been a question with her, any agreeableness he had was so much gain. Poor Gwendolen had no awe of unmanageable forces in the state of matrimony, but regarded it as altogether a matter of management, in which she would know how to act" as she "devised little schemes for learning what was expected of men in general" (262). She has perfect faith in "her future influence as an omnipotence in managing" (465). She has no idea that Grandcourt intends to hold onto "his mastery" (271).

Grandcourt is one of "those who prefer command to love" (493). Although the woman normally controls the socializing in the home, it is Grandcourt alone who determines who can be invited, overruling his wife's objection to Lush and his wife's preference for Deronda. Nor does he allow his wife's family to visit—and family proximity is one of the main benefits of neighbor marriage. Grandcourt absolutely does not want Gwendolen to manage domestic, community, or political life for him. He has Lush to work through his personal arrangements, and he has no intention whatsoever of going into politics. It is bitterly ironic when Mr. Gascoigne suggests that Gwendolen "use your influence with Mr. Grandcourt to induce him to enter Parliament," assuring her that "a wife has great influence with her husband. Use yours in that direction, my dear" (464). Gwendolen, of course, has no influence whatsoever. The neighbor plot promises power, but in a terrible irony, in this novel, the husband who already enjoys that power uses it on the wife. His keenest pleasure is her awareness of her bondage: "What he required was that she should be as fully aware as she would have been of a locked hand-cuff, that her inclination was helpless to decide anything in contradiction with his resolve" (492).

Finally, Grandcourt is a squire who has no interest in his land or community. Although he is responsible for Diplow, Ryelands, and Gadsmere, he is indifferent to them all. Raymond Williams cites Cobbett's distinction, fifty years before *Daniel Deronda*, between

> a resident *native* gentry, attached to the soil, known to every farmer and labourer from his childhood, frequently mixing with them in those pursuits where all artificial distinctions are lost, practising hospitality without ceremony, from habit and not on calculation; and a gentry, only now-and-then residing at all, having no relish for country-delights, foreign in their manners, distant and haughty in their behaviour, looking to the soil only for its rents, viewing it as a mere object of speculation, unacquainted with its cultivators, despising them and their pursuits, and relying, for influence, not upon the good will of the vicinage, but upon the dread of their power.[128]

Grandcourt is such a landowner, and he certainly has no interest in establishing an organic community. The notion of a landlord who regards the estate simply as a source of profit is someone we might identify with Henry Wilcox in *Howards End* (1910), but he shows up in *Daniel Deronda* in 1874 and, indeed, in Cobbett's remarks in 1821, reminding us that the constituent conditions of modernity can be found whenever we choose to look for them.

Gwendolen's neighbor plot is therefore shorn of the significance, the agency, the power, and the social centrality that she might well have expected. Far from achieving power, the marriage disempowers her profoundly. She loses the ability to form her own friendships or express her own mind. Instead of a permeable influence, Gwendolen must contract within herself, making her face a mask hiding her feelings. Gwendolen's "belief in her own power of dominating—was utterly gone. Already, in seven short weeks, which seemed half her life, her husband had gained a mastery which she could no more resist than she could have resisted the benumbing effect from the touch of a torpedo" (357).

Gwendolen's helplessness is symbolized by the fact that instead of running the estate, she is hauled onto a yacht and made to move around aimlessly in an environment entirely controlled by her husband. "Grandcourt had an intense satisfaction in leading his wife captive after this fashion: it gave their life on a small scale a royal representation and publicity in which everything familiar was got rid of and everybody must do what was expected of them whatever might be their private protest—the protest (kept strictly private) adding to the piquancy of despotism" (566). Yachting forces Gwendolen into exactly the opposite values from the ones normally associated with neighbor marriage. Like Wentworth's ship, Grandcourt's yacht strongly contrasts with the landed estate. Grandcourt makes her adopt mobility instead of stasis, privacy instead of social orientation, and a life of pointless pleasure instead of one of moral influence. Moreover, the yacht is already outfitted, so there is nothing for Gwendolen to manage. The life on the yacht is the epitome of the kind of individualism Victorian subjects disliked, the isolation and anomie in the aimless pursuit of self-interest; it is as far as possible from the sort of organic community, or even meaningful moral action, for which they so often yearned.

Nell's problem in *Cometh Up as a Flower* had been that she was unable to recognize the advantages of the neighbor marriage, but Gwendolen's problem is different; knowing this plot perfectly well, she nonetheless finds that its iconography of permeability and influence actually makes it unenforceable. When thinking over her marriage, she recognizes the contract: she would get Grandcourt's money in exchange for herself. But her additional expectation of enjoying power in marriage had not, could not, have been spelled out. Gwendolen realizes that "she could not excuse herself by saying that there had been a tacit part of the contract on her side—namely, that she meant to rule and have her own way" (563). Similarly, when things go wrong with the Wilcox marriage in *Howards End*, Margaret suddenly discovers that all her intellectual and cultural superiority can simply be put aside by her husband, who insists on his own power. At key points, then, the man keeps the power.

If one's expectations derive from something as impalpable as a cultural expectation, or as indirect as the workings of influence, one cannot itemize them or insist on their fulfillment. If, on the other hand, one's expectations derive from the concrete workings of recognized power in economic and political venues, it is very easy to insist on their continuance. The fantasy of female power in the neighbor plot is an impalpable, vulnerable one, perhaps obeyed by husbands during courtship (as Grandcourt humors Gwendolen's pretty airs of mastery) but without any necessity for respect in real married life. These late novels of the neighbor plot, *Daniel Deronda* and *Howards End*, demonstrate what all modern readers recognize about influence: it does not really work. Money and the vote are better.

Daniel Deronda and *Howards End* do not mark the end of the neighbor marriage plot, however. (Similarly, we shall see that *The Mill on the Floss* does not end disability marriage; in both cases Eliot only prefigures a consensus that would come much later). Mary Ward's *Marcella* and Sarah Grand's *The Heavenly Twins*, both published in 1894, depict young women who marry landowner neighbors and who struggle to make the estate a site for personal empowerment and political change. *Howards End* is of course a classic neighbor plot, in which Margaret Schlegel, facing imminent homelessness, marries Mr. Wilcox, a kindly older neighbor who can offer her a central role on a country estate. This narrative persists long past the point at which the landed gentry had ceased to be a significant political presence, long past the point at which English country homes could be seen as the stable heart of England.

This continuation in fiction—itself, perhaps, a ghostly and tenuous perpetuation of a figure that had lived long before—indicates that the neighbor marriage continued to serve imaginative needs long after its constituent terms had been individually rejected. The neighbor plot's long afterlife confirms, for me, that it is not really about perpetuating the squirearchy, but rather a dream about power for women. Until suffrage, until women could exercise meaningful participation in political and social organization, this fantasy would persist in fiction. Female power was tenuous and vague and contingent, ghostly indeed, in this model, but it had one advantage: it is hard to kill a ghost.

In its nostalgic embrace of past values, in its social orientation, in its insistence on a wider and more meaningful life for the woman, neighbor marriage exemplifies the work of familiar marriage. Familiar marriage implies a permeable, interactive, extensive selfhood. In subsequent chapters we will move through the varieties of familiar marriage, starting in the smallest unit—the family (cousin marriage in Chapter 4)—through the moderate scale of friendship circles (disabled marriage in Chapter 5), and to the largest realm—the public and the nation (vocational marriage in Chapter 6). At each level, familiar marriage works to guarantee a woman's continued enmeshment in her world and a life that she finds meaningful, significant, and secure.

At each level, too, we can see what is frightening about romantic marriage. Romantic marriage was extremely threatening in its exclusive focus on a quality of feeling, rendering all other emotions, skills, and experiences irrelevant, and refusing basic prudent safeguards for a lifelong connection. When the handsome stranger sweeps you off your feet and takes you far away to live together in private ecstasy forever, what happens to your family, your friends, your skills? Familiar marriage made it possible to imagine marriage as a continuation, not a denial, of those qualities—and even if the novel did plump for romantic marriage in the end, that romantic marriage might well be fundamentally improved by competition with a familiar possibility. After hundreds of pages dwelling on the heroine's attachment to her work, care, or family—after the heroine is shown to be so committed to those interests that she is willing to consider a marriage to a man whom she only mildly likes, simply to protect them—it should not surprise us when the romantic hero suddenly shows a heretofore unguessed-at predilection for whatever the heroine had originally wanted, facilitating the happy marriage at last. The familiar marriage prospect has successfully kept these needs before the reader's eyes, making us want them fulfilled by the end of the novel. Thus the category of the familiar marriage is crucial to Victorian marriage plots, regardless of whether the familiar lover triumphs. In grappling with it, rejecting it, embracing it, and modifying it, these narratives were able to interrogate women's lives and relationships. The Victorian novel does not always endorse familiar marriage by any means, but its presence acted like a dark background to the blazing light of the romance plot, defining its negative spaces, its absences, its risks, and its failures. Romantic marriage is travel into an unknown country. But familiar marriage is the estate next door, the solid, capacious space into which the woman herself—small, vulnerable, precarious—finds a home at last.

4

Cousin Marriage

READING ON THE CONTRARY

Cousins probably know all or most of your little family secrets. Cousins, perhaps, have romped with you, and scolded you, and teased you, when you were young. Cousins are almost the same as brothers, and yet they may be lovers. There is certainly a great relief in cousinhood.

ANTHONY TROLLOPE, The Vicar of Bullhampton[1]

And I do not want a stranger—unsympathizing, alien, different from me; I want my kindred: those with whom I have full fellow-feeling.

CHARLOTTE BRONTË, Jane Eyre

IF THERE IS anybody closer than a neighbor, it would be a family member. This chapter moves from marrying into the house next door to marrying into one's own home. In Chapter 3, we saw that neighbor marriage allows women the fantasy of constructing an organic community around themselves. Endogamous marriage shares that interest in using marriage as the basis of a social network, but it starts with the already existing clan, reinforcing and consolidating family ties that may have been frayed. While neighbor marriage operates simultaneously and diffusely at domestic, communal, and national levels, endogamous marriage dwells at the scale of the family, where it performs intensive repair work. To marry a relation, then, is to yearn for one's marriage to initiate a harmonious social organization—but that organization should be the family, not the nation.

Perhaps the most familiar form of familiar marriage, cousin marriage is notoriously common in Victorian fiction. There are courtships or marriages within the family in novels by virtually every author of the period, including Dickens, Eliot, Brontë, Trollope, Thackeray, Yonge, Gaskell, and Oliphant. In many of these novels, cousinship is reinforced by adoptive sibhood, intensifying the union's endogamous charge. From *Mansfield Park*'s Fanny and Edmund through *Wuthering Heights*'s Catherine and Heathcliff, we grapple with one family relationship after another. Whether we insist on the cultural difference that once made these unions seem acceptable, or read them for buried clues to their participants' covert sexual uneasiness, modern critics almost always read them in relation to a modern culture in which family marriage is primarily understood as incestuous. But this is not the way Victorians understood cousin marriage. Mary Jean Corbett remarks that the process of inventing the incest charge was slow:

> [It] took place over the course of the entire nineteenth century. Like heterosexuality itself, exogamy and endogamy had to be invented and have to be understood as having a history, one that begins around Austen's moment. We forget too easily the force and scope the now-anomalous alternative plot of marriage within the family had for Austen's original audience. Its erasure from our histories of domestic fiction prematurely forecloses the possibility that there might have been something valuable for some female characters, and their authors, in that plot.[2]

In this chapter, we will try to recover what was "valuable" in cousin marriage. If neighbor marriage foregrounds a fantasy of female empowerment, turning outward to local and national social worlds, we shall find that family marriage encourages a countervailing dream of safety, deeper enmeshment within the kin network.

If neighbor marriage's dream of female power works against the dominant theoretical understandings of the public sphere and perpetuation of lineage, so too does cousin marriage stubbornly oppose a powerful theory: Victorian anthropology. Anthropological discourse emerged at mid-century to explain kin unions, but it took the opposite approach to the one we find in novels. Victorian anthropology moved toward identifying endogamous marriages as incestuous and regarding organic communities as relics of a primitive past, whereas Victorian novels usually celebrated familial marriages and yearned to reconstruct such communal life. Victorian anthropology imagined marriage with males as the agents, while Victorian novels more often than not vested marital choice in females. The anthropological "family" and "marriage" are thus as much a fiction as any novel of the period, but they move in the opposite direction, as anthropological work regendered, pathologized, and archaicized the values held dear by fictional narratives. By looking at three novels that predate the anthropological era, *Mansfield Park* (1814), Charlotte M. Yonge's revision of *Mansfield Park* in *Heartsease* (1854), and *Wuthering Heights* (1847), we can elicit a different model, drawing out their shared assumptions about a good marriage, a healthy family, and generational change. These three works from the first half of the nineteenth century converge on a common story, one that became increasingly difficult to enunciate as the century wore on. Anthropological understandings of family, which merged with Darwinist thought and led to psychological discourse, became normative by the end of the century. Recovering the previous way of thinking—and seeing moments when it survives in spite of this critique—will demonstrate a strong mode of Victorian fictional thinking that we misrepresent when we rush to diagnose incest.

Nineteenth-Century Family Marriage

To Victorians, cousin marriage felt quite natural. Florence Nightingale remarked in 1860 that one way people marry was if "accident or relationship has thrown them together in their childhood, and acquaintance has grown up naturally and unconsciously. Accordingly, in novels, it is generally cousins who marry; and *now* it seems the only natural thing—the only possible way of making an intimacy."[3] As Nightingale points out, novels helped train individuals to see cousin marriage as natural, but this relationship also flourished because the cousinship allowed for free communication over a lifetime, as opposed to the scripted and surveilled conversation possible under a chaperone's eye in public venues. Charlotte Yonge wrote, rather wistfully, that "the intercourse between cousins is so pleasant, that it almost naturally leads to something warmer."[4]

Family marriage was economically and emotionally useful. It kept property within the clan and cemented kin bonds. Claudia Nelson explains that cousin marriage offered a chance to get to know your partner without chaperones, the promise of harmonious relations with in-laws, and the reassuring prospect of keeping money within the family.[5] Who could be more trustworthy than someone known since childhood; someone who shares the same family background, memories, traditions, and rules; and someone who is likely to have similar status and finances? The cousin may be a worrisome option if one sees marriage solely as a sexual partnership, but an ideal choice in a culture that imagines marriage in terms of a future of shared work and familial stability.[6] For Victorian readers, emotions like familiarity, trust, and companionability might have been more appealing than desire. This is not to say that cousin marriage, in fiction or in fact, was sexless, but simply that cousin marriage is orthogonal to desire. It may or may not include desire; its point is to pursue a different end.

Cousin marriage was a common practice in nineteenth-century Britain, as Nancy Fix Anderson and Adam Kuper have shown.[7] Kuper points out that more than one out of every ten marriages in the bourgeoisie (three times more than in the working class) was with a cousin.[8] These interconnected clans, including the

Darwins/Wedgwoods or the Coleridges, exercised enormous influence in the literary, artistic, and scientific worlds of Victorian England. Cousin marriage had, after all, been legally and religiously permitted since the Henrician statute of 1540. "English contemporaries did not generally regard such [cousin] marriages as abnormal or as verging on the incestuous, and novelists typically represented them as calm, safe, rational arrangements."[9] Indeed, their own monarch was a living advertisement for cousin marriage, since Victoria and Albert were cousins, as were most royal families. Similarly, the small pool of aristocratic families was intricately interconnected by multiple intermarriages. At the lower level, too, it was sometimes hard to avoid marrying a relation. "According to sociologist Robin Fox, for much of the Victorian period 'the radius of the average isolate, or pool of potential spouses, was about five miles, which was the distance a man could comfortably walk twice on his day off, when he went courting.' Consequently, England was full of villages in which generations of intermarriage had resulted in a community tied together by a complex network of blood relationships."[10] Thus at every class level, from the nobility to the middle-class intelligentsia to the rural poor, people were limited to potential partners who were often already connected with them in various ways. Add to this demographic situation the emotional and financial security afforded by marrying within the family, and we can understand why it was so widespread.

Cousin marriage enabled the couple to retain their natal families instead of moving into an isolated partnership. Victorian living arrangements accommodated a much larger range of relationships than the modern definition of family suggests. As George K. Behlmer has pointed out, "in 1851 just 36 percent of households contained a married couple, at least one child, and no one else."[11] The majority of households contained multiple individuals: servants, apprentices, poor relations, maiden aunts, grandparents, lodgers, and pupils. To move from this kind of population to the twentieth-century norm of the nuclear family was an enormous change, writes Elizabeth Rose Gruner: "Definitions of the family underwent a shift from a fluid network of family relations in the early part of the nineteenth century to an increasingly naturalized nuclear unit by about the middle of the century. The negotiation between seeing the family as an affiliative network of friends, neighbors, servants, and distant kin and seeing it as a privatized domestic unit was neither easy nor complete by mid-century."[12]

In Chapters 2 and 3, we saw how terrifying it felt for women to move into the married state. In a sudden transition, the woman lost her name, her birth family, her home, and her community. In *Novel Relations*, Ruth Perry argues that women in the eighteenth and early nineteenth centuries experienced a traumatizing decline in status as inheritance, marital, and dowry law converged with a new belief that conjugal, not consanguineal, identity was what truly mattered.

This situation made women into economic burdens on their natal families, yet also made them vulnerable in marriage. The marriage ceremony suddenly made a woman completely reliant on a man whom she may not have known well. Part of the value of cousin marriage was that it eased that shift. Cousin marriage reconciled women's two identities. Marrying a cousin reinforced one's place in the original consanguineal network, whereas to marry an unrelated person meant being ripped away from one's family and sent into an unknown world.

Inventing Primitive Marriage: The Anthropological Anti-Novel

Although cousin marriage was common, in the second half of the nineteenth century a new discourse began to rewrite it as a form of pathology. The new anxiety about cousin marriage literally and figuratively descended from Darwin. Not only did a Darwinist anxiety about heritability generate challenges to cousin marriage, but Charles Darwin himself, who had married a cousin, part of a long line of intermarried Darwin-Wedgwood clans, asked his son to investigate cousin marriage. George Darwin concluded that cousin marriage posed no risks to offspring.[13]

Anthropological theories of the history of marriage employed Auguste Comte's idea of progressive development and universal stages of human growth. Henry Sumner Maine and John McLennan both speculated on how marriage moved from an original state of primitive promiscuity and sexual violence toward the modern "civilized" state of monogamous couples protected by contract law.[14] John McLennan, whose *Primitive Marriage* was published in 1865, focused on the primal scene of marriage, not its development over time.[15] He emphasized a fundamental difference between marriage within the group ("endogamous") and marriage outside the group ("exogamous").

McLennan posited an original state in which marriage was endogamous and therefore peaceable: "It is clear, that if members of a family or tribe *are forbidden* to intermarry with members of other families or tribes, and free to marry among themselves, there is not room for fraud or force in the constitution of marriage. The bridegroom and bride will live together in amity among their common relatives."[16] In these endogamous unions, relations approve of the marriage and there is no "foreign interest," for everyone is kindred and tribal members share "common interests and possessions" so that "obviously within such a group there can be neither barter nor sale."[17]

However, not all groups are endogamous. And McLennan's real interest in *Primitive Marriage* is in the endogamous group's warlike counterparts/successors, the exogamous tribes, whose marital life consists of kidnapping and raping their neighbors' women, having first murdered their own. (McLennan perceives female infanticide as widespread because daughters are "a source of weakness."[18]) This "primitive-marriage" activity begins the dynamic of different communities sorting out clans and setting marriage laws in place.

Fellow anthropologists Henry Sumner Maine, Sir John Lubbock and Friedrich Engels concurred with McLennan that primitive marriage was based on the abduction of women.[19] This assumption was soon taken for granted; writing twenty years later, Engels is only surprised that McLennan makes so much of this "capture." He claims that "the abduction and barter of women" should really be regarded as "widespread symptoms, and nothing but that, of a new and much more profound change."[20] As Kathy Psomiades points out, primitive marriage is based on violence against women, who become mute, passive prizes in violent exchanges between men who are strangers to them.[21] At its best, in McLennan's account, mating with strangers is facilitated by purchasing a bride, and at its worst, it operates via the murder, assault, kidnapping, and rape of females, an experience so traumatically memorable that leaves its imprint upon the marriage ceremony worldwide.[22]

Interestingly, McLennan does not treat these two forms of marriage as equivalent. Rather, he briefly describes harmonious endogamous marriage and then spends the rest of the book on gruesome tales of exogamous marriage, which he assumes to be, in some sense, the real form of marriage, the ancestor of modern marriage.[23] For McLennan, mating within the clan leaves no symbolic trace. Like good women and happy families, it generates no story. This rivulet of human history sinks underground, and the populous surface landscape shows little evidence of its subterranean current. For it is the contact with strangers that produces social interaction. The exchange of women across the borders of the clan makes the rest of history narratable. We move into the modern marketplace once women become objects of exchange; we move into the decoding of marital and historical relationships once women can be imagined to be stolen rather than amicably entering new cohabitations.[24]

If familial marriage has no story, neither does the woman in an exogamous union. Utterly passive, she is merely an object to be circulated, by trade or violence. McLennan's follower, Sir John Lubbock, surmised that women wanted to be captured, but even such minimal speculation on women's agency is absent from *Primitive Marriage*.[25] As Psomiades cannily points out, these theories of women as passively circulated objects emerged during the great ferment over women's agency, legal status, and property ownership in marriage in the 1860s, the years between Britain's first Matrimonial Causes Act (1857) and the Married Women's Property Act (1870), and—I would add—the period whose political discourse about work for women created a powerful new kind of female persona, as we shall see in Chapter 6. Thus, just as Victorian activists were reconfiguring marriage as a legal, sexual, and political act, Victorian anthropologists reacted by making it the foundation of the modern marketplace.[26] Just as activists created a vision of women needing work, anthropology reimagined women as passive mute objects. "That these years were also very nearly the exact period of the anthropological debate over the evolutionary priority of 'matriarchal' marriage seems scarcely a historical coincidence," Stocking comments; it was precisely when marriage seemed most variable that anthropologists most wanted to fix a "real" story of marriage.[27]

If we read Victorian anthropology as reacting against mid-Victorian ideas of female agency, we can understand why it does not match the female marriage plot very closely.[28] In 1865, the year McLennan's book appeared, recent novels included *Aurora Floyd*, *Wives and Daughters*, and *Our Mutual Friend*—hardly featuring passive female victims of marauding male raiders—and readers enjoyed sensation fiction plots in which strong women exulted in bigamy, crime, even murder. "Primitive marriage" was a reaction against all this upheaval, as it restored men and women to their "proper" places and asserted that such roles constituted immutable historical fact. In posthumously published notes, McLennan remarked that marriage was, quite simply, "the union of one man and woman in a consortship for the whole of life—an 'inseparable consuetude' of life between husband and spouse, with interests the same in all things civil and religious. That idea, despite all woman's rights movements to the contrary, is that destined to prevail in the world."[29]

We should remember, however, that even in the midst of McLennan's roiling waters of murder and rape, his map keeps a safe space for the calm underground lake of harmonious endogamy. Given the strength of his interest in exogamous primitive marriage, the fact that the endogamous haven appears at all shows how powerful this nostalgic attachment to family marriage must have been.

Sigmund Freud imported these tenets of Victorian anthropology into *Totem and Taboo*, placing them at the heart of psychology.[30] He employed the widespread Victorian assumption of a universal human nature that moves in progressive stages toward civilization. But Freud also picked up the idea of an originary moment that involves love within the family. The difference is that for Freud, endogamy ends because of the great taboo—incest—whereas for McLennan and his ilk, endogamy is simply how people lived before marital violence erupted.

Incest, for Freud, is at the heart of both the individual's psychosexual maturation and at the core of the society's historical development. For the individual, it is the incest taboo that makes the Oedipal complex work. Pollak rightly calls it a "gender-instituting prohibition."[31] Heterosexual desire and gender identity operate because the incest taboo forces the psyche to swerve away from the original parent toward a new object of desire. Similarly, in *Totem and Taboo*, Freud ensconced incest at the anthropological heart of historical development. Like McLennan, Freud imagines a traumatically violent originary scene whose traces can still be pieced together via residual symbolic elements. But whereas McLennan's originary scenario was the rape of the stranger, Freud's was the murder of the father. In *Totem and Taboo*, he imagines an ancestral crime in which a band of brothers killed their father to get sexual access to their sisters. Overcome by guilt, they reacted by deifying the dead father and declaring sisters forbidden. This primal murder structures later religious thought. Thus if McLennan saw sex at the origin of society, Freud saw the refusal of sex. In both cases, males have to seek sexual partners beyond the family. For McLennan, however, this is a fall that produces violence, whereas for Freud, it is the prohibition that produces society. Both imagine that history—violence, interaction, religious scruples—begins only when men push outside the family for sexual objects.

The key point is the sexualization of marriage. Victorian anthropology has no category for familiar marriage, defined by companionable, affectionate, mutually helpful partnership. By the end of the nineteenth century, family marriage was defined as sexual, and its sexual relationship was taboo. Havelock Ellis writes: "For persons who have grown up together from childhood habit has dulled the sensual attraction of seeing, hearing, and touching and has led it into a channel of quiet attachment, robbing it of its power to call forth the necessary erethistic excitement required to produce sexual tumescence."[32] In Ellis's analysis, "quiet attachment," far from being the basis of marriage, has become its opposite. No longer can affectionate, familiar companionship serve as the basis of marriage if marriage requires sexual excitement. Indeed, Ellis redefines courtship (rather shockingly for a Victorian) as "the process by which powerful sensory stimuli proceeding from a person of the opposite sex gradually produce the physiological state of tumescence, with its psychic concomitant of love and desire, more or less necessary for mating to be effected."[33] Turning courtship into a synonym for arousal, then making it depend on heterosexual coupling and specifically on male pleasure, Ellis makes "tumescence" rather than companionship the test of marriage. Freud quotes this passage approvingly; its vision of male heterosexual sexual drive is one that he endorsed.

After Freud, in the twentieth century, it became impossible to read familial union without seeing it as incest. Indeed, Freud made incest so important that he could retroactively criticizes his predecessors for failing to notice it, complaining about "the manner in which the incest problem is here [in McLennan] entirely neglected."[34] McLennan uses the word "incest" occasionally, to denote particular tribal practices, not a universal principle. But McLennan is an emissary from a mid-Victorian time when marriage within the family could be understood on grounds other than incest. Without denying that sex occurs in familiar unions, he does not seem unduly bothered by it; it is simply not central to his model. But with the Freudian turn of the century, it becomes the core of marriage.

The person who picked up the Victorian anthropological legacy in the twentieth century was Claude Lévi-Strauss, who dedicated his *Elementary Structures of Kinship* (1949) to Lewis Henry Morgan, and who brought back a theory that Edward Burnet Tylor had advanced in 1889.[35] "Claude Lévi-Strauss used the observations of nineteenth-century precursors like McLennan, Morgan, and Engels to develop an overall model of marital practices," explains Elsie Michie.[36] Lévi-Strauss credits the incest prohibition with developing social relations. People have to accept an exchange in which they entrust their female family members to outsiders and adopt female outsiders into their own families.[37] The incest prohibition produces the exchange of women, which generates social circulation, the harmonious interaction of men. "The prohibition of incest is less a rule prohibiting marriage with the mother, sister, or daughter, than a rule obliging the mother, sister, or daughter to be given to others. It is the supreme rule of the gift," Lévi-Strauss writes.[38]

It is hard to read this account of women as the "gift" with the kind of reverence that Lévi-Strauss evidently wanted us to accord to it. As Gayle Rubin has famously pointed out in "The Traffic in Women," if women are only the material being exchanged then women themselves are not fully human, but merely counters to promote male social interactions.[39] It is the men who experience social relations, and the women whose trading among men promotes it. Moreover, as Rubin explains, Lévi-Strauss's theory rests on women being unable to express desire or to choose another woman. Thus all society is predicated upon women's obligatory heterosexuality and complete powerlessness.[40] This assumption reveals the extent to which Lévi-Strauss has inherited McLennan's fantasy that social relations among men begin with women's circulation (whether via gifts, kidnapping, or trade). Lévi-Strauss explicitly acknowledges McLennan as a precursor.[41]

This is the point at which a critic, having explained the anthropological theory, would normally "apply" it to the novels. But I want to do the opposite here. I want to analyze just why Victorian anthropology, with Lévi-Strauss as its heir, does not seem to work for the Victorian marriage plot. If we want a story of marriage by abduction, rape, or barter of women, we could look at eighteenth-century Gothic and seduction novels, or the occasional Victorian novel in which a female character complains that she was sold in marriage (like Edith Dombey, Gwendolen Harleth, or Estella Havisham), but in none of these cases do social interactions between the groups occur as a result of this transfer, and the marriages do not even work as marriages; in eighteenth-century fiction the woman is either raped or escapes, but rarely marries her seducer, while Edith's,

Gwendolen's, and Estella's marriages collapse. Instead, if we seek a story of social interaction generated by one group's abduction of another group's member, what fits best are industrial novels and adventure stories, where a modern young person is suddenly plunged into a foreign culture (Jacobite rebels, pirates, the industrial north) and must learn to appreciate it enough to mediate between the two cultures. However, it is significant that these genres do not accomplish the social work Lévi-Strauss foretold via marriage, but rather through almost any other mechanism: parental mobility, adoption, kidnapping, or cultural misunderstanding.[42] The absence of Lévi-Strauss's key transaction, marriage, as the agent of social interaction in the nineteenth-century novel is notable. What fulfills the vision of *Elementary Structures of Kinship* in nineteenth-century fiction are the genres focused on generically male experience: war and industrialism.[43] What we often find—as we shall see in *Mansfield Park* and *Wuthering Heights*, for instance—is a situation in which the man assumes he is in something like an anthropological plot, but the woman does not recognize it. She is certain that marriage performs very differently.[44] Edgar, Heathcliff, and Sir Thomas Bertram may attempt to trade in women, to give a woman as a "gift," but she resists, insisting on a different kind of story. Catherine and Fanny insist on their own feelings and their own kind of endogamous unions.

Lévi-Strauss mistrusts endogamy, insisting that

> exogamy provides the only means of maintaining the group as a group, of avoiding the indefinite fission and segmentation which the practice of consanguineous marriage would bring about. If these consanguineous marriages were resorted to persistently, or even over-frequently, they would not take long to "fragment" the social group into a multitude of families, forming so many closed systems or sealed monads which no pre-established harmony could prevent from proliferating or from coming into conflict.[45]

Fragmentation into a multitude of families that come into conflict: what could be a better description of the Bertrams, or the Earnshaws and Lintons? These central nineteenth-century texts demonstrate just the kind of familial congealing and conflicts that Lévi-Strauss sees as antagonistic to harmonious society. Such "closed systems or sealed monads" might well describe the English class system in the nineteenth century: self-contained families in an intricate dance of mutually conflicted social relations. Just as Lévi-Strauss notes, endogamous marriage did reinforce the dominant social order and the elites' power by consolidating families and preventing the circulation of their property.[46] This is also the work that Lord Hardwicke's Act tried to do, as we saw in Chapter 2.

What Lévi-Strauss is criticizing here is the precise dynamic for which so many Victorians yearned: small, closed, homogeneous organic communities. He is instead validating a world of individualist free circulation—a notion that, as we saw in Chapter 3, actually worried most nineteenth-century writers.

Lévi-Strauss was writing *The Elementary Structures of Kinship* from 1943 to 1949, as a French intellectual working at the New School in New York while fleeing the Nazis. It makes sense that he would have prized interaction, diversity, and social alliances across groups.[47] "Lévi-Strauss's preoccupation with social integration . . . is manifest throughout *The Elementary Structures of Kinship*," notes Marcela Coelho de Souza.[48] But writers in the British nineteenth century had different values, perpetuated through other mechanisms. Cousin marriage did the work that Lévi-Strauss felt was inimical to social functioning, but for the Victorians, that work *was* social functioning: it was the maintenance and reproduction of a stable system of closed families, into which the reader could imagine himself/herself. In McLennan's minor, neglected dynamic of endogamous marriage, we see the same dream of communal bliss within a small, connected group that we see in Austen, not to mention Eliot, Carlyle, Morris, and Ruskin. Meanwhile, McLennan's depiction of an exogamous world of violence expresses the Victorian fear of individualist, self-interested atomization. Victorians were yearning for small collectives, and Lévi-Strauss's valorization of diverse social fabrics comes from a very different era, responding to very different stimuli.

Lévi-Strauss, like Freud, imagines marriage as a system of sexually bonded, exclusively monogamous couples. "As soon as I am forbidden a woman, she thereby becomes available to another man," he explains, "and somewhere else a man renounces a woman who thereby becomes available to me."[49] In other words, the woman cannot be available to more than one person. She is available only to a male, and her "availability" must be specifically sexual, since presumably familial or friendship affection could be widely shared. "Availability," for Lévi-Strauss, is faithfully and exclusively monogamously heterosexual, with men as sexual agents and women as sexual objects.

Yet women were "available" to other people in multiple ways in the nineteenth century novel. Take Shirley Keeldar, for instance. She is "available" to her tenants as an estate owner, "available" to Caroline as a loyal friend, "available" to Mr. Yorke as a sparring partner, "available" to Mrs. Pryor as a daughter-figure, "available" to her cousins as a host, "available" to Robert Moore as a business consultant, "available" to Henry Sympson as a romantic ideal, and "available" to Louis Moore as a pupil and eventually a wife. As an unmarried woman, Shirley lives, at different times, with Caroline, Louis, Henry, and Mrs. Pryor, and in each of these nonsexual cohabiting relations she performs crucial emotional and economic services. In this respect Brontë is more radical than Lévi-Strauss. Whereas

Lévi-Strauss reduces a woman to one man's exclusive sexual property, Brontë writes her as an agent with multifarious affective relationships in fluid family configurations over decades.

Shirley is typical of characters in fictional situations, not to mention real nineteenth-century living arrangements. Spinster aunts and poor relations lived with host families, adult siblings cohabited, and elderly parents resided with grown children. From Ruth and Tom Pinch in *Martin Chuzzlewit*, to the sisters in Oliphant's *The Doctor's Family* and Martineau's *Deerbrook*; to the three siblings at Marsh End; to the siblings in *East Lynne* (the Carlyles), *Ruth* (the Bensons), and *Bleak House* (the Smallweeds); and to Maggie and Tom Tulliver, scarcely a Victorian novel does not show adult family members living together. If we expand this consideration to include unrelated roommates, we can add Mr. George and Phil, Esther Summerson and Ada, Eugene Wrayburn and Mortimer Lightfoot, Pip and Herbert Pocket, Shirley Keeldar and Caroline Helstone. Even if some of these pairings seem incestuously or sexually charged to modern readers, in no case are we supposed to believe a sexual relationship is actually occurring. Sex is not the point; helpfulness is.

Lévi-Strauss does not consider endogamous living situations like Shirley's—cohabitations that emulate marriage in every way except for the sexual—nor does he consider marriages in which sex is in abeyance. These nonsexual arrangements do not force the woman out of the family; they do not make her available or institute exchange. They "use" the woman not for her sexuality but for her other qualities: her work potential, her political ties, her kin, her property, her kindness to elders and children, her managerial skills. And it is this nonsexual, amicable, intrafamilial coupledom—something outside Lévi-Strauss's conception of couples—that the Victorian novel especially likes to feature. While Rubin has made the dehumanization of women in Lévi-Strauss's theory hard for anyone to miss, there has been far less notice of the extent to which Lévi-Strauss assumes that marriage is primarily sexual—a sign of our modern assumption that marriage is all about sex and our difficulty seeing an alternative in the past.

What I hope I have shown here is how McLennan's endogamous/exogamous marriage theory starts as a fairly standard Victorian opposition of safe, harmonious, closed communities versus dangerous, violent social openness, analogous to a *Gemeinschaft* versus a *Gesellschaft*, but then, through Freud's and Lévi-Strauss's development, turns into a different kind of tale: exogamous marriage as the basis of social formation, with endogamous marriage pathologized as incestuous. By the twentieth century, marriage is supposed to be sexual, and social organization is supposed to be diverse and liberatory. This is the narrative we have inherited, and it is a story that entirely reverses the emphasis in Victorian fiction.

Mansfield Park without Incest

The sex-centered view of marriage is particularly visible in the history of critical assessments of Fanny's and Edmund's marriage in *Mansfield Park*, where a cousin relationship is heightened by adopted sibship, rendering it doubly endogamous. The incest accusation has been ubiquitous in *Mansfield Park* criticism since the 1930s, according to Tuite.[50] Johanna Smith sees Fanny and Edmund's relationship as "incestuous paralysis."[51] James F. Kilroy worries about the ending violating "the implied, but not actual, taboo against sexual relations within the immediate family."[52] Some critics see incest as the open secret of *Mansfield Park*, to which apparently quite unrelated statements really point. Thus Eileen Cleere interprets Fanny's distress at the "disorder" of her family's home in Portsmouth as a covert allusion to incest, and then goes further to read Fanny's dismay at Maria's elopement with Henry Crawford as incestuous too.[53] Any unusual exclamation of horror must necessarily point to a hidden sexual taboo which it is the work of this novel to relocate, cover, and render acceptable. Fanny's disgust at working-class living conditions and her revulsion at adulterous betrayal within the family have no currency in themselves but are covers for something else. Nancy Fix Anderson goes so far as to assert that all cousin marriage, whether in fact or fiction, manifests "strong unconscious incestuous feelings." She reads "love for a cousin [as] a convenient and fitting displacement of love toward a family member," "a psychologically safe outlet for incestuous feelings."[54]

A more recent, although less common, reading of the cousin marriage is to see it as a political act aimed at preserving the squirearchy, as we saw in Chapter 3. For instance, Clara Tuite explains:

> Endogamy in *Mansfield Park* symptomatizes both a desire and a fear of self-closure on the part of an aristocracy whose social, cultural and economic ascendancy is becoming increasingly tenuous in the early nineteenth century, due to the rise of the bourgeois class to economic, cultural and social power. This is not, therefore, the old kind of aristocratic survival strategy of improvement through dynastic alliance and aggrandizement; it is a defensive patrilineal plot of regeneration and incorporation.[55]

The way in which the family marries itself constitutes a retrograde strategy on the part of an already failing system.[56] In *Mansfield Park*, cousin marriage therefore exemplifies precisely what Lévi-Strauss was afraid of: "forming so many closed systems or sealed monads."[57] It extends an outmoded aristocratic system, reinforcing existing power structures while deterring diversity, social mingling, individualism, and progress. Thus when we declare Fanny and Edmund's marriage incestuous, we are rejecting this closed aristocratic self-reinforcement, diagnosing a conservative political resolution as a pathology. In that respect, "incest"—a term and an idea that is not present in *Mansfield Park*—acts as a way of expressing our own commitment to progressive democratic diversity.

A "non-incest" reading of *Mansfield Park* engages in what Sharon Marcus calls "just reading," respecting the surface of the text instead of suspiciously viewing it as a cover for a buried always-sexual secret. Marcus remarks, "Taking friendship in novels to signify friendship . . . highlights something true and visible on the text's surface that symptomatic reading had ironically rendered invisible."[58] Similarly, taking familial affection to signify familial affection may actually open up the novel, while the incest reading may be misdirecting our attention and foreclosing our capacity to note a wider range of feeling.

Almost every Austen novel features endogamous marriages. Cousins/foster-siblings marry in *Mansfield Park*; brother-in-law and sister-in-law marry in *Emma*; in *Sense and Sensibility* a woman marries her brother-in-law and her sister's husband, Colonel Brandon, originally wanted to marry his cousin/foster-sister Eliza; cousins Henrietta and Charles Hayter marry in *Persuasion*, where William Elliott pursues his cousin Anne; Anne de Bourgh and Mr. Collins both seek cousin marriages in *Pride and Prejudice*.[59] Glenda Hudson eloquently explains that "in [Austen's] novels, the in-family marriages between the cousins and in-laws are successful because they do not grow out of sexual longing but are rooted in a deeper, more abiding domestic love which merges spiritual, intellectual, and physical affinities. Moreover, such unions form a new chapter in the fictional depiction of male/female relationships in that the participants are temperamentally equal."[60] Fanny and Edmund do not marry *in spite* of being related; they marry *because* they are related. "Idealizing first affections and critiquing their disruption, the narrative voice of *Mansfield Park* implies that marriage should support rather than nullify sibling ties."[61] If we focus on agape rather than eros, *Mansfield Park* can be read as a paean to family love, instead of a problematic vision of marriage.

Mansfield Park starts with only one viable relationship, the endogamous affection between Fanny and William, and this becomes the germ for all the reforms in the novel. George Haggerty explains that in *Mansfield Park*, "only the cozily familiar love of quasi-siblings can be depended on as sustaining and meaningful."[62] This healthy sororal love offers an alternative to the cold, formal, and embittered family relations among the three original sisters, the Crawford household, and the Bertrams. To read sibling love as incest is to render pathological what the novel presents as emotional sustenance. In *Mansfield Park*, Austen prizes cousin marriage to the extent that it succeeds in replicating sibling affection. An exogamous union may have a harder time emulating the fraternal/

sororal bond; cousinship, particularly when reinforced by foster-siblinghood, has a natural advantage.

It is notable that the novel begins, almost uniquely in Austen's *oeuvre*, with the previous generation.[63] When Miss Maria Ward weds Sir Thomas Bertram, the narrator remarks that the marriage does not benefit her sisters. The inception of this novel is a tale of sisterhood gone awry, where Miss Frances's disastrous marriage leads to "an absolute breach between the sisters," and Mrs. Norris has "no real affection for her sister."[64] Sisters who ignore and despise each other do not have the emotional resources to nurture the children in their care or to model good relationships within the family. The novel's opening two pages feature only two sentences about Mrs. Norris's marriage but half a page describing Mrs. Norris's reactions to Mrs. Price. It is her behavior as a sister—not as a wife—that indicates something crucial about this character.

No wonder, then, that Mrs. Norris's prediction about sibling relations for the second generation proves incorrect. When Sir Thomas Bertram worries that hosting Fanny might be dangerous to Tom or Edmund, Mrs. Norris replies:

> You are thinking of your sons—but do not you know that of all things upon earth *that* is the least likely to happen; brought up, as they would be, always together like brothers and sisters? It is morally impossible. I never knew an instance of it. It is, in fact, the only sure way of providing against the connection. Suppose her a pretty girl, and seen by Tom or Edmund for the first time seven years hence, and I dare say there would be mischief. The very idea of her having been suffered to grow up at a distance from us all in poverty and neglect, would be enough to make either of the dear sweet-tempered boys in love with her. But breed her up with them from this time, and suppose her even to have the beauty of an angel, and she will never be more to either than a sister. (4–5)

Mrs. Norris's logic relies on the difference between a sister and a beloved. She regards these as mutually exclusive categories, so that once Fanny moves into the sister category, she must perforce exit the beloved category.[65] Her construction of love here relies on the conventions of romantic fiction: the woman should be "pretty" or have "the beauty of an angel," and the man should feel sympathy for her ("the very idea of her having been suffered to grow up . . ."). These are, indeed, the qualities that later name Edmund's attraction to Mary Crawford; he sympathizes with a pretty woman who comes from an uncongenial home. But Mrs. Norris does not have a similar vision of sisterhood. Lacking real experience of that state, she cannot imagine the emotions it involves. Mrs. Norris imagines no story, no qualities for her protagonists; like McLennan, she believes there is nothing to tell in a state of familial union. Mrs. Norris actively advises the Bertrams to evade sisterliness, warning Maria and Julia, "on the contrary, it is much more desirable that there should be a difference" (16). Fanny will be kept, in Mrs. Norris's casual but revealing expression, "on the contrary."

Mansfield Park is in fact the story of two generations, each of which absorbs a poor female relation to very different effect. In the first generation, the Bertram family takes in Mrs. Norris. At the beginning of *Mansfield Park*, she forms part of an older, expansive, permeable sense of family that can admit Fanny and William as well as herself. In this older form of family, the patriarch has the right to decide on his female dependents' marriages. At the end of the novel, however, the family circle narrows. Initially Sir Thomas thought that Mrs. Norris "seemed a part of himself, that must be borne for ever," but he finds to his delight that he can renegotiate his family boundaries to keep her out (424). Just as the Darcys are able to construct a newly filtered, selective family at the end of *Pride and Prejudice*, so too the Bertram family is reconstituted as a condensed, chosen version of its original capacious extension. And Sir Thomas Bertram must relinquish his marital authority, learning, instead, to respect young women's growing right to consensual choice.

The second generation's female outsider becomes the agent of this reeducation, this modernization. At first the Mansfield Park ménage simply cannot comprehend Fanny's mourning for her family ("Her feelings were very acute, and too little understood to be properly attended to" [11]). For "when to these sorrows was added the idea of the brothers and sisters among whom she had always been important as play-fellow, instructress, and nurse, the despondence that sunk her little heart was severe" (12). Note that Fanny's emotional ties are to her siblings, not to her parents, in spite of Edmund's assumptions ("You are sorry to leave Mamma, my dear little Fanny," he decides, wrongly [12]).

This multifaceted sibling love will come to be—although the Bertrams cannot yet know it—the force that transfigures their own home. The first step occurs when Edmund befriends Fanny. After she explains her true sorrows, he generously responds: "Let us walk out in the park, and you shall tell me all about your brothers and sisters" (12). Edmund's willingness to learn about sibling affection marks him as potentially lovable. When Edmund "wrote with his own hand his love to his cousin William, and sent him half a guinea under the seal. Fanny's feelings on the occasion were such as she believed herself incapable of expressing; but her countenance and a few artless words fully conveyed all their gratitude and delight, and her cousin began to find her an interesting object" (13–14). Sibling love animates Fanny's face, makes her visible in a new way to Edmund. He, in turn, proves capable of expressing family affection. Their love begins here.

What siblinghood means is shown by Fanny and William's mutual love. The narrator remarks that "Fanny had never known so much felicity in her life, as in this unchecked, equal, fearless intercourse with the brother and friend," with whom she can share plans, communicate feelings about family members, and reminisce. To the earlier qualities of sibship—nursing and instructing and playing—we can add siblings' shared perspective on their shared past. In the narrator's famous description: "An advantage this, a strengthener of love, in which even the conjugal tie is beneath the fraternal. Children of the same family, the same blood, with the same first associations and habits, have some means in their power, which no subsequent connection can supply, if such precious remains of the earliest attachments are ever entirely outlived" (211–212).

The narrator's remark strongly rebuts Mrs. Norris's. Real siblinghood means "unchecked, equal, fearless intercourse," a description poignantly revealing a life in which ordinary speech is fearful, constrained, and subservient. Hudson writes, "These sibships, as we may call them, embody a literary as well as a social innovation. Based on mutual respect, individual worth, and shared beliefs and concerns, they herald a new dimension in the English novel to the extent that they are relatively egalitarian societies."[66] Tuite may see *Mansfield Park* as maintaining an archaic aristocratic framework, but from inside that milieu, Austen's sibling characters perceive something like a democratic haven.

This form of love offers a new model for marriage. Just as Edmund was first stirred by seeing Fanny's love for William, so Henry Crawford makes the same discovery. "Fanny's attractions increased—increased two-fold—for the sensibility which beautified her complexion and illumined her countenance, was an attraction in itself. He was no longer in doubt of the capabilities of her heart. She had feeling, genuine feeling. It would be something to be loved by such a girl." (212). It would be easy to say that both Edmund and Henry are aroused by Fanny's love for William, but it is not exactly arousal; it would be more precise to say that they are stirred to emulation. They desire not so much Fanny herself, but Fanny's feeling. Henry wants to provoke an equivalent of sibling love for himself. In this new sight, familial affection, the tired roué finds a better alternative than the stories of seduction, flirtation, and escape that had previously occupied him. And when he decides to propose to Fanny, he cites this scene as one of his motives. "To see her with her brother! What could more delightfully prove that the warmth of her heart was equal to its gentleness?—What could be more encouraging to a man who had her love in view?" (266).

Fanny, Edmund, and Henry's love triangle is a foundational model for the familiar-romantic rivalry that would come to dominate the Victorian marriage plot. Edmund holds the familiar post—he is cousin, foster brother, and cohabiter with Fanny—but Henry has to learn to reform his romantic-suitor persona.

He actually covets the role of a familiar suitor, but to achieve it he must slough off his earlier rakish tendencies and learn the new emotional ideal. (As readers know, he does not quite manage the transformation.) Like Darcy, like Marrable, Henry Crawford will only succeed in marrying the woman he wants if he learns to emulate the qualities of familiar union.

However, the Crawfords' model derives from a different world of emotional interactions, which favors the immediate satisfaction of desire, followed by the polite release of the once-beloved. Their temporal idea is visible in their behavior, in which the siblings may collude for a shared goal temporarily, may separate themselves for indefinite periods, and come together only for their mutual interest. For instance, they plot together to trick Fanny into accepting Henry's necklace for the ball. But this chain is both empty in itself (signaling the lack of real feeling) and a representative of a twisted form of sibling feeling, a careless gift valued by neither the giver nor the receiver. Like Henry's unsatisfactory letters, "done in the fewest possible words," there is no real emotional content (53).

The Bertrams present a similarly diseased endogamous situation. If the Crawfords have a careless alliance, the Bertrams' fraternal feeling is mainly characterized by animosity. Maria and Julia enact a toxic rivalry over Henry Crawford, and Tom and Edward, although remaining courteous, must work to maintain their truce in spite of the real strain of being structurally situated as rivals for the same diminishing estate.[67] In short, the Bertram household is one of insufficient resources and greedy children; the sisters fight over the one romantic prospect, and the brothers fight over the one inheritance.[68] Their sibships are competitive rather than cooperative.

But Fanny's combination of Edmund's chain with William's cross reveals a better alignment. They are "those memorials of the two most beloved of her heart, those dearest tokens so formed for each other by every thing real and imaginary" (245). Sibling love is here warmly embraced as the basis of a love made for marriage. They go together; they were formed for each other. In Susan Lanser's words, "sisterhood in Austen's novels constitutes the prototype for marriage itself; the ideal marriage, finally, may be modeled upon the ideal sisterhood."[69] This modeling occurs in Fanny's childhood, when we find that "she loved [Edmund] better than any body in the world except William; her heart was divided between the two" (19). No wonder Haggerty writes that "fraternal love" is posited in this novel as an alternative to erotic love. William and Edmund play analogous roles in Fanny's life, and she is devoted to each in a similar fashion. The novel abounds in misdirected erotics—between Maria and Henry, Edmund and Mary, even Henry and Fanny—but all those relations collapse before the intensity of fraternal bonds. Toward the end of the novel, when he arrives in Portsmouth to take Fanny home to Mansfield, Edmund says: "My Fanny—my only sister—my only comfort now" (405). A more powerful statement of affection, in this novel at least, can hardly be imagined.[70]

Because the fraternal relation embraces so much, it is the richest form of emotional bond in the world of *Mansfield Park.* No need to answer Edmund's query "whether it might not be a possible, an hopeful undertaking to persuade her that her warm and sisterly regard for him would be foundation enough for wedded love" (429). In this novel, it is by far the best foundation for wedded love, embracing as it does shared memories, freedom, egalitarianism, play, instruction, and nursing. Since one cannot marry a biological brother, the closest one can get is a cousin. Indeed, as the narrator asks, "what could be more natural than the change?" And that key word is repeated: "I only intreat every body to believe that exactly at the time when it was quite natural that it should be so, and not a week earlier," that Edmund wanted to marry Fanny (429). In a Romantic-era novel, "natural" is not a word to be overlooked. Family love is "natural"; it is the same word used by both Charlotte Yonge and Florence Nightingale in their accounts of cousin love, cited earlier. Sibling love is the natural basis for marriage, cousin relations mimic it, and all the other marital motives this novel has presented—the marriages for money, for position, for erotic desire—are perforce unnatural. This is the lesson Sir Thomas Bertram finally learns: a young woman like Fanny is not property he can transfer to a promising buyer, but a subject whose feelings can transform a family.

Fanny and Edmund's relation is precisely the extent of the novel itself; we are interpolated into feeling their love because we have shared its formative moments and watched its texture thicken throughout their story. Just as Fanny had played, instructed, and nursed her siblings, so Edmund had loved, guided, and protected her. Years of care for Fanny constitutes a history of love to which the addition of a romantic element is not a transformation but only a final minor detail: "What was there now to add, but that he should learn to prefer soft light eyes to sparkling dark ones" (429). Hudson sums up:

> Even more important for Austen is the idea that conjugal love should be patterned after fraternal love, that the perfect marriage should be like the ideal sibling relationship with its shared trust and understanding, love and esteem, high regard and loyalty, and that the partners should come not only from the same social circle but also, if possible, from the same family . . . . Fraternal rather than sexual love preponderates in Austen's fiction, and, in many regards, the romantic scenes are domestic scenes.[71]

The narrator enumerates the advantages of marrying a cousin/foster sibling. Edmund knows Fanny's character intimately and has no doubts of either

her moral merits or her mental superiority. "Their own inclinations ascertained, there were no difficulties behind, no drawback of poverty or parent" (430). (This may remind us of McLennan's pronouncement that in endogamous unions, "the bridegroom and bride will live together in amity among their common relatives."[72]) By contrast, there are virtually no happily married exogamous couples in this novel. When we consider the Bertrams, the Grants, the Prices, the Rushworths, Admiral and Mrs. Crawford, and even the Norrises, marriage in the first generation (plus Maria and Rushworth in the second generation) is characterized by the partners' indifference, irritation, violence, fear, or dislike.[73] Nor do passionate romantic couples have a future: Maria and Henry Crawford's pairing fails. Only endogamy teaches how to love. The second generation can, at last, achieve harmonious cousinly marriage.

No wonder, then, that the end of the novel is a festival of siblings. "Indeed, the breach between sisters created by the unequal alliances described at the opening of *Mansfield Park* is repaired in one branch of the next generation," explains Corbett, "as the felt need for proxy daughters ultimately enables two of the Price sisters to renew their attachment."[74] Mrs. Price and Lady Bertram repair their bond, Susan and Fanny live together, and the younger set of sisters serves the elder. The real resolution of *Mansfield Park* is not the marriage between Fanny and Edmund but the restoration of appropriate family feeling in two generations (parents and children) and two families (Prices and Bertrams), all based on the model of good sibling affection. In this respect, *Mansfield Park* colludes with the sororal companionship that, as we have seen, constitutes the happy endings of *Sense and Sensibility* and *Pride and Prejudice*. The famously suspiciously hasty tone of Austen's description of Fanny and Edmund's marriage is often read as revealing Austen's own skepticism about cousin marriage.[75] What it really shows, I think, is a haste to get the marriage out of the way to get back to the siblings. In this regard the last page matches the first, in which marriages get minimized while the narrator dwells on family relations. Fanny can finally be "available" to all people: a sister, a daughter, a wife, a friend. Here is the real happy ending: "In *her* [Susan's] usefulness, in Fanny's excellence, in William's continued good conduct, and rising fame, and in the general well-doing and success of the other members of the family, all assisting to advance each other"—Mansfield Park has finally become not an estate but a family (431).

Becoming the Brother's Wife

Six years after Austen died in Winchester, Charlotte M. Yonge was born in the neighboring town of Otterbourne. Members of Austen's circle were among Yonge's closest friends: the Biggs, Lefroys, and Austen-Leighs.[76] Like Austen,

Yonge wrote novels about young women growing up in middle-class families in country villages. The two writers were often associated with each other, as for instance in an 1854 review commenting that Yonge "in common with Miss Austin [. . .] is chiefly remarkable for truthful delineations of character."[77] Austen heavily influenced Yonge, and throughout her life she revised her predecessor's plots.[78] Biographers Margaret Mare and Alicia Percival mention that Yonge could spend an evening reciting Austen quotes from memory; Austen was her greatest literary love other than Sir Walter Scott.[79]

It is perhaps fitting that while Yonge's first novel was clearly influenced by Scott, with its rugged northern castle, rival clans, and ancestral curses, her second novel, *Heartsease* (1854) is a meditation on *Mansfield Park*.[80] June Sturrock summarizes *Heartsease* in a way that reveals its relation to its predecessor text:

> A very young, timid, but highly-principled and religious girl from a large and humble family is taken into a rich, upper-class household, whose money comes mainly from large estates in the West Indies. In this cold and formal family, she is neglected, snubbed, and often made to feel like a vulgar and uneducated outsider, especially by the beautiful but passive lady of the house, by a self-possessed daughter of the house—and most of all by a spiteful, hostile, and mercenary aunt. One of the two sons shows her great kindness, but all the same, she suffers greatly through a number of trials, and is often unwell. She is brought into direct rivalry for the affections of her beloved with a richer, livelier, and better-born young woman. Eventually, after a series of family disasters, her strict adherence to her own ethical code places her as the moral center of her household, a household that is made more humane by her central role in it.[81]

What Sturrock's summary does not mention is that when our heroine competes with a livelier rival, that lady is actually the beloved's sister. For *Heartsease* has, in a sense, *Mansfield Park*'s plot written backward. Whereas in *Mansfield Park* fraternal affection proves to be the best basis for marriage, in *Heartsease*, marriage constitutes a destabilizing disturbance in an ongoing sibling relationship. In this respect, *Heartsease* describes the opposite dynamic from the one Sharon Marcus describes in *Between Women*, in which female relationships facilitate marriage; here, marriage is mostly notable because it complicates those relationships.

Heartsease presents a different model of literary reworking from the one we examined in Chapter 3. Where *Cometh Up* critiques Austen, *Heartsease* appreciates and extends Austen's emotional logic.[82] Perhaps appropriately, while *Cometh Up* is like a rebellious adolescent flouting parental rules, *Heartsease* is a dutiful daughter or sister text.

Such homage fit Yonge's views of how the literary world ought to work. Yonge was committed to mentoring younger writers.[83] This is a case of an author consciously helping construct a tradition of women's writing, featuring grateful appreciation of her predecessor. Moreover, Yonge's Tractarian beliefs taught her to see herself linked to others in a larger pattern. Allusiveness, Charlotte Mitchell explains, "was not seen as feebly derivative, but creative, as an emulation of the divine patterns which transcend temporal reality. [Yonge's religious mentor] Keble's watchword, Yonge tells us, was 'Don't be original.' "[84]

In *Heartsease*, Yonge shows her credentials as an astute reader of Austen by making the story much more explicitly about sibling love—and, a century and a half before Edward Said, emphasizing the devastating effect of a family fortune derived from slavery in the West Indies. When Theodora learns that her beloved brother Arthur has married, "Theodora awoke to sensations of acute grief. Her nature had an almost tropical fervor of disposition; and her education having given her few to love, her ardent affections had fastened upon Arthur with a vehemence that . . . made the loss of the first place in his love painful."[85] Theodora's love is part of her essential (somewhat racialized) nature and fostered by her poor education. This language makes it clear that we are supposed to disapprove of her passions, not because of any kind of sexual pathology, but because they exceed the bounds of feminine decorum. Throughout the novel, Theodora struggles with this "perverse jealousy," which makes her act proudly indifferent to Arthur whenever she is most miserably desperate for his favor (114). Only by gradually coming to appreciate, and then even to adore, Arthur's wife, Violet, can Theodora conquer her passionate nature. In so doing, she also achieves a healthier sororal love. By the end, Arthur gives her a "look of affection," and she realizes that "he had never given her such an [*sic*] one in the days when she deemed his love a thing exclusively her own, she had now gained something far better than his heart had then to offer. The best spot in it then had nothing half so deep, fond, and unselfish as what he gave her now" (496). Thus this novel centrally concerns Violet retraining Theodora to enhance her relationship with Arthur. It is as if the main purpose of Fanny marrying Edmund was to help Julia become a better sister.

As with *Mansfield Park*, however, modern readers of *Heartsease* find the incest issue unavoidable. Valerie Sanders, who appreciates the intense sibling ties in Yonge's fiction, describes *Heartsease* chiefly in terms of what is not there, the "relationships [that are] almost sexual."[86] It is no longer possible to parse sibling love without reference to incest, and if the incest is not there ("*almost* sexual"), that absence is what we note.

For *Heartsease* depicts a world of lateral ties. Parents are absent, dead, or incompetent. As in much of *Mansfield Park*, it is the siblings whose loyalties, loves, quarrels, and reunions make up the novel's emotional life. Every character is understood primarily as a sibling, entangled with other siblings. For instance, Arthur's brother John suffered the death of his beloved sister when he was five.[87] Their neighbor Helen Fotheringham was brought in to supply the place of his lost companion (145). Explicitly presented as a sister-substitute, Helen is someone whom it is safe to adore. "She was exactly of my own age, but with all the motherly helpful kindness of an elder sister, and full of pretty, childish compassion for the little wretched solitary being that I was" (145). Helen therefore becomes John's lifelong love. Similarly, a neighbor named Lady Lucy adores her brother, Lord St. Erme, as much as Theodora loves Arthur, but Lucy expresses her love in a more acceptably feminine style, with clinging, meek, submissive expressions of devotion. As a friend notes, "there was never fonder love between a brother and sister; she hardly had a thought that did not centre in him. . . . how often we have seen them walking arm in arm together, and said they might be taken for a pair of lovers" (420). This description is true not only of St. Erme and Lucy but also of John and Helen, or Arthur and Theodora. Virtually all sibling pairs could be taken for lovers in *Heartsease*. If sisterhood is not the same as being a lover, it is only because—on the evidence of this novel—being a lover is a far more fraught, miserable, and complicated proposition.

Lovers are bad substitutes for siblings. When Theodora first contemplates marriage, she thinks, "there was another kind of affection, not half so valuable in her eyes as fraternal love; it made fools of people, but then they were happy in their blindness, and could keep it to themselves. She would condescend to lay herself open to the infection. It would be satisfying if she could catch it," but, on finding her suitors unsatisfactory, she realizes that "one 'Hollo, Theodora, come along' would have been worth all the court paid to her by [other] men" (141). Romantic love is figured here as a disease, contrasted with the frank, jovial comradeship afforded by a brother. As Sanders perceptively writes, "One never entirely loses the sense in Yonge's novels that to marry is to settle for something inferior to sibling love—something coarser—however necessary it must be in a realistic world."[88]

Although Theodora contracts a turbulent engagement to her lifelong friend and neighbor, Percy Fotheringham (himself the brother of Helen, who was engaged to Theodora's elder brother John), their relationship seems mainly predicated on his rather sadistic (or elder-brotherly?) desire to "tame" her, and her rather masochistic desire to be disciplined. Their on-again, off-again engagement is a penitential period of frequently expressed mutual self-hatred, and, perhaps understandably, they seem in no hurry to wed.

Sanders suggests that "Theodora's dismissal of non-fraternal love implies a fear of sexuality. . . . Yonge's repeated emphasis on brother-sister dyads as nurturing, reassuring and safe suggests, too, a shrinking from the physical commitment to an outsider that pervades her fictional families."[89] However, Theodora is written as a highly sexually suggestive subject. The novel opens with Theodora's nineteen-year-old body, tall and regal, which boasts "a complexion of gypsy darkness" and "fresh, healthy red lips," with hands "very soft and delicate, though of large and strong make" (2). Her strong coloring, her "tropical fervor" and "West Indian constitution," and her towering rages all seem to suggest someone who, in Victorian iconography, is too liable to passion in every sense (40, 145). Theodora resembles Bertha Mason more than any other mid-Victorian female character.[90] Sanders is right that *Heartsease* prefers safe fraternal bonds to sexual commitments to outsiders, but this preference is not due to Theodora's character; it is, rather, a structural preference that determines the novel, from the title onwards, and the type of familiar marriage plot genre in which it participates.

Just as *Cometh Up as a Flower* puts its female character into a neighbor marriage she does not comprehend, *Heartsease* fixes its female character in a romantic union she fails to understand. Each marriage is an odd case in a novel that otherwise endorses the competing model. In *Heartsease*, we are expected to believe that Violet—the shy, sweet, pious, self-doubting fifteen-year-old girl whom we meet in the opening pages—should have fallen overwhelmingly in love with a careless handsome guardsman after dancing with him once at a ball, and have married him almost immediately. Neither Violet nor her family ever bother to investigate this stranger's moral credentials, financial situation, personal history, or family connections. Arthur, a typical romantic lover, is a stranger and a soldier, swooping in on a vulnerable impoverished, local teenage beauty—a Wickham or Willoughby, a M'Gregor or Marrable.

The not-so-secret secret of *Heartsease* is that this marriage is a disaster. It may not be a coincidence that the husband shares a name with Arthur Huntingdon, and Violet's second name (and the name shared by other significant characters) is Helen. Like Anne Brontë's Arthur Huntingdon, Yonge's Arthur Martindale is a careless and irreligious flirt, a gambler, and a drinker with bad companions and dangerous ways, who impoverishes his family and endangers the well-being of his son before (nearly) perishing of disease brought on by his degraded lifestyle.[91] Like Helen Huntingdon, Violet is a religious woman driven to reform her husband partly by anxiety for the welfare of her son. *The Tenant of Wildfell Hall* was published in 1848, and in *Heartsease*, which Yonge had written by 1851, Yonge may have been rewriting Anne Brontë's story in order to prove that perfect feminine goodness could eventually overpower male dissipation.[92]

Violet, like Fanny, comes from a large lower-class family that seems mainly composed of siblings; her greedy father and her downtrodden mother are largely ignored. On her first appearance she can barely say a word about herself, referencing her sisters' reactions in lieu of her own (11–12).[93] Violet's especial sororal partner is Annette, with whom she had enjoyed "twin-like companionship" (335). Annette is, in fact, so much like Violet that Percy Fotheringham feels entitled to assume they are substitutable. "The same stamp as her sister," he muses, and sends her a note which reads "in knowing your sister, and seeing your resemblance to her, I know you" (343). In Annette, Violet sees a mirror of herself, a mutually nurturing partner with whom she shares formative experiences and crucial feelings.

Where Violet's consanguineal home is the site of mutually sustaining relationships, her conjugal home is associated with neglect and depression.[94] Arthur cannot establish a supportive relation with Violet because he has had no such family experiences himself. The Martindale clan is as dysfunctional as the Bertrams on whom they are modeled. As in *Mansfield Park*, an interloper has poisoned the first generation. The Mrs. Norris figure, Mrs. Nesbit, is a controlling aunt who has made the Lady Bertram-like Lady Martindale into an automaton who only fulfills her aunt's wishes and appears indifferent to the rest of her family. Mitchell writes, "More openly than in *Mansfield Park*, the childlessness of the aunt is associated with her usurpation of power—she exercises power illegitimately, neither a parent nor a landowner or householder. She is a cuckoo who has crept into the Martindale nest, and upset its god-ordained systems of power and responsibility."[95] One might argue that the West-Indian plantation holder Lord Martindale is doing something similar on a global scale, exercising power illegitimately in a realm not rightly his own. Like Sir Thomas, Lord Martindale is stately and detached from his children's concerns, and he spends much of his time managing a dwindling estate in the West Indies.[96] Into a household tainted by slave ownership, with no familial affection, with an absent heir and a destructive alliance between a headstrong sister and a self-indulgent brother, steps Violet, importing a different model.

The fact that it was possible to write a well-received love story about siblings indicates something important about mid-Victorian readership. *Heartsease* complicates our assumptions about the inevitable triumph of romantic love. At mid-century, it was not at all clear which way of thinking about marriage readers ought to adopt. Romantic and familiar marriage were both accessible fantasies about marriage, and *Jane Eyre, Cometh Up as a Flower, The Vicar of Bullhampton*, and *Heartsease* all teach different variants of it, some working to create compromise formations, some endorsing one model, and some exploring how to recalibrate one model to acquire the values traditionally associated with the other. To read *Heartsease* is to be reminded that Victorian readers found it perfectly pleasurable to have a novel without passionate romantic love.

There is no serious critical disagreement about the importance of siblinghood in *Mansfield Park* and *Heartsease*.[97] But analyses of relationships too often devolve into diagnoses of incestuous pathologies, followed by speculation on why the author was oblivious to the perverse desires the critic can so easily spot. Reading endogamous marriage in terms of the late-Victorian fascination with the incest prohibition simply does not work for early and mid-Victorian fiction. Perhaps a better clue comes from the McLennan model of endogamy, in which familial union simply means social harmony. For this is the dynamic in Austen and Yonge: a sibling model of mutual love harmonizes those at odds, repairs a damaged social structure, and compensates for a disastrous history. Endogamous love retrains neglectful parents, abusive spouses, and competitive siblings, and rectifies the damage done in the previous generation. Nineteenth-century authors want us to read these unions as emotionally reparative, not sexually diseased or politically retrograde, and if we want to know what family marriage plots meant for Victorian readers, we need to recognize this alternative perspective.

Wuthering Heights*: Contrary Readings*

Wuthering Heights (1847) may seem like the great exception to the rule of reparative family union, for this is a novel in which an endogamous relationship exacerbates the bad feelings already existing within the family, doubling what was already dark and twisted by making it marry itself and reproduce. In fact, however, *Wuthering Heights* follows the same logic of cousin marriage as *Mansfield Park* and *Heartsease*: a first generation in which a vicious outsider ends up corrupting familial relations, with a second generation that excises the outsider in order to reformulate itself along more affective, domestic lines as ratified by a cousin marriage in the younger generation. In this sense we might read *Wuthering Heights* not as the exception to the norm of Victorian fiction but as its exemplar.

Wuthering Heights does not just chart a particular family's situation, but uses it as a representative case for reading the history of family structures. The novel charts the shift from an older model of aristocratic lineage to a newer idea of a nuclear family, showing how the transition generated fundamental doubts about the nature of the family. *Wuthering Heights* asks: In moving toward the closed nuclear family, what happens to those people who might once have been included in the household, like servants, foster children, illegitimate offspring, and poor relations? What emotional and economic benefits are conferred by membership in a family, and conversely, what kind of liberty is enabled by exclusion from one? Like *Mansfield Park, Wuthering Heights* asks the question constantly, "Pray, is she out, or is she not?"[98]

In *Wuthering Heights*, the first generation cannot get "out." They live in suffocating isolation. Jerome Bump argues that in "focusing on the family as a unit at Wuthering Heights, we discover one of the best illustrations of a closed system in literature. Its members are not merely extremely isolated from others; they are actively hostile."[99] Certainly the family's imperviousness to outsiders is what fascinates Lockwood, making him identify it as a good subject for narrative. In his celebrated reading of *Wuthering Heights*, Leo Bersani argues that the project of this novel is to tie up all the characters in an unbreakable family circle. It imagines intense sibling closeness, the love of oneself as embodied in another person.[100] In a world consisting virtually only of family, all one can do is replicate and perpetuate that family.

In this Hobbesian state of nature, it is not surprising that the family's relationships take what McLennan would soon delineate as the two alternatives in primitive marriage: rape and incest.[101] While Heathcliff's sexual violence against Isabella is all but explicit, it is Heathcliff's quasi-incestuous relation to Catherine that grabs most readers' attention.[102] Kathryn B. McGuire asserts, for instance, that "an unconscious incest taboo impeded [Heathcliff's and Catherine's] expectations of normal sexual union and led them to spiritualize their attachment, eventually leading them to believe that they could find union only after death."[103]

Within the world of the novel, however, Heathcliff and Catherine are not described as incestuous. Brontë herself never invokes this term. "Despite this presumptive readerly drive to anchor relationships in blood connection," Corbett remarks, accurately, "the bar to marriage between Heathcliff and Catherine nowhere registers in the text as incest: however sibling-like their bond may appear to critics, it is clearly not on the ground of their already being brother and sister, either by blood or informal adoption, that they do not marry."[104] It is quite possible for Catherine to marry Heathcliff. It is, in fact, an option that Nelly, Catherine, and Heathcliff all consider. She refuses, not because of their sibling relationship, but because "it would degrade me to marry Heathcliff, now."[105] What prevents their marriage is a recent development, "now": Heathcliff's catastrophic class fall. If shared experiences and the same "soul" connect Catherine and Heathcliff, class is what divides them. The reason they do not marry is not that they're too similar, but that they're too different.

The real problem is not an incestuously closed family but the invasion of these closed families by outsiders. In other words, we are not in McLennan's harmonious endogamous state. Instead, we are in his harsher world of exogamous primitive marriage, where the Grange and the Heights are like rival tribes, with the men kidnapping each other's women. "The two families exchange their daughters/sisters," Drew Lamonica points out, although neither Catherine nor Isabella (nor, in the next generation, the younger Cathy) necessarily want to be exchanged.[106] As Victorian anthropology predicts, sexually driven men buy Catherine or abduct Isabella. The novel can be read as an exposé of the damage done by outsiders invading a closed endogamous tribe. After all, the rough world of the Earnshaws goes on well enough until interrupted by the silken civilities of the Lintons, unsettling Catherine with alien loyalties. Meanwhile, the Lintons' peaceful haven is ruined by Earnshaw violence. One might argue that the problem in *Wuthering Heights* is that families aren't closed *enough*.

However, the problem is more basic: What makes a family? Heathcliff may be adoptively part of the family—and Maine stressed the importance of adoption in composing clans—but he is exogamous in race and class terms. Meanwhile, Linton is not biologically related but he is endogamous in terms of race and class.[107] Who is more "like" Cathy? If she seeks similarity, whom should she wed? Heathcliff is like her in upbringing and personality; Edgar is like her in being white gentry. "Family" is a fluid concept here, and so is the question of who is in or out of the group. Because of this variability, it is impossible to decide whether *Wuthering Heights* is depicting the pathology of a stiflingly closed family, or the dangers of invasion by an exogamous stranger. Is Heathcliff the dark heart of the Earnshaws, or the invading other?

This uncertainty becomes, literally, fatal. Catherine is a prototypical victim of primitive marriage, passively torn apart between men who are trying to claim her. The agonizing undecidability of Catherine's deathbed comes, in part, from her being forced to choose one family but not knowing which family she belongs to. Catherine experiences a catastrophic version of the romantic-familiar rivalry, with a demonic romantic lover in Heathcliff and a weak familiar lover in Edgar. Lyn Pykett clarifies:

> The story of the first Catherine hinges—as do most novels of the period—on her choice between two men. Choosing the correct husband is the central moral task set for the heroine of most eighteenth- and nineteenth-century novels, particularly those written by women. Catherine's choice of Edgar is socially sanctioned and conforms to the dominant fictional pattern (seen most clearly and familiarly in the novels of Jane Austen) according to which heroines are led to make the rational choice of the sensible, educated man of property and standing in the community.[108]

Pykett appreciates the extent to which *Wuthering Heights*, in spite of its status as a novel unlike any other in the nineteenth century, in fact shares the dominant rivalry plot this book explores. In Catherine's case, the contrast is sharp. Is she part of the consanguineous family with Heathcliff, or the conjugal family with

Edgar? Which man is an intruder from an outside realm, violently taking her away from her true circle?

For *Wuthering Heights* can be read as an anthropological document, a contact zone where the ethnographer Lockwood discovers a tribe and finds a native interpreter, Nelly, to explain its ways. If the novel is a kind of ethnological report, what it records is an unmistakably savage state, something that Emily Brontë might have thought about when she read a nearly twenty-page review of Auguste Comte's positivist philosophy in *Blackwood's Edinburgh Magazine* in 1843 discussing his theories of primitive theology.[109] The last two pages of this review focus on Comte's ideas of fetishism and primitive religion, giving a sense of a savage perspective in which nature itself is animated, a notion which may have contributed to her conception of Heathcliff's non-Christian worldview.

However, if *Wuthering Heights* depicts the anthropological state of savagery, it also enshrines anthropology's antithesis: the idea of female character made possible in the marriage-plot novel. Catherine may seem like a victim of male sexual exchange, but she views herself as a person in a social context that they are inexplicably violating. Patsy Stoneman explains that "only if we regard Catherine as Edgar's 'possession' is there any logic in Heathcliff's equalizing the situation by stealing his other 'possession'—that is, Isabella." [110] Rather, Catherine wants inclusivity, access to both men. She believes she could "be available" (to use Lévi-Strauss's term) to more than one person. As the carvings in her bedchamber show, she imagines that she can simultaneously be Catherine Linton and Catherine Heathcliff, without losing Catherine Earnshaw. These selves coexist; "the air swarmed with Catherines" (20). Lamonica points out that "Catherine's decision to 'choose both' (and, thereby, to 'be both') is ultimately an attempt to dodge the operations of marital exchange."[111] But I would say that Catherine is not trying to "dodge the operations of marital exchange," as if marital exchange were an immutable fact, but rather to stand for an alternative form of human relations that has warrant in another kind of text.

Catherine imagines what I am reading here as the literary alternative to the anthropological myth: being "available" to more than one person, a model that understands more forms of love than eroticism and more forms of marriage than possession. She understands herself through books; we see her library and her writings when Lockwood visits her bedroom. Meanwhile, Heathcliff gives up language, his hard work extinguishing "any love for books" while he enters what Nelly tartly calls "an almost idiotic excess of unsociable moroseness" (68). Exiled from reading, Heathcliff will gain his adult knowledge from legal and economic structures of power. He will be unable to comprehend Catherine's embrace of multiple social relationships.

Stoneman has identified Catherine's wish to have both Heathcliff and Edgar as a literary artifact in itself, a free-love imperative deriving from Emily Brontë's reading of Shelley's "Epipsychidion."[112] Yet the text gives us no warrant for assuming Catherine intends her relation to both men sexually. What she wants is not so much free love as what we might see, pitiably, as free society: the company of more than one person. Catherine wants different, and not necessarily sexual, forms of companionship from each man. She wants a familiar, mutually respectful relationship with Edgar and a romantic, passionate connection with Heathcliff. If critics assume that what Catherine wants is monogamous sexual relationships simultaneously, they are being less imaginative than Catherine herself.

Through Heathcliff and Edgar, *Wuthering Heights* interrogates specifically early nineteenth-century changing models of the family and demonstrates that they converge in their treatment of women. The first-generation Earnshaw family understands itself in terms of an older family type similar to the one that Lawrence Stone has dubbed "the Open Lineage Family," characterized by permeability of space and lack of privacy.[113] Stone claims that this family type ended in the sixteenth century (befitting a family whose lintel carving offers a founding date of 1500). Indeed, Maja-Lisa von Sneidern sees the Heights as a predominantly fifteenth-century environment.[114] It is a family configuration that defines itself by its ancestral history and operates according to the needs of the larger kin network, not individual wishes. Its population is flexible, accommodating people like Nelly and Heathcliff, whose status is part servant, part foster child.[115] The Earnshaw house is permeable to the outdoors; wind, snow, dead rabbits, mud, and hunting dogs all move in and out. There is little privacy, as most events occur in the great kitchen, and Heathcliff and Catherine share a bed.[116] The house's characteristic products—guns, straw, dogs, hams, and oatmeal—are elements in an agricultural economy.[117]

Meanwhile, the Linton family represents the emergent nuclear-family model, similar to what Stone calls "the Closed Domesticated Nuclear Family."[118] The Lintons are a closed unit, a husband and wife with two children, living in a comfortable house that is impervious to the elements. Cloaked with curtains, shielded with doors, and guarded from outsiders by servants and dogs who know their places as defenders of (but not participants in) the family—unlike the servants and dogs who range all too freely at the Heights—the Grange is a building which we first glimpse from the point of view of those outside, excluded from its warm embrace. The Grange is part of a consumer economy, not an agricultural economy; as Stoneman points out, it boasts sweet cakes, chandeliers, and carpets.[119] Part of what *Wuthering Heights* stages is the confrontation of these two modes of imagining the family, and the eventual triumph of the nuclear-family model once it has been strengthened by incorporating elements of the aristocratic lineage paradigm. The novel "traces the emergence of the modern family."[120]

However, another part of what *Wuthering Heights* reveals is the way both systems dehumanize women. Heathcliff, who becomes the owner and representative of Wuthering Heights, views marriage in a way that is characteristic of this older lineage system. He arranges marriages—his own, his son's—solely for dynastic benefit and property transmission. As Heathcliff matures, he becomes imbued with Earnshaw assumptions about marriage, entitlement, and property. "Heathcliff becomes, in one critic's view, 'more an Earnshaw than the Earnshaws themselves.' "[121] Named after "a son who died in childhood," Heathcliff becomes the spirit of that house, and by the end of the novel, quite literally so (38). Instead of being the exogamous stranger, he becomes the embodiment of that family's worst aspects, the Earnshaw lineage come to life, stalking the earth in apparently inhuman unstoppability.

Because Heathcliff adheres to the older lineage model, he sees people as static objects. He has no model of human development, in spite of the fact that this subject forms the heart of the nineteenth-century realist novel, including his own. Heathcliff assumes that Hareton will "never be able to emerge from his bathos of coarseness, and ignorance" (219). Linton he regards as "my property," a dynastic guarantor who gives Heathcliff "the triumph of seeing *my* descendent fairly lord of their estates; my child hiring their children." Linton's own wishes are irrelevant, and his personality is positively distasteful to his father (207, 208). Heathcliff's tendency to regard individuals as property gets reinforced during his years away from Wuthering Heights. Whether he went into the army, as Nelly guesses, or got involved in the slave trade, as some critics surmise, he had an experience of seeing powerless bodies treated as objects, their physical suffering demanded as instruments for a ruler's will.[122]

Interestingly, Edgar, although coming from a closed nuclear family, agrees with Heathcliff here. He wants his descendant to return "to the house of her ancestors; and he considered her only prospect of doing that was by a union with his heir" (259). Modern marriage and inheritance law—and perhaps proto-anthropological thinking—teach Edgar to disregard women's feelings. He too assumes that women are unchanging objects for men to move around. Thus he can demand that Catherine ignore Heathcliff, and Edgar feels perfectly justified locking his daughter in his grounds. As a manager of an estate, Edgar sees women as among the objects to be itemized and retained. Heathcliff and Edgar have both learned to treat women (and children) as property, rather like Sir Thomas Bertram (and Grandcourt, as discussed in Chapter 3). In these novels, male assumptions about marriage often diverge terrifyingly far from the women's point of view. These men assume that they are independent, mobile, autonomous agents, controlling females who are merely mute pieces of property. This idea connects to the story of primitive marriage, but it was also supported by the Victorian legal system. Frances Power Cobbe pointed out that "the notion that a man's wife is his PROPERTY, in the sense in which a horse is his property . . . is the fatal root of incalculable evil and misery. Every brutal-minded man, and many a man who in other relations of life is not brutal, entertains more or less vaguely the notion that his wife is his *thing*, and is ready to ask with indignation (as we read again and again in the police reports), of any one who interferes with his treatment of her, 'May I not do what I will *with my own*?' "[123] It is a sentiment entirely characteristic of Heathcliff.

Heathcliff's instrumentalist view of human beings is only possible in a life lived without novels. Under his rule, Wuthering Heights is a place where it is almost impossible, as Isabella finds, "to preserve the common sympathies of human nature" (136). He has the greatest contempt for anyone "picturing in me a hero of romance," interestingly objecting to the way many readers have responded to him (149). Yet the fact that he is in a novel, and the fact that *Wuthering Heights* is a realist novel as well as a Gothic thriller, guarantee that characters will develop.[124] Jerome Bump reads the second generation as a precise replica, a stagnant repetition, of the first.[125] But in fact the second generation grows beyond their elders' recognition. Hareton proves educable; Linton and the younger Cathy show qualities that their elders do not expect. Heathcliff lacks the capacity to understand his own fiction. Edgar, too, who can see Heathcliff only as a runaway servant, cannot possibly offer the kind of complex reading Catherine requires (96).

For this novel enacts a much more Victorian idea of psychological depth than anything Heathcliff (or Edgar) can comprehend. Perhaps this is because its narrator, Nelly, points out, "I have read more than you would fancy, Mr. Lockwood. You could not open a book in this library that I have not looked into, and got something out of also" (63). Women who tell the story ultimately demonstrate fidelity to a more affective kind of narrative than the men, with their property-based views of female exchange. Whether the self-taught Nelly, the romantic literature reader Isabella, or the writer Catherine, the women inhabit a textual tradition that neither Edgar nor Heathcliff share.

Significantly, the only male who wants to read is Hareton. Kate Flint remarks that "it is Cathy who teaches Hareton to read, thus giving him the key to unlock literature, the very thing which, the novel demonstrates by its own existence, has the potential to unsettle, to pose questions rather than provide answers."[126] Hareton, not Heathcliff, thus grows to be capable of comprehending his own novel. For we track Hareton's tentative shame about his illiteracy, his painstaking efforts at self-education, his eagerness to offer books to Cathy, and his yearning to have Cathy read to him.[127] Learning to read, Hareton comes to understand character in every sense: he intuits Cathy's underlying kindness in spite of her cruel behavior. Cathy and Hareton share fidelity to a world of rich imagination that Heathcliff never knows. And it is their cousin marriage that will repair the damage of the antagonistic first generation.

What Cathy teaches Hareton, specifically, is to turn the word "contrary" into a harmony. "'Con-*trary*!' said a voice, as sweet as a silver bell—'That for the third time, you dunce! I'm not going to tell you again—Recollect, or I pull your hair!' 'Contrary, then,' answered another, in deep, but softened tones. 'And now, kiss me, for minding so well'" (307). They enact the emotional ambiguity of love in *Wuthering Heights* in this scene: kisses and hair-pulling, sweetness and insults at once. But the scene is also a microcosm of the novel as a whole. It references the "contrary" families of the nuclear-family Lintons and the open-lineage Earnshaws, learning to harmonize in their descendants, turning their violence into affectionate play. It is also, of course, the story of Hareton and Cathy's courtship, their opposition dissolving into affection. When Hareton mispronounces the word, stressing the first syllable, he emphasizes "con," which means "with," but also "against." His mispronunciation situates him between classes and generations.[128] By "conning" his lesson, he learns that opposites can chime in together. The misreading of "contrary" is a kind of performative misrepetition that reveals the union at the end of the rivalry.

Emily Brontë's novel describes the way the modern family gets instituted. How do you invent a family that is a domestic haven? You work through and kill off its unruly members—its racially and classed others, its rebellious women—and you marry the remaining cousins to one another. Purified and winnowed down, this version of the family is a prize that takes two generations to achieve. We don't know whether Heathcliff/Catherine suffered from excessive endogamous closeness or excessive exogamous invasive difference, but there is no question that Hareton/Cathy achieve a legitimate, regular, culturally appropriate cousin marriage, featuring shared care for their shared estate. Moving to cousin marriage in the second generation repairs the family. But there is an unresolved residue. The ghosts of Catherine and Heathcliff still walk. The new life of endogamous harmony is haunted by the old violence.

This violence helps inform the post-anthropological story of marriage. Catherine and Heathcliff fit what we regard as the truth of romantic union, with their fierce, exclusive erotic passion; Cathy and Hareton seem disappointingly quaint, conventional, old-fashioned types. But what I have been arguing in this chapter is that the system they embody had value too, and it is a value we ought to recognize. The familiar marriage of the second generation is as important as the romantic passion of the first generation. Cousin marriage joins in holy matrimony those who had previously been opposed to one another and overwrites the violent monogamous anthropological narrative with social harmony. Instead of female abduction, we get the cousin marriage plot: the sound of a voice like a "silver bell," a wedding bell, gets the last note in the story.

Conclusion: Going Contrary

In this chapter we have seen how the anthropological and literary accounts of familiar marriage emerge through the nineteenth century. In *Wuthering Heights* they are located in two generations, one undoing the work of the other. But we can also see their opposition in a larger sense. The two stories are, as it were, mirror images of each other: they speak each other's contraries.

In the anthropological story, social organization begins when a man carries a woman away from her natal family, regardless of how she feels about it. The man enters social relations by buying or abducting her from other men. Thus the woman is understood as the property of men in her home tribe and acquired solely as a sexual object by another man. Can she marry someone in her home tribe? Such an endogamous marriage offers harmony, but it is mainly a blockage in circulation, a hoarding of what should be traded. The incest taboo arises to force her circulation outside her natal group. Marriage becomes a name for heterosexual sex driven by male desire: "tumescence," in Havelock Ellis's description. Marriage is defined by monogamous heterosexual allegiance, rendering its participants' social loyalties, emotional attachments, friendships, skills, histories, and wishes irrelevant.

In the literary story, almost every one of these elements gets reversed. Where the anthropological story starts with marriage, the Victorian marriage novel often ends there, spending most of its energies on the courtship period. Where the anthropological story has a male actor, the Victorian marriage plot usually centers on a woman. The woman's feelings are paramount, and she makes the marital choice. In the familiar plot that I discuss in this chapter, she chooses an endogamous partner. This marriage repairs the original family, previously damaged by an exogamous intruder who introduced violence, hostility, and dehumanization. This marriage reaffirms emotional values: mutual help, respect, kindness, shared skills, and social networks. Its sexual component is not necessarily absent, but it is considered less important, subordinated to affective qualities.

The two stories not only differ but actually reverse each other's trajectories. Each begins with a dangerous situation to be rectified by the next generation's marriage, but they reverse their sense of which is which. Anthropology answers incestuous self-replication with marital exchange; literature repairs foreign invasion with cousin marriage.

The anthropological story may work with some novels. *Dracula*, for instance, can be read as men fighting over the sexual ownership of women. Certainly anthropological work informs those later nineteenth-century narratives that are interested in savagery, male sexual aggression, and female sexual passivity, because it naturalized those identifications as basic to human development. Certainly, too, male characters like Heathcliff often read their own marriage plots from this perspective. But when the marriage plot is focalized through a woman, this primitive-marriage perspective gets depicted as a pathological, dangerous approach that destroys women. Cousin marriage suggests other values. Fanny weds Edmund, Cathy unites with Hareton, Ada decides to marry Richard, Esther agrees to wed her foster-father Jarndyce, Emma realizes she must marry Mr. Knightley, Jane seriously considers St. John, Dorothea yearns for Will Ladislaw, and Sue consents to cohabit with Jude. In each case, the family marriage compensates for a problematic elder generation, marked by legal battles, disinheritance, ineptitude, futility, or cruelty. In each case, the woman believes that what she can bring to the marriage—fortune, devotion, teaching skills, loyalty—will repair the previous damage. They look forward to a future of companionable mutual respect. The endogamous union may or may not actually occur, but when it follows the narrative I have outlined above, it has a powerful appeal as a mutually reparative act.

It also had appeal because nineteenth-century women, forced into marital situations regardless of their preferences and denied economic, amatory, or professional outlets, were able to retain some control over their identity by imagining a fictional situation in which they might choose their own family. Opting to stay in existing networks may not feel like much self-determination for us, but it was a poignantly powerful fantasy for Victorian female readers. It enabled them to imagine maintaining existing emotional affiliations, providing a welcome antidote to the terrifying prospect of marrying a romantic stranger and thereby losing identity and relationships.

This appeal, however, would not last. The endogamous marriage remained popular until the last few decades of the century, when cousin marriage plots began to be troubled by fears about heredity and incest. Charlotte M. Yonge, whose novels of the 1850s, *The Heir of Redclyffe* and *Heartsease*, solely featured endogamous marriages, turned against cousin marriage by the time she wrote *Womankind* in 1878. Worried about inherited diseases, she warned that "those tales which treat of the marriage of first-cousins as simple and unobjectionable do no kindness," for "young people cannot understand why [parents block first-cousin marriages], point to the instances among their friends, and those with which novels unfortunately provide them, and try to wear out opposition."[129] Thomas Hardy's *Jude the Obscure* and Elizabeth Robins's *The Open Question* similarly express concerns about cousin marriage intensifying unwanted hereditary conditions. Through the turn of the century, cousin marriages persisted in fiction but often remained unconsummated, an uneasy attempt to retain the emotional relief of endogamous marriage without the risks of heredity. Such unconsummated unions characterize Lucas Malet's turn-of-the-century novels, *The History of Sir Richard Calmady* and *The Wages of Sin*, and can also be seen in high-Victorian cousin courtship plots like Henry James's *The Portrait of a Lady* and Anthony Trollope's *Can You Forgive Her?* The need for a companionable partnership persisted, but its relation to marriage had become problematic; endogamous unions had come to mean incestuous pathology instead of harmonious reparation.

5

Disability Marriage

COMMUNITIES OF CARE IN THE VICTORIAN NOVEL

A sick chamber may often furnish the worth of volumes.

JANE AUSTEN, Persuasion

A new sort of way, this, for a young fellow to be making love, by breaking his mistress's head!—is not it, Miss Elliot?

JANE AUSTEN, Persuasion

Hitherto I have hated to be helped—to be led: henceforth, I feel I shall hate it no more. I did not like to put my hand into a hireling's, but it is pleasant to feel it circled by Jane's little fingers.

CHARLOTTE BRONTË, Jane Eyre

THROUGHOUT THIS BOOK we have seen how profoundly familiar marriage is tuned toward the social world. Whether the woman imagines marriage as the opportunity to constitute an imagined community or a chance to repair family bonds, the marriage is less about the person of the husband than about the larger network that the marriage makes possible. Whereas modern readers may intuitively recognize the social content of familial or neighborhood matches, we may have more trouble distinguishing the social components of the marriage plot that this chapter analyzes: marriage to a physically disabled subject.[1]

Today disability is deeply involved in what disability scholars call the medical model, in which bodies are assumed to be normatively perfect and disability is a flaw that requires medical intervention. Instead, disability advocates fight for a social model, in which one can accommodate a range of functions for diverse bodies and minds. To create social expectations and architectural arrangements that only validate a single type of person is to disenfranchise (in fact, to disable) the rest of the world. This chapter, however, asks readers to reach back before the medical model was securely in place and to recover a different way of understanding disability. What if disability was not construed as failure to fit a social organization but rather as the cause of social organization itself? What if the Victorians themselves had something that we might call a social model?

In this chapter, I argue that the disabled subject of the nineteenth century was the center of a social network. Because a disabled person required carers, this person was normally surrounded by others: parents, friends, servants, nurses. For a lonely person, a disabled partner could be the entry into a ready-made world, offering the intimate community ties for which so many Victorians yearned. Of course, this vision might have been true in fiction, but the reality for disabled subjects in the nineteenth century was not necessarily socially enabling. Victorian novels, however, not only imagine but also interrogate the notion of a community of carers, parsing the variety of ways one might receive and give care, and exploring the adverse effects of poor care relations.

In order to parse this disabled sociality, I use a theoretical apparatus borrowed from feminist ethics: the theory of ethics of care. Ethics of care asserts that human relations should be understood as interdependent exchanges of caregiving and care-receiving, rather than the monadic persona of classic liberal thought, often equated with *Homo economicus*, the rational subject of economic theory who makes decisions to further his own interest.[2] David Wayne Thomas explains that, "at a general level, liberalism indicates a doctrine whereby individuals bear equivalent rights of free thought and action within a sociality to which they adhere through their own volition." But, he continues: "So understood, liberalism has been widely criticized as a naïve voluntarism, a perniciously atomistic individualism, and an unduly abstracting subscription of agency to universalizing moral perspectives."[3] Ethics of care critiques this "perniciously atomistic individualism," arguing instead that humans are always mutually dependent, enmeshed in social ties from birth. The disabled person and the caretaker (the cared-for and the caregiver), or the mother and child, offer models of the kind of intimate dependency on which all human relations depend. Victorianists may recognize something like this as "this particular web," in George Eliot's words, in which "certain human lots" are "woven and interwoven."[4]

Readers of Victorian disability marriage plots often assume the disabled male suffers a failure of power that affiliates the character with a female experience of confinement, discomfort, weakness, and dependency. He is, in short, symbolically castrated.[5] Thus the female reader can identify with the disabled male, and the female character enjoys equitable status when the suitor is brought down to her level. This reading, however, makes what may be an anachronistically modern assumption that the normative state of the body is whole, and that a disabling event is a traumatic loss. Given the practice of nursing sick family members at home, and the range of disfigurements publically visible, Victorian subjects may well may have viewed bodies as perennially vulnerable to periodic problems rather than normatively healthy. Martha Nussbaum reminds us that disability is a fluid and frequent condition:

> The relative independence that many people sometimes enjoy looks more and more like a temporary condition, a phase of life that we move into gradually and all too quickly begin to leave. Even in our prime, many of us encounter shorter or longer periods of extreme dependency on others - after surgery or a severe injury, or during a period of depression or acute mental stress.[6]

This is an understanding of the body that Victorians may have found easier to accept than we do.

Indeed, our tendency to assume that disabled men suffer from symbolic (or actual) castration and that their marriages are relatively sexless belies the real complexity of these fictional depictions. In Victorian fiction, disabled marriages show a wide variation of sexual activity. Like cousin marriage, disability marriage accommodates erotic desire but does not make it the main reason to wed; in both cases, the marriage is about personal social relations. When modern critics condemn these marriages for "incest" and "castration," they are condemning the fact that the union fails to match our current understandings of appropriate sexual behavior. However, familiar marriage challenges us to cease policing desire as the core of marriage. Instead, we must understand a marriage as a scene of multiple affective needs, ties, relations, and gratifications. In this chapter I want to read disability marriage positively, stressing that it offered particular pleasures—pleasures that were social above all, with sexual pleasures not excluded, but not nearly as important. What if we view the Victorian physically disabled man, not as worrisomely asexual, but as attractively befriended?

In fact, in much Victorian fiction, what the male disabled subject loses in autonomy, he gains in sociality. Debarred from competing in the male world of self-interested striving, he is inducted instead into a female-associated system of mutual caretaking. Romney Leigh, for instance, insists on enacting his own plans without regard to others' feelings until he is blinded. Then he recognizes how catastrophically his arrogance hampered his attempts at social justice.[7] Rochester spends much of the novel trying to trick or overpower Jane; only when disabled can he can express pleasure in dependency. In these cases, it is the weakened male body that accomplishes mutual social relations. More conventional attempts at male domination fail.

At the same time, women get resocialized in relation to these men. Characters like Jane Eyre and Lizzie Hexam, who spend most of their respective novels fleeing from their suitors' sexual aggression, can now initiate contact, soothing and ministering to the men's bodies, touching hands, stroking hair. Empowered to care for the men, the woman finally have an avenue for the tactile expression of caring that was denied to them previously.[8]

This chapter will show how Austen maps out networks of care in *Persuasion* (1817), while Charlotte Yonge extends such care communities to a remarkable degree in *The Clever Woman of the Family* (1865). These authors use the physically disabled body to pull characters into relations of mutual care centered on a person who needs nursing. It is not a society consisting of rational individuals occasionally colliding while pursuing self-interested goals. Indeed, when such men turn up in these novels, they are criminalized. (Familiar marriage fears men who act according to our mainstream theories of marital behavior, whether they are squires trying to perpetuate their class, cousins trying to trade women in primitive-marriage ways, or *Homo economicus* trying to maximize self-interest.) This pattern of care communities extends, as we shall see, through novels by Dickens, Gaskell, and Craik. But this chapter ends with *The Mill on the Floss* (1860), which I argue instantiates a significant revision of the genre of disabled marriage. The novel no longer presents a disabled man's body as a social opportunity for networks of care; instead, Philip Wakem becomes a pathological case study. George Eliot, both the foremost advocate of relationality in the Victorian novel and the most profound liberal novelist, brings these opposing worlds together. While keenly appreciating the sociality of disabled caring, Eliot nonetheless implacably relegates it to the past. In modernity, everyone is an isolated being, and disability is a matter for diagnostic intervention, not an opportunity for communal kindliness.

I do want to stress that disabled marriage, like all forms of familiar marriage, is a literary construct. Real women certainly did marry disabled men during this period—as real women obviously did marry cousins and older squires—but it would certainly be dangerous to assume that such unions always delivered the communal satisfactions afforded their fictional exemplars. A case for the real-world benefits of disabled marriage could probably be made, but only after significant immersion in private documents of the period, and even then, individual experiences probably differed considerably depending on class, region, and personalities. Thus it is safer, and truer, to read these social marriages as imagined worlds rather than a reflection of lived experience. Indeed, the fact that a culture would dream of marrying disabled men is itself fascinating enough to require its own treatment.

Extraordinary Victorian Bodies

Victorian fiction uses certain conventions for disabled representation, and some of these ways of describing the body may seem strange to us.[9] Modern disability studies generally assumes what Robert McRuer has labelled "compulsory able-bodiedness," in which able-bodiedness is the norm, the unmarked case, and any divergence from that norm is problematic.[10] Indeed, McRuer, Tobin Siebers, and Ato Quayson—three of the deftest contemporary theorists of disability—all perform their analysis of disability from the premise that the disabled body is customarily regarded as socially and physically inferior.[11] But this was not necessarily the case in fiction of the nineteenth century, where disability and illness are consistently associated with social success.[12]

In this chapter, I look at any condition that invited care, without making the distinctions common in contemporary disability theory among illness, physical disability, sensory impairment, cognitive disability, acute trauma, and chronic conditions. There are two good reasons for including a broad range of conditions. First, in the Victorian imagination, these categories were not necessarily distinct. When someone was lying on a sickbed with a fever, it was not necessarily clear whether it was the fever itself that disabled her or whether her illness arose from some deeper injury, invisible in the days before X-rays. Moreover, for Victorians, it was not easy to predict whether physical disabilities might be short-term or permanent, while cognitive and emotional conditions were understood in ways that diverge significantly from our lexicon.[13] It makes little sense to limit ourselves to one type if our subjects understood impairments differently. Second, ethics of care focuses on the way one cares for others, without much regard to what specifically provokes the care. Thus the theory encourages a radical reassignment of our perspective. In ethics of care, we shift away from diagnosing the cared-for's body, reorienting toward the relationship between carer and cared-for. Instead of asking what is wrong with a person, we ask how care relations operate in that person's life. In discussing, say, illness and trauma, I do not treat them as fundamentally distinct experiences but rather as sometimes-overlapping ways to produce certain kinds of care.

Generally speaking, illness in Victorian fiction tended to provoke tender social relations, particularly when the sick person was bedridden and confined to the sickroom. For men and women, "the consoling community of the sickroom" was a special space that allowed acknowledgment and satisfaction of one's bodily appetites, personal relationships, and individual needs.[14] Joe nurses Pip in *Great Expectations* so tenderly that Pip can remark, "I feel thankful that I have been ill."[15] Similarly, Mr. Rochester, Romney Leigh, and Arthur Clennam suffer from fevers that burn out the remnants of their pride and allow them to reaffirm their love for the humble person who might nurse them.[16] The sickroom fostered ties that normally had no chance to form if a man was bent on the competitive, self-interested work of economic success. Indeed, because the traumatic illnesses destroy the men's careers, they are nursed into convalescence by people who nurse them for love, not money, a more emotionally authentic relation.

Sometimes the carers can become acolytes; Victorian fiction has many saintly dying women, whose nurses regard their patients with loving appreciation.[17] Illness allows the cared-for and the carer to express their mutual feelings, and it strengthens social ties that ordinary life had eroded. In much Victorian fiction, "the nurse-patient bond effectively supplants marriage as the preferred means to formal closure and societal consolidation," writes Miriam Bailin.[18] It is carework that expresses patient, continuous love of the other. However, such sustained care is also true when the cared-for has a long-term physical disability; in this regard, chronic incapacitation, whether caused by disease or disablement, is the key to ongoing care. Such an ongoing situation enmeshes the person in complex ongoing relations with multiple carers over time. Two people, bound together in tender ministrations over decades, is not unlike a marriage.

While carers in realist fiction are often deeply attached, in other types of fiction the carer and cared-for may relate in terms of mutual entertainment. This is especially evident in the case of Dickens's "grotesques," descended from the carnival or the freak show, in which the disabled individual proudly displays the body for others' enjoyment. Although today we would deplore this kind of voyeuristic gaze, disabled subjects like Phil Squod in *Bleak House* relish attention.[19] Minor characters like Phil often evince an overpowering sense of gratitude, a passionate loyalty, even love, toward the able-bodied main character who befriended the "freak."[20] While these characters are not usually involved in marital plots themselves, Melissa Free argues that their function is to facilitate the heteronormative marriage plot from which they themselves are debarred.[21] Miss Mowcher in *David Copperfield*, Jenny Wren in *Our Mutual Friend*, and Miserrimus Dexter in *The Law and the Lady* mediate between their friends and the persons they love, relaying messages and offering hints. They form a crucial part of the main character's social network.

Nursing bound people together, much like kinship, but—importantly—it was an elective form that could override and correct the bonds of biology. Bailin explains:

> Nurses and patients may be parents and children, masters and servants, husbands and wives, lover and friends, but these particularized forms of relationship are subsumed under the generic roles and functions which

> illness prescribes. The nurse-patient relation preserves and intensifies the significance of familial and communal ties, but refigures them as immune to the economic, political, or sexual considerations that complicate and distort those ties outside of the sickroom enclave.[22]

In fact, nursing often appears in fiction when a character loses family; for instance, through nursing, the orphaned Romola and Ruth make new bonds, winning love through their selfless devotion to others.[23] Disabled marriage thus functions as an elective form of the older familial network. "Often, rather than reuniting kin, illness summons a society suited to one's own specifications and substitutes for the coercions of blood and marriage a physical tie as voluntary as friendship and as essential as survival."[24]

Caretaking also had an advantage in that it constituted an alternative form of physical contact that could be initiated by the female caregiver. Where cousin marriages in fiction often simply ignored the question of sex, disability marriages allowed readers to imagine another kind of feeling. Instead of the stark choice of either responding to or refusing male sexual overtures, the woman now could generate touch herself, in a different way. When Rochester is able-bodied, for instance, Jane complains about his sexual aggression: "His hand was ever hunting mine, vigorously, and [I] thrust it back to him, red with the passionate pressure."[25] However, once Rochester is disabled, Jane can trim Rochester's hair and cut his nails, a form of intimate physical management that would have been out of the question before his accident. As Bailin notes, "sexual passion is transformed into what Charlotte Brontë calls in *Villette* 'the passion of solicitude' and to the bodily intensities of convalescence."[26] Similarly, in *Our Mutual Friend*, Lizzie Hexam tries to evade Eugene Wrayburn's careless, domineering pursuit, but when he is severely hurt, Lizzie can initiate contact: she places her hand upon his and draws her arm under his head.[27] Lizzie and Jane touch in caring ways, marking an end to the kind of harassment that has forced each woman to flee earlier in the novel. Bronwyn Rivers explains that "the nurse is required to engage in intimate bodily observation—a directive contrasting the prohibition on such intimacies in the outside world—and thus learns a language foreign to mere visitors to the sickroom."[28] Intimacy provides a different somatic vocabulary for Victorian women, one that makes them less vulnerable to predation. And because both Eugene Wrayburn and Rochester continue to experience physical and sensory impairments after they leave the sickroom, the caring marital relationships that nursing initiates will continue.

It is important to recognize that disabled men in Victorian fiction experience nursing as an *additional* form of contact, not a *replacement* for some kind of lost, castrated sexuality. Rochester, for instance, has not been desexualized.

His immediate reaction to suspecting Jane's presence is to grope her body. He is as sexually aggressive as he ever was, a fact that certainly complicates readings of Rochester as symbolically castrated. Collins's Miserrimus Dexter kisses his female visitor with burning lips and wraps his arms around her waist. Romney Leigh journeys to Aurora's home in order to propose to her. Eugene is desperate to marry Lizzie.

Indeed, in nineteenth-century fiction, male disabled bodies are often hypersexualized rather than desexualized. For every angelically weak child, there is a perversely powerful male dwarf. For every Tiny Tim, we have a Quilp, or a Miserrimus Dexter, or indeed a Sir Richard Calmady.[29] Female disabled bodies are also sexualized. As Martha Stoddard Holmes points out, quite often the disabled woman is "too feeling, too expressive, and potentially too sexual for matrimony."[30] Mobility seems to have been a key variable; characters whose disabilities immobilize them can evoke loving caregiving, but people who retain independent movement seem to have achieved heightened sexual appeal. Somatic markers like dueling scars or Byron's club foot draw attention to the body and such characters might even have unusual physical prowess or exceptional musculature to enable mobility in spite of the apparent impairment.

The caregiver's acquaintance with the rhythm of symptoms, the intimacy of pain, and the constraints of capability create bodily familiarity without necessarily generating sensuality. Sensuality can coexist with caretaking; caretaking does not replace but runs parallel to it. It is the pleasure of having this alternative that the de-eroticized disabled plot makes possible. By assuming that a traumatic injury constitutes a symbolic castration, we unthinkingly buy into a contemporary assumption that disabled people have (or should have) no sexuality.[31] We also use an anachronistic notion of marriage centered on erotic attraction. But the Victorian novel allows marriage to center on other ties and imagines bodies commanding multiple responses. Oversimplifying disabled marriage as a scene of deprivation or sacrifice imposes reductive (and ablist) modern assumptions on a period that actually entertained a touchingly rich range of possibilities about love.

Ethics of Care

In the last few decades, theorists have begun to outline something that looks like a good explanation for the Victorian disabled marriage. "Ethics of care" theory (part of a way of thinking called "relational ethics") is founded on the belief is that everyone needs others—most obviously in infancy, in old age, and in periods of disability—and everyone has a right to receive as well as give care. Thus instead of imagining individuals engaged in rational social-contract making with equal peers, we need to imagine human beings as profoundly interdependent. Virginia Held contrasts caring relations with "the splendid independence, self-sufficiency, and easy isolation of the traditional liberal ideal of the autonomous rational agent."[32] From a Victorian point of view, this might well mean a contrast between a dangerously autonomous individual and a safely organic community.

Ethics of care was first explored by Carol Gilligan in *In a Different Voice* (1982) and then given fuller development by Nel Noddings in her 1984 book *Caring: A Feminine Approach to Ethics and Moral Education.* Noddings often identifies caring with parenting, teaching, and nursing relationships. However, she also sees it as the primary ground of moral relations. Noddings writes that "the relation of natural caring will be identified as the human condition that we, consciously or unconsciously, perceive as 'good.' It is that condition toward which we long and strive, and it is our longing for caring—to be in that special relation—that provides the motivation for us to be moral."[33] Although caretaking is hard work, it is also, Noddings claims, profoundly rewarding to be using one's energy to help a person one cares for: "I *care*, and that means that my consciousness is turned to the cared-for. I have little need to reflect on this consciousness, and I may be but dimly aware of a euphoria, ranging from a mild 'all's well' to ecstasy, that accompanies my activity with the cared-for."[34] Eva Feder Kittay agrees that "precisely because of the significance of both affect and trust in these relations, the ties formed by relations of dependency are among the most important ones we experience. It often seems that to infuse caring labor into such a relationship . . . relaxes our own boundaries of self, which makes way for a emotional bond that is especially potent."[35] Such connections offer the deepest experience of goodness that we can achieve.

Ethics of care allows us to look at disability without being dogged by our culture's often counterproductive stress on autonomy.[36] "Our culture's excessive emphasis on independence leads to a frustrated and frustrating belief by both parties that at least an illusion of independence for the disabled person must be maintained regardless of the expense to the quality of her relationship with the one or ones on whom she depends."[37] Barbara Hillyer asks why we see dependency as problematic when in fact we are all dependent on others, and all we can do to repay this is to be ready to give help to others in turn.[38]

Such skepticism about autonomy is "an exciting development in ethical theorizing," writes Susan Wendell. "I believe that if everyone with a disability is to be integrated fully into my society, without being 'the Other' who symbolizes moral failure, then social ideals must change in the direction of acknowledging the realities of our interdependence and the value of depending on others and being depended upon."[39] In this theory, what now makes the disabled extraordinary would then constitute their claim to representativeness. For if "being human" is defined as "that which needs help," then the disabled become the clearest type of humanness. They are not the exception; they are the exemplar.

Care ethicists try to formulate the theory in a way that prevents the exploitation of the carer. Noddings insists that nobody is perpetually a carer; everyone must learn to care and to receive care. "Parties are not stuck in their positions as carers or cared fors. As carer I contribute in one way to the relation, as cared for, in a different way . . . this requires each of us to be sensitive cared fors (to accept gifts joyfully without always trying to cancel the debt) as well as responsible carers."[40] Care must be mutual, Kittay stresses, whether or not a severely disabled individual can be the one to return care. Instead, she advocates "a chain of obligation linking members of a community"; neighbors, friends, family, even passers-by should be willing to respond to anyone who needs care.[41] This crucial idea of the community of care allows care relations to extend beyond a particular dyad, and instead to characterize a local way of life.

Real care demands "motivational displacement": helping the cared-for do what he or she wants, not necessarily what the carer might want.[42] Noddings warns us to avoid "the projection of one's own personality into the personality of another in order to understand him better; intellectual identification of oneself with another."[43] Care relations need to leave a space between the carer and the cared-for, allowing for respect, difference, even conflict. Noddings cites the definition of "sympathy" from physics: "a relation of harmony between bodies of such a nature that vibrations in one cause sympathetic vibrations in the other."[44] This does not mean merging into one, or a community enforcing its values upon an unwilling recipient, but thinking and moving sympathetically.

The problem is that in contemporary, urbanized Western culture, most people do not live in nurturing small communities whose members have leisure to recall and repay moral debts with a fine reciprocity, nor are we always able to offer care to those we love. Ethics of care remains somewhat utopian in a society that regards caretaking as a labor-intensive, self-sacrificing, low-status exhausting chore often performed by vulnerable low-income and migrant workers. There is little discourse in our contemporary culture that values the work done by these nurses, nannies, and aides.[45] We exalt independency, and we tend to regard dependency as a mark of shame.

But there is one place where an ethics of care is not just a naïve hope. There is one place where people are bound into small communities observing one another's behavior; where vast numbers of the population have no gainful employment and therefore have leisure to care for one another; where caretaking is profoundly approved of; and where nursing occurs within the home, not the institution. That place is the Victorian novel. "3 or 4 Families in a Country Village is the very thing to work on," not only in novels, but also, as it turns out, in ethics of care.[46]

If we want to see ethics of care in action, we should visit St. Ogg's, Cranford, or Highbury.

Critics have recognized this special relationship. Brigid Lowe writes that "the mid-Victorian realist novel is the medium par excellence for an exposition of a sympathetic politics of care, and an effective vehicle for the perpetuation of the conditions for its realization."[47] Martha Stoddard Holmes agrees that Victorian women's novels specifically "narrate the human situation as one of sequential and sometimes nested dependencies, through plots and characterization that normalize and valorize relationships built on vulnerability and need. While dyads of care are a common character development structure, ensemble plots construct disability as a feature of community life . . . Thematically, the fictions engage disability as a force that brings people into a wide range of complex relationships, transforming social institutions like marriage in the process."[48] Not only do Victorian novels exemplify a politics of care, but, as Stoddard Holmes writes, they use the narrative structures that care suggests to transform social structures.

Disability marriages could generate the kind of *Gemeinschaft* for which Victorians yearned. As we have seen, neighbor marriage assumed that a neighborhood centered on the squire constituted a satisfying sort of community. But the disability marriage plot offers an alternative view of communal life. It pays attention to the specific daily acts—the gifts, the words, the physical help—afforded by one person to another. It imagines an intimate, ongoing, everyday interrelationship. The persons in such a care relation need not be related to each other. Anyone can offer care, regardless of gender, age, or status; relationships are formed through the performance of care acts, not through the essential identity of participants. A care community can be composed of a military regiment, or the tenants of a boarding house, or those who encounter each other by chance in Chancery or the Inns of Court.

Ideally, such a close-knit bond would generate loving helpfulness on the carer's part and grateful affection on the cared-for's part. However, Victorian fictions also show care ethics gone wrong, in which care becomes abusive, carers are exhausted, and cared-fors are resentful. When parenting, teaching, and nursing relationships sour, the result is not so much an organic community as a situation of mutual imprisonment. And one of the most important functions of such scenes in Victorian fiction is to show the ways care can go astray.

This craving for a kindly community of care is particularly acute if the woman is isolated—deprived of a home, a family, and social ties. In a neighbor marriage, the woman is often threatened with imminent homelessness, but she generally marries the squire before she actually loses her home. In a cousin marriage, the woman is often embedded in a dysfunctionally conflicted family, but her endogamous union reconciles the warring branches. The woman of the disability marriage, however, has often already lost it all. Jane Eyre, Lizzie Hexam, John Halifax, Ruth Hilton, Amy Dorrit, Caroline Helstone are without relations or friends; they are orphaned, homeless, and estranged from any guardians they may have.[49] The orphan recovers from this devastatingly dangerous solitude by finding a new network. Those who don't have the luck to collapse on the doorstep of heretofore unknown cousins, or to bewitch the local gentry, do it through nursing: Eugene Wrayburn, Phineas Fletcher, Thurstan Benson, Arthur Clennam in his fever, Robert Moore when injured by the rioters. To enter a marriage that is entirely enmeshed in care ethics means that the couple "went down into a modest life of usefulness and happiness. Went down to give a mother's care, in the fulness of time, to Fanny's neglected children no less than to their own, and to leave that lady going into Society for ever and a day. Went down to give a tender nurse and friend to Tip for some few years."[50] In this story, to marry is not to propel oneself forward but to return to the perennial needs of others; lonely orphans achieve the emotional pleasures of being needed and appreciated; outsiders become thoroughly, intimately, enmeshed.

If these are not all marriages in a legal sense, they function narratively like marriages, with deep affective ties and lifelong cohabitation. The absence of a legal marriage tie makes us readers stress their ongoing daily relationality rather than their erotic desire. Indeed, this lack of marriage in so many disabled marriage plots is meaningful: it signals the difficulty of correlating an increasingly romanticized notion of marriage with the care relations around disability, but it also frees authors to imagine alternative relations, radically democratic, same-sex, and unusual unions that cut across normative gender and age and class lines. The nonmarital nature of most disabled unions is therefore both progressive and disturbing; it indicates that marriage was evolving in a way that felt incompatible with the qualities of gratitude, love, and care that a nursing relationship highlighted, but it also allows readers to imagine situations in which such affective relations could flourish outside heteronormative pairs.

John Halifax, Gentleman—*and Others*

Dinah Mulock Craik's wildly popular *John Halifax, Gentleman* (1856) tells the inspirational story of how a penniless, starving orphan, John Halifax, becomes a wealthy magistrate. *John Halifax, Gentleman* is generally read as an allegory of the ideal Victorian masculinity, a novel that "openly extols the values of self-help and economic individualism."[51] Yet John is not an isolated being making decisions in his own self-interest. Rather, his famous intensely homoerotic lifelong relationship with the crippled Phineas Fletcher gives John the personal and professional help he needs.[52] *John Halifax, Gentleman* demonstrates just how much a union with a disabled subject can benefit both partners. Rather remarkably, it manages to be the ultimate allegory of both the self-made man and the relational self, simultaneously and in the same character.

John's relationship with Phineas can be seen as a quasi-marital partnership, inasmuch as it involves a lifetime of cohabitation and shared property as well as mutual love. As we have seen, familiar marriage can include cohabiting sibling pairs that are not technically married, like Tom and Ruth Pinch in *Martin Chuzzlewit*, Marianne and Elinor in *Sense and Sensibility*, Tom and Maggie Tulliver in *The Mill on the Floss*, and Felix and Geraldine in Yonge's *The Pillars of the House*. Familiar couplehood can also include a cared-for and a carer: Ruth and Mr. Benson, Clennam and Little Dorrit, Jenny Wren and Lizzie Hexam. John and Phineas are a similar pair. Disabled unions are not usually explicitly marital. Sometimes the disabled man expresses love openly, but the woman shrinks from the union and the man may consider himself debarred from marriage. This is the case with Ralph Touchett and Isabel Archer, Philip Wakem and Maggie Tulliver, and Duke (Viscount Fordham) and Barbara Brownlow in Yonge's *The Magnum Bonum* (1879). In such unconsummated relationships, marriage is replaced by an intensified adoration, a passion of tenderness that imbues the couple with an almost unbearable affective charge. This is also true of John and Phineas, whose love for each other is the most profound feeling of the novel.

In fact John and Phineas are socially and psychologically typical, not unusual, for a disabled marriage pair. John is a homeless orphan, craving the companionship afforded by the invalid's circle. Phineas has a father and a nurse but feels somewhat estranged from them. Thus both boys are ready to adopt one another. John has recently lost his mother when he meets Phineas, and Phineas—an older, weaker, loving person who teaches and cares for John—takes on a quasi-maternal function. At the same time, John, who is taller and stronger, carries Phineas around like an infant. Nursing, argues Bailin, reconstructs a shattered self in terms of "a reassuring relation to others—a relation which explicitly evokes the attachment of parent and child."[53] They call each other "my brother," showing how disabled marriage can provide the elective affiliations that its members lack in their biological kin.

Although I read John and Phineas's relationship as a form of familiar marriage, Karen Bourrier offers an important argument about the narrative function this pair serves in *The Measure of Manliness: Disability and Masculinity in the Mid-Victorian Novel*. Bourrier claims that the disabled man's sensitive nerves make him the emotional center of the mid-Victorian novel. He is able to articulate feelings for the strong, taciturn man of business. Phineas Fletcher affectionately narrates *John Halifax, Gentleman*, just as Arthur softens Tom Brown's school progress. Even Tom Tulliver is paired (against his own will) with the sensitive, imaginative Philip Wakem, and the unbending Caspar Goodwood becomes the last attendant on the dying Ralph Touchett. The hard businessman of the nineteenth century requires such an affectionate interpreter, made sensitive by his disability, if the reader is to sympathize with him.

In the disabled marriage plot, or in Bourrier's friend pairs, the partner not only provides emotional focalization but also contributes a social network. Whereas John is a rootless stranger, with neither family nor friends, Phineas is deeply established in the town of Norton Bury and shares with John his own social status, career prospects, and connections (including Phineas's father and ex-nurse, who go on to give John substantive assistance). As Colella puts it, "broadly speaking, Halifax gets a chance to prove his worth in the capitalist game because Phineas has willingly opted out."[54] Phineas rents a room for John; tutors him in reading and math; and gets John a job in his father's tannery, eventually engineering John's rise to become the head of the business. Meanwhile, John gives Phineas the emotionally meaningful gift of affectionate attention: carrying him up stairs, pushing his carriage, taking him on outings, and generally bringing "into my pale life the only brightness it had ever known."[55] As a result of John's nursing, "sickness did not now take that heavy, overpowering grip of me, mind and body, that it once used to do. It never did when John was by. He gave me strength, mentally and physically. He was life and health to me, with his brave cheerfulness" (124).

After cherishing Phineas, John uses nursing as the template for his most intense adult relationships. His method of courting Ursula March follows this model. John helps her through her father's final illness and death, and his first lover's kiss is on "that wrist which was hurt" (189). Separated from Ursula by class difference, he comes down with a wasting fever and a "soul-sickness" which will make him die unless Ursula intervenes (212–218). Thus Ursula's first visit to John is as a nurse, and their mutual care provides the kindness that would normally have come from relatives; as John declares when ratifying their engagement, "we have no parents, neither she nor I" (226). Nursing also characterizes John's fathering. His beloved daughter, Muriel, is blind, and his care for her both expresses and enhances his love. Muriel's colorlessly angelic nature and somewhat unmotivated decline make her into a generic icon of childhood (she is simply called "sister" or "the child") that functions to show up John's fatherhood. To be a father is to be a nurse; to show John as a good father therefore requires a sick child whom he can nurse.

Thus this supposedly self-made, autonomous man has to meld with disabled partners in order to get what he needs at every point in his life. As a teenager, he needs to enter into relations of mutual care with Phineas; as a young marriageable man, he needs to care for Ursula and have her nurse him in turn; and as a mature father, he needs to comfort his dying daughter. John's virtues become visible through such relations. Modern readers may regard Ursula's healed cut as quite a different situation from a child's blindness and a friend's chronic illness. But these differences do not matter for the kind of disability narrative that *John Halifax* exemplifes. As long as John can act as nurse, any disabling incident serves his need. John receives not only emotional reinforcement but also pragmatic benefits from offering care. His quasi-marital relationship with Phineas gets him a career; his marriage with Ursula brings him the money to buy the mills that make his fortune; and his nursing of blind Muriel teaches him how to be a good master to his workmen, since the workers accept steam power in the mill, "partly owing to their strong impression of Mr. Halifax's goodness as a father, and the vague, almost superstitious interest which attached to the pale, sweet face of Muriel" (334).

John Halifax, Gentleman does not show how to be a self-made man. In fact, it shows that one cannot be a self-made man. To find a novel in which an upwardly mobile man succeeds by cutting his emotional ties, we must go back much earlier. We must learn to read Mr. Elliot.

Mrs. Smith and Mr. Elliot

Jane Austen's last completed novel, *Persuasion* (1818), has an "autumnal" quality—its attention to ill health, fading, and suffering—that paradoxically makes it a significant innovation.[56] Whereas *Mansfield Park* knits its heroine into a loving network through cousin marriage, *Persuasion* does it through disability marriage. In this novel Austen imagines how affliction can increase affection, and she rejects those who embody the atomized individualism usually seen as the marker of modernity. Anne and Wentworth, who nurse, are rewarded; Mrs. Clay and Mr. Elliot, who do not, are demonized. Anne is the typical isolate of the disability marriage, enduring unsatisfactory consanguineous ties and craving congenial company. When estranged from Wentworth, Anne gazes longingly at his fellow officers. "'These would have been all my friends,' was her thought; and she had to struggle against a great tendency to lowness."[57] Monica Cohen points out that in this scene, "company substitutes for property." Anne Elliot longs for social ties in having refused Wentworth, unlike her predecessor Lizzie Bennet, who covets Pemberley.[58] Both are forms of familiar marriage, but Lizzie's centers on the power of the manager of the estate, while Anne's dwells on the pleasures of a network of friends.

As with *Mansfield Park*, modern readers often find themselves baffled by a key element in the supposedly triumphant union. Just as we have trouble reading *Mansfield Park*'s cousin marriage outside the lens of incest, critics often have difficulty comprehending why *Persuasion*'s final union needs to be mediated by an outsider, Mrs. Smith. Modern readers tend to find this kind of union revolting rather than triumphant. Sexual consummation in marriage, we feel, should be reserved for a pair who fulfill rather precise criteria; they cannot be too close in consanguinity or upbringing (the problem of *Mansfield Park*), but they also cannot be so distant that others are included in their marital decisions (and this is the issue in *Persuasion*). If *Mansfield Park*'s couple is too tightly sealed, *Persuasion*'s couple is too porous to the outside world. Marc Cyr goes so far as to accuse Mrs. Smith of having "actively pimped for the man [Mr. Elliot]" and sums up that "what she *meant* to do was prostitute Anne for financial gain."[59] However, Cyr's reading is just as anachronistic as the incest accusation in *Mansfield Park*. Cyr's accusation assumes that *Persuasion*'s characters are pursuing marriage as an intimate erotic partnership, in which an outsider's intervention is scandalous. But they are, in fact, pursuing marriage as the constitution of a beneficial social network. Mrs. Smith is not an outsider organizing someone else's intimate life for her own selfish needs, for she is already part of any marital arrangement involving Anne. She is, after all, the dowry Anne brings to the match, one of the few friends Anne can present to Wentworth in return for his wealth of connections. The Mrs. Smith episode climaxes and finalizes the sociality that Austen has been propounding throughout the novel—and it is crucial that Austen does so through a disabled woman.

We can see how innovative *Persuasion*'s treatment of caretaking is if we compare it to a novel published just two decades earlier, Fanny Burney's *Camilla*, which has an idealized disabled woman rewarded with marriage.[60] In *Camilla*, Eugenia is loved *in spite of* her appearance. Her short stature, her pockmarked face, and her hobbled leg are merely physical coverings concealing her lovely soul. Nor do characters have to take care of her physically; she experiences no pain or weakness as a result of her condition.[61] Thus Eugenia's disability acts as a filter that allows us to separate the shallow characters from the virtuous ones; only good characters can see her real qualities beneath the unattractive appearance.

In *Persuasion*, disability is neither limited to a single person nor is it a physical envelope concealing a precious soul. Rather, most characters experience intermittent periods of weakness. Courtship is conducted through alleviating others' suffering, and friendships are formed through mutual assistance. As John Wiltshire comments, "illness then features in the novels of Austen as a mode of social circulation."[62]

Anne is constantly nursing connections who are emotionally or physically unwell: her querulous sister, Mary; her nephew with his broken collarbone; the grieving Captain Benwick; and Louisa with her head injury. The capacity to care for others propels Anne into different locales and imbues her with value.

The nephew's tumble, of course, prefigures Louisa's fall, the central event of the novel.[63] When Louisa falls, Wentworth exclaims, "If Anne will stay, no one so proper, so capable as Anne!" He pleads to her directly, "'You will stay, I am sure; you will stay and nurse her;' cried he, turning to her and speaking with a glow, and yet a gentleness, which seemed almost restoring the past" (106). This thrilling moment marks his returning love. As Wiltshire explains, "it is precisely as a nurse that she values herself most and is most valued by those around her."[64]

If Anne is a superlative nurse, Wentworth is her match.[65] Wentworth's fellow-feeling for a body in pain leads him to nurse Captain Benwick. He "never left the poor fellow for a week; that's what he did, and nobody else could have saved poor James" (101). Wentworth cares for Anne when she is weary, once by detaching a clinging toddler and once by placing her into a carriage. As she notes, "he could not see her suffer, without the desire of giving her relief," a warm impulse that, although neither consciously acknowledges it, constitutes his covert courtship (84). In these scenes Wentworth is acutely aware of Anne's body, not in an erotic sense but rather as a body akin to his own—a body that can be tired, worn, and hurt, and that he springs to relieve from an emotion of sympathy.[66]

Anne and Wentworth are fitted for each other by their exceptional capacities to care for others, and their social circle is formed by others with similarly empathetic responses to pain. The time in Lyme knits all of Louisa's nurses closely and focuses intensely affective emotions on the subject of that care: "Mrs. Harville and [Mary] quite agree that [they] love [Louisa] the better for having nursed her" (155). Such love particularly affects Anne: "Mrs. Musgrove's real affection had been won by her usefulness when they were in distress. It was a heartiness, and a warmth, and a sincerity which Anne delighted in the more, from the sad want of such blessings at home" (207). Given the isolate's lack of consanguineal ties, nursing is a priceless alternative opportunity for forming tender bonds. As Anne herself comments, "when pain is over, the remembrance of it often becomes a pleasure. One does not love a place the less for having suffered in it" (173).

For Anne's home offers the opposite of the warm sociality of these caretaking circles. The Elliot family offers a parody of caretaking values. Obsessed with cosmetically pleasing exteriors, Sir Walter and Elizabeth assess beauty instead of evaluating the person's somatic condition, cataloguing freckles instead of feebleness. They pursue patronage instead of mutual interdependency. The Darymples and the Elliots have only the most attenuated, intermittent, and formal sense of cousinship. Mr. Elliot and the Elliot family, similarly, have been estranged for years, although they are cousins. They enact a cold version of the cousinship that is practiced as a warm relationship between the Musgroves and the Hayters.[67] The sibling adoration that provides the model of a viable relationship for the characters of *Mansfield Park* is absent from *Persuasion*, in which sororal relations among the Elliot sisters are indifferent at best and the novel has no interest in improving them. There is no need for reparative familial unions, because the familial impulse can be provided through carework instead.

Persuasion flirts with such a plot in imagining a cousin marriage between Anne and Mr. Elliot. Indeed, Anne is momentarily "bewitched" by Lady Russell's vision: "You are your mother's self in countenance and disposition; and if I might be allowed to fancy you such as she was, in situation, and name, and home, presiding and blessing in the same spot, and only superior to her in being more highly valued!" (150). Lady Russell articulates an older idea of marriage, in which a good spousal choice is characterized by birth, money, and status, and a union reinforces the family. But Anne, while not entirely endorsing romantic marriage, nonetheless is aware that in the modern world, a conjugal prospect must be judged on the basis of personal qualities, not preexisting position. Wentworth's self-made man qualities—his confidence, courage, and eagerness—make him a good prospect in a world in which fortunes can be made and not just inherited.[68] In Mr. Elliot's case, it takes Anne only a moment to realize that "she never could accept him" (150). This is a novel that forms its ties through care, not through kin, and the rejection of Mr. Elliot reinforces this preference for affiliative rather than biological networks. Although technically related, Mr. Elliot and Anne have no qualities or memories in common that would make it a true familiar marriage; she is in fact far more familiar with the exogamous Captain Wentworth, whose feelings she can intuit without even a glance.

Mr. Elliot is worthy to be the heir of Sir Walter because he has the same kind of self-regard as his family head. When appointed as executor of Mr. Smith's will, he categorically "would not act" (196). His letters "all breathed the same stern resolution of not engaging in a fruitless trouble, and, under a cold civility, the same hard-hearted indifference to any of the evils it might bring on her" (196). In this respect Mr. Elliot is a perfect example of *Homo economicus*, the crudely self-interested caricature of the liberal subject. If Anne represents unselfish caretaking of others, Mr. Elliot embodies the opposite: self-regard without caring for anyone else's interest. No wonder the two cannot mate.

Captain Wentworth, however, is also initially drawn to the *Homo economicus* model. When Wentworth famously exhorts Louisa to admire a hazelnut, he notes that the nut has "not a puncture, not a weak spot any where," and, "my first wish for all, whom I am interested in, is that they should be firm" like the nut (81). This view, intriguingly, resembles a liberal ideal of personhood, as described by Mary Midgeley:

> This model shows human society as a spread of standard social atoms, originally distinct and independent, each of which combines with others

> only at its own choice and in its own private interests. This model is drawn from physics, and from seventeenth-century physics at that, where the ultimate particles of matter were conceived as hard, impenetrable, homogenous little billiard balls, with no hooks or internal structure. To see how such atoms could combine at all was very hard.[69]

To be "firm" is all very well, but how might a hazelnut melt, yield, unite with another? Wentworth, adhering to this atomistic view, cannot imagine a social, let alone a marital, kind of contact—he can only imagine "firm" resistance to others. It is no wonder that he later claims he was surprised that everyone interpreted his behavior to Louisa as a suitor's; by embracing the "nut" model, he loses his capacity to understand interaction.

It makes sense that Wentworth is powerfully drawn to the language of self-determination. As we saw in Chapter 3, Austen's men tend to enact modernity and mobility, as compared with the more static and familially entrenched women. Wentworth, however, has a particular emotional attachment to this story of autonomy. As Susan F. Feiner explains, autonomous narratives "carry foward the humanist project in which Man (the conscious, knowing, unified, and rational subject) is the master of his fate"—a very good description of how Wentworth wishes to view his life, and an explanation for his rage when Anne dares to frustrate his intentions.[70] This is the narrative Wentworth likes to tell about himself. But his real interest is in an ethic of care.

We see this layering when Wentworth narrates his career to the Musgroves. On the one hand, it is a self-made man's story: he is hardworking and deserving, thus he made captain early and got good ships. This story is confirmed by the public record of the naval list that the group is studying. But elements of Wentworth's narrative complicate this apparently triumphant progress, offering a more private, experiential, care-based history. His first ship, the Asp, was "quite worn out and broken up. I was the last man who commanded her.—Hardly fit for service then" (60). When his listeners exclaim, however, Wentworth recalibrates his language. "Ah! she was a dear old Asp to me. She did all that I wanted. I knew she would" (61). His affectionate nostalgia for the ship in spite, or because, of its bad condition, shows something other than self-interest. A fully self-made man could not afford to be tenderly loving to older, damaged, unwanted female bodies, whether belonging to ships or suitors. Wentworth's tenderness toward broken bodies indicates his fitness for a narrative of mutually caring stasis instead of (or as well as) one of self-achievement.

Like Wentworth, Anne is a transitional figure, attracted to modern discourses yet unwilling to relinquish traditional ways of thinking. Eight years previously, Anne implicitly obeyed her parental figure in dictating her engagement. But the early nineteenth century, this period of acute change in marital ethics, has altered Anne too, and she now feels, in tune with the emerging cultural consensus, that her marriage is her own personal choice. Anne's agonized attempts to work out her personal preferences versus her duty to Lady Russell offer us a snapshot of the confusion during this intensely transitional period of marriage history. Both Anne and Wentworth are tortured by changing mores: Just how much self-interest was permitted, and how much duty to one's social network? While Anne says she was right to obey Lady Russell, the entire novel betrays her covert insurgency. While Wentworth claims to enact the self-sufficient monadic persona, his acts demonstrate his fundamental allegiance to the needs of others.

Although Wentworth is usually read as the new man of the nineteenth century, the professional who rises by his own meritocratic exertions, it is Mr. Elliot who is truly the new man, the self-interested rational agent. Mrs. Smith says that Elliot is "a designing, wary, cold-blooded being, who thinks only of himself. . . . He has no feeling for others" (187) And Mrs. Clay is his perfect match, with her "self-interested, profit-oriented, and not entirely honest spirit and drive."[71] It is appropriate that these two modern figures end up together, in an alliance that is more of a mutual conspiracy than a sexual bond.

Austen dislikes this monadic persona.[72] Marilyn Butler writes: "In Jane Austen it is the villain who has always in some form or other embodied self-sufficiency, a whole intellectual system of individualism or self-interest that the more social and outward-turning ethic of the novel was designed to counter."[73] Yet Mr. Elliot is not really punished for being "a disingenous, artificial, worldly man, who has never had any better principle to guide him than selfishness" (195). In fact he ends up getting everything Sir Walter wanted: money, the title, Kellynch Hall, and even Mrs. Clay. In *Sense and Sensibility*, Willoughby tries to acquire such coldly driven selfishness, but it is an agonizing misfit with his real drive of ardent pleasure-seeking, so that he achieves material comfort only at the cost of emotional distress. In *Persuasion*, not quite a generation later, the cold new world is one in which such men can thrive without a look backward. It is perhaps because Mr. Elliot represents modern man—and a specifically masculine sensibility, the self-disciplined, self-interested, cool persona required for the industrial magnate—that critics are often anxious to exculpate him. Cyr and Smith ask what is so bad about what Mr. Elliot has done, and indeed, if it is criminal behavior to criticize Sir Walter, pursue pleasure, and appreciate Anne, who is safe?

Only from the point of view of a network of care is Mr. Elliot evil—and so it makes sense that it is Mrs. Smith, the central figure in that network, the person who condemns him most thoroughly. Nameless, almost classless, the poorest figure in the Austen oeuvre, she seems an unlikely candidate to dominate the end of this novel. Yet her prominence is undeniable. As Anne is the center of the love plot, Mrs. Smith is the center of the caretaking plot. Structurally, these two plots appear side by side, as if they are of equal importance.

The nephew's fall is the event of the novel's opening, Louisa's fall is the catastrophe of the novel's center, and Mrs. Smith is the episode of its close. As the sufferers get older, Anne's role in nursing them becomes more abstract—she literally lifts and carries the boy, but she only calls for help for Louisa, and she accepts that Mrs. Smith's physical care will be provided by Nurse Rooke. Similarly, the social circles around each injury become wider. The nephew's social circles comprise his immediate family; Louisa's social circles extend to both her family and her friends (Wentworth, the Harvilles). But Mrs. Smith's social circles are wider still, involving persons who have no idea they are even in relation to her: Mrs. Wallis, Mrs. Clay, Mr. Elliot, the servants and caretakers, the personnel of Bath itself. Thus Austen starts with a small sufferer and a small circle and makes both larger with Louisa in order to broaden both out to a vision of a society linked by networks of information and interest: a whole city.

Mrs. Smith's manners also represent the climax of what other characters do. She presumably supports herself by selling her small handicrafts, although for face-saving reasons she tells Anne she uses them for genteel philanthropy. In this respect she resembles the other characters.[74] Everyone in this novel puts up a façade to conceal real financial needs, beginning with Sir Walter and Elizabeth, who will not admit the need for retrenchment, or Charles Hayter, who presents himself as a gentleman and a scholar even though his family owns only a deteriorating farmstead. Even the sympathetic Harvilles insist on hosting the whole party, refusing to admit their house is too small.

Similarly, Mrs. Smith's reluctance to criticize Mr. Elliot until the very end makes her typical. Anne, the recipient of everyone's confidences, smiles and keeps her own feelings about the Musgroves private ("she could do little more than listen patiently" and counsel forbearance [44]); nor does she criticize Lady Darymple, Mrs. Clay, or Mr. Elliot to her father. In Austen's novels, willingness to criticize another person proves the critic's untrustworthiness, as Elizabeth realizes belatedly about Wickham, or Emma about Frank Churchill; circulating nasty speculations does serious damage. Indeed, Mrs. Smith's bravely swallowing the prospect of Anne's union with Mr. Elliot without a hint of demurral must be seen as proof of her mastery of gentry manners, a gratifying demonstration of her real politeness. The moment Anne's frank admission that she does not care for Mr. Elliot releases Mrs. Smith to be honest; she cannot stop communicating. In this respect, too, Mrs. Smith simply enacts what everyone else in the novel does: respects others' social entanglements.

The worst sufferer, the most helpful caretaker, the most baldly rapacious, the most visibly polite: Mrs. Smith intensifies the currents of social and economic behavior in *Persuasion*. But it is particularly interesting that the way she takes care of Anne is by telling stories. D. A. Miller sees her as a proto-novelist:

> What has come to rescue Mrs. Smith, of course, is not some Captain Wentworth, but her own proto-novelistic love of news, of managing its acquisition and distribution, and most of all, "of telling the whole story her own way" in a world where, as Anne herself has had occasion to note, "men have had every advantage of [women] in telling their own story."[75]

Like any writer, Mrs. Smith uses multiple sources. Here is how she describes the "acquisition and distribution" of her news:

> [The information] does not come to me in quite so direct a line as that; it takes a bend or two, but nothing of consequence. The stream is as good as at first; the little rubbish it collects in the turnings, is easily moved away. Mr. Elliot talks unreservedly to Colonel Wallis . . . [who] has a very pretty silly wife, to whom he tells things which he had better not . . . She, in the overflowing spirits of her recovery, repeats it all to her nurse; and the nurse, knowing my acquaintance with you, very naturally brings it all to me. (192)

But there is nothing "natural" about this; to make this "stream" flow, Mrs. Smith has to do some things that nothing in her class or her life could have prepared her for. She has to be willing to befriend a servant—someone Anne does not even notice when she opens the door (186). She has to invite rather than snub servants' gossip; among Smith's sources are a laundress and a waiter. "*Persuasion* makes room for the ways in which social circles interconnect through invisible channels and accepts that servants and nurses observe shrewdly and can unravel plots," Gillian Beer explains.[76] She has to violate the laws of honor that require confidentiality between male comrades and between husband and wife. If she meticulously follows the rules of polite conversation with Anne, she also reveals herself able to perform the rules of quite other classes, quite other social arrangements—to go undercover, to explore networks of sociality to which nobody else has access. In these ways, Mrs. Smith ceases to represent the other characters—she becomes something new, something like an investigative reporter. And what teaches her this technique is disability. Mrs. Smith explains, "I think differently now; time and sickness, and sorrow, have given me other notions" (189). It is her long experience of requiring care that teaches Mrs. Smith to become a new kind of character.

What Mrs. Smith shows is that the most active, successful social manager of this novel is a disabled, impoverished woman of no name, the most "socially 'reduced' figure in Jane Austen's fiction."[77] She and Mr. Elliot are profoundly opposed to one another. Unlike *Homo economicus*, individualist Mr. Elliot frozen into implacable self-regard, she represents an entirely fluid and networked sensibility that regards class as irrelevant to her needs. And that this care-ethics heroine is a revolutionary one is evident from the amount of critical hostility she has incurred.[78] Critics like Cyr and Smith work to salvage the autonomous self by praising Mr. Elliot and calling Mrs. Smith reprehensible. Yet in *Persuasion*, disability, far from immuring or immobilizing, creates a peculiar form of freedom. It generates love and friendship. It propels the networking of stories, in which information circulates as a linguistic equivalent of what people do in a community of care.

Clever Woman of the Family

Fifty years later, Charlotte Yonge would create a new version of Mrs. Smith: Ermine Williams in *The Clever Woman of the Family* (1865). As we have seen, Yonge was intimately acquainted with Austen's novels and members of Austen's circle, and may well have considered herself Austen's successor in both regional and narrative terms. Just as Yonge intensified Austen's logic of endogamous love in *Heartsease*, so too, in *Clever Woman*, she underlined the virtues of the relational heroine and the evil of the atomistic villain.

Ermine Williams is an updated, professionalized version of Mrs. Smith, someone who can actually make a living from circulating stories. Like Mrs. Smith, Ermine's capacity to communicate actually derives from her lack of physical mobility, as if a static body compensatorily sets information free. When an editor invites Ermine to write for his magazine, he describes her disability as her best credential: "When I said I saw the world through a key-hole, he answered that a circumscribed view gained in distinctness."[79] Ermine writes a column under the name of "The Invalid" and eventually becomes the acting editor of the journal.

Mrs. Smith and Ermine each live in a dark room, in poverty, unable to move without help. Yet each woman enjoys an "elasticity of mind," feeling "joyous-tempered" (*Persuasion*, 145; *Clever*, 140). Each woman becomes the heroine's closest friend, giving her particularly vital advice about marital choices. Each woman experiences some improvement in her health as she begins to feel valued by friends and suitors, and each achieves some financial comfort, but there is no indication of a cure.

Each, however, has been ruined by the selfish financial machinations of her closest male connection's advisor. Each woman watched helplessly as a man that her husband or brother trusted stole her fortune. Yonge's Mr. Maddox, like Austen's Mr. Elliot, is a handsome, plausible stranger, who spots the heroine by the seashore and tries to effect an alliance with her by smoothly agreeing with whatever he imagines to be her opinions. Will the disabled best friend warn the heroine in time? In each case, his bad character is finally revealed through a damaging letter in his own handwriting. The villain also keeps a lower-class mistress (Mr. Elliot has Mrs. Clay, Mr. Maddox has Maria Hatherton). In his self-interested greed, his appetite for money and sex beyond legal boundaries, the man represents the worst of *Homo economicus.*

Structurally, *Persuasion*'s Anne and *Clever Woman*'s Rachel are parallel figures: an unmarried, intelligent woman in her twenties, bored and frustrated by her family. Her surviving parent and her elder sister have a strong sense of correct social deportment, and her younger sister-figure is frequently ill and is absorbed in her children. *Clever Woman*'s setting in a seaside resort (an unusual place for a Yonge novel) may be intended to recall Lyme. In both cases, characters can visit the town because a military campaign has just ended, whether Napoleon's capture in *Persuasion*, or the Rebellion of 1857 in India in *Clever Woman*. In Chapter 3, we saw that the soldier is often a dangerous romantic lover, but, interestingly, in a care-based system the soldier's experience in nursing the wounded reconfigures him into an acceptable familiar suitor. In *Clever Woman* and *Persuasion*, the soldiers do not import violence, but domestic skills. As Monica Cohen points out, Wentworth oversees cooking, sewing, and the hiring of schoolmasters on board ship; the navy is a fine tutor in home management techniques.[80] In *Clever Woman*, Alick's and Colin's military service teaches them to give dinners, nurse the sick, organize balls, set up charities, collect ornaments, respect their social superiors, and maintain harmonious relations within the regiment. Kate Lawson points out that in *Clever Woman*, the British colonial army is needed to reform an England that is decaying due to the scourge of liberal autonomy.[81]

However, Yonge reworks the marriage plot she inherited from Austen by transferring some of Anne Elliot's experiences to Ermine. Rachel has Anne's unsympathetic family structure and affiliation with a money-grubbing man, but Ermine gets Anne's love plot, enduring years of silent fidelity to a man in military service who was considered too poor to marry her in the first place, although he soon proved himself capable of a sterling career. She meets him again, years later, when she considers it too late for them to wed. By giving the love plot to Ermine, Yonge affiliates it to disability even more than Austen did. For in *Clever Woman*, both members of the couple suffer near-fatal bodily traumas. Colin's damaged lungs and Ermine's burned legs leave their bodies altered forever. Where Austen's heroine merely experiences a certain amount of ladylike fatigue, Yonge's heroine is what she herself describes as an "old cinder" (94).

As disability is more profound in *Clever Woman*, it is also more widespread, and the nursing required is more extensive. Everyone in *Clever Woman* is disabled. Conditions include nervous disorders, blindness, insanity, internal bleeding, illness in childbirth, amputations, recurrent fevers, fragile lungs, disabling burns, diphtheria, child abuse, and starvation. Even the dog suffers a broken paw; even the child's doll has legs that will not bend (165–166, 205–206). Indeed, the only extraordinary bodies are the healthy ones, and they are clearly destined to fail so that they can be brought into conformity with the system of nursing that becomes the social realm of *Clever Woman*.

Avoncester society, in *The Clever Woman of the Family*, initially consists of single women: Fanny Temple, Rachel Curtis, Grace Curtis, Mrs. Curtis, Ermine Williams, and Alison Williams. They are all widows or spinsters who do not expect to wed and who are often hostile to one another. At the beginning of the novel, their social ties are easily frayed. Rachel tyrannizes over Fanny and despises the Williams sisters; Fanny tells Rachel to stop teaching Fanny's sons, Ermine and Alison dread Rachel's visits, and Grace slyly pokes fun at Rachel. Mrs. Curtis and Grace extort observances of social conventions that Rachel despises.

This atomized, mutually mistrustful crowd finally begins to coalesce once it has suffering bodies in its midst. It coheres into a community of care around, first, the feeble Fanny Temple. When her son and cousin spar over who will take care of her, Fanny sobs and responds, "There's plenty of care for you both to take . . . The Major says I need not be a poor creature, and I will try. But I am afraid I shall be on all your hands" (45–46). Attracted by Fanny, the two wounded Keith men soon arrive: Colin with shot lodged in his lungs; Alick with malarial fever, shrapnel embedded in his side, and amputated fingers.

If ever there was a symbolically castrating impairment in Victorian fiction, it is Alick's. Physically weakened and missing crucial "members," this is a male body with permanent deficits. When Rachel's hands collide with Alick's in trying to catch a fly, her hands descended on "what should have been fingers, but they gave way under her—she felt only the leather of the glove between her and the newspaper" (182). Alick immediately jokes.

> "Inferior animals can dispense with a member more or less," . . . and as he spoke he removed the already half drawn-off left-hand glove, and let Rachel see for a moment that it had only covered the thumb, forefinger,

> two joints of the middle, and one of the third; the little finger was gone, and the whole hand much scarred. (182)

Yet Alick's "missing member" does not render him sexless, as Rachel will find when he becomes doggedly determined to marry her; their marriage will produce at least two children. Indeed, in spite of their severe wartime injuries, both Alick and Colin demonstrate relentless determination to marry, a ruthless discipline that awes observers. Colin spends years quietly and inexorably setting up the material conditions that will make his union with Ermine possible. Alick, although advertising his laziness, maintains an almost terrifying level of control over Rachel. Both soldier on, one might say, in their immovable determination to wed (and, in Alick's case, retrain) their chosen brides. Their physical frailty therefore does not correlate to a failure of masculine power. Instead, it moves them into a relation of care.

Yonge scholars agree that interdependence was central to Yonge's thought. As Brigid Lowe writes, "Yonge demands not that women should become as independent as men in all arenas but the conjugal bond, but rather that men should become as relational and altruistic as women, and that 'Familial' affective, irrational bonds of mutual reliance should spread as widely as possible among human beings who, in the last analysis, want and need each other."[82] Although Lowe is not explicitly addressing *Clever Woman* here, she describes precisely what this novel does: Rachel needs to be trained out of her mistaken drive for independence, into bonds of mutual reliance. In *Clever Woman*, writes Martha Stoddard Holmes, happy relationships require "mutual weakness and mutual nursing," and "in heterosexual courting couples, [infirmity] catalyzes rather than precludes marriages."[83] As we saw in *Persuasion*, weakness provokes caretaking, which in turn draws people together. But in *Clever Woman* all these elements are exaggerated: suffering is virtually universal, and every person participates in the caretaking required as a result.

In an important article, Tamara Silvia Wagner has argued that mutual dependency deriving from disabilities is at the heart of Yonge's work:

> What can be termed Yonge's religion of domesticity, a grounding of her spiritual agenda in everyday responsibilities, is rooted in this ideal of mutual dependence and, ultimately, in the dependability provided by a caretaking that is never unidirectional. Most importantly, this ideal of interrelationships at home seeks to highlight, not erase, the individual's role while stressing each family member's need and, by implication, natural right to depend on others, to be dependent as well as dependable, to be

> depended *on*, that at the same time implies a defence of dependencies as the connecting elements of any functioning community.[84]

Mutual dependency has to be defended against what Wagner calls the Victorians' "rampant idealization of the self-made, self-reliant, and also self-sufficient, individual."[85] In this respect Yonge extends Austen's initial opposition between Mr. Elliot and Mrs. Smith into a whole social system.

For the couples who marry in *Clever Woman*, the main motive is caring. Perhaps Wagner describes it best when she notes that "the novel ultimately sees both heroines married to such doubly desirable nursing heroes."[86] What they experience is the euphoric interdependency that Nel Noddings described as the heart of care. The emotion that drives a marriage is the most targeted, intense version of the emotion that drives all social relations in Yonge's novelistic world.

Love, in Charlotte Yonge's "radically relational conception of human nature," is demonstrated by caregiving.[87] Characters court each other by wheeling chairs to windows, smoothing pillows, and changing dressings. Invalidism and romance are synonymous, because Yonge uses them to express the same aim: loving interdependency. As Lowe points out, "not one of Yonge's own novels takes marriage, sexual choice or love as its primary concern or structuring force."[88] In fact, Yonge disliked the idea of romantic passion as formulated in *Romeo and Juliet*, calling their love "disobedient, passionate, and culminating in suicide."[89] Yonge did not believe that Englishwomen experienced romantic passion at all:

> It is not right to represent love as a lawless, in fact, sensual passion, excited by mere chance, and entirely unconnected with esteem. It might be so in the untaught woman, with the more violent passions of southern climates. It is not so in the average woman of the north. She has discrimination and control of herself, and she can learn that there are some whom she ought not to love.[90]

Yonge's opposition between lawless passion and self-controlled esteem comes straight out of eighteenth-century conduct manuals and indeed reveals just how long these earlier models continued to affect Victorian writers. She prefers to envision marriage on a parental model, with a "paradigmatic relationship" "between mother and child."[91] The two marriages of *Clever Woman* depict love as a childlike dependence on a nurturing parent figure.[92]

Clever Woman has several points at which the reader's expectation of romance gets baffled during the events we would normally expect to be charged with desire: proposals and marriage nights. In these scenes, Yonge uses disability as the switch that flips us off the rails on which we thought we were riding, onto the familiar marriage track.

Ermine and Colin woo each other with concern about each other's condition. Ermine habitually turns aside his queries about her invalidism to ask about his infirmity.[93] Similarly, when Alick falls in love with Rachel, she is physically weak and mentally fragile. Yet Alick proposes not in spite of her condition but, in a sense, because of it. As Stoddard Holmes reminds us, for Yonge, "disability, nursing, and interdependence are not bars to courtship but its bases."[94] He offers himself first as a "son," to help Rachel's mother, and then asks Rachel to "come and help" him with the needs of military families. When Rachel objects that she can help nobody, he responds that "these last weeks have shown me that your troubles *must* be mine" (410, 411). Not a word of love or desire escapes Alick's lips. What he wants is quite precisely to share her troubles and to enlist her in helping others. In this typical familiar-marriage move, he aims to join her social network, de-emphasizing the personal desire that might be seen as disruptive in favor of a more diffused loyalty to the entire clan.

The immediate effect of Alick's proposal is to win the love, not of Rachel, but of her mother. Mrs. Curtis's "surrender of judgment was curiously complete. 'Dear Alexander,' as she thenceforth called him, had assumed the mastery over her" (413). Rachel, meanwhile, is feverish, resentful, and resistant. As her sister astutely remarks, "her mother was more in love with 'dear Alexander' than Rachel was" (417). It is tempting to read this as an unconsciously comical quasi-incestuous substitution, but such a reading misses the point: the mother's approval confirms that this marriage respects and upholds familial ties. And Rachel first imagines Alick as a suitor when she muses, significantly, that it would be good to have "a near relation like him" (378).

In other words, marriage means inducting another family member into the network, and the virtue of a marriage can be measured by how well the newcomer performs his familial relations and whether family members endorse the newcomer's inclusion.[95] Alick woos Rachel's mother, but Colin and Ermine similarly require the approval of Colin's brother and Ermine's sister before they can wed (520–522). Marriage is a communal arrangement, and the whole clan must approve of the alliance.

Importantly, that clan is not a nuclear family. The only living parent in this novel is Mrs. Curtis; almost everyone gets parented by an avuncular relation.[96] Alick grew up in the care of Mr. Clare, Fanny lived with her aunt, Ermine and her sister Alison are raising their niece, and an orphaned boy has been adopted sequentially by an aunt on each side of his family.[97] *Clever Woman* has a remarkable number of children cared for by people who are not biologically their parents. Indeed, biological ties do not create the necessary interdependence. Rachel's mother is notoriously inept in the sickroom, Lord Keith's grown daughter is a terrible mother, and Alick's sister dislikes and avoids nursing.[98] These functions are met by exogamous people, attached through choice instead of blood, which proves their caregiving credentials.

Alick gives his fiancée physical pleasure, but not in the way we might expect. He sits "beside her couch, with a stillness of manner that strangely hushed all her throbbings; and the very pleasure of lying really still was such that she did not at once break it. The lull of these few moments was inexpressibly sweet" (418–419). This restfulness is in some sense the opposite of the "throbbings" of erotic desire.[99] In fact, the "lull" seems to be Yonge's ideal. When Alick begs Rachel to describe her feelings for him, she itemizes "such rest, such kindness, such generosity" (420). Alick works hard to "soothe and rest her spirits," to achieve "a tranquillity that was balm to the harassed spirit," a "dreamy repose" so as "to lull her on in this same gentle, unthinking state of dreamy rest" (421, 431, 445, 446). Amid mental and physical pain, the desire is not for more excitement but for blessed relief, and love is the name for the sufferer's attitude toward the person who provides it. Rachel's gratitude for care is not substituted for love, it *is* love, an alternative form of love.

Ermine and Colin, like Rachel and Alick, crave "lulls." They achieve one in their joyful reunion: "they gazed into each other's faces in the untroubled repose of the meeting, exclusive of all else" (119). On their wedding evening, they merge into an even deeper haven of rest, a kind of infantile presymbolic union:

> The patient spirits had reached their home and haven, the earthly haven of loving hearts, the likeness of the heavenly haven, and as her head leant, at last, upon his shoulder, and his guardian arm encircled her, there was such a sense of rest and calm that even the utterance of their inward thanksgiving, or of a word of tenderness would have jarred upon them. (536)

Perfect bliss is perfect stillness, silence, and immobility. If this is their true moment of union, it is one whose physical components are more paternal than sexual, with Colin protectively putting his arm around Ermine. But it is also an explicitly disembodied image. They are not physical bodies but "patient spirits" and their union is more like death than like marriage. Ghostly, disembodied, nonsexual—their union is too blissful for words. The home is (almost literally) heaven.[100]

Alick and Rachel achieve a homelike trance of peace when they visit Alick's blind uncle, Mr. Clare, during their honeymoon. Rachel feels that finally "she had her childhood's heart again" (477). Mr. Clare lives in loving fellowship with Mr. Lifford, his worn-out curate, who is a caretaker twice over, caring for blind

Mr. Clare in his work, and for a wife who is confined to an asylum in his vacations (visits which he considers "rest" [448]). Clare and Lifford model marital behavior for Rachel and Alick. For all practical purposes, they are a married couple, whether or not their relationship is sexual.[101]

Clare and Lifford, like John and Phineas, are perhaps an even more radical version of a same-sex couple than one would expect, because they are a same-sex couple whose loving cohabitation is not in the least controversial, a couple whose very ordinariness is important. Just as ethics of care makes the extraordinary body into the typical body, ethics of care can also make unconventional living arrangements perfectly unremarkable. If the issue is the quality of care between two people, not their biological relationship or marital status, then all relationships—adoptive, sexual, platonic, friendship, and marital—are simply enunciations of the same fundamental principle. Anyone can mother, anyone can husband, anyone can friend, and everyone can nurse.

In *Clever Women*, nursing is not affiliated to the female sphere, for in fact men have impressive nursing ability. Alick, though suffering from recurrent attacks of fever, nonetheless makes a special point of taking care of the elderly Lord Keith in his "tedious and painful illness" so as to spare Lord Keith's brother Colin from his incessant caregiving (505). "There cannot be a better nurse than Alick Keith," Colin admits, but he worries that Alick is overexerting himself (524, 529). "In fact," Colin says afterward, "I never knew much he was going through rather than summon me," although Rachel soon arrives to care for Alick (538). In this paradigmatic care community, every person in the society is ill, and every person nurses. Even those not directly involved in the Colin-Alick-Lord Keith triangle watch out for the men, making sure that the caregiver is not exhausted or exploited.

This episode of male nursing has the effect of interrupting the honeymoon idyll for both couples. When Alick is bedridden, shaking, feverish, and headachy—and, in his free time, nursing Lord Keith—he is evidently sexually unavailable (505). In this case, Alick's illness is not necessarily meant to signal a sexless marriage, since they do have children later. But his absence makes us focus on the nonsexual aspects of the union.

Similarly, the moment his wedding service is over, Colin rushes off to his brother's deathbed, and "Ermine had to continue a widowed bride for full a fortnight" (535). Kim Wheatley reads this absence as symptomatic, arguing that "the absence of sex in Colin's and Ermine's marriage is hinted at by the fact that Colin and Ermine are forced to spend their first two weeks of marriage, including their wedding night, apart."[102] By so obtrusively baffling the sexual aspect of their union, Yonge forces us to consider what a nonsexual romance might be like. But it is not just an absence of sex; it is a presence of nursing. Lord Keith's dying request precipitates the proposal, and Colin's care for Lord Keith characterizes the honeymoon. In this respect, the proposal and honeymoon do exactly what they are supposed to do: they represent the acme of the emotional bliss of this couple, which, in this novel, derives from caring for those they love.

The opposite of this networking is the criminal selfishness enacted by Maddox, who pursues economic self-interest, even to the point of starving his own child. His independence is absolute; although he has accomplices, they do not know his whole character and he can renounce them when he chooses. He craves excitement (he is addicted to gambling) rather than yearning for lulls. Susan F. Feiner summarizes this sort of character: "Certainly for a hundred years, and on some readings since the days of Adam Smith, the *dramatis personae* of mainstream economics have been self-interested and egoistic actors for whom the dual spurs of competition and pleasure-seeking have motivated all behavior. *Homo economicus (a.k.a.* Rational Economic Man), [was] reared in the Cartesian nursery, nourished by a diet long on atomism and short on empathy."[103] Indeed, *Homo economicus* "seems to epitomize the competitive, self-interested, isolated individual—shrewd, calculating, and devoid of sentiment, the personification of capital."[104] In this novel, it is not enough to expose Maddox's villainy, he must be put behind bars in a campaign that requires the now-consolidated members of Avoncester society, from children to adults, to join forces in a final great community of care to testify against him. *Homo economicus* is criminalized, isolated, and expelled from the social realm. As Lowe writes:

> Yonge is certainly no advocate of the self-owning rights and independence of individual women. But neither is she an advocate of the rights of the individual as an ultimate principle more generally; such priorities would be radically inconsistent with her assessment of what human subjects are like, and how their interaction should thus be viewed and conducted. Her "good" characters are, definitively, conscious of being emotional creatures who are radically dependent on one another.[105]

The final work of the novel is to set up a new home: not a happy marital haven, but a convalescent home for military invalids, attended by girls being trained for domestic service. In this institution, *Clever Woman* envisions a larger version of the disabled-marriage home, a permeable realm open to visitors, guests, and the public, a space in which multiple disabled men can be attended by multiple caretaking women. The institution is an updated version of the squire's estate or the home of the extended family. The two Keith households become alternative versions of this larger convalescent home. Moreover, setting up that institution is a collective endeavor, not one person's independent initiative. The novel's final vision is of an enlarged community of care, one that has been expanded to include lower class members, servants, and common soldiers. Mrs. Smith drew on this class for her stories, but Charlotte Yonge makes them part of the story themselves.

Medicalizing Disability in The Mill on the Floss

If *The Clever Woman of the Family* has arguably the most disabilities per capita of any Victorian novel, it is, nonetheless, not the most famous Victorian depiction of a disabled suitor. That honor goes to *The Mill on the Floss* (1860), in which the weak, pale, hunchbacked, sensitive Philip Wakem courts the queenly Maggie.[106] And although *Clever Woman; John Halifax, Gentleman*; and *The Mill on the Floss* were all published within the same decade, *The Mill on the Floss* points the disabled marriage narrative in a different direction from the other two novels. Philip is perhaps the first modern case study of the psychology of a disabled individual in British fiction. He is not a nodal point for networks of care but a personality whose insecurities, hopes, self-hatreds, and needs are intimately formed by the experience of growing up with an extraordinary body. Philip is not in the novel for other characters to cluster around, but to be diagnosed and found lacking.

In this respect, Philip Wakem marks the moment that the disabled-marriage path we have been following comes to a dead end, shunting travelers onto a different trail. From *Persuasion* through such novels as *Ruth, Our Mutual Friend, Shirley, Romola, The Clever Woman of the Family*, and *The Portrait of a Lady*, Victorian fiction depicts invalids as offering a social opportunity attractive to isolated individuals, a marriage prospect that could enmesh her in an affiliative network that replaces the lost kinship group. But in *The Mill on the Floss*, Philip has no such network. Karen Bourrier argues that "in *The Mill on the Floss*, Eliot makes the struggle to bring Philip Wakem out of the morbid introspection caused by his deformity and into a sympathetic bond with the community a central point in his character," but this struggle fails: his disability isolates him from his community instead.[107]

It is instructive to compare Philip to Phineas. The two disabled, sensitive best friends appear in novels published only four years apart (and Elaine Showalter speculates that Eliot may well have intended *The Mill on the Floss* as a corrective to *John Halifax, Gentleman*).[108] Phineas's and Philip's fathers resent their sons' intellectual orientation and incapacity to follow them in business. But in social respects, Philip is very different from his predecessor. Phineas had nurses and servants, but we never hear of anyone taking care of Philip. Instead, we are told that he has no experience of a mother's love, and he disapproves of his father

(344). Moreover, Philip has "no friend to whom I can tell everything—no one who cares enough about me" (315). Philip and Stephen Guest merely maintain occasional companionship. Indeed, Philip craves solitude, frequently rushing off to evade Stephen at moments of emotional drama, an immersion in a private psychological world that would have been utterly foreign to Phineas (437, 452).

Philip is not only alone, he infects others with his isolation. For the terrible fact is that if Maggie marries him, she gains no social network through Philip and she loses the only social network she already has, her consanguineous family. As Mary Jean Corbett remarks, *The Mill on the Floss* is the supreme testimony to the strength of the first-family bond.[109] Ripped away from the networks of care, what advantage does the disabled suitor offer in marriage? He must now be assessed solely on the basis of his own body and mind, both of which are perceived as irreversibly damaged according to the medical model.

The Mill on the Floss still promotes the values of caretaking, affection, and affiliative (non-biological) bonds that we have seen in every disabled marriage novel of the nineteenth century. It is, after all, set nostalgically in the early years of the nineteenth century, supposedly the last period of real *Gemeinschaft*.[110] Moreover, *The Mill on the Floss* is based in Eliot's famous humanism, the recognition that others possess an "equivalent centre of self."[111] For "caring involves stepping out of one's own personal frame of reference into the other's. When we care, we consider the other's point of view, his objective needs, and what he expects from us. Our attention, our mental engrossment is on the cared-for, not on ourselves."[112] This latter passage comes from Nel Nodding's description of ethics of care, but any Victorianist will recognize it as an apt description of Eliot's idea of sympathy.[113] Philip enunciates what this kind of love does:

> The new life I have found in caring for your joy and sorrow more than for what is directly my own, has transformed the spirit of rebellious murmuring into that willing endurance which is the birth of strong sympathy. I think nothing but such complete and intense love could have initiated me into that enlarged life which grows and grows by appropriating the life of others. (523)

Noddings would have agreed—and so would Yonge, and Eliot herself.

In Eliot, the Victorian novel finds its greatest advocate for the care ethics narrative—and, ironically, the author whose novel refuses to enact it—just as Eliot speaks most eloquently for women's fantasies of power and capacity for work, yet writes narratives in which women are blocked from both. Nobody was better at delineating a world of fulfilling possibility that she would not allow her characters to enter. Eliot uses at least three of the major forms of familiar marriage—neighbor, disability, and vocational—but sets the plot in motion only to frustrate it. Gwendolen, Maggie, and Dorothea think they know what narratives their marriages initiate. But Eliot reverses the terms on them, giving them relationships characterized by the precise opposite of what they coveted.

St. Ogg's is no Avoncester. It is a community of care, but the care it offers is bad, based on revulsion and disavowal of shared responsibility. Tom describes Philip's "puny, miserable body" (359); Lucy says regretfully, "I'm very fond of poor Philip, only I wish he were not so morbid about his deformity. I suppose it *is* his deformity that makes him so sad—and sometimes bitter" (390). Lucy uses a medical model, blaming a failed body or mind. After all, if one assumes everyone to be an autonomous subject, disability simply means the physical failure to be autonomous enough, and the mental bitterness that results. The family is frequently hostile, and there are virtually no friends outside the family.[114] *The Mill on the Floss* is a tragedy because in a world that still holds ethics of care as a value, conditions have made it impossible to enact or even to recognize it. In Eliot's novel, Mr. Elliot or Mr. Maddox is no longer a solitary villain threatening to invade the community, but the closest connection one has—one's brother, for instance. Iris Marion Young's description of the atomistic subject describes Tom perfectly: "The impartial subject need acknowledge no other subjects whose perspective should be taken into account and with whom discussion might occur. Thus the claim to be impartial often results in authoritarianism. By asserting oneself as impartial, one claims authority to decide an issue, in place of those whose interests and desires are manifest."[115]

Maggie reverses the fate of the disabled-marriage female subject, as she moves not from isolation into sociality but from sociality into isolation. "As I chop away at the chains that bind me to loved others, asserting my freedom, I move into a wilderness of strangers and loneliness, leaving behind all who cared for me, and even, perhaps, my own self."[116] Noddings's *cri de coeur* might have been an epigraph for the last third of *The Mill on the Floss.* Enmeshed in family at the beginning of the novel, Maggie increasingly becomes an isolate.

Maggie, however, has the impression she is in an ordinary care-ethics familiar marriage plot, as she, like Anne Elliot or Rachel Curtis, learns to nurse and to be valued for her nursing in the time-honored manner of the good Victorian girl. In Book Four, Maggie becomes her parents' caretaker, and both her nursing experience and her emotional isolation predispose her toward disabled marriage. As the narrator sums up, "she had a moment of real happiness then—a moment of belief that if there were sacrifice in this love—it was all the richer and more satisfying" (350). In accepting Philip, she is doing precisely what her culture has taught her is appropriate.

Readers may also think we recognize Maggie's later predicament, which seems just as conventional: the familiar versus the romantic suitor. Stephen is the classic romantic suitor: erotically thrilling, untrustworthy, and wealthy. Philip, however, provokes a feeling that is just as potent.

> Her tranquil, tender affection for Philip, with its root deep down in her childhood, and its memories of long quiet talk confirming by distinct successive impressions the first instinctive bias—the fact that in him the appeal was more strongly to her pity and womanly devotedness than to her vanity or other egoistic excitability of her nature—seemed now to make a sort of sacred place, a sanctuary where she could find refuge from [Stephen's] alluring influence. (427)

As she tries to explain to Stephen, her feelings for both men are authentic, but fundamentally different. "I *do* care for Philip—in a different way," she cries (499). Just like Catherine in *Wuthering Heights*, Maggie insists that she is capable of "being for" others, that she is not just a prize for one man. Her love of Tom fits into this situation as well. Surely it should be legitimate to have deep love for a brother, fondness for a disabled friend, and erotic attraction to a romantic suitor all at the same time. Yet, just like *Wuthering Heights*, *The Mill on the Floss* depicts a society in which widespread skepticism as to a woman's capacity for multiple relationships destroys her.

Interestingly, early reviewers of *The Mill on the Floss* despised Stephen Guest. A reviewer in 1861 could not comprehend why Maggie "would have let herself be wholly drawn away from her love for the deformed and suffering Philip by a mere outside fancy for the good-looking, sweet-voiced coxcomb, Stephen Guest" who offered nothing but "animal feelings."[117] Dinah Mulock Craik (predictably) agreed, lamenting that "the only love that might have at once humbled and raised [Maggie], by showing her how far nobler it was than her own—Philip's—is taken from her in early girlhood."[118] Even Swinburne, not usually known for repudiating sexual scenes, found Stephen appalling, a "thing" (not a man) that generated "bitter disgust and sickening disdain," while Leslie Stephen called Stephen "indefensible," as compared to the "lovable" Philip.[119]

Today, in an era that sees sexual attraction as the core of marriage, critics tend to reject the prospect of marrying Philip. Elaine Showalter calls him "sexually unattractive" and accuses him of "entrapp[ing]" Maggie "in an exploitative and oppressive relationship."[120] But Showalter is right; Eliot does indicate Maggie's suppressed sexual uneasiness with Philip.[121] In *John Halifax, Gentleman*, John adores Phineas's body, praising his height, paleness, delicacy, big eyes, and "bewitching" long black hair (79). But in *The Mill on the Floss*, the invalid's body becomes a sexual problem rather than a social opportunity, and that invalid's history of suffering becomes a reason for avoiding human ties rather than a rationale for gathering a network of carers.

In an earlier novel, Stephen would have been the tempter, whom she should resist to stay true to the good man to whom she is plighted, the subplot that tested her spiritual strength and moral duty. On the other hand, in a later novel, Stephen would have been the virile stranger who frees her from a tiresome engagement to a weakly prig. Philip would have been the subplot that represented her tepid bourgeois entanglements, falling away before a blast of natural manhood. But Maggie is neither Annie Strong in *David Copperfield* nor Lucy Honeychurch in *A Room With a View*. Caught in the middle, Maggie sees the benefits and problems of both. At this historical moment, the choices are so finely balanced as to be impossible. Both familiar and romantic suitors get some kind of love. As Maggie herself puts it, "love is natural—but surely pity and faithfulness and memory are natural too" (469). She is at the fulcrum of a perfectly undecidable choice.

Blocked from either the familiar or the romantic union, Maggie must fall back upon kin, a relationship that hurts more than it sustains her. Suzanne Graver explains that "the kinship ties dramatized in the family gatherings of *The Mill on the Floss* suggest not brotherly and sisterly love, but exclusive, intolerant, and unloving clannishness."[122] The Dodsons' family traditions have curdled into rigid rules of minor etiquette that ignore deeper emotional needs. They "favor a good business investment over family sentiment when the two are at odds."[123] This sterile form of family consciousness dooms the family to peter out; the Dodson sisters have no descendants, except for Tom and Lucy (Maggie, all agree, is a Tulliver). Nor is the Tulliver side much better. Mr. Tulliver's irritable, reluctantly nostalgic tie to his sister is the only kinship relation he recognizes beyond his nuclear family. Disliking the avunculate, he is nevertheless tied to them against his will. One of his first declarations in the novel is, "I shall ask neither aunt nor uncle what I'm to do wi' my own lad" (12). This is very different from the loving adoptive aunts of Yonge's novel. As the family turns in on itself, each Dodson or Tulliver pair becomes a small center of its own financial management. What's more, the famously evolutionary language of the novel replaces endogamy with a discourse of "breeds," a coolly scientific consideration of the workings of heredity and the unpredictability of survival in a harsh world.[124]

Cousin marriage is no longer viable in this new world. Tom would like a cousin marriage with Lucy, but Lucy's "nature supplied her with no key to Tom's" (475). Where other Victorian novels show cousins as people who share memories, kindnesses, and mutual respect, the world of *The Mill on the Floss* forecasts a future of independent nuclear-family financial rivals, squabbling over who begs, borrows, or owes money to whom. They are not unified but rather operate like species competing to survive, the Tullivers versus the Deanes versus the Gleggs. Atomism is the new situation, and (as in Wentworth's hazelnut model) there is no possibility of recombination. In *Clever Woman* and *Persuasion*, Maddox and Elliot were villains invading a harmonious *Gemeinschaft*, but in *The Mill on the Floss*, Tom is a citizen and representative of the new world, *Gesellschaft*.

If *The Mill on the Floss* rethinks cousin and disabled marriage, it also makes Wakem's decision to hire Tulliver into a grotesque updating of the neighbor marriage. A newly homeless woman is provided for by the wealthy local neighbor, but in this case, it is a vengeful transaction between men, not an expression of love for a woman. *The Mill on the Floss* takes the forms of marriage that allowed people to express their yearning for a larger, richer sociality and argues that modernity is transforming them into individualizing, isolating experiences. In *The Mill on the Floss*, neighborliness is poison, cousinship is competition, and disability is pathology. And yet there is no way out, for Stephen—the figure outside of all this, the glamorous exogamous suitor of the romantic marriage plot—offers little in himself and precipitates the crushing betrayal of those connections one does possess. This is a tragedy, of course, for Eliot, the great advocate of networks. Graver argues that Eliot wants to remake the network through art and abstract thought; be that as it may, Eliot writes the end of a tradition in which it can be made through marriage.[125]

Conclusion: The Portrait of a Sick-Nurse

The Mill on the Floss marks the turn toward a new way of seeing the disabled suitor. It pioneers some of the main avenues through which disability itself will come to be understood: as a case study of psychological problems, as a medical issue foregrounding diagnosis and prognosis, as an inadequately sexual choice for a marital partner.[126]

However, the future predicted by *The Mill on the Floss* did not arrive for half a century. Late-Victorian fiction continued to read the disabled suitor in terms of care ethics; *Clever Woman* and *Our Mutual Friend* both postdate *The Mill on the Floss*, as do important disabled suitors in later novels. In Charlotte Yonge's *The Magnum Bonum*, Barbara Brownlow refuses to marry the consumptive young man Duke because he is, she declares, "such a muff!"[127] But Duke brings the Brownlows into his social circle together. When a boy meets his schoolfriend abroad accidentally, the two families form lifelong ties, and Duke oversees and commemorates their union through editing a journal called "The Traveller's Joy" on his deathbed. This bound volume includes a representative piece of writing from each member of the circle, and each has a personal inscription from Duke.

Having accomplished this collection, literally binding together the two families, Duke gracefully expires. Barbara considers herself "almost his widow" and regards her relation with him as the glory of her life.[128]

Two years later, Henry James's *The Portrait of a Lady* (1881) would use a similar plot, with a consumptive man using his last strength to pull together a community of care. Ralph Touchett endures a protracted-enough dying to give him the capacity to weld the unpromising particles of disparate characters together, miraculously managing to unify Caspar Goodwood, Henrietta Stackpole, Mrs. Touchett, Lord Warburton, and Isabel into one loving community. Ralph is cared for, but he also gives care back. As Ralph's father remarks with delight, "I call him my sick-nurse because he's sick himself."[129] Thus he exemplifies Noddings's explanation that "parties are not stuck in their positions as carers or cared fors. As carer I contribute in one way to the relation, as cared for, in a different way . . . this requires each of us to be sensitive cared fors (to accept gifts joyfully without always trying to cancel the debt) as well as responsible carers."[130] As the "sick-nurse," one can be both sick and a nurse, both cared-for and a carer. Ralph, the fulcrum of a community of care, creates the euphoric ties that Noddings recommended, rising to an almost unbearable crescendo of tenderness, adoration, and sympathy through mutual nursing.

It is Ralph, then, not Philip, with whom this chapter will end. Before the suitor's suffering was pathologized, it was appreciated as a public concern, the opportunity for the making of a social world. Before the disabled body was seen as a medical problem to be solved by a surgeon in an institution, it was seen as a situation to be managed collaboratively by an extended family in the home. Thus the mid-Victorian disability plot gives us a subjectivity and a story to counterpoint the better-known liberal agent: the relational self instead of the monadic persona, lulls instead of achievements. It offers a vision of a voluntary, affiliative social network that avoids the exclusivity of the romantic pair while prioritizing tenderly intimate feelings.

Throughout this book we have seen that familiar marriage is the shadowy other self to romantic marriage. For each element of romantic marriage, familiar marriage substitutes something else. Instead of marriage with a stranger, familiar marriage advocates marriage with neighbor or family; instead of feeling erotic desire for another's body, familiar marriage advocates sympathetic helpfulness; instead of demanding a private dyad, familiar marriage wants a larger social network; instead of valorizing the self-made man, familiar marriage prizes unselfish participation in a system of mutual care. Familiar marriage offers a social vision and a form of subjectivity the Victorians were not yet willing to lose.

But by pursuing familiar marriage, we can also see the larger shadow narratives of our culture's intellectual history. In Chapter 3 we saw that the idea of marrying so as to perpetuate the squirearchy does not do justice to women's fantasies of an ineffable form of power based in influence—a model that helps explain the persistence of the parliamentary ghostwriter union throughout nineteenth-century fiction. Similarly, in Chapter 4 we saw that the understanding of women as mute sexual prizes in rivalry among men does not match women's roles in Victorian marriage plots, where women's multifarious relationships become the center of the novel. This chapter adds a contrast between the dominant story of the individual—a public, rational, self-serving monad—and a socially enmeshed, relational, affective figure. Familiar marriage generates fantasies of other social worlds: extended families, *Gemeinschaft* neighborhoods, communities of care.

This intensely felt need for a safe social environment, however, became increasingly detached from the marriage plot by the end of the nineteenth century. The social bonds of neighbor marriage began to fray after 1880, due to growing interest in psychology and ebbing faith in the landed estate. Cousin marriage felt viable until post-Darwinist anxiety about heredity set in after 1870. Disabled marriage began to be unsettled by the medical model after the 1860s. In the next chapter, we will look at a form of familiar marriage that had an even shorter lifespan. Vocational marriage stories altered in the 1850s, and it is the story of their fall, not their triumph, that shall occupy us next. What happens to a dream of marriage that barely lasted long enough to be realized, that almost from its inception had to be expressed in comic asides, in minor characters, in delusions, and in tears?

6

Vocational Marriage, or, Why Marriage Doesn't Work

He continued—"God and nature intended you for a missionary's wife. It is not personal, but mental endowments they have given you: you are formed for labour, not for love. A missionary's wife you must—shall be. You shall be mine: I claim you—not for my pleasure, but for my Sovereign's service."

"I am not fit for it; I have no vocation," I said.

CHARLOTTE BRONTË, Jane Eyre

Introduction: Women Working at Marriage

Neighbor marriage, cousin marriage, and disabled marriage all function to keep the woman oriented to a wider world—a local community, a family, a network of friends. The subject of this final chapter, vocational marriage, similarly places the woman into larger social relations: in this case, the public. Vocational marriage means a marriage contracted in order to get meaningful work. The woman imagines her future in terms of parishioners, customers, students, clients, employees, patients, or colleagues. She sees herself as an aide or partner in the joint occupational project of her married life. What she dreams of is a larger usefulness to the world.

For examples of nineteenth-century vocational marriage plots, we might think of St. John's proposal to Jane Eyre when he asks her to run an Indian school with him, Mr. Collins's assurance that Lizzie will be acceptable as a clergyman's wife, Casaubon's wish for an assistant to "supply that need" of which he had become conscious, George Vavasor's proposal of a political partnership with his cousin Alice, or Phillotson's requesting a schoolmistress to work with him.[1] In these cases, the woman is asked to perform a certain kind of work rather than given romantic reassurances. Indeed, in the case of Jane, Alice, or Sue, the woman may resent protestations of adoration as unwarranted, inauthentic interferences with a business arrangement. The woman of the vocational marriage enjoys the sense of her own capacity, the exercise of her own talents. Ideally, she strides fearlessly into a useful life. She is like Mrs. Proudie, relishing ecclesiastical politics; like Jane Eyre, enjoying nursing Rochester; like Phoebe Junior, eager to coach Clarence into Parliament; like Mrs. Bagnet or Mrs. Croft, thriving in naval campaigns.

Yet the inclusion of Mrs. Proudie in the list above might give us pause. Although perfectly satisfied with her own leadership of the diocese, her social world despises her. Similarly, if Mr. Collins and St. John Rivers are the best examples of a vocational marriage plot, then that is hardly an advertisement for the genre. For the fact is that the proposed vocational marriage fails, whether women want to marry to assist with research (Dorothea Brooke), to help collect beautiful objects (Isabel Archer), to participate in politics (Alice Vavasor), or to co-run a school (Miss Peecher). Either the vocational marriage will never get realized, or it will turn out to be a terrible mistake.

Although vocational marriage's fantasy of female centrality resembles squire marriage, in terms of sexual contact, vocational marriage is actually closer to disabled marriage. The business partnerships of vocational marriage resemble the nonsexual cohabitations of disabled couples, like Phineas Fletcher and John Halifax, or Ruth and Thurstan Benson. All three forms of familiar marriage are progressive inasmuch as they play out alternative social arrangements—same-sex partnerships, affiliative rather than biological ties, women's political power, women's public work. All three use the marriage plot to create a kind of shadow version of this ideal, one that sadly lacks "real" power. A care dyad is not the same thing as a same-sex marriage. Influence is not the same thing as the vote. Marrying a clergyman in order to minister to others is not the same thing as becoming a member of the clergy oneself. The marriage plot helped people imagine what might be possible, but did not help them achieve it.

This tug between what was possible and what was desirable may help explain an odd element of vocational marriage. What we have is a plot that keeps recurring and yet keeps getting rejected. The fact that vocational marriage plots continually appear indicates a continuing need for imagining meaningful work in middle-class women's lives, but the fact that women are rarely allowed to enjoy such lives indicates a certain hopelessness in trying to envision the real conditions that might make such futures possible.

However, there is another reason that vocational marriage plots are plots of failure. Oddly enough, Victorian feminism itself wrote this story. In this chapter we shall see how mid-Victorian women's activism, ironically, required readers to believe that married women could not work.

Vocational marriage had not always seemed shameful. Marrying for work, like other familiar-marriage forms, is a survival from an earlier idea of marriage. Yet as Ruth Perry points out, "the ideology of romantic marriage served to de-legitimate earlier pragmatic motives for marriage such as providing care for orphaned infants, young children, or aging parents; prudent management of households; the addition of new wealth or property; avoiding sin; the production of new progeny."[2] Vocational marriage, like neighbor, cousin, and disability marriage, fulfilled older goals that were becoming suspect in the nineteenth century when marriage increasingly came to be associated with romantic love.

As late as the seventeenth and eighteenth century, the working class or middling sorts married (at least in part) to get help running a farm, staffing a shop counter, transcribing notes, working in a parish, manufacturing small items, or taking care of a household. Women formed an essential part of this economy, and, according to Ivy Pinchbeck, "marriage was, in fact, as much a business partnership as it was among the small clothiers and the farming classes."[3] Historians traditionally trace a shared "family economy" that gave way to the single male wage-earning breadwinner sometime between 1600 and 1800, leaving women with little to do at home (although Amanda Vickery has influentially challenged this model).[4]

The "helpmeet" remained a common notion in nineteenth-century marital arrangements. M. Jeanne Peterson argues that marriage offered a chance for women to join the husband's job. St. John Rivers and his ilk are not asking for anything unusual, according to Peterson:

> The details of Victorian married life, and in particular the urban gentry's arrangements of men's and women's work, confirm what marriage proposals and Victorian generalities suggest. Wives were assistants, colleagues, and partners in the work that men did. Their husbands took the public credit for the tasks performed—these were not "dual careers," nor was there any ideology of equality. These were "single-career families," but both husband and wife partook of that single career.[5]

This was particularly true of clerical, academic, and business professions. Letters and diaries show that, historically, women managed parish work for clergy husbands, advised about personnel decisions, negotiated the husband's social status, transcribed the husband's correspondence and manuscripts, assisted with research if he was writing, communicated messages to and from him, and negotiated on his behalf with others. Peterson concludes that women participated fully in public life.[6]

Peterson's view may be too rosy—those shared careers, after all, were ones in which women had no ability to choose or alter their work, no recognition, and no pay—but she makes an important point that in the nineteenth century, middle-class women expected marriage to initiate a kind of work. Being invited to run a household or operate a school, to work in a parish or help copy manuscripts, was a perfectly legitimate part of courtship transactions. Of course, not all forms of work were equally acceptable for middle-class women. Philanthropy, art, and political activity were the careers most frequently imagined.[7] Properly feminine work had to adhere to tacit rules, Jordan explains. The woman had to be working in a domestic space, and the work had to be both clean and sedentary.[8] In each case the woman has to undertake the vocation for higher goals—as Alan Mintz writes about vocation in George Eliot, it means aiming for "the disciplined accumulation of ambitious good deeds rather than material goods or capital."[9]

Yet in most Victorian fiction, married women cannot be depicted as working, let alone marrying in order to work. St. John Rivers, Archibald Carlyle, John Jarndyce, and Mr. Collins all propose marriage that will involve work. They may regard their vocational proposals complacently, but in each case, the woman is dismayed. The only vocational proposal that anyone welcomes is Casaubon's, and this is presented as Dorothea's delusion (the narrator provides the critique that Dorothea cannot, inquiring, "How could it occur to her to examine the letter, to look at it critically as a profession of love?" [44]). Flora May's vocational marriage to George Rivers in *The Daisy Chain* is similarly problematic. Generally, career-oriented proposals are often treated as lacking (Jarndyce), risible (Mr. Collins), dismaying (Casaubon), or even insulting (St. John) because they eschew romantic authenticity. Yet those careerist proposals are still offered, and still tempt the heroine. The impulse to vocationalism is fully acknowledged by Victorian fiction. But that impulse, by and large, cannot be fulfilled through a main character's marriage. If accepted, it is relegated to minor, comic, eccentric characters. This chapter will explore some of the reasons that vocational marriage almost inevitably fails in Victorian fiction after mid-century. Novels in the second half of the nineteenth century may make space for vocation and space for marriage, but it is not the same space.

Separating vocationalism from marriage worked toward a particular ideological goal. To have a vocation meant to have something interior, a hidden talent, a psychological drive that needed to be elicited, respected, and followed. It meant, in short, to be the kind of character that the novel was all about. By presenting the heroine as a woman who wants a career, the vocational novel presented her as a modern figure. But the woman's deep individual psychology is supposed to get satisfied through romantic marriage, not vocational unions. Thus the vocational marriage plot actually works to enhance its rival, romantic marriage. Who would marry a Collins, a Jarndyce, a Casaubon, a George Vavasor? They function to express the woman's inner need for appreciation of her skills or status, a need that the romantic suitor must then evolve to meet.

Vocational marriage began to look bad in fiction partly because of the novel's orientation toward an aspirational upper-middle-class lifestyle. Couples hoped to achieve a life of shared *leisure*, not labor. After marriage, women were expected to reduce their work to an occasional amateur hobby, unless a dire need—like the husband's financial failure or death—drove the woman to try to provide for her family. In this case, her work could be represented as a regrettable necessity. Davidoff and Hall explain, "For a middle-class woman of the early nineteenth century, gentility was coming to be defined by a special form of femininity which ran directly counter to acting as a visibly independent economic agent."[10] Critics since Ian Watt have noted how centrally the eighteenth- and nineteenth-century novel form focused on middle-class subjectivity.[11] In Victorian fiction, upwardly mobile lower-middle-class figures—farmers like Mr. Cheesacre in *Can You Forgive Her?* and grocers like Mr. Joe Jiffin in *East Lynne* or Mr. Tozer in *Phoebe Junior*—look forward to a world in which their wives or daughters would no longer have to work.

Vocational marriages are virtually never treated as admirable options for main characters, but they can sometimes be acceptable fates for comic side-kicks. In many novels, minor characters vicariously act out the wishes that the protagonist cannot allow herself to articulate. Thus, for instance, in Trollope's Barsetshire novels, Mrs. Proudie's devastating strategies in the wars of ecclesi-astical politics allow Eleanor and other women to seem gentle and detached by comparison.[12] Kate Vavasor, who pushes Alice to marry George in order to help his career; Henrietta Stackpole, whose intense journalistic curiosity about the world undergirds Isabel's; Cornelia Carlyle, who directly demands information Lady Isabel is too genteel to request; Caddy Jellyby, whose uncomplaining cheer-fulness about her conjugal labors spurs Esther to emulation—these characters are too strange, unattractive, ludicrous, or humble to emulate directly, but they become surrogates to express the vocational needs of the main characters. Quite often, the surrogate character is working class, and her plot functions primarily as comic relief to offset the main character's higher-class marriage plot. This is particularly true in Trollope's fiction; both *Can You Forgive Her?* and *The Way We Live Now* sport working-class marriage plots that act as exaggerated, buf-foonish versions of the main characters' stories, but also sometimes allow for intriguingly different endings.[13]

Occasionally, a character who contemplated vocational marriage may be saved if she can repent her careerist drive in time. If she marries properly—that is, for love—she can get rewarded via a small job routed through her husband.

Dorothea experiences such a belated spousal career through Ladislaw, as do Flora in *The Daisy Chain*, Rachel in *The Clever Woman of the Family*, and Alice in *Can You Forgive Her?* Sometimes a woman's vocational marriage could become acceptable if it taught her that she could not do the job by herself, like Bathsheba Everdene, who finally concedes that she needs Gabriel Oak to help her run the farm in Hardy's *Far from the Madding Crowd*. Sometimes work was viable if it could be ascribed to a larger and more generally admirable force: artistic genius, saintly care for the poor, familial loyalty. Craik's artist Olive, Eliot's ardent Dorothea, and Dickens's hard-working Caddy Jellyby Turveydrop all consider marriage compatible with work for these reasons. Working after marriage, in these cases, becomes relational, a sign not of the woman's innate drive to develop her own skills but of her willingness to sacrifice herself for higher causes.

But what if women pursued scholarship, politics, medicine, the law, or philanthropy with reference to their own interest instead of their men's? Marrying for such a goal seemed cold-blooded, because it overrode the person of the spouse with the prospect of the career, and unfeminine, because it introduced women into male realms. In vocational mode they might act in a prototypically male fashion, as self-willed subjects negotiating for advantage in the public sphere, or they might develop themselves through work instead of marriage.[14] Moreover, in expecting payment, the women indicated either that their men failed to earn enough for the family or that they had an unfeminine hankering for money or ambition. There was almost no socially acceptable way of remunerating women's work, a fact that famously affected real women writers trying to negotiate decent contracts with publishers.[15]

Generally speaking, Victorian fiction enshrines the hope for a calling, a vocation. Female characters do not want work, per se; they virtually never crave the jobs that were actually available to women: domestic service, agricultural work, governessing, or housekeeping. Copeland points out that the professions of companion or governess "raise universal horror across the entire range of [Regency] women's fiction."[16] Jane Eyre, Agnes Grey, and Lucy Snowe certainly show that the repulsion against such paid household roles persisted into mid-century. Household labor seems like it might have been more attractive. In *Professional Domesticity in the Victorian Novel*, Monica Cohen points out how closely housekeeping matched the goals of men's artistic and intellectual professions. In housekeeping, Cohen argues, a woman's vocation is not "abandoned, it is simply relocated."[17] After all, housekeeping involved the renunciation of selfish goals, a kind of spiritual mission, as Sarah Stickney Ellis opined when she exhorted women to tell themselves every morning, "I will meet the family with a consciousness that, being the least engaged of any member of it, I am consequently the most at liberty to devote myself to the general good of the whole."[18] Similarly,

Elizabeth Langland has shown that middle-class household management involved the acumen of a business owner.[19] Writers of household and conduct manuals often stressed that housekeeping, like any profession, needed discipline and training and skill.[20]

However, in spite of Cohen's and Langland's cogent accounts of the real skills involved in household management, it is rare to find a fictional character motivated by the desire to start housekeeping. After all, if a character enjoys domestic management, the kind of household assistance she might render a husband was not particularly different from what she was probably already doing as an unmarried daughter. Characters like Emma Woodhouse, Lucilla Marjoribanks, and Esther Summerson are already running households when they wed, so marriage gives them no new domestic vocation. When Dorothea vows to find out what everything cost, the reader is meant to feel it as a sad fall from her vocational dreams rather than an eager embrace of a new professional challenge. As Harriet Taylor remarked in *The Enfranchisement of Women*, "numbers of women are wives and mothers only because there is no other career open to them, no other occupation for their feelings or their activities."[21]

Instead, those advocating work for women endorsed careers in such fields as education, medicine, art, literature, drama, music, philanthropy, ornamentation, cookery, and management.[22] What they wanted was to achieve something like professionalism. Professionalism showcases trained expertise, specialization of tasks, the subdivision of time and space, a full-time occupation that is devoted to service. It requires commitment to the work and solidarity with others doing similar work.[23] The professional was a sort of self-made man, living on his own labor, yet getting cultural cachet for his specialized skills and working intellectually instead of physically. Susan Colón has argued that the period between the 1850s and the 1870s was the key era for the development of professionalism and professional self-scrutiny. Such work included a moral component, an idealistic "service ethic" in which the professional devoted himself to helping others and distanced himself from the market by accepting honoraria rather than wages.[24] As Dorice Williams Elliott writes, "it was difficult to tell the difference between the spiritualized vocation considered appropriate to women and the professionalized sense of vocation that male professionals claimed."[25]

The rise of the professional, along with what Harold Perkin calls "the entrepreneurial ideal," formed part of the period's growing idealization of work.[26] In *The Duke's Children*, one of the wealthiest aristocrats in England, the Duke of Omnium, tells his children that it is work "that makes the happiness. To feel that your hours are filled to overflowing, that you can barely steal minutes enough for sleep, that the welfare of many is entrusted to you, that the world looks on and approves, that some good is always being done to others,—above all things some good to your country;—that is happiness."[27] The capacity for self-disciplined, unrelenting productivity in the face of adverse circumstances guaranteed a man's probity, confirmed the middle class's superiority to the debilitated aristocracy, and endowed its practitioner with spiritual benefits. Bronwyn Rivers sums it up:

> From Thomas Arnold's injunctions to Rugby students that work was the prime human calling, to Thomas Carlyle's dictate that "Work is alone noble," writers elevated work as a prime virtue in itself. Religious beliefs were closely tied to this valuing of work, particularly through the influence of the Protestant work ethic, which connected work to the acquisition of a state of grace. Work was also said to bring the personal benefits of self-improvement and happiness.[28]

Of these claims, the most famous was Thomas Carlyle's oft-cited claim in *Past and Present* (1843): "For there is a perennial nobleness, and even sacredness, in Work. Were he never so benighted, forgetful of his high calling, there is always hope in a man that actually and earnestly works: in Idleness alone is there perpetual despair. . . . The latest Gospel in this world is, Know thy work and do it."[29] Such exhortations must have felt peculiarly acutely poignant to a class of persons consigned to "Idleness" for the duration of their adult lives. Living as they did in a culture that revered work, middle-class women mourned their helplessness. In 1851, Charlotte Brontë insisted, "After all—depend upon it, it is better to be worn out with work in a thronged community, than to perish of inaction in a stagnant solitude."[30]

Thus Victorian novels often passionately insisted on women's "calling" to exercise their talents, improve their society, and engage in meaningful occupation—not to mention getting paid—and to that extent, emulate their professional male brethren. However, Victorian novels did not often imagine a plot in which those women could succeed. If single women did male-identified work in novels, they were often strangely defeminized, unmarriageable beings, like the female lawyers Sally Brass, Cornelia Carlyle, and Judy Smallweed, or the female bankers Mrs. Clennam and Catherine Vernon. If married women tried to work, they were punished by miserable unions or by the death or suffering of family members that their attention might have prevented; such erring women include Dorothea Casaubon, Flora Rivers, and Mrs. Jellyby. These are generalizations, of course, but they name the dominant, if not necessarily exclusive, vocational plots available to women. The vocational novel thus presents the odd combination of a powerful call for women's work, matched by an equally strong tendency to punish, deny, or suppress women for pursuing that work in marriage.

Women are made to crave professional work that they cannot get, continue, or do well. It is a plot that is set up to fail.

Vocational Rhetoric: The Langham Place Writers

The vocational marriage plot was set up to fail because of a major discursive shift in the mid-Victorian period. A particular kind of rhetoric about work began around 1855 and lasted through the late 1860s. It was the sustained campaign for work for women centered on the reformers associated with the Langham Place group. It was not that these writers invented the cause of work for women, which, after all, was eloquently expressed in earlier texts including *Jane Eyre* and *Aurora Leigh*; it was, rather, that they codified, centralized, and turned this urge into a narrative form. The Langham Place advocates essentially marketed the notion of vocation for women and, like other forms of marketing, made it ubiquitous. They organized work into a genre, with a recognizable character experiencing predictable stages in a predetermined narrative. Key vocational marriage plots of the 1860s—*Middlemarch, Can You Forgive Her?, Miss Marjoribanks*, and *The Clever Woman of the Family*—engage explicitly with the Langham Place model, naturalizing and disseminating what amounts to a newly codified notion of womanhood.

Until the mid-1850s, Victorian fiction offered a wide spectrum of ideas about women and work. In Charlotte Brontë's novels, published between 1847 and 1853, Jane Eyre, Lucy Snowe, and Caroline Helstone want work desperately. Yet Emily Brontë's female characters remain quite indifferent to the possibility, while Anne Brontë's protagonists, Agnes Grey and Helen Huntingdon, tend to take it for granted as a necessary part of daily labor, sometimes rewarding, sometimes grueling. In Dickens's novels, particularly *David Copperfield* (1850), *Nicholas Nickleby* (1838), and *Bleak House* (1852–1853), many women want and expect to work. Sophy Traddles, Dora, and Agnes all seem to enjoy working; Kate Nickleby works; Esther, Caddy, and of course Mrs. Jellyby see themselves as inherently working subjects.[31] Meanwhile, Judy Smallweed in *Bleak House* (1853), and Sally Brass in *The Old Curiosity Shop* (1841) helped disseminate the mid-century image of the monstrous female worker, who was unsoftened by the relational demands of marriage and had an unhealthy, parasitic attachment to a professional brother.[32] Similarly, Elizabeth Gaskell has sympathetic working-class women, a nurse in *Ruth* (1853) and a dressmaker in *Mary Barton* (1848). But her later novels, *North and South* (1854) and *Wives and Daughters* (1865), written during the years of the Langham Place rhetorical explosion, showcase women of the gentry class who have no such recourse and suffer for their lack of ability to intervene effectively in the lives of the men they care for.

It is this robust pragmatism and flexibility that would drop out of the vocational narrative in the next few decades. Most of the time, in 1840s and 1850s novels, work is respectable and nondescript. Some jobs are acceptable, while others aren't. Work's necessity is taken for granted as a means to make a living and keep oneself occupied. It may or may not continue after marriage, depending on the couple's needs and their class status. Work is as individuated as any other part of the characters' biographies.

Aurora Leigh (1856), which was published just as the Langham Place campaign got underway, offered what may have been an even more inspirational vocational tale than *Jane Eyre*. Aurora refuses to marry her cousin until he learns to respect her work as a poet. There is not the slightest expectation that she will give up her career upon marriage; rather, the marriage is a partnership between his philanthropic and her poetic genius. In its calm assertion of women's genius, and their need for a professional exercise of that capacity, *Aurora Leigh* was groundbreaking and deeply influenced members of the Langham Place circle, including Bessie Rayner Parkes, Barbara Leigh Smith (later Bodichon), and Millicent Garrett Fawcett.[33] Another of Barrett Browning's friends was Anna Jameson, a prominent writer on art and history, who, born in 1794, was a kind of elder statesman for young women like Parkes and Leigh Smith. These women formed the nucleus of the Langham Place group, named after the address of their headquarters.

The members of the Langham Place group initially worked for the Matrimonial Causes Act of 1857, but once that passed, they had to decide what their next campaign would target. Parkes and Leigh Smith decided that reforming women's access to work was more pragmatic than trying to redress discrimination generally and more likely to win public support than fighting for divorce or suffrage.[34] Their vocational campaign is generally seen as starting with Jameson's lectures of 1855, published under the title of *The Communion of Labour* in 1855–1856.[35] *Aurora Leigh* may be the last major text that imagined a married women's successful career, since it appeared just before *The Communion of Labour* initiated a flood of vocational writings that would forever change the discourse of women and work.

The extent and significance of the Langham Place group's writings on work can scarcely be exaggerated. Rosemary Feurer writes, "One need only read the titles of the books of leading early feminists to realize the centrality of the issue of work to them." She cites Barbara Leigh Smith, *Women and Work* (1857), as well as Bessie Raynor Parke, *Essays on Woman's Work* (1866); Josephine Butler, *The Education and Employment of Women* (1868); Josephine Butler, ed., *Woman's Work and Woman's Culture* (1869); Emily Faithfull, *Women's Work, With Special Reference to Industrial Employment* (1871).[36] Even this list understates the number of people involved, since it leaves out Dinah Mulock Craik's *A Woman's Thoughts about Women* (1858), centrally concerned with work for single women, and Anna Jameson's formative *The Communion of Labour: A Second Lecture on the Social Employments of Women* (1855), as well as important books by John Duguid Milne, Jessie Boucherett, and Mary Taylor, not to mention numerous articles in the Langham Place group's periodicals, the *English Woman's Journal* (succeeded by *The Englishwoman's Review*) and *Victoria Magazine*. Moreover, several of these books were worked on by different authors; thus George Eliot helped Barbara Leigh Smith Bodichon with *Women and Work*, and Butler's *Woman's Work and Woman's Culture* included articles by nearly a dozen different writers, including Frances Power Cobbe, Jessie Boucherett, Sophia Jex-Blake, and Elizabeth C. Wolstenholme.

In so large a movement, there was, of course, considerable variation, but certain shared ideas became central to the work of the Langham Place group. Jordan notes, "It was during this brief period [from 1855 to 1857] . . . that the belief that women should earn their own livings ceased to be the odd cranky solution proposed on occasion by a number of people to diverse social problems, but coalesced into a discourse, a body of argument whose truth might be contested or defended, but whose existence *as* a discourse was known and acknowledged."[37] "Work" centralized all the disparate problems previously associated with the Woman Question. Coeducation? Coeducation was good because it would train women for jobs. Prostitution? Prostitution would be eradicated when women could do other kinds of work. Marriage property? Property issues would be resolved when women could earn their own keep. In Jordan's words, the "features entangled in the diverse and contradictory debates over the woman question were melded together to form the coherent discourse of women's work in the world as it came to be promulgated by the Women's Movement, a discourse that argued a single structural cause for the various problems facing women, and proposed a social solution."[38]

However, the new advocacy constructed work as an activity that stopped at marriage. Helsinger, Sheets, and Veeder argue that "in part this emphasis must have been a deliberate decision by feminists: to focus on work for single women was to avoid the threat to home and family perceived in the employment of married women."[39] Indeed, Jordan surmises that the writers formulated this strategy in order to answer W. R. Greg's article "Why Are Women Redundant?," in which Greg expressed anxiety that if single life was made economically easy for women, they would never get married at all.[40] In response, the women of Langham Place stressed that once women wed, their primary career had to be caring for their homes and families. This position was taken by Bessie Rayner Parkes, Frances Power Cobbe, Emily Davies, Emily Faithfull, and even John Stuart Mill, who wrote that "like a man when he chooses a profession, so, when a woman marries, it may in general be understood that she makes choice of the management of a household, and the bringing up of a family, as the first call upon her exertions."[41] Even if a woman did find work, it was only for the limited and uncertain period before marriage, as Julia Wedgwood warned, making it impossible to settle down because everything might have to stop at any moment if the great event happened.[42]

This married-woman deadline usefully facilitated fidelity to domestic ideology. As we saw in Chapter 3, the notion of the domestic sphere developed as an originally feminist innovation, an attempt to give women their own realm. Thus Victorian activists did not necessarily see their role as fighting domestic ideology. Rather, by insisting that women's primary responsibilities remained familial, private, domestic ones, activists maintained continuity with the main current of feminist thought in the period.

The campaign's decision to limit work to unmarried women also derived from the 1851 census, which found more women than men in Great Britain. The numbers were startling: "By 1851, for every one hundred women in Britain there are only ninety-six men; of every one hundred women over twenty, only fifty-seven are married—thirteen are widowed, and thirty have not married. Nearly one half of the adult women in Britain—two and a half out of six million—have no spouse to support them."[43] Clearly some women would not be able to rely on men to support them and would be required to earn their own way. This demographic discovery, dubbed the "odd woman" debate, powerfully fueled the drive for work. However, this argument tacitly defined work as something women did in lieu of marriage, an activity reserved for single women.

However, there was a second precept in Langham Place writing that pulled away from domestic ideology and toward egalitarian rights discourse. These advocates argued that work was a basic tenet of human development, a fundamental right. Jameson wrote firmly, "In a free country, and a Christian community, a woman has the rights which belong to her as a human being, and as a member of the community, and she has no others. I think it a dangerous and a fatal mistake to legislate on the assumption that there are feminine and masculine rights and wrongs."[44] Women's rights to labor and to legal protection, Jameson insisted, "are her rights, not more or less than the rights of the man."[45] Similarly, Craik demands something for women that she calls a "right": "the right of having something to do."[46]

In an odd way, women became visible to the law as egalitarian subjects only insofar as they worked. If women were now to be understood as autonomous agents, and if that identity was developed through work, then work became the key to their existence in the new discursive regime. "To obtain a firmer footing on the earth's broad surface, to acquire some weight in affairs, to be taken into some real account as the half of humanity, women must work," insisted one writer.[47] Similarly, John Duguid Milne wrote that "the mind is in its nature active, and can be formed only in activity; the character is in its nature active, and can be formed only in activity."[48] In the era of the Gospel of Work, work made women visible as half of humanity, literally forming their minds and characters. Work is the mechanism through which personhood forms. In 1855, J. W. Kaye wrote an article called "The Non-Existence of Women" in which he argued that married women's status as legal nonentities had a catastrophic ripple effect through the rest of their lives.[49] "The effect of this [non-existence] is to limit the aspirations, to paralyze the energies, and to demoralize the characters of women," Kaye warned. "They are born and educated, as it were, for total absorption."[50] Deterred from working, they spent their lives in querulous idleness, having ceased to exist psychologically, socially, or legally.

The problem is that these two positions conflicted. If domestic-ideology advocates assumed that only unmarried women needed work, then they framed work as an economic necessity rather than a quality of personal fulfillment. If work was about earning, it could be relinquished; once a woman had a husband to support her, she could stop working, and in fact she ought to be eager to stop inasmuch as her natural place was in the home.[51] But egalitarian arguments claimed that one's vocation could never be surrendered: it was a bedrock right and a lifelong need. The period's marital reforms, particularly the Married Women's Property Act and the Matrimonial Causes Act, inculcated the idea that women were egalitarian individuals whose marital relationship was a secular contractual partnership, not a sacred duty or a relational merging into a shared identity. If the capacity to work was the basis of modern identity and the guarantor of social existence, then it had to be retained. Vocationalism became a space in which a prior domestic separate-sphere ideology had to consort uneasily with a newer discourse of women's legal and philosophical rights, and this coalition was highly unstable.[52]

These manifestos notably construct the denial of work as a health issue. Virtually every writer on the subject asserts that failure to work destroys the body and the mind. Frances Power Cobbe warned that idle women become tiresome and incompetent, while Julia Wedgwood claimed that such women live unreal lives and see their powers wither away.[53] Bodichon warned that "she will surely be ill, miserable, or go mad if she has no occupation."[54] The articles vividly warned of dissipated idleness, wasted years, and withered abilities. [55] "Doomed to such death in life, for these long and dreary adult years," Milne warned, "the pain suffered, the diminished energy, the sleepless nights and useless days, are a serious drag on women's usefulness and happiness."[56]

Significantly, all three of these causes—unmarried women's poverty, liberal self-determination, and personal health—were rhetorically formulated to focus on the effects, not of working, but of failing to work. Thus readers were most frequently exhorted to imagine not the pleasure of achievement but the pain of being denied self-determination, being unable to support oneself, and experiencing one's body and mind failing. These publications depict vocational need thwarted (whether by marriage or by a cruel world), and the woman suffering as a result.

It was understandable that feminist advocates focused on current suffering instead of future hope. Most middle-class Victorian women did not have paid work outside the home, so it was easier to critique the current situation than to imagine a different future. This choice also opened up rhetorical options. Readers of melodrama, sentimental fiction, and Gothic novels enjoyed weeping over novels depicting middle-class women as people doomed to "die young, cramped, and thwarted," condemned to misery as a "a hostage in the home."[57] Sentiment had a history of mobilizing political involvement; it was invoked on both sides of the slavery debate in the Romantic period, and it was intended to move people toward right action.[58] From the helplessly imprisoned Gothic or melodramatic heroine, to the agonized sensation-fiction sufferer, to the miserably repressed authoress, suffering had been a major way of constructing Victorian female narratives.[59] Ann Cvetkovich argues, however, that by the Victorian period, sentimentality actually disciplined and retrained readers into merely personal expressions of feeling, foreclosing actual political action.[60]

Whether efficacious or not, this rhetorical choice had long-reaching consequences. This writing placed failure at the heart of feminism. To suffer and be still meant to be a woman. Although it was Martha Vicinus's groundbreaking collection of 1972 that popularized this phrase, Sarah Stickney Ellis invented "suffer and be still" in 1842. Deploring the fact that men must give up the poetry of their nature in order to work, Ellis reminds female readers that they must keep their poetic sensibility alive, for a woman's life "is one of feeling, rather than of action; whose highest duty is so often to suffer, and be still; whose deepest enjoyments are all relative; who has nothing, and is nothing, of herself; whose experience, if unparticipated, is a total blank."[61] Because women are non-existent (to use J. W. Kaye's term), they must find their compensation in imaginative life.

The Suppressive Hypothesis

It is not particularly novel to regard being a middle-class woman as a state of suppression, denial, stasis, decline, and failure. But what is unusual about Langhamite rhetoric is that it made vocational identity into something that competed with romantic love. To be a woman who wanted to work (and who was doomed not to work) was to occupy a particular model of subjectivity. That model was a different one from the marital ideal.

One useful way to understand this identity is to use Foucaultian sexuality as a parallel. In *The History of Sexuality*, Foucault noticed that in the nineteenth century, the oft-expressed belief that sex was being repressed offered an excuse for talking about it constantly: "sex became something to say, and to say exhaustively."[62] The "repressive hypothesis," then, named the notion that repression was both widespread and damaging, and had to be evaded by increasingly complete revelations. The result was a "discursive explosion" by the 1890s that sustained multiple medical, psychoanalytical, and juridical institutions. Sex gained a privileged status as the truth of a person, the basis of an identity, most notoriously in the invention of the homosexual: "the sodomite had been a temporary aberration; the homosexual was now a species."[63]

For 1860s Langhamite writers, work operated like sex did for 1890s Foucaultian subjects. Like sex, work was the subject of a discursive explosion, conferring new importance on what had previously been seen as an ordinary practice, and not a particularly dignified or interesting one. It offered a new template for a different understanding of identity: a person who worked became a person fundamentally different from one who did not. Middle-class women often regarded their desire for work (like sex) to be a source of shame—the work itself hidden from strangers, done in odd hours, denied by families—so that work for women was associated with a furtive, embarrassing, private drive.

Work and sex, both vitally important, had to be performed correctly. Fiction showed what might happen if one got it wrong. Female vocationalism had its perversities, its forbidden pleasures associated with queer individuals (perhaps we should call them vocational inverts), people like Sally Brass, Judy Smallweed, or Cornelia Carlyle. It had its version of erotomania (employomania?) in work-obsessed figures like Mrs. Jellyby or Mrs. Clennam. Yet one couldn't opt out, either, since eschewing this activity inevitably caused dysfunction: hysteria, dullness, apathy, emotionalism, failure to concentrate. Experts were necessary to guide the middle-class subject in the right ways of doing what had previously been done without too much thought.

We might call the vocational rhetorical explosion the "suppressive hypothesis," for it claims that women's natural urge to work gets suppressed, just as the repressive hypothesis posits that a natural erotic drive gets repressed. In both cases, these claims are constructs that serve particular interests. The suppressive and the repressive hypothesis are both policed by medical threats. Foucault argues that the sexual drive was justified in the name of physical and psychological health. As we have seen, the vocational drive (for women) was similarly invoked for the sake of their mental and economic health. Just as reproductive heterosexual sex became the norm, from which all divergence was pathological, so too feminized professional work (particularly artistic and philanthropic work) was defined as the ideal for women, from which divergence was problematic. Just as sexualized medicine threatened anyone who diverged from heterosexual reproductive marital intercourse with a diagnosis, so too did failure to work "properly" create a pathology—and in both cases it was the same convenient illness.[64] Bodichon wrote that "idleness, or worse than idleness, is the state of tens of thousands of young women: in consequence . . . that one terrible disease, hysteria, in its multiform aspects, incapacitates thousands."[65] At the same time, vocational desire could move and rouse youths; in Bodichon's peroration, in fact, arousal to vocational desires replaces susceptibility to marital hopes: "Oh young girls! waiting listlessly for some one to come and marry you. . . . Arouse yourselves! Awake! Be the best that God has made you."[66] Unmarried women were essentially comatose, needing to stir their deeper drives if they were to become fully healthy.

To modern readers, Bodichon's peroration may seem inherently erotic, but I want to question our hastiness to assume that sex constitutes the real truth of any discussion of thrilling feelings. Indeed, historically, the vocational discursive explosion preceded the sexual one, so it makes at least as much sense to think that seem like erotic dynamics really refer to underlying discourses of work. Work desire and erotic desire coexist in nineteenth century writing. Sometimes one stands in for the other, sometimes they act in parallel. And although our critical history of emphasizing desire makes us assume that the underlying reality is always erotic, we also need to be aware that sometimes love is the cover story, and the need to work is the hidden content. St. John Rivers and George Vavasor, for instance, have to propose marriage instead of what they really want, a business partnership. We need to make sure we privilege neither sex nor work as the real story to which the other always points. Both are the subject of crucial Victorian discourses through which institutions and identities that became fundamental to modernity could develop.

We also need to make sure that we read vocational desire the same way we have been able to read sexual desire. Literary critics have developed extraordinary sensitivity to the remotest traces, the subtlest signs, of erotic desire, which we tend to regard as foundational to literary texts. William Cohen, for instance, argues in *Sex Scandal* that sex generates the rich, polyvalent kind of discourse that we call "literary."[67] Peter Brooks's groundbreaking narrative theory relies on the idea that plot works like the male sex drive, through accumulation, climax, and release. Feminist criticism, too, still focuses on erotic drives, as Elliott points out: "Curiously, most discussions of women's desires, even now, equate the word 'desire' with sexual passion or longing."[68]

If we know how to trace desire for erotic pleasure, why not use that same skill to trace the desire for a busy, meaningful, successful life? Repression, need, and pleasure—and the dire hysterical effects of the denial of such pleasures—emerge in a vocational discourse as much as they do in a sexual one. In other words, work in the 1860s acts very much like sex in the 1890s. Elliott points out that "like unfulfilled erotic desires . . . unused ambitious desires might lead to illness and hysteria" (163). Vocation, indeed, may have laid down the pattern that eroticism would subsequently follow.

Both discursive explosions established a normative self. If sex instituted a medicalized, psychologized self, vocation implemented a liberal identity, an independent agent bound to fulfill her private needs without regard to familial or marital expectations. The suppressive hypothesis assumes that the natural state of affairs involves women's free participation in the public sphere, and that this would have happened if not for an unfair suppression, a choking off of opportunity. Vocationalism helped writers conceptualize both a natural state of freedom and a societally imposed suppression.

It is important to note that neither work nor sex single-handedly accomplished the transition to a new model of personhood. They were just the most visible and powerful mechanisms winching a larger cultural turn. In the case of work, vocationalism got support from legal reforms and educational access, for changes to marriage law in the second half of the nineteenth century were based on, and in turn reinforced, an idea of women as egalitarian individuals whose marital relationship was a secular contractual partnership, not a sacred duty or a relational merging into a joint identity. Legal reform thus plays a similar role for vocation in the 1850s and 1860s that medical discourse played vis-à-vis sex in the 1890s.

However, one of the most important elements of the vocational explosion, at least in terms of its influence on the literature of the 1860s, was the fact that while it demanded women's work, it also insistently read that work as a necessary failure. The Langham Place rhetoric argued that women all naturally wanted to work, but (like sex) this natural drive was being frustrated by powerful social mechanisms that repressed and denied its outlet.

Foucault's model offers us one more insight: how a discourse establishes its other. Foucault taught us not to ask "Why are we repressed?" but rather, "Why do we say, with so much passion and so much resentment against our most recent past, against our present, and against ourselves, that we are repressed?"[69] Similarly, the suppressive hypothesis might prompt us to stop asking "Why were we imprisoned by domestic ideology?" Rather, we might inquire, "Why do we say, with so much passion and so much resentment, that we were imprisoned in domestic ideology?"

Although we have seen that the Langham Place writers tried to hold on to domestic separate-sphere ideology, their advocacy of the "rights of women" set in motion the trend that would ultimately undermine this ideal. As modern liberal feminism emerges, domestic feminism becomes cast as its opposite. Additionally, as we saw in Chapter 4, resentment of the newly empowered autonomous female subject was one of the factors that drove the anthropological counter-theory of primitive marriage. John McLennan and Henry Sumner Maine argued that "primitive marriage" involved speechless, passive women, traded or stolen in transactions between men, their only value a sexual one and their experience founded in violence from infanticide to rape. The rise of the Victorian liberal, autonomous, egalitarian female subject left collateral damage in the form of these two alternative models of femininity, both reductive and archaic: woman as domestic drudge or woman as sexual pawn. In the case of domestic ideology, particularly, this late-Victorian dismissal became the normative way to read the movement, obscuring its origins in feminist advocacy and rendering its real achievements in the first few decades of the nineteenth century very difficult to see. For modern scholars (not to mention modern students), the idea that separate spheres might have seemed good for woman at one point now seems completely counterintuitive.

Thus, just as Foucault taught us to see the 1890s as the era when repression got demonized, so too we might see the 1860s as the period when domestic ideology was repudiated. Plenty of 1890s writers still strongly advocated repressing one's erotic desires. Plenty of 1860s writers still strongly advocated restraining one's vocational desires to the home. But in both cases, the discursive explosion began a trend that would eventually make the older position seem unhealthy and outmoded. The repressive hypothesis made the homosexual become a species; but the suppressive hypothesis worked the other way, pushing the woman from a distinct species toward a new status as an egalitarian liberal subject. As such a subject, capable of working, holding property, and entering contractual relations, she was generically indistinguishable from a man, and the markers of her special status—coverture and a separate sphere—increasingly seemed like unforgivably archaic, unfair ideas.[70]

Vocational Narratives

In order to trace the influence of the suppressive hypothesis, I want to move back to Austen and to changing fashions in Austen criticism. Austen's novels manifest the kind of variability we saw in other pre-Langham Place writers, with different vocational fates for different heroines. In *Persuasion, Pride and Prejudice*, and *Mansfield Park*, the female characters seem to look forward to active, useful, busy married lives, whether spent running a ship, managing Pemberley, or organizing the parish.

However, as Edward Copeland has noted, *Emma* expresses horror of work.[71] In *Emma*, Emma Woodhouse has no work, acquires none through marriage, and in fact is the agent of others losing their vocations. Emma's only possible ending is to continue exactly as she is, catering to her father. Her new life as a wedded woman does not provide her with a fresh access of duties; instead, her marriage means that Mr. Knightley must for some period give up his own work.[72] Jane will marry Frank instead of governessing. Harriet will live in the quasi-genteel environs of the Martins' home (where they will be hiring a boy) rather than managing the farm herself.

Post-1850s Victorian critics found this cessation of work deeply worrisome. As readers steeped in the suppressive hypothesis, they had no doubt about what was wrong with Emma. She was, above all, a vocational subject: stifling for lack of employment, failing in crucial ways as a result. An anonymous reviewer in 1870 commented irritably that "at the present day a girl of higher mind would make an occasional exception to the rule, employing her intellect upon better things, and not, as is the case with Emma, using her superior intelligence to do base things with superior vigour."[73] Nor could this writer comprehend Emma's distaste for Jane Fairfax's governessing. Her governessing was "an intention which proceeded from a high sense of honour, and which any right-minded girl would have known how to appreciate. But Emma is always Emma."[74] Indeed, Margaret Oliphant extended this critique to Jane Austen herself, speculating that Austen's humor "is the natural result of the constant, though probably quite unconscious, observation in which a young woman, with no active pursuit to occupy her, spends, without knowing it, so much of her time and youth."[75] In this respect Austen's very style is shaped by her excessive leisure; ironically, her occupation is shaped by her lack of occupation.

For suppressive readers, Emma is an irresistibly apt example of what can go wrong. Emma's bad qualities support a lot of the claims in Langhamite rhetoric. For instance, Emma's aimless, self-indulgent leisure leads her into mischief, into the matchmaking fantasies that damage her friends' lives and risk her own happiness. It makes her into an unsatisfactory dilettante, never finishing her books or paintings, never practicing her music adequately.[76] "She will never submit to any thing requiring industry and patience," Mr. Knightley pronounces (32). This is precisely the kind of deterioration predicted for victims of enforced middle-class leisure. Yet in Austen's novel, Emma, oddly, prospers. A happy Emma—an Emma who is "handsome, clever, and rich, with a comfortable home and happy disposition"—an Emma whose continued life of leisure suits her perfectly—violated the key precepts of the vocationalist era (3). Where was her hysteria, her idleness, her deterioration? The problem with Austen's Emma is that she fails to fail.

Interestingly, after the 1860s vocational explosion got superseded by the 1890s explosion of sexual discourse, *Emma*'s problem ceased to be read as a lack of work and began to be read as a lack of desire. Briefly comparing *Emma* criticism of the nineteenth and twentieth centuries shows that the same critical moves get made, first in the vocational register, then in the sexual one. Both discourses develop the same theory: Emma's character is damaged by a crucial absence, of which she is complacently unaware, and she gets a happy ending only insofar as she unconsciously manages to fill that gap.

Claudia Johnson notes that *Emma* criticism is characterized by "a lively and explicit interest in the sexual irregularities of Emma Woodhouse."[77] From the 1950s through the 1970s, critics speculated on Emma's supposed frigidity. "Postwar discussions of Emma Woodhouse . . . were fixated on Emma's lack of heterosexual feeling to such a degree that Emma's supposed *coldness* became the central question of the novel: was Emma responsive to men? could she ever really give herself in love, and thus give up trying to control other people's lives? would marriage 'cure' her?"[78] Since then, Jill Heydt-Stevenson, Nicholas Preus, and Maureen M. Martin have swung to the other extreme, seeing Emma as ardently (hetero)sexualized.[79] Preus, indeed, sees virtually all of the elements in the novel as clues to Emma's incipient sexualization, including Jane's piano playing, which he regards as a sign that "Jane has discovered her sexuality and Emma seems to recognize this almost subliminally."[80] In this genre, Emma's apparent indifference to sex becomes itself the clinching proof of the extent of her problem, whether that problem is frigidity or powerful desire. Eve Sedgwick notes, "Even readings of Austen that are not so frankly repressive have tended to be structured by what Foucault calls 'the repressive hypothesis'—especially so, indeed, to the degree that their project is avowedly *anti*repressive."[81] In order to liberate Emma, it is necessary first to argue that she is repressed.

Like Margaret Oliphant, D. A. Miller regards the author's lack as crucial, but the missing piece is no longer occupation, but consummation. In *Jane Austen, or, the Secret of Style*, Miller ends up triumphantly ascribing Austen's style to her status as a spinster.[82] For Miller, exclusion from sexual knowledge is the central irritant, the grit around which the pearl of Austen's style coagulates. If Oliphant saw the problem as Austen's lack of work, Miller sees the problem as Austen's lack of sex.

In both the nineteenth century's suppressive and the twentieth century's repressive hypotheses, *Emma* gets read identically, structurally speaking. She suffers a catastrophic secret lack in spite of her explicitly contented prosperity. Each reading depicts Jane Fairfax as a rival who successfully negotiates what Emma does not have. In fact, Austen herself achieves her inimitable style through her similar lack, which, ironically, provokes her to feats of great style. *Emma* criticism gives us a microcosm of the way vocational readings taught us how to perform sexual ones. It also demonstrates that in the character of Austen's who is most full of joyful, triumphant plenitude, failure had to be generated somehow. Ironically, one great achievement of the invention of modern liberal feminism at mid-century was that by emphasizing suffering it deterred us from recognizing female success.

As June Sturrock has shown, three major novels of the 1860s rewrite *Emma: Miss Marjoribanks, Middlemarch,* and *The Clever Woman of the Family.*[83] Yet I want to add that these three rewritings each work to bring an uncomfortably successful woman more in line with the suppressive hypothesis. Oliphant, Eliot, and Yonge thus rewrite Austen to create a story of shameful work and ultimately failure. In each novel, a strong, intelligent woman stuck in a small provincial society desperately wants to improve her neighbor's well-being with well-intentioned schemes of social engineering. Each woman craves a vocation, a need that she struggles to express. That urge may propel her toward ill-chosen unions. Quashing those drives produces mental and physical breakdowns. Each woman suffers terribly if denied work, and she changes fundamentally as a result of the collapse of her vocational wishes. Each subsides into a happy marriage that will redirect and subdue her vocational impulses into the more socially acceptable role of the helpmeet. In each case, she gets some modest work after marriage, but it is now properly rerouted through the husband and made part of marital duties.

Thus Dorothea, Lucilla, and Rachel all undergo a narrative conditioned by the vocational explosion's stress on ambition, suppression, misery, failure, and subsidence into domesticity. *Middlemarch, Can You Forgive Her?,* and *The Clever Woman of the Family* explore what it means to be women defining herself by work that is implacably denied to her. In Margaret Oliphant's *Phoebe Junior* and *Miss Marjoribanks,* Oliphant translates this narrative into a comic register. But whether comic or tragic, these quite different novels show the existence of a vocational narrative that did not exist for *Emma.* These authors had rich social and intellectual ties to the Langham Place circle. Trollope was friendly with Emily Faithfull, Oliphant's dearest friend was Anna Jameson's adoptive daughter Geddie Macpherson,[84] and Eliot was very close to Barbara Bodichon. Such ties did not guarantee sympathy, since most of these writers harbored complicated objections to vocationalist aims. Although these authors range politically from Eliot's eager involvement to Yonge's decided rejection of the vocational campaign, in each case, as we shall see, the suppressive hypothesis dominates their fiction, determining the way they depict middle-class female characters.

The suppressed female subject became the template for imagining a character. A brief examination of these novels will reveal why vocational marriage became impossible after 1860.

Vocational Novels of the 1860s, or, Why Women Don't Work

Margaret Oliphant's *Miss Marjoribanks* is a rarity: a comic, unsentimental account of a woman's desire for a career. In an article published in 1858, Oliphant boldly asserts that meaningful work is a more important need than marital love.

> If a woman is certain that she is more fitted to be the mistress of a house, and the mother of a family, than anything else, and that this is her true vocation—spite of all natural human prejudices in favour of the natural preliminary of marriage, we are bound to declare that her first duty, as it seems to us, is to *be* married, even though it should be quite impossible for her to persuade herself that she is "in love" before.[85]

Marrying without love in order to pursue vocation characterizes many of Oliphant's female characters. Hester, Kirsteen, Phoebe, and Lucilla—to name only the best-known female characters in her oeuvre—either eschew marriage or make practical, vocational choices, marrying for a future of useful work rather than romantic love.

However, what is particularly unusual about Oliphant's novels is that the men get the vocational narrative as well. In *Miss Marjoribanks* (1866), Lucilla Marjoribanks's willingness to contemplate marriage with scions of the Church, Parliament, and the Navy is matched by the men's equally non-romantic appreciation of her skill as a manager of their careers. Men and women alike recognize that marriage simply presents a field for the exercise of Lucilla's managerial genius. With scrupulous fairness, Oliphant gives romantic-familiar rivalries to both Mr. Cavendish and Miss Marjoribanks. In a later novel, *Phoebe Junior*, she has a character who marries for love and finds himself out of work as a result. His newfound leisure "was a drawback to him, and cramped his mental development; but he was happy in his home with his pretty Ursula, which is probably all the reader will care to know."[86]

In *Miss Marjoribanks*, Lucilla Marjoribanks marries her hapless cousin Tom out of a kind of exasperated familiar affection, not a romantic passion. What's more, a major drawback to the marriage, in Miss Marjoribanks's viewpoint, is that Tom has no job and intends to save her from working. "I mean to take care of you, Lucilla; you shall have no more anxiety or trouble. What is the good of a man if he can't save the woman he is fond of from all that?" Tom cries, but "Lucilla could not but cast a despairing glance round her, as if appealing to heaven and earth. What was to be done with a man who had so little understanding of her, and of himself, and of the eternal fitness of things?"[87] Ceasing to work is the last thing she wants. Instead, Miss Marjoribanks instructs Tom to buy an estate so that she can design improved cottages and eventually get Tom into Parliament. Lucilla Marjoribanks offers an example of a rare success story in the vocational marriage trajectory.

Ten years after *Miss Marjoribanks*, perhaps in irritated response to novels that depicted vocational marriage as doomed, Oliphant pushed her sturdy advocacy of pragmatic vocational marriage even further. In *Phoebe Junior* (1876), the heroine contemplates the proposal Clarence Copperhead is about to make. A classic familiar suitor, he has known Phoebe all her life; they played together as children and he attends her father's church, and he is competing with a romantic suitor—a handsome, idealistic, charming stranger named Reginald May. Phoebe thinks: "She did not even take the trouble of saying to herself that [Clarence] loved her; it was Reginald who did that, a totally different person, but yet the other was more urgent. What was Phoebe to do? She did not dislike Clarence Copperhead, and it was no horror to her to think of marrying him. She had felt for years that this might be on the cards, and there were a great many things in it which demanded consideration" (300).

The reason to marry is not that she loves him but that he offers a capacity for meaningful work that uses her talents:

> He was not very wise, nor a man to be enthusiastic about, but he would be a career to Phoebe. She did not think of it humbly like this, but with a big capital—a Career. Yes; she could put him into parliament, and keep him there. She could thrust him forward (she believed) to the front of affairs. He would be as good as a profession, a position, a great work to Phoebe. He meant wealth (which she dismissed in its superficial aspect as something meaningless and vulgar, but accepted in its higher aspect as an almost necessary condition of influence), and he meant all the possibilities of future power. Who can say that she was not as romantic as any girl of twenty could be? only her romance took an unusual form. It was her head that was full of throbbings and pulses, not her heart. (300)

Just as Oliphant recommended in "The Condition of Women," careers matter more than love. Here we see the vocational marriage endorsed with dazzling courage. "He would be a Career, but he was not a Passion, she said to herself with a smile" (302).

Phoebe, like Miss Marjoribanks, get the typical post-Langham Place job of the parliamentary ghostwriter to her husband. In both cases, however, these women make their husbands' careers possible. As Clarence says, she is "the only one in the world that can do the business instead of coaches. Phoebe knows I'm fond of her, but that's neither here nor there. Here is the one that can make something of me. I ain't clever, you know it as well as I do—but she is. I don't mind going into parliament, making speeches and that sort of thing, if I've got her to back me up. But without her I'll never do anything" (403). Love is irrelevant, "neither here nor there." What's important is that she will facilitate his career. Phoebe and Miss Marjoribanks remain two of the only characters who achieve successful vocational marriages after Langham Place. Oliphant manages this fate partly through comedy, although it remains unclear exactly what work Oliphant's irony does. Is she satirizing her self-sufficient heroines, or a world that would, absurdly, expect them to give up "Careers" for love?

Ironically, it was perhaps Oliphant's hostility toward the Langham Place writers that enabled her to formulate a narrative of female vocational success. By the 1870s, to show a woman triumphing and finding a robust career—and valuing her career more than her love life—was, oddly, a sign of one's non-allegiance to the feminist narrative of female suppression. Yet this robustly pragmatic narrative would have no successors. No heroines in any major novels of the late nineteenth century follow Phoebe's example.

If Oliphant was ambivalent about Langham Place ideas, George Eliot was so sympathetic to their campaign that one might almost consider her a member. She had been friends with Barbara Bodichon and Bessie Rayner Parkes since the early 1850; Bodichon was, indeed, "the most constantly valued friend of her adult life."[88] Eliot helped her compose *Women and Work*, and Eliot's reviews for the *Westminster Review* provided the model for *Victoria Magazine*, although Eliot did not approve of the quality of the journal.[89] Eliot used Bodichon as the model for Romola, and in Gillian Beer's words, perhaps "Bessie Parkes and Barbara Bodichon provided models of Dorothea's possibilities, and measures of her curtailment."[90]

Eliot's political commitment to Langham Place campaigns echoed throughout her fiction. From her first full-length novel, *Adam Bede* (1859), through *Daniel Deronda* (1876), Eliot depicts intelligent, passionate, driven women who nonetheless fail to achieve meaningful work. As Dorothea Barrett notes, Eliot "was a woman whose vocation was to explore again and again the question, how can women satisfy their need for vocation?"[91] Critics since Florence Nightingale have deplored the fact that Eliot consistently depicts professional fulfillment as impossible for women, in spite of her own eminently successful career. What I want to suggest here is that this narrative should be read as the most profoundly influential and successful instantiation of the suppressive hypothesis. Placing female failure at the heart of women's narrative, Eliot both popularizes and perpetuates the story that Langham Place was starting to tell.

Adam Bede, written in the first ardent years of the vocationalist campaign, expresses some of the ideas that were beginning to get an airing. Dinah is "the only heroine in any of the George Eliot novels who has a definite vocation [yet] chooses a marriage which is bound to conflict with her work, relinquishes her work without apparent pain, and subsides into the role of helpmate and mother."[92] Dinah does not seem to suffer when her occupation gets foreclosed, and no other female characters languish for lack of meaningful work. This emphasis on successful vocation, with relative indifference to the effects of its later failure, indicates that this novel emerges at a very early moment in the discursive explosion.

Indeed, *Adam Bede* may have been written in a period of hopefulness and excitement about female vocation. Eliot composed it between October 22, 1857, and November 16, 1858.[93] Jennifer Stolpa points out that in 1852, Eliot had met with Florence Nightingale on her return from Kaiserwerth. Moreover, Eliot was friendly with Anna Jameson between 1852 and 1854.[94] Dinah Morris's marriage to Adam Bede can be seen as exemplifying Jameson's theory in which feminine skills (cherishing and purifying) meld with masculine skills (working and providing) to provide a perfectly crafted "communion of labour."[95]

Adam Bede was inspired by Eliot's aunt, Elizabeth Evans, a fierce Methodist preacher who had once counseled a girl in prison for infanticide. She continued her preaching even after the Methodists forbade female ministers in 1803, simply moving to the allied group of Primitive Methodists. According to Stolpa, in fact, many Methodist women defied the injunction and continued to preach for decades, not being fully silenced until 1850.[96] While Eliot wrote this novel, she and Lewes called it "My Aunt's Story."[97] At some point, however, Eliot decided to give it a new title that centered the narrative on a male character, and she rearranged the chronology of the novel to make Dinah's marriage and motherhood coincide with the injunction forbidding preaching. Elaine Lawless views these choices as a betrayal. "In the novel Eliot undermines the right of Dinah to be the central figure, has extreme difficulty allowing this woman preacher to be a strong character, and, in the end, forces her to submit to the will of a male character, Adam Bede, in a completely unsatisfying conclusion called 'Marriage Bells.' "[98]

Instead of Dinah's vocation assisting her husband, her marriage marks its retreat into a private hobby, a personal activity performed in her spare time. Dinah's post-marital work becomes privatized. She continues her vocation in the form of visiting, teaching, and cottage preaching, but these are quite appropriately feminine avocations, being unpaid, morally improving work conducted in private homes. The one part of her vocation that placed her in the public sphere stops in a way that curiously and suspiciously coincides with her marriage, especially since her husband endorses her suppression.

The gratuitous nature of this cessation is, typically, expressed by a minor character who can safely express rebellious dissatisfaction so as to leave the main characters luminously contented. Seth Bede insists that it is "a sore pity" Dinah stopped; she ought to have continued her vocation.[99] His one dissenting voice—"This was a standing subject of difference rarely alluded to"—is allowed to stand as the moment that troubles the supposedly serene ending, the problem unresolved.[100] Meanwhile, Adam Bede, who is equally defined by his vocation, never has to relinquish his work. Instead, he moves up inexorably through favors shown by neighbors and employers, getting better and better jobs. Adam's private relationships conduce to his work, as his friendship with Arthur and his possible marriage to Mary Burge both advance his career. But Dinah's private relationships coincide with the curtailment of her work. Their moment of "communion of labour" marks the crossover of two different trajectories, moving in opposite directions.

Even if we are not yet encouraged to read Dinah's ending as tragic, the important fact is that Eliot wrote her vocation as incompatible with her marriage. "The only interpretation that makes sense of this equivocal ending," Barrett argues, "is that which sees vocation and sexual fulfilment as mutually affecting but essentially separate needs which, in the case of women, because of various internal and external impediments . . . can rarely be simultaneously fulfilled."[101] *Adam Bede*'s ending importantly institutes erotic and vocational success as parallel, incompatible narratives.

In order to do this, Eliot had to deliberately alter her source narratives. Her aunt's real-life example offered Eliot two possibilities. Like Elizabeth, Dinah could have kept on preaching even after the Conference decision of 1803. Also like Elizabeth, Dinah could have married a devoted Methodist and worked with him in joint exercise of their religious mission. Elizabeth was married to Eliot's uncle Samuel, the source for Seth's character. Seth's strong support of Dinah's continued preaching makes it clear that marrying him would have perpetuated, not ended, her public speaking. Alternatively, Eliot could have imagined a "communion of labour" in which Dinah's special skills combine with Adam's in order to perpetuate the best work of both, perhaps showing a scene of village visiting in which Adam constructed needful furniture or shelter, while Dinah ministered to the inhabitants' feelings. Instead, Eliot created an abrupt, uneasy ending, focusing on loss—the cessation of Dinah's work—and dissension within the family, as the brothers argue over it. Although Dinah herself does not articulate the characteristic lassitude, dissatisfaction, and decay associated with suppression, Lawless has argued that we see it in the text, as Dinah anxiously gazes out for Adam and begs him to come in, replicating Lisbeth's querulous dependency.[102] This silencing, this unexpected thwarting of the heretofore successful working woman via marriage marks an early emergence of the Langham Place narrative, which would be fully realized in *Middlemarch*.

Dorothea Brooke is thwarted far more profoundly, and with far more extensively explored consequences, than Dinah. In moving from Dinah to Dorothea, what we see is the development of the suppressive hypothesis, from the rudimentary hints of trouble at the end of Dinah's story to the material of an entire life's tragedy in Dorothea's. Dorothea is the iconic victim of the suppressive hypothesis. After all, the novel is, according to Gillian Beer, "about work and the right to work, about the need to discover a vocation which will satisfy the whole self and to be educated to undertake it."[103] Eliot famously sets up parallel gendered stories of vocation. But at every moment, Dorothea's story is bent by the Langham Place narrative in particular ways, ways that her male counterpart eludes.

Where Adam's vocational story is one of inexorable improvement facilitated by an old-boy network, Lydgate's vocational story is one of professional certainty and delight. Lydgate experiences a blinding flash of certainty, "the moment of vocation had come . . . the world was made new to him" (144). The moment he sees the anatomical entry, he recognizes his future. By contrast, Dorothea never has a specific calling but seems equally happy to draw up architectural plans, contribute to a hospital, visit the poor, learn Greek, transcribe notes on myths, or assist a Member of Parliament in his reformist political activities.[104] This changes Dorothea's story subtly but importantly. If she were driven by a specific vocation, like Lydgate, it would be a case of genius that must find expression. Because Dorothea's need is for any kind of work, however, she can function as Everywoman, as one of many Theresas (in the words of the finale). All that she requires is that her work be ethically admirable according to the middle-class female ideal. Thus her life becomes a study of work in itself rather than women's fitness for a particular kind of work, or women's need to support themselves through that work.

Alan Mintz explains:

> As a woman, Dorothea is not allowed the direct access to the world possible for men. Despite this fact, what she wants most in life is to do some great good for the world, and, although there is no adequate vehicle for this desire, it remains in George Eliot's eyes unequivocally vocational. The impossibility of its satisfaction does not change its nature. In fact, Dorothea's womanhood, instead of being an anomaly, is simply the most extreme example of the variety of constraints and contingencies that frustrate the urge to alter the world.[105]

Yet it is not "Dorothea's womanhood" that prevents her, but a society that imagines womanhood to mean one thing rather than another—a world that assumes women possess only what Casaubon calls "the purely appreciative, unambitious abilities of her sex" (279).

Eliot's use of free indirect discourse also allows her to use the vocational ideas of the 1860s to define a character who is living through the 1830s.[106] Barbara Hardy notes that *Middlemarch* "is written from an authorial viewpoint of the late 1860s, when the woman's movement started."[107] When Dorothea mourns "the stifling oppression of that gentlewoman's world, where everything was done for her and none asked for her aid" and "the gentlewoman's oppressive liberty" (274), she "experiences what by midcentury was 'the fashionable feminine complaint of occupational vacuity'—she has 'nothing to do.'"[108] Feeling the miserable idleness that the Langham Place writers associated with joblessness, Dorothea seeks the kind of vocations they advocated. Dorice Williams Elliott points out that Dorothea's involvement in philanthropy and cottage housing are mid-Victorian causes.[109]

Dorothea's hunger for meaningful work leads her to marry Casaubon in the most famous example of a failed vocational marriage in nineteenth-century fiction. "It always seemed to me that the use I should like to make of my life would be to help some one who did great works, so that his burthen might be lighter," Dorothea muses. This "use" is marital as well as occupational, the two intertwined: "She was looking forward to higher initiation in ideas, as she was looking forward to marriage, and blending her dim conceptions of both" (363, 86).

Yet Eliot is so wedded to the suppressive hypothesis that she *cannot* show successful female work associated with marriage. She depicts Dorothea as a good woman with an ethically admirable ideal of marriage, who, unfortunately but innocently, picks an inferior specimen. Casaubon's failings doom Dorothea's hope for meaningful work in marriage. But after Casaubon dies, Dorothea's vocational hopes are equally blighted, in spite of the apparently propitious conditions of being well provided with a great fortune and endless time to read and learn. As Celia remarks, with her characteristic sense, "I think it is very nice for Dodo to be a widow . . . she can have as many notions of her own as she likes" (536).

The figure of the wealthy and powerful widow was in fact a cultural commonplace. Karen Bloom Gevirtz notes that in the eighteenth century "the widow was, of all women, the best situated for making full use of the new economic opportunities."[110] Legally protected, able to own property and enter into contracts, and head of the household, the widow had a uniquely powerful position.[111] Indeed, when Dorothea becomes a widow, her new status unsettles and intimidates Ladislaw.

Although there is no certain precursor for Dorothea as there is for Dinah, both Barbara Bodichon and Jane Senior have been suggested as models.[112] Both were energetic reformers who achieved success and fame—Bodichon as the driving force of the Langham Place movement, Senior as the first female civil servant in Britain—and both were close friends of Eliot's. Barbara Hardy argues that Dorothea is based not on the mature, successful Jane Senior of the mid-1870s but on the Jane Senior Eliot met in 1869, the frustrated wife trapped in an uncongenial marriage.[113] Q. D. Leavis was the first to argue that Dorothea is based on Oliphant's managerial Lucilla Marjoribanks, pointing out that Eliot would have read the novel in *Blackwood's Edinburgh Magazine* two years before she began *Middlemarch*.[114] Thus one would expect Dorothea's narrative to propel her toward vocational triumph in several registers: structurally, as a wealthy, independent widow; historically, as a figure based on two of the most successful female activists of the period; and literarily, as a character whose prototype was an almost comically successful woman. As in the case of Dinah, Eliot had to alter the trajectory of her character. She had to force her figure into failure.

Dorothea's married life must be a period of failure in order to fit the suppressive hypothesis. As she herself remarks sadly, "I have never carried out any plan yet" (820). At the beginning of the novel we see Dorothea studying Loudon's plans in order to design cottages, learning passages of Pascal and Jeremy Taylor by heart. But when Casaubon tries to teach her Greek, she is "shocked and discouraged at her own stupidity" (65), and after Casaubon's death, she has trouble learning the geography of Asia Minor. Eliot shows us Dorothea failing to concentrate on political economy, even though it was the "never-explained science" always used to extinguish her ideas (18) and therefore something she has long wished to learn. Instead, Dorothea pronounces the names on the map aloud in a kind of "chime." "She looked amusingly girlish after all her deep experience—nodding her head and marking the names off on her fingers, with a little pursing of her lip, and now and then breaking off to put her hands on each side of her face and say, 'Oh dear! oh dear!'" (805–806). Dorothea's inattentive girlishness and silliness, the chiming and pursing, seem to bely the serious mental energies with which Eliot has initially presented her. It is particularly difficult to believe that the woman who enjoyed drawing up architectural plans at the beginning of the novel is having serious difficulty with the spatial organization of a map at the novel's end.

Dorothea's "Oh dear! oh dear!" marks her descent into the kind of dilettantism and degradation that activists regarded as nonworking women's doom. Thus she experiences what Catherine Judd calls "vocational martyrdom," even though her material conditions and the historical situation of her originals would seem far more likely to facilitate a period of vocational triumph.[115]

Dorothea's failure propels her toward romantic marriage. Had her widowhood seemed like a period of intellectual and financial power, readers might not have wanted to see her end it. Yet, like most Victorian novelists, Eliot does not wholeheartedly endorse the romantic marriage. After all, Dorothea's first failed marriage and her equivocal second marriage register the difficulty and the costs of moving from familiar to romantic marriage. Marrying for love is hardly a triumph in *Middlemarch*, but it is a difficult necessity. Ladislaw and Dorothea's engagement is marked by Dorothea's tears, Will's exasperation, and Dorothea's renunciation of her fortune and her hopes (811).

Vocationalism characterizes *Middlemarch*'s ending, but in reformed, displaced, and minimized ways typical of the vocational marriage plot. Serious Dorothea ends up essentially idle, and it is the dilettantish Will Ladislaw who supposedly acquires a real vocation in the end. Dorice Williams Elliott argues that Ladislaw enacts Dorothea's displaced vocational desires.[116] It is as if readers want the vocational urge, once raised, to be sated, even if it can only be resolved by transferring it to a male character. Dorothea ends up with a minor job routed through her husband to reward her for giving him her larger plans. She will help write his parliamentary speeches, the kind of indirect political participation most often vouchsafed to vocationalist female characters. The parliamentary wife redirection offers a vision of political work achieved through language rather than through direct representation.

In the finale, Eliot stresses that Dorothea's is not a personal but a generic tragedy. Dorothea's failure is that of the general social organization, an "imperfect social state" that "we insignificant people with our daily words and acts" prepare for "many Dorotheas, some of which may present a far sadder sacrifice than that of the Dorothea whose story we know" (838). Catherine Gallagher argues that Eliot uses all the characters of *Middlemarch* as types, a generic quality that works in tension with their own particularity.[117] Dorothea, in other words, is already iconic, representative of a type, one of "the number who lived faithfully a hidden life" (838). Thus Dorothea should be read as the embodiment of the feminist rhetoric of work, enacting in every iconic moment the generic situation of women according to this discursive regime. In every stage, Dorothea is exemplary: in her frustration at her gentlewomanly leisure, in her difficulty achieving self-improvement, in the suppression of meaningful work, in her redirection into marriage and motherhood, in her final role as wifely supporter of a Member of Parliament.

Like other nineteenth-century vocationalist novels, however, *Middlemarch* can depict female vocational success in minor, eccentric characters, the saintly protagonist's sidekicks. Mary Garth and her mother are too robust, wry, and unattractive to carry the full romantic freight of the protagonist. Therefore they are allowed to write books and teach children while successfully making pies (243). Comedy—particularly the bodily/sexual adventures of lower class women—becomes one mode for alternative vocationalism, the way of carrying on the older tradition of pragmatic marriage and successful post-marital occupation in fiction.[118]

Middlemarch is the most powerful instantiation of Langham Place rhetoric, but it is important to note that in writing this compelling case study Eliot influenced and revised the Langham Place narrative. By so powerfully envisioning a symbol of female martyrdom, Eliot overrode whatever more hopeful stories might have been visible in the earlier rhetoric and whatever alternatives might have been envisioned by texts like *Aurora Leigh*. Both Florence Nightingale and Barbara Bodichon deplored the ending of *Middlemarch*, although Bodichon's claim that the ending was "unbearably sad" might be read as praise for Eliot's artistry and indeed a recognition of the affective potential of the story of female failure.[119] Failure may not necessarily have been something the women of Langham Place themselves initially saw as central to vocational narratives, particularly when we recall the initial influence of *Aurora Leigh*. It was Eliot who made failure the crucial element of the story. Thus Eliot was not merely reflecting a narrative emerging elsewhere, but actively shaping it, sometimes to the dismay of its originators. Gillian Beer sums up, "What is remarkable is the extent to which the feminist issues of the work were recognized as crucial, and quite specific, by the book's first readers . . . It is tonic to recognise how fully this work was in touch with the issues being debated in the women's movement of the 1850s and 1860s, and how thoroughly it entered the debates."[120]

Turning Dinah aside from the prosperous married career of her original, turning Dorothea away from the kind of mastery associated with widowhood, Eliot institutes a powerful story. If Dinah's and Dorothea's failures seem inevitable and preordained, that is a mark of Eliot's great skill, for historical and material conditions would seem to precipitate them toward successful vocations compatible with marriage. Eliot may not have created this narrative. But she naturalized it and, in that respect, tied it into a longstanding literary tradition of the emotive sympathy with women who suffered and were still (arguably dating from *Clarissa*) moving through sensation fiction's dramatic presentation of emotional agony and looking ahead to the New Woman novels' enshrinement of professional disaster. In that respect, the vocational narrative gained power from a long history of vicarious sentimental pleasure in female pain, but also lost the chance to imagine an alternative sort of story for women.

While Eliot's sympathetic and intimate engagement with the Langham Place campaign led her to extend their ideas, Anthony Trollope's vocational fiction was explicitly designed to critique Langham Place rhetoric. On the one hand, Trollope had a close relationship with reformer Kate Field, and he was willing to contribute to two Victoria Press publications produced by Langham Place.[121] On the other hand, his own published articles on female employment express skepticism, arguing that marriage was a better solution to female boredom than work.[122]

Trollope's *Can You Forgive Her?* (1864–1865) ends up essentially reinforcing the cultural consensus that was forming in the 1860s over the necessity and yet impossibility of work for middle-class women. Alice is surrounded by "a flock of learned ladies" asking "What should a woman do with her life?"[123] Margaret F. King confirms that "Alice's story is partly a narrative response to a specific 'flock of learned ladies,' headquartered by late 1859 in London's Langham Place."[124] Indeed, Trollope locates Alice and her father on Queen Anne Street, only a few streets away from Langham Place.[125] In Alice Vavasor, Trollope—like Eliot—is thinking about how to imagine the generic subject of the Langham Place publications. Alice "had by degrees filled herself with a vague idea that there was a something to be done—a something over and beyond, or perhaps altogether beside that marrying and having two children—if she only knew what it was" (92). What she knows is that she wants real work—an urge no doubt fed by watching her father's unsatisfactory, unproductive career.

Just as Eliot makes Dorothea hunger for any kind of appropriate employment, Alice's vocational yearning is carefully constrained so as to make her a somewhat generic subject. First, Alice is an ordinary middle-class woman, not a radical. Alice is "not so far advanced as to think that women should be lawyers and doctors, or to wish that she might have the privilege of the franchise for herself; but she had undoubtedly a hankering after some second-hand political maneuvering" (93). In this respect she can remain representative, like Dorothea. She is neither a genius requiring an outlet for her heaven-sent skills, nor a perishing woman desperate to support herself—two extreme cases in which readers might be willing to countenance work.

Trollope sets Alice between two marital choices: "the worthy man" John Grey versus "the wild man" George Vavasor (21). Alice feels romantic love for John Grey and vocational passion for George Vavasor. In setting romantic and vocational urges in competition, Trollope concedes that they are parallel feelings of comparable strength. But he also tacitly depicts them as incompatible, for he vests them in different men, associated with divergent futures. Moreover, both are shameful: just as Alice cannot comfortably articulate her erotic desire for John Grey, she also cannot bring herself to pronounce her vocational needs. If it feels unfeminine to own up to her love, it is equally shameful to express her wish for a political career, with an "undefined ambition that made her restless" (92), asking herself "what had she wanted in life that she should have thus quarrelled with as happy a lot as had ever been offered to a woman?" (124).

It is evident that what Alice wants is "a husband whose mode of thinking is congenial to my own . . . a husband who proposes to himself a career in life with which I can sympathize" (287). Although Trollope makes this motive vividly clear to the reader, Alice herself often has trouble articulating or justifying it; she is in a culture in which the yearning for a meaningful life seems like an embarrassing private urge. Reflecting on her decision, she can only berate herself as "an idiot and a fool, as well as a traitor" and asks herself if she had been "mad" to send him away (123–124). Moreover, John Grey is so fundamentally skeptical of this motive that he simply decides she is mentally ill and refuses to break off the engagement, indeed surreptitiously managing her monetary affairs as if he is already her husband in an act that infantilizes Alice, undercutting her own independent will (97–98, 306). Alice's father and the members of Alice's social circle are equally incredulous. *Can You Forgive Her?* shows how misapprehension and skepticism and disapproval (including her own) would undermine a vocationally driven woman at every turn.

The competition between the two suitors structures the plot differently from *Middlemarch*, where Dorothea marries each man sequentially. Here Alice *accepts* each suitor sequentially but because she does not actually marry George, vocational marriage remains a possible idea rather than a lived experience.

George Vavasor's suit reveals how closely vocational marriage resembles other forms of familiar marriage in abjuring romance. Like Jane Eyre, "Alice could not love her cousin and marry him; but she felt that if she could do so without impropriety she would like to stick close to him like another sister" (94). As a comrade, aide, and business partner, George seems acceptable, but the problem is that the romantic component increasingly expected in marriage is not seen as compatible with vocational partnership. "As for that girl's dream of the joys of love which she had once dreamed,—that had gone from her slumbers, never to return. How might she best make herself useful,—useful in some sort that might gratify her ambition;—that was now the question which seemed to her to be of most importance" (263). For women at mid-century, vocational satisfaction might quite legitimately be more compelling than erotic fulfillment. Alice tells George, "Without passion, I have for you a warm affection, which enables me to take a livelier interest in your career than in any other of the matters which are around me. . . . I do feel that I can take in it that concern which a wife should have in her husband's affairs" (274). This line reveals a sense of shared concern about career in marriage, the kind of understanding M. Jeanne Peterson found in real couples.

Moreover, vocational marriage continues familiar marriage's important function of providing arrangements that satisfy pragmatic or social needs. Sharon Marcus argues that Alice "rejects one kind of marriage in order to embrace another; she turns from John, an indomitable superior who insists on the permanence of marriage promises, to George, who allows Alice to define marriage as dissoluble, egalitarian, and contractual."[126] Familiar marriage allows ideas of marriage outside the model of the passionately, indissolubly wedded romantic dyad. As Marcus points out, the fact that Alice could keep her own last name in this marriage symbolizes her continued sense of self, an attractive proposition in the world of vocational marriage.[127] (Similarly, Lucilla Marjoribanks marries a cousin and keeps her own name.) Although familiar marriage sustains a wide range of marital norms, in this case, the Vavasor cousins' arrangement is a characteristically liberal one, involving two equal and separate subjects entering into a well-defined partnership negotiated in writing and predicated on economic exchange rather than emotional need.

The problem is that the vocational suitor does not stay in the box to which she has consigned him. George does not remain a familiar figure, but becomes, horrifyingly, eroticized. He insists on a romantic relation with Alice, demanding that she kiss him. "Was she to give herself bodily,—body and soul, as she said aloud in her solitary agony,—to a man whom she did not love? Must she submit to his caresses,—like on his bosom,—turn herself warmly to his kisses? 'No,' she said, 'no,'—speaking audibly, as she walked about the room; 'no;—it was not in my bargain; I never meant it'" (309). Having envisioned their relationship as a pure partnership, she is appalled by the marital expectation of erotic relations, much like Jane Eyre imagining the horror of St. John's scrupulous performance of a love he does not feel. Jane and Alice agree that there is nothing wrong with a frankly platonic, egalitarian work partnership, but when it fraudulently mimics its rival, romantic marriage, it becomes unspeakable. The growing expectation of romantic marriage taints the original pragmatic arrangement, forcing it to contort itself to mimic something that it is not. Like *Jane Eyre* or *Middlemarch*, this novel contemplates vocational marriage with dismay and then turns inexorably toward a climactic romantic union. These novels' depiction of romantic union as inevitable and passionately desirable, a fitting culmination for a woman's life, helped consolidate the ascendency of the new paradigm.

Although in this chapter I focus on Alice's story, it is worth noting that Trollope plays out the vocational/romantic rivalry three times in the novel. Kate Flint describes "the triumvirate of unmarried woman, wife, and widow, each forced to discriminate between 'the worthy man and the wild man' in their lives."[128] Alice's marriage plot is the middle-class version and the main one, but Glencora has an aristocratic plot, caught between her humdrum, hard-working familiar husband, Palliser, and her exciting, beloved, untrustworthy passionate suitor, Burgo. Meanwhile, in the comic lower-class register, the widow Mrs. Greenow chooses between prosperous but boring Mr. Cheesacre and dashing, shabby Captain Bellfield. In a move that should feel familiar by now, it is only the lower-class comic character who is allowed to satisfy her own wishes, while the middle- and upper-class women get chastened.

In Alice's case, as in Dorothea's case, vocational marriage is a disaster. But whereas Dorothea picked an inept vocational suitor, Alice chooses a villain out of melodrama. Her cousin George Vavasor shows himself to be a vicious, violent, dishonest man who attacks his sister, attempts to murder John Grey, and then flees to America under a false name. Alice finds herself entrapped in a kind of seedy mock marriage, giving away her property without getting any influence in the man's career in return. Instead of a career, she is fleeced—ransacked for property, her own wishes disregarded. Instead of being an egalitarian liberal subject in a contractual relation, as Marcus had optimistically noted, Alice becomes the victim of a tyrannical or savage marriage, the anthropological notion of the 1860s, in which a strong man essentially kidnaps a passive, silent woman for his own purposes.[129] The futuristic form of marriage reverts to the most prehistoric. Compared to the cruelty of George Vavasor, John Grey's absolute rule—which is at least conducted courteously—seems preferable.[130]

Meanwhile, the happiest marriage at the end of *Can You Forgive Her?* appears to be one between two men. As Plantagenet and Glencora Palliser travel with John Grey and Alice, the women discuss their prospective lives as wives and mothers and the men achieve "close intimacy," "intent upon politics" (643). It is Palliser who convinces Grey to go into Parliament. Nervously, Palliser tells his partner, "I hope you'll like it," and assures him that once he takes to the work, he will "get to feel it as I do" (674). This is the vocational equivalent of the wedding scene, companions who will share work, the elder helping introduce the other into his world.

We should not read this scene as an encoded enactment of homoerotic desire, a same-sex marriage plot, because that would be mean casting vocation merely as a cover story for a sexual "real." That is the mistake George Vavasor makes about Alice, assuming her offer to partner with him professionally stands in for coded sexual desire. The men show no signs of an erotic attraction, but a genuine shared bonding experience in talking about Parliament. Indeed, vocation is as strong as sex. The women are consigned to sex—becoming wives and mothers—while the men are assigned to vocation. Both urges, having been strongly evoked in *Can You Forgive Her?*, require narrative resolution. But because Trollope is conservatively unwilling to sate a woman's urge for work, he has to suddenly generate a heretofore unsuspected readiness to change in a character whose primary quality has always been his utterly unyielding self-satisfaction, and a somewhat fairy-tale opportunity ("you might easily find some quiet little borough . . . if you like to spend a thousand pounds, the thing isn't difficult" [618]) in a series that is profoundly committed to depicting the realistic difficulties of electioneering. John Grey's happy ending violates probability, his character, and the work of the rest of the Palliser series that was to come. It can only be justified by the inexorable logic of the vocational urge, which requires to be resolved, much as a story that begins with romantic desire must, in the nineteenth-century novel, move toward a marriage. John Grey and Will Ladislaw are the fortunate recipients of the happy endings their wives wanted, in spite of the fact that the men never wanted them at all.

If the vocational happy ending is less than convincing, so is the romantic happy ending, just as it is not entirely joyful in *Middlemarch*. Alice finally returns to John Grey in a marriage that disempowers her much as her entanglement with George Vavasor had. As King remarks, "at the end of the novel, as Alice accepts Grey's forgiveness and his offer of marriage, the punishment and extinction of her desire for autonomy are completed" (316). When Grey tells Alice that he plans to go into Parliament, she is "afraid to speak" lest she show too much enthusiasm. She finally asks, "Oh, John, what right can I have to say anything?" (644). Tellingly, Alice's last words in the novel are in heartbreaking response to the announcement that her husband has indeed gone into Parliament: "I hope nothing that I have ever said has driven you to it" (675). Renouncing her influence, doubting her right to express wishes, Alice ends in a place of radical self-doubt.

Alice achieves final status as wife to a Member of Parliament, the same ending Glencora gets, and the one we have seen given to Dorothea. The spousal parliamentary ghostwriter becomes the final job of the energetic, dissatisfied, and talented women in other novels: Lucilla in *Miss Marjoribanks* (1866), Phoebe in *Phoebe Junior* (1876), and Angelica in Sarah Grand's *The Heavenly Twins* (1893). Silenced themselves, they speak only through their husbands' voices, much as Dinah's decision to quit preaching is announced for her by her husband, and Rachel Curtis's philanthropic redirection into a local institution gets set up by her husband.

Alice Vavasor is, like Dorothea, a subject of the suppressive hypothesis. Afflicted by idleness and uncertainty, she tries to find meaningful work via marriage, an attempt that ends disastrously. Reformed and reunited with her romantic lover, she gets silence and failure as her portion, except for the minor, mediated role of the political ghostwriter. Alice is more aware than Dorothea of the ways that vocationalism parallels eroticism, perhaps accounting for the fact that she is much more tongue-tied than Dorothea about her wish for work. Free, indirect discourse helped Dorothea express more than her own generation could know, but Alice's characteristic mode is not speech extended impossibly across generations, but inarticulateness. From her inability to speak her vocationalism, to her final denial of a "right to say anything" and renunciation of anything "I've ever said," Alice is finally suppressed. King comments that "Trollope first voices and then attempts to silence the discourse of mid-century feminists."[131] The irony is that, in doing so, he furthered their cause.

Perhaps the novel most critical of the Langhamites was Charlotte Yonge's *The Clever Woman of the Family* (1865), which also "first voices and then attempts to silence the discourse of mid-century feminists." "With *The Clever Woman of the Family* Yonge brings the debate over women and work into a religious context."[132] In *Clever Woman*, like *Can You Forgive Her?*, a woman driven to find meaningful work ends up cowed, silenced, and grateful to be married to a masterful man who teaches her that work belongs in the male homosocial realm. Yet, like Trollope, Yonge accepts the suppressive hypothesis and creates a sympathetic portrait of a woman aching for meaningful work, thus making the vocational figure feel real in spite of its author's personal antagonism to the cause.

Yonge's novel "directly satirized SPEW, the Victoria Press, and *Victoria Magazine* by attributing folly and pomposity to women like the Langhamites," notes Jennifer Phegley.[133] Rachel Curtis's determination to offer vocational training to women in printing and her adoption of a dubious acronym for her job-training organization made it clear that Yonge was specifically targeting Langham Place. And yet Rachel is allowed a heartfelt plea for work. "Here is the world around one mass of misery and evil! Not a paper do I take up but I see something about wretchedness and crime, and here I sit with health, strength, and knowledge, and able to do nothing, nothing—at the risk of breaking my mother's heart!"[134] Rachel laments her enforced dilettantism, a *cri de coeur* reinforced by the narrator's sympathetic commentary a few pages later (38, 42). Yonge offers a convincing, detailed account of the suppressive hypothesis, allowing us to enter Rachel's painful mindset—an act of identifying with her otherwise uncongenial heroine that creates sympathy where we would not normally expect it. Indeed, Yonge praises Rachel's energies, while also giving admiring depictions of other working women, including the Williams sisters, one a governess and the other an editor. The novel strongly supports women's right to work but insists that it be the right kind of work, performed the right way.

The problem is Rachel's "self-sufficiency," a term used repeatedly.[135] Sturrock notes that self-sufficiency was "a commonly used Tractarian diagnostic term," but its opposite is not reliance solely on God but also on other humans—the kind of intersecting network of relationships fostered by disability.[136] Humbled by her own suffering, sensitized to others' pain, Rachel can become a member of a community of care. This reformation also has the effect of perpetuating the suppressive hypothesis, however. Suffering becomes the key to Rachel's reformation, and it also becomes the agent of her story.

Both Alice Vavasor and Rachel Curtis are so eager for work that they ignorantly end up bankrolling unreliable, compelling men who steal their money yet make no political improvements; indeed, in both cases, the man physically abuses those closest to him. Alice and Rachel both suffer as a result, losing their reputations, their money, and indeed suffering so a traumatic change in their prospects that they can only feel incredulous gratitude that a good man is still willing to take them after all. Safely married off to John Grey and Alick Keith, the women are granted the small recompense of projects suitable for wives, funneled through the husbands. While Alice gets to be a parliamentary ghostwriter, Rachel is allowed to help with a convalescent home her husband has established. Her blazing drive for philanthropic improvement is exposed as merely self-serving ambition that must be redirected into motherhood and diffused into the general glow of the shared communal nursing ethos that dominates *Clever Woman*. Alice ends her novel by asking her husband whether she has any right to speak, and Rachel ends hers by demonstrating how her husband silences her. Like Dinah and Dorothea, the women lose their voices and their hopes of careers.

In all these cases, romantic marriage is the enemy of vocation. The woman has to develop shame about her life of useful work and then evince admiration and gratitude for the man whose espousal ends it. *Clever Woman, Can You Forgive Her?*, and *Middlemarch* all start with profound sympathy for an energetic middle-class woman who is wasting her life, but they all demonstrate her catastrophic failures, punish her deeply, engage the reader in voyeuristic enjoyment of her suffering, and depict romantic marriage as her salvation inasmuch as it renders her silent and grateful at last. As we have seen in each chapter in this book, familiar marriage offers alternatives for women's lives that have significant benefits, and the turn to romantic marriage can reasonably be read as tragic. Rachel, Alice, and Dorothea are three exceptional women who could have fulfilled important social functions. But the romantic marriage plot forces them to relinquish the difference they could have made, turning inward to a private dyad, exiled from the larger networks for which they yearned.

The suppressive hypothesis I have been outlining here gives us a way of thinking about what happened to depictions of women by the 1860s. As mid-Victorian feminists transformed woman from a domestic-sphere denizen to an individual liberal agent, they made new kinds of reforms possible—but they did so by associating women with failure. Given the very real legal and political advances made possible by liberal feminism, it may seem petty to note that this form of feminism entailed a cost as well, especially when it is only the loss of an imagined alternative. But any history of feminism must register the reverberations of its decisions. And it seems worthwhile to note that the move to liberal feminism instituted its powerful rhetorical campaign by insisting that happy, successful, working married women could not exist. To some extent, suffrage, coeducation, marriage reform, and employment law came to depend on the constitution of women as suffering, suppressive victim.[137] How might this bending of women's narratives have impacted both the emergent feminist movement and the history of the novel?

We have come, in a sense, to the end of the marriage plot. In vocational marriage, the attempt to achieve familiar marriage is always disastrous. The marriage can never occur, or the marriage is doomed when it does occur, or the story gets shunted off onto comic subsidiary characters, or the woman must be retrained. By the end of the nineteenth century, the fundamental goals of familiar marriage have become recast as personal, perverse, humiliating drives. Vocational marriage's drive to interact with the larger public becomes pathologized as a suppressive-hypothesis hysteria, while disability marriage's yearning for care communities gets diagnosed as attraction to asexual bodies, and cousin marriage's wish to remain close to family is called incest. The Freudian model descends on the familiar marriage and stifles it.

Familiar marriage did not die, but it lost its status in Anglo-American culture. In the twentieth-century Western novel, a character would seek fulfillment through erotic passion, a desire that might or might not be associated with marriage. It is true that familiar marriage persists today, as I mentioned in the Preface, in popular genres like romantic comedies and children's films. But the vision of marriage that had lasted three centuries, the idea of a union that served social needs, no longer received cultural respect. Novels no longer tried to articulate why one might marry for another kind of future, for a different sense of love.

I want the last word to be Maggie Tulliver's plea, which is also a plea to us: "Love is natural—but surely pity and faithfulness and memory are natural too" (469). Throughout this book I have used topographical metaphors to place familiar marriage in relation to its better-known rival. I have described it as the shadowy valley, the side path, and the subterranean lake. But in Maggie's world map, those spaces get reversed. For it is familiar marriage that provides solid, known ground, and romantic marriage that sweeps her dangerously away into powerful currents, unknown waters, fatal floods. Maggie might move ahead to romantic marriage—it is the future, and everything is pushing her toward it. Indeed, today we know: that ship has sailed. In the history of the novel, there is no heading back. But from its deck today perhaps we can look back and regard, with a kind of wondering respect, Maggie's achievement of an almost impossibly difficult mission, her slow, grueling journey to home, to community, to St. Ogg's. We can acknowledge that when choosing a brother or neighbor or disabled suitor, a female character might not be a victim of false consciousness or sexual pathology or trafficking; a woman might have her reasons. The ending of *The Mill on the Floss* requires us to respect Maggie's success in choosing her own path and asks us to pity her as a helpless victim of larger currents. For Maggie's movement attests both to the difficulty of moving against the romantic tide and the need so many Victorian women felt to find a safer harbor.

Notes

CHAPTER 1

1. Charlotte Brontë, *Jane Eyre*, ed. Q. D. Leavis (1966; repr. London: Penguin, 1988), 428. Further references will be to this edition and will be listed parenthetically.
2. A. C. Grayling, *Meditations for the Humanist: Ethics for a Secular Age* (New York: Oxford University Press, 2002), 68.
3. See Ruth Perry, "Introduction," in *Novel Relations. The Transformation of Kinship in English Literature and Culture, 1748–1818* (Cambridge: Cambridge University Press, 2004) for a good review of disputes amongst historians of the family, especially pp.14–21. Also see chapter 2 for an analysis of the family history debates.
4. William Jankowiak, ed., *Romantic Passion: A Universal Experience?* (New York: Columbia University Press, 1995), 4.
5. Deborah Lutz, *The Dangerous Lover: Gothic Villains, Byronism, and the Nineteenth-Century* (Columbus: Ohio State University Press, 2006).
6. Mikhail Bakhtin, "Forms of Time and of the Chronotope in the Novel," in *Narrative Dynamics: Essays on Time, Plot, Closure, and Frames*, ed. Brian Richardson (Columbus: Ohio State University, 2002), 15–24.
7. Lutz, 40.
8. Lutz, 49.
9. Anthony Giddens, *The Transformation of Intimacy: Sexuality, Love and Eroticism in Modern Societies* (Stanford, CA: Stanford University Press, 1992), 38–45.
10. Jean E. Kennard, *Victims of Convention* (Hamden, CT: Archon Books, 1978), 12. Kennard addresses the convention of the untrustworthy vs. the exemplary suitor in Austen, although she reads them somewhat differently than I do. She sees them as embodying qualities that the heroine must embrace or relinquish, and does not connect them to familiar or romantic models.

11. Notice of *The Belton Estate, Saturday Review* xxi, February 3, 1866, 140–142. Cited in David Skilton, introduction to *The Claverings*, by Anthony Trollope (New York: Oxford University Press, 1986), x.
12. Wendy Jones, *Consensual Fictions: Women, Liberalism, and the English Novel* (Toronto: University of Toronto Press, 2005), 7.
13. Elaine Hatfield, "Passionate and Companionate Love," in *The Psychology of Love*, ed. Robert J. Sternberg and Michael L. Barnes (New Haven, CT: Yale University Press, 1988), 191. Elaine Hatfield's earlier research in relationship theory was published under the name of Elaine Walster.
14. William Jankowiak and Thomas Paladino, "Desiring Sex, Longing for Love: A Tripartite Conundrum," in *Intimacies: Love and Sex Across Cultures*, ed. William Jankowiak (New York: Columbia University Press, 2008), 2–3.
15. Raymond Williams, "Dominant, Residual, and Emergent," in *Marxism and Literature* (Oxford: Oxford University Press, 1977), 123.
16. Michel Foucault, *The History of Sexuality: Vol 1, An Introduction*, trans. Robert Hurley (New York: Vintage Books, 1990), 78.
17. Jay Clayton, "Narrative and Theories of Desire," *Critical Inquiry* 16 (Autumn 1989), 36. In Chapter 6, I explore one discursive explosion about a different kind of "craving"—work—but it might be useful to try to perform something like queer readings dedicated to tracing the other objects of desire Clayton mentioned: religion, money, or power.
18. Ros Ballaster, *Seductive Forms: Women's Amatory Fiction from 1684 to 1740* (Oxford: Clarendon Press, 1992); Katherine Binhammer, *The Seduction Narrative in Britain, 1747–1800* (Cambridge: Cambridge University Press, 2009).
19. Elsie Michie, *The Vulgar Question of Money: Heiresses, Materialism, and the Novel of Manners From Jane Austen to Henry James* (Baltimore: Johns Hopkins University Press, 2011).
20. Of course, there are exceptions to the rule, like the rape in *Tess*, or the disastrous money-based Grandcourt marriage in *Daniel Deronda*. My point is simply that most novels stop short of actually enacting these plots, since the mere threat is enough to mobilize the narrative. I am grateful for Helena Michie for a conversation at Dickens Universe in 2014 in which she elucidated this idea.
21. See Claudia Nelson, *Family Ties in Victorian England*, Victorian Life and Times Series, ed. Sally Mitchell (London and Westport: Praeger, 2007); Leila Silvana May, *Disorderly Sisters: Sibling Relations and Sororal Resistance in Nineteenth-Century British Literature* (Lewisburg, PA: Bucknell University Press, 2001); Valerie Sanders, *The Brother-Sister Culture in Nineteenth Century Literature: From Austen to Woolf* (Hampshire, UK: Palgrave, 2002); Joseph A. Boone and Deborah Epstein Nord, "Brother and Sister: The Seductions of Siblinghood in Dickens, Eliot, and Brontë," *Western Humanities Review* 46, no. 2 (Summer 1992): 164–188.
22. Sanders, 100.

23. Mary Jean Corbett, *Family Likeness: Sex, Marriage, and Incest from Jane Austen to Virginia Woolf* (Ithaca, NY: Cornell University Press, 2008), 116.
24. Boone and Nord, 165.
25. Boone and Nord, 165. Also see May and Sanders, and Leonore Davidoff, "Kinship as a Categorical Concept: A Case Study of Nineteenth-Century English Siblings," *Journal of Social History* 39, no. 2 (Winter 2005): 411–428. Davidoff agrees that "brothers and sisters became the archetype of relations between men and women but unsullied by sexuality" (414).
26. Lady Audley marries twice for security, preferring her second husband inasmuch as he gives her a better position. She is quite uninterested in, and perhaps incapable of, romantic feeling. Aurora Floyd's marital suitors, similarly, present various degrees of reassuring affection and moral reliability that is clearly meant to contrast favorably with the presumably erotically tempestuous secret match in her past.
27. Florence Nightingale, "Cassandra," *Florence Nightingale's Cassandra* (1860; repr., New York: Feminist Press, 1979), 49.
28. Joseph Allen Boone, *Tradition Counter Tradition: Love and the Form of Fiction* (Chicago: University of Chicago Press, 1987), 74.
29. I have, for instance, argued that Mr. Venus's love for Pleasant Riderhood in *Our Mutual Friend* is a middle-class norm, inappropriately projected onto people with very different needs. See chapter 4 in *Novel Craft.*
30. Coontz points out that many working-class marriages resisted romantic norms well into the twentieth century. Stephanie Coontz, *Marriage, A History: How Love Conquered Marriage* (New York: Penguin, 2006), 147.
31. Vlasta Vranjes argues that the marriage plot generated a sense of "Englishness" in *English Vows: Marriage Law and National Identity in the Nineteenth-Century Novel* (forthcoming).
32. See Lisa Surridge, *Bleak Houses: Marital Violence in Victorian Fiction* (Columbus: Ohio University Press, 2005); A. James Hammerton, *Cruelty and Companionship: Conflict in Nineteenth-Century Married Life* (New York: Routledge, 1992); and Hammerton, "Victorian Marriage and the Law of Matrimonial Cruelty," *Victorian Studies* 33, no. 2 (1990): 269–292.
33. See Carolyn Vellenga Berman, *Creole Crossings: Domestic Fiction and the Reform of Colonial Slavery* (Ithaca, NY: Cornell University Press, 2006).
34. Susan Meyer, *Imperialism at Home: Race and Victorian Women's Fiction* (Ithaca, NY: Cornell University Press, 2006).
35. Jane Austen, *Mansfield Park* (New York: Oxford University Press, 2008), 220.
36. A word about *Jude the Obscure* may be relevant here. In some ways it is the most trenchant version of the romantic-familiar plot, with the animalistically sensual Arabella versus the non-erotic cousin Sue. Yet Hardy uses this plot in order to eviscerate it. He takes apart the erotic/vocational divide with a vengeance, demonstrating skepticism about female vocation and placing sexuality at the center

of both relationships. In this respect it really needs to be read as part of the fin de siècle's revision of the marriage plot into a plot about sexuality.

37. Lois E. Bueler, *The Tested Woman Plot: Women's Choices, Men's Judgments, and the Shaping of Stories* (Columbus: Ohio State University Press, 2001), 4.
38. Michael McKeon, *The Origins of the English Novel, 1600–1740*, 15th anniv. ed. (Baltimore: Johns Hopkins University Press, 2002), 20.
39. Lawrence Stone, *The Family, Sex, and Marriage in England, 1500–1800* (New York: Harper and Row, 1977). A much more nuanced account of "the integration of love and marriage" and the role of the novel in "providing instruction and orientation in affairs of the heart" can be found in Niklas Luhmann's *Love as Passion: The Codification of Intimacy*, trans. Jeremy Gaines and Doris L. Jones (Cambridge, MA: Harvard University Press, 1986), 10, 11.
40. Stone did modify his claims ten years later. See "Love" in *The Past and Present Revisited.*
41. Helen Berry and Elizabeth Foyster, *The Family in Early Modern England* (Cambridge: Cambridge University Press, 2007), 8.
42. For examples of critics continuing to grapple with Watt, see Kelly Hager, *Dickens and the Rise of Divorce: The Failed Marriage Plot and the Novel Tradition* (Burlington, VT: Ashgate, 2010); and Helen Small, "Against Self-Interest: Trollope and Realism," *Essays in Criticism* 62, no. 4 (2012): 401.
43. Ian Watt, *The Rise of the Novel: Studies in Defoe, Richardson and Fielding* (Berkeley and Los Angeles: University of California Press, 1957), 18.
44. Watt, 65–88.
45. Watt, 92.
46. Watt, 177.
47. Watt, 113.
48. Nancy Armstrong, *Desire and Domestic Fiction: A Political History of the Novel* (New York: Oxford University Press, 1987), 4.
49. Armstrong, 8.
50. Armstrong, 9.
51. Armstrong, 21.
52. Armstrong, 21.
53. Pamela and Jane Eyre directly reform their suitors; Evelina does it indirectly, by choosing the one respectful male over the rakes who continually menace her, showing that a good woman will not choose a dangerous lover.
54. It is, however, worth noting that Jennifer Golightly comes to exactly the opposite conclusion. Golightly believes that eighteenth-century fiction cast an idealized conjugal family as an answer to the flaws of the biological kin. Jennifer Golightly, *The Family, Marriage, and Radicalism in British Women's Novels of the 1790s: Public Affection and Private Affliction* (Lewisburg, PA: Bucknell University Press, 2012).

55. For a more extensive review of relevant recent work on Victorian family studies, see the introduction I co-authored with Kelly Hager in "Extending Families," a special issue of *Victorian Review* 39, no. 2 (2013): 7–21. For eighteenth-century studies, see Joanne Bailey, "Favored or Oppressed? Married Women, Property, and 'Coverture' in England, 1660–1800," *Community and Change* 17, no. 3 (2002): 351–372; Naomi Tadmor, *Family and Friends in Eighteenth-Century England: Household, Kinship, and Patronage* (Cambridge: Cambridge University Press, 2001); Amanda Vickery, *The Gentleman's Daughter: Women's Lives in Georgian England* (New Haven, CT: Yale University Press, 1998).
56. For instance, Corbett explains, "incest" became a way of naming the poor as bestial figures grappling in dark hovels, while in the Deceased Wife's Sister controversy, it was idealized as a way of maintaining maternal and domestic order with a perfect substitute mother.
57. Corbett, vii.
58. Leonore Davidoff, *Thicker Than Water: Siblings and Their Relations 1780–1920* (New York: Oxford University Press, 2012), 163.
59. Davidoff, 90.
60. Sharon Marcus, *Between Women: Friendship, Desire, and Marriage in Victorian England* (Princeton, NJ: Princeton University Press, 2007).
61. Holly Furneaux, *Queer Dickens: Erotics, Families, Masculinities* (New York: Oxford University Press, 2009), 10.
62. Furneaux, 14.
63. Elizabeth Thiel, *The Fantasy of Family: Nineteenth-Century Children's Literature and the Myth of the Domestic Ideal* (New York: Routledge, 2007), 8.
64. Thiel, 8.
65. Hager, 5.
66. Michie.
67. Maia McAleavey, *The Bigamy Plot: Sensation and Convention in the Victorian Novel* (Cambridge: Cambridge University Press, 2015).
68. Marcus, 88–90. Indeed, Marcus is so interested in amity that she disregards the rise of romantic marriage completely.
69. Jennifer Phegley, "Victorian Girls Gone Wild: Matrimonial Advertising and the Transformation of Courtship in the Popular Press," *Victorian Review* 39, no. 2 (Fall 2013): 130–131; Mary Lydon Shanley, *Feminism, Marriage and the Law in Victorian England, 1850–1895* (Princeton, NJ: Princeton University Press, 1989), 7.
70. Perry, 198.
71. It may be historically true that separate spheres emerged during the era of companionate marriage, but the couple's companionability or lack thereof would not have affected this arrangement. Nancy Armstrong, *Desire and Domestic Fiction: A Political History of the Novel* (New York: Oxford University Press, 1987), 41.

72. Helena Michie notes that "there are as many names for the new marital style as there are dates for its triumph over older models. It has been variously referred to as 'affective marriage,' companionate marriage,' less formally as 'marriage for love,' and even 'egalitarian marriage.'" She tries to circumvent the confusion by inventing her own term, "conjugal marriage." Helena Michie, *Victorian Honeymoons: Journey to the Conjugal* (Cambridge: Cambridge University Press, 2007), 20.
73. Eve Kosofsky Sedgwick, *Between Men: English Literature and Male Homosocial Desire* (New York: Columbia University Press, 1985), 172.
74. For an informative critique of Sedgwick's treatment of female characters, see Marjorie Garber, *Vice Versa: Bisexuality and the Eroticism of Everyday Life* (New York: Simon and Schuster, 1995), 423–428.
75. Sedgwick, 167.
76. Sedgwick, 164.
77. On Jenny's choice of name, see Sara D. Schotland, "Who's That in Charge? It's Jenny Wren, 'The Person of the House,'" *Disability Studies Quarterly* 29, no. 3 (Summer 2009): n.p.; and Elaine Ostry, *Social Dreaming: Dickens and the Fairy Tale* (New York: Routledge, 2002), 74.
78. Charles Dickens, *Our Mutual Friend,* ed. Adrian Poole (1865; repr., New York: Penguin, 1997), 222, 224, 232, 239, 241, 243.
79. Denis de Rougemont, *Love in the Western World,* trans. Montgomery Belgion (1940; repr., Princeton, NJ: Princeton University Press, 1982), 5.
80. See, for instance, Rita Felski, "Context Stinks!," *New Literary History* 42, no. 4 (Autumn 2011): 573–591.
81. Honor McKitrick Wallace, "Desire and the Female Protagonist: A Critique of Feminist Narrative Theory," *Style* 34, no. 2 (Summer 2000): 176–187.
82. Interestingly, Yonge also uses the term "elf" to name a woman who is perceived according to Creole norms, Elvira de Menella in *The Magnum Bonum.* It is as if the woman's early immersion in a slave-owning society has dehumanized her.
83. He remarks that "when a dependant does her duty as well as you have done yours, she has a sort of claim upon her employer for any little assistance he can conveniently render her" (279).
84. Charles Lindholm, "Love and Structure," *Theory Culture Society* 15, nos. 3–4 (August 1998): 248.

CHAPTER 2

1. Helen Berry and Elizabeth Foyster, *The Family in Early Modern England* (Cambridge: Cambridge University Press, 2007), 3.
2. Joseph Allen Boone, "Chapter Two: The Emergence of a Literary Ideal of Romantic Marriage: A Historical Perspective," *Tradition Counter Tradition: Love and the Form of Fiction* (Chicago: University of Chicago Press, 1987), 31–64.

3. R. Howard Bloch, *Medieval Misogyny and the Invention of Western Romantic Love* (Chicago: University of Chicago Press, 1992), 8–9.
4. In this period, "a suitable marriage, especially among the propertied classes, was one which gave the individual and those closest to him potentially useful new kinsmen," according to historian Ralph A. Houlbrooke, *The English Family 1450–1700* (London and New York: Longman, 1984), 73.
5. Frances and Joseph Gies, *Marriage and the Family in the Middle Ages* (New York: Harper and Row, 1987), 9.
6. Gies, 11. Also see Diana O'Hara, *Courtship and Constraint: Rethinking the Making of Marriage in Tudor England* (Manchester, UK: Manchester University Press, 2000), 2–3.
7. There is no question that medieval marriages often involved affection, in spite of Stone's claim to the contrary. Letters and wills amply attest to marital love (Gies, 299). "In David Herlihy's words, 'The medieval family was never dead to sentiment; it is only poor in sources'" (Gies, 297).
8. Frederik Pedersen, *Marriage Disputes in Medieval England* (London: Hambledon, 2000), 155. Pedersen explains that William Aungier "is the only litigant in the surviving fourteenth-century marriage cases from the archbishop's court in York who explained that he expected marriage to be based on affection. His case is unique because the choice of words reported in his statements make it clear that he had an notion of marriage which included fidelity and a lasting emotional involvement with his partner."
9. Martha Howell, "The Properties of Marriage in Late Medieval Europe: Commercial Wealth and the Creation of Modern Marriage," *Love, Marriage, and Family Ties in the Later Middle Ages*, ed. Isabel Davis, Miriam Müller, and Sarah Rees Jones (Turnhout: Brepols, 2003), 18–19.
10. Houlbrooke, 69.
11. Houlbrooke, 77.
12. Stephanie Coontz, *Marriage, A History: How Love Conquered Marriage* (New York: Penguin, 2006), 15–18.
13. Wendy Jones, *Consensual Fictions: Women, Liberalism, and the English Novel* (Toronto: University of Toronto Press, 2005), 25.
14. Shannon McSheffrey, *Marriage, Sex, and Civic Culture in Late Medieval London* (Philadelphia: University of Pennsylvania Press, 2006), 19–20.
15. McSheffrey, 19.
16. Bloch, 8–9.
17. Cited in Robert C. Solomon, *Love: Emotion, Myth, and Metaphor* (New York: Prometheus Books, 1990), 56.
18. Andreas Capellanus, *The Art of Courtly Love* (c.1180), cited in Boone, 31.
19. In *Conduct Becoming: Good Wives and Husbands in the Later Middle Ages* (unpublished manuscript), Glenn Burger argues that the medieval idea of sacramental marriage aimed to remake the married state into a holy situation by focusing on

partners' marital affection and mutual moral/religious improvement. Also see Emma Lipton, *Affections of the Mind: The Politics of Sacramental Marriage in Late Medieval English Literature* (Notre Dame, IN: University of Notre Dame Press, 2007).

20. Glenn Burger, *Conduct Becoming: Good Wives and Husbands in the Later Middle Ages.*
21. Gies, 129.
22. McSheffrey, 21.
23. Burger.
24. Tine de Moor and Jan Luiten van Zanden, "Girl power: The European Marriage Market and Labour Patterns in the North Sea Region in the Late Medieval and Early Modern Period," *Economic History Review* 63, no. 1 (2010): 1–33.
25. O'Hara, 10–11. However, Lena Cowen Orlin regards O'Hara's position as overly tendentious, with the evidence amenable to other interpretations. See Orlin, "Rewriting Stone's Renaissance," *Huntingdon Library Quarterly* 64, nos. 1–2 (2002): 189–230.
26. O'Hara, 3.
27. Edmund Leites, *The Puritan Conscience and Modern Sexuality* (New Haven, CT: Yale University Press, 1986); Margo Todd, *Christian Humanism and the Puritan Social Order* (Cambridge: Cambridge University Press, 1987).
28. Carol Thomas Neely, *Broken Nuptials in Shakespeare's Plays* (New Haven, CT: Yale University Press, 1985), 9.
29. Laura Gowling, *Domestic Dangers: Women, Words, and Sex in Early Modern London* (Oxford: Clarendon, 1996), 187.
30. Lawrence Stone, "Love," *The Past and Present Revisited* (Abingdon, UK: Routledge, 1987), 327–343. Reprinted from *Passionate Attachments: The Essential but Fragile Nature of Love*, ed. E. S. Persons and W. Gaylin (New York: Free Press, 1987), 328.
31. In "The Doctrine and Discipline of Divorce," Milton contrasts loveless animalistic fornication to the mutual solace of well-matched souls, which he regards as the true meaning of marriage. This position clearly develops out of the Puritan tradition.
32. Martha Howell, "The Properties of Marriage in Late Medieval Europe: Commercial Wealth and the Creation of Modern Marriage," *Love, Marriage, and Family Ties in the Later Middle Ages*, ed. Isabel Davis, Miriam Müller, and Sarah Rees Jones (Turnhout, BE: Brepols, 2003), 36–37.
33. Howell, 17–61.
34. C. B. Macpherson, *The Political Theory of Possessive Individualism: Hobbes to Locke* (Oxford: Clarendon, 1962), 59, 61, 88.
35. J. G. A. Pocock, "The Myth of John Locke and the Obsession with Liberalism," *John Locke: Papers Read at a Clark Library Seminar* (Los Angeles: William Andrews Clark Library, 1980), 16.
36. Joan Tronto, *Moral Boundaries: A Political Argument for an Ethic of Care* (New York: Routledge, 1993), 29. Tronto traces the development of British liberal

thought through Shaftesbury, Hume, and Adam Smith, showing how they increasingly articulated an awareness of a need to move in larger and larger collectives.

37. However, Iris Marion Young has argued that the universalist state idealized in the eighteenth century is actually a reaction against the wildly heterogeneous class-mixing public that Habermas has described. Iris Marion Young, "Impartiality and the Civic Public: Some Implications of Feminist Critiques of Moral and Political Theory," *Feminism as Critique: On the Politics of Gender* (Minneapolis: University of Minnesota Press, 1987), 64.
38. See Dympna Callaghan, "The Ideology of Romantic Love: The Case of Romeo and Juliet," *The Weyward Sisters: Shakespeare and Feminist* (New York: Wiley-Blackwell, 1994), 80–81.
39. *Romeo and Juliet* was published in 1597 and was based on Arthur Brooke's "The Tragical History of Romeus and Juliet" (1562), itself based on an Italian tale translated into French in the mid-sixteenth century. See Dympna Callaghan, *Romeo and Juliet: Texts and Contexts* (New York: Bedford/St. Martin's, 2003), 8–10.
40. Callaghan, "Ideology," 62.
41. David Blewett, "Changing Attitudes Toward Marriage in the Time of Defoe: The Case of Moll Flanders," *Huntingdon Library Quarterly* 44, no. 2 (Spring 1981): 80.
42. John Stockwood, "A Bartholomew Fairing for Parents" (1589), in Callaghan, *Romeo and Juliet*, 262–263.
43. Cited in Katherine Sobba Green, *The Courtship Novel 1740–1820: A Feminized Genre* (Lexington: University Press of Kentucky, 1991), 50.
44. Margaret Magdalen Jasper Althens, *The Christian Character Exemplified From the Papers of Mrs. Frederick Charles A—s, of Goodman's Fields* (Hartford, CT: Lincoln and Gleason, 1804), 96, 99.
45. Houlbrooke, 76.
46. See Charles Gibbon, from *A Work Worth the Reading* (1591), and Thomas Hilder, from *Conjugal Counsel: or, Seasonable Advice, Both to Unmarried, and Married Persons* (1653) in Callaghan, *Romeo and Juliet*. Hilder writes, "Now in the fear of God let parents be admonished to beware of this sin, of enforcing their children to accept of such husbands, and wives, as themselves only chose without, nay, against the free consent of their children" (279).
47. George Savile, Marquis of Halifax, *The Lady's New Years Gift, or, Advice to a Daughter*, 3rd ed. (London, 1688), 25–26.
48. *The Gentlewoman's Companion; or a Guide to the Female Sex: Containing Directions of Behaviour in All Places, Companies, Relations, and Conditions, from Their Childhood to Old Age* (London, 1675), 89. This compilation was ascribed to Hannah Wolley, one of the first professional writers of conduct and household management manuals, but it appears in fact to have been an anonymous compilation of works plagiarized from multiple writers. See Katherine Ellison, "Introduction to the *Gentlewoman's Companion*," Emory Women Writers Project, 1999, http://womenwriters.library.emory.edu/essay.php?level=div&id=gc_complete_000.

See also Elaine Hobby, *Virtue of Necessity: English Women's Writing, 1646–1688* (London: Virago Press, 1988).

49. John Milton, "Preface," *The Doctrine and Discipline of Divorce*. The copytext for this edition of *The Doctrine and Discipline of Divorce* is a copy of the 1644 (second, expanded, and revised) edition owned by Rauner Library at Dartmouth College (Val. 824/M64/P8), http://www.dartmouth.edu/~milton/reading_room/ddd/book_1/.
50. Milton, chapter 12.
51. Cited in Joshua Phillips, *English Fictions of Communal Identity, 1485–1603* (Burlington, VT: Ashgate, 2010), 1–16. On the theory of possessive individualism, see Macpherson.
52. Wendy Jones, 4–5.
53. Goode, *World Revolution and Family Patterns*, cited in Ruth Perry, *Novel Relations: The Transformation of Kinship in English Literature and Culture, 1748–1818* (Cambridge: Cambridge University Press, 2004), 220.
54. Martha Nussbaum, *Frontiers of Justice: Disability, Nationality, Species Membership* (Cambridge, MA: Harvard University Press, 2007), 104.
55. For cogent critiques of the way possessive individualism relates to slaves, the laboring classes, and disabled subjects, see Jennifer Rae Greeson, "The Prehistory of Possessive Individualism," *PMLA* 127, no. 4 (October 2012): 918–924; Macpherson, 222; Nussbaum, 98. I focus on women here for purposes of the marriage plot, not by any means because they are the only subjects assigned irrational emotionalism in Western history.
56. Linda J. Nicholson, *Gender and History: The Limits of Social Theory in the Age of the Family* (New York: Columbia University Press, 1986), 114.
57. Seyla Benhabib, *Situating the Self: Gender, Community and Postmodernism in Contemporary Ethics* (New York: Routledge, 1992), 157.
58. McSheffrey, 194.
59. Gal Gerson, "Liberal Feminism: Individuality and Oppositions in Wollstonecraft and Mill," *Political Studies* 50, no. 4 (2002): 794.
60. Iris Marion Young, *Justice and the Politics of Difference* (Princeton, NJ: Princeton University Press, 1990), 110. Ruth Perry puts it well: "In theorizing individuals as ontologically prior to society, their model of an abstract individual leaves the mother out of the process and ignores the essential interdependence which is a sociological and physiological fact of life for women. In supposing that individuals exist separately before they come together in society, these theorists ignore the work that women do in bearing and tending the young and in caring for the bodily needs of their families. The world of possessive individualism projected from such skewed conceptions about human society is a world in which the only players who matter are adult white men, competing with one another and adjudicating their disputes with contracts. Love, trust, friendship, art, invention—all are irrelevant to instrumental disagreements about the distribution of property."

Ruth Perry, "Mary Astell and the Feminist Critique of Possessive Individualism," *Eighteenth-Century Studies* 23, no. 4 (Summer 1990): 454.

61. Nancy Yousef, *Isolated Cases: The Anxieties of Autonomy in Enlightenment Philosophy and Romantic Literature* (Ithaca, NY: Cornell University Press, 2004), 19.
62. Lawrence Stone claims (rather outrageously) that it was Mary's dislike of "poor Mr. Pendarves" which drove him to drink (311). Mary, he concludes, was "basically frigid" (313). *The Family, Sex, and Marriage in England, 1500–1800* (New York: Harper and Row, 1977).
63. Laura E. Thomason, *The Matrimonial Trap: Eighteenth-Century Women Writers Redefine Marriage* (Lewisburg, PA: Bucknell University Press, 2014), 93–94.
64. Mary Delany, *The Autobiography and Correspondence of Mary Granville, Mrs. Delany* was based on her 1740 correspondence with the Duchess of Portland. See Thomason 179, n. 1, and Mary Delany, *The Autobiography and Correspondence of Mrs. Delany, vol. 1*, ed. Sarah Chauncey Woolsey (Boston: Roberts Bros., 1879).
65. Thomason, 102.
66. On the problem of consent as a basis for marriage, see Sandra Macpherson, "Lovelace, Ltd.," *ELH* 65, no. 1 (Spring 1998): 99–121.
67. The Cambridge Group for the History of Population and Social Structure, led by Laslett, endorsed the new idea of computerized data, focusing on statistical analysis of quantifiable demographic elements and scorning the "attitudinal" or "literary" readings of historians who derived ideas about people's beliefs from the writings they left behind; they therefore refused to speculate on the emotions that underlay these statistically visible practices and delivered no opinion on the degree of marital love in the past.
68. While this dispute was passionate at the time, it had died down by the late 1980s. See Naomi Tadmor, *Family and Friends in Eighteenth-Century England: Household, Kinship, and Patronage* (Cambridge: Cambridge University Press, 2001), 4. My own sense is that the family history diatribes derived much of their edge from historians' reactions to the sexual revolution of the 1960s and 1970s; discussions of medieval and early modern pairings were really driven by the authors' enthusiasm or dismay at the sexual freedoms of their own era. Stone and Shorter in particular freely interlard their analysis with condemnations of female frigidity, paeans to sexually liberated maidservents, and dire warnings about uppity women destroying their children's egos. The not-so-covert aim of the family history of the 1970s was to provide a backstory for the sexual efflorescence of modernity. Since fighting over the merits of the sexual revolution no longer feels particularly urgent, the energies driving the dispute have died down.
69. In the heat of the family history debates, Alan Macfarlane's scorching review revealed Stone's selective use of evidence and his decision to ignore enormous quantities of data that do not fit his theory, including medieval and Tudor documents and the entire literary tradition. (Alan Macfarlane, "Review of *The Family,*

Sex, and Marriage," History and Theory 18, no. 1 (February 1979): 103–126. Also reprinted in *Early Modern Europe: Issues and Interpretations.*) Stone himself subsequently modified the claims put forth in *The Family, Sex, and Marriage.* "Love," *The Past and Present Revisited* (Abingdon, UK: Routledge, 1987), 327–343. Reprinted from *Passionate Attachments: The Essential but Fragile Nature of Love*, ed. E. S. Persons and W. Gaylin (New York: Free Press, 1987).

70. Thomason, 3.
71. On the origins of the novel and its relation to other genres like conduct manuals, spiritual autobiographies, sermons, travel narratives, and even accounting manuals, see Ian Watt, *The Rise of the Novel: Studies in Defoe, Richardson and Fielding* (Berkeley and Los Angeles: University of California Press, 1957); Nancy Armstrong, *Desire and Domestic Fiction: A Political History of the Novel* (New York: Oxford University Press, 1987); Poovey; and Stone. See also Michael Mascuch, *Origins of the Individualist Self: Autobiography and Self-Identity in England, 1591–1791* (Stanford, CA: Stanford University Press, 1996).
72. See discussion in Green, 2–3.
73. Faramerz Dabhoiwala, *The Origins of Sex: A History of the First Sexual Revolution* (New York: Oxford University Press, 2012), 178.
74. Katherine Binhammer, *The Seduction Narrative in Britain, 1747–1800* (Cambridge: Cambridge University Press, 2009), 6.
75. Binhammer, 137.
76. Perry, 245; Wendy Jones, 6.
77. Perry, 237.
78. In Edgeworth's *Belinda*, for instance, Belinda works herself up to rational esteem for a suitor named Mr. Vincent, but when she discovers he has gambled, she breaks off their engagement. Her feelings are so admirably under her control that they can be arrested the moment he fails the moral test.
79. Dabhoiwala.
80. Ingrid H. Tague, "Love, Honor, and Obedience: Fashionable Women and the Discourse of Marriage in the Early Eighteenth Century," *Journal of British Studies* 40, no. 1 (January 2001): 76–106.
81. John Gregory, *A Father's Legacy to His Daughters* (London: H. D. Symonds, 1793), 100.
82. Thomason, 9.
83. Stone, *Family*, 281.
84. Cited in Green, 141.
85. See n. 48 about the disputed authorship of this collection.
86. Gregory, 95.
87. Samuel Richardson, *Clarissa: Or, the History of a Young Lady: Comprehending the Most Important Concerns of Private Life, and Particularly Showing the Distresses That May Attend the Misconduct Both of Parents and Children, in Relation to Marriage*, ed. Angus Ross (1747–1748; repr. New York: Penguin, 1985), L32.1, 148–149. Future references will be noted parenthetically within the text, by letter number.

88. Mary Patricia Martin identifies this stalemate but reads it as a failure of Richardson's literary performance rather than a cultural crisis in "Reading Reform in Richardson's *Clarissa*," *SEL* 37, no. 3 (Summer 1997): 602. In criticism written out of the understanding that sex is the secret to everything, the rape is instantly recognizable as a formal success. She writes approvingly that "from this point forward the difference between Lovelace's and Clarissa's stories comes sharply into focus. A rush to closure breaks through the interpretative malaise, and generic conflict is now clear" (603). But the "interpretative malaise that marks the first half of *Clarissa* [features] lengthy negotiations," with "no clear sense of what kinds of choices will shape this narrative, or of what kind of story this is going to be" (602). Martin's perplexity over the categories of marital consent, and her palpable relief when the story turns to sex, indicate the ways that our emphasis on sex has foreclosed other kinds of readinggs.
89. T. C. Duncan Eaves and Ben D. Kimpel, *Samuel Richardson: A Biography* (Oxford: Clarendon, 1971), 92–99. Eaves and Kimpel also identify two broadsides on marital duty that Richardson seems to have written in the 1730s and early 1740s, although no copies have survived (50).
90. Laura E. Thomason, "Hester Chapone as a Living Clarissa in *Letters on Filial Obedience* and *A Matrimonial Creed*," *Eighteenth-Century Fiction* 21, no. 3 (Spring 2009): 339. Also see Mary Vermilion, "Clarissa and the Marriage Act," *Eighteenth-Century Fiction* 9, no. 4 (July 1997): 395–414 for a consideration of the complicated ways the novel both inspires and contests elements of Hardwicke's Act.
91. For an account of the critical consensus on Clarissa's inactivity post-rape, see Frances Ferguson, "Rape and the Rise of the Novel," *Representations* 20 (Autumn 1987): 107.
92. Bonnie Latimer, *Making Gender, Culture, and the Self in the Fiction of Samuel Richardson* (Burlington, VT: Ashgate, 2013).
93. Terry Eagleton offers an unforgettable summary of critics' eagerness to demonstrate Clarissa's secret desire for Lovelace in *The Rape of Clarissa: Writing, Sexuality and Class Struggle in Samuel Richardson* (Minneapolis: University of Minnesota Press, 1982), 64–70. Yet as recently as 2012, Will Pritchard devoted several pages of his article, "Pope, Richardson, and 'Clarissa'," to discussing whether Clarissa secretly loves Lovelace. See *Literary Imagination* (June 20, 2012), 8–12.
94. Binhammer, 22–23.
95. Jean I. Marsden testifies to the popularity of *Romeo and Juliet* in the seventeenth and eighteenth centuries in "Improving Shakespeare: From the Restoration to Garrick," *The Cambridge Companion to Shakespeare on Stage*, ed. Stanley Wells, Sarah Stanton (Cambridge: Cambridge University Press, 2002), 21–36. Richardson was particularly interested in Shakespeare, using references and quotes to the plays to structure *Clarissa*. See Thomas Keymer, "Shakespeare in the Novel," *Shakespeare in the Eighteenth Century*, edited by Fiona Ritchie and Peter Sabor (Cambridge: Cambridge University Press, 2012), 118–140.
96. On Richardson's construction of threatening urban space, see Watt, 181.

97. Watt, 222.
98. Latimer, 3.
99. Hina Nazar, *Enlightened Sentiments: Judgment and Autonomy in the Age of Sensibility* (New York: Fordham University Press, 2012), 68.
100. Binhammer, 28.
101. See Dabhoiwala and Tague.
102. Latimer opines that in fact "it is not so much rape as the incremental violations of individual will involved in marital tyranny that form the primary paradigm for female oppression in *Clarissa*" (182).
103. Eagleton, 88–89.
104. Whether or not modern readers accept Grandison as a moral icon, it is incontestable that this is what Richardson was trying to write.
105. Binhammer, 27.
106. Binhammer, 34.
107. For examples of Richardson's characters' imitators, and Richardson's own testimony that he wished his novels to be read as conduct manuals, see Sylvia Kasey Marks, *Sir Charles Grandison: The Compleat Conduct Book* (Cranbury, NJ: Associated University Presses, 1986), 14–17.
108. David Lemmings, "Marriage and the Law in the Eighteenth Century: Hardwicke's Marriage Act of 1753," *The Historical Journal* 39, no. 2 (June 1996): 342.
109. Lemmings, 339–360.
110. Erica Harth, "The Virtue of Love: Lord Hardwicke's Marriage Act," *Cultural Critique* 9 (Spring 1988): 123–154.
111. Harth, 133.
112. Eve Tavor Bannet, *The Domestic Revolution: Enlightenment Feminisms and the Novel* (Baltimore: Johns Hopkins University Press, 2000), 111.
113. Dabhoiwala, 207.
114. Stone deals with the problem that history does not show a smooth progression towards marrying for love by citing only the opponents of Hardwicke, giving the misleading impression that they represented the winning side.
115. See Deborah Lutz, *The Dangerous Lover: Gothic Villains, Byronism, and the Nineteenth-Century* (Columbus: Ohio State University, 2006).
116. See, for instance, Sir Walter Scott's memory of his seventeen-year-old self reading *Emmeline* and strongly wishing for Delamere's passion to be rewarded. In Charlotte Smith, *Emmeline, or, The Orphan of the Castle*, ed. Loraine Fletcher (1788; repr. Peterborough, ON: Broadview, 2003).
117. Binhammer, citing Laura Kipnis, 9.
118. See Ian Bradley, *The Call to Seriousness: The Evangelical Impact on the Victorians* (New York: Macmillan, 1976); and Callum Brown, "The Salvation Economy," *The Death of Christian Britain: Understanding Secularisation 1800–2000* (New York: Routledge, 2001).
119. Bradley, 179.

120. Mary Brunton, *Self-Control* (New York: Pandora Press, 1986), 87–89.
121. Jillian Heydt-Stevenson, "Northanger Abbey, Desmond, and History," *The Wordsworth Circle* 44, nos. 2–3 (Spring–Summer 2013): 142.
122. Mary Waldron, *Jane Austen and the Fiction of Her Time* (Cambridge: Cambridge University Press, 2004), 27.
123. Anne Henry Ehrenpreis, "Northanger Abbey: Jane Austen and Charlotte Smith," *Nineteenth-Century Fiction* 25, no. 3 (December 1970): 347.
124. See Ehrenpreis; Rachel Brownstein, *Why Jane Austen?* (New York: Columbia University Press, 2011), 137–140; Heydt-Stevenson, "*Northanger Abbey*"; William H. Magee, "The Happy Marriage: The Influence of Charlotte Smith on Jane Austen," *Studies in the Novel* 7, no. 1 (Spring 1975): 120–132; Frank W. Bradbrook, *Jane Austen and Her Predecessors* (Cambridge: Cambridge University Press, 1966), 105.
125. Magee, 120.
126. Jane Austen, *Northanger Abbey, Lady Susan, The Watsons, and Sanditon*, ed. James Kinsley (1818; repr. New York: Oxford University Press, 2003), 38, 79–81. All future references will be to this edition and will be noted parenthetically in the text.
127. Nancy Yee, "John Thorpe, Villain Ordinaire: The Modern Montoni/Schedoni," *Persuasions* 31, no. 1 (Winter 2010), http://www.jasna.org.ezproxy.gc.cuny.edu/persuasions/on-line/vol31no1/yee.html.
128. Jillian Heydt-Stevenson, *Austen's Unbecoming Conjunctions: Subversive Laughter, Embodied History* (New York: Macmillan, 2008), 121.
129. Miriam Rheingold Fuller, "Let Me Go, Mr. Thorpe; Isabella, Do Not Hold Me!: *Northanger Abbey* and the Domestic Gothic," *Persuasions* 32 (2010): 96–97.
130. George Justice, "*Northanger Abbey* as Anti-Courtship Novel?," *Persuasions* 20 (1998): 191.
131. Justice, 193.
132. As many critics have pointed out, of course, this assumption that England is a secure, transparent, law-abiding society where publicity makes bad behavior impossible is only true if one happens to be a wealthy well-born white male like Henry Tilney. Eleanor and Catherine both experience the horrors of the General's domestic tyranny, riots, and unrest that characterized 1790s British life, while it is precisely the "neighbourhood of voluntary spies" who endangered British people by reporting on supposed treason and pro-French Revolutionary sympathies. See Austen, *Northanger Abbey*, 371, n. 145.

CHAPTER 3

1. Stephanie Coontz, *Marriage, A History: How Love Conquered Marriage* (New York: Penguin, 2006), 145–146.
2. Wendy Jones, *Consensual Fictions: Women, Liberalism, and the English Novel* (Toronto: University of Toronto Press, 2005), 6.

3. Eve Kosofsky Sedgwick, *The Epistemology of the Closet* (Berkeley and Los Angeles: University of California Press, 1990), 47–48.
4. Coontz, 147. Diaries and memoirs confirm this pattern. In Laurel Thatcher Ulrich's *The Midwife's Tale*, eighteenth-century Maine midwife Martha Ballard rarely refers to her husband as anything other than Mr. Ballard in her private diary, and they acted as co-workers, each in charge of a different segment of household labor, rather than romantic lovers. Two centuries later, in a memoir of a family in the Lower East Side in New York, we see records of two non-romantic marriages contracted as late as the 1910s. In the first, the woman married to escape her boarding house and the man married because he felt "sorry for her." When she died in the influenza epidemic of 1919, the widower married a woman he had just met in order to secure a mother for his three young children. (Jack Waldman, *Memories, Life in the Twentieth Century in America* [privately printed], 3, 19.)
5. Pat Jalland, *Women, Marriage, and Politics 1860–1914* (Oxford: Oxford University Press, 1986), 75.
6. T. S. Arthur, *Advice to Young Ladies on Their Duties and Conduct in Life* (London: J. S. Hodson, 1855), 152.
7. H. W. H., *How to Choose a Wife* (London: Partridge, Oakey, 1855), 18.
8. Sarah Stickney Ellis, *The Daughters of England: Their Position in Society, Character, and Responsibilities* (New York: D. Appleton, 1842), 223.
9. *The Etiquette of Love, Courtship and Marriage* (London: Simpkin, Marshall, 1847), 18.
10. "Relatively stable societies with solidified extended families, age-sets and other encompassing social networks that offer alternative forms of belonging and experiences of personal transcendence through participation in group rituals are not prone to valuing romantic involvement." Charles Lindholm, "Love and Structure," *Theory Culture Society* 15, nos. 3–4 (August 1998): 257.
11. Lindholm, 243.
12. Mike Featherstone, "Love and Eroticism: An Introduction," *Theory Culture Society* 15, nos. 3–4 (August 1998): 5.
13. Michael J. Freeman, *Railways and the Victorian Imagination* (New Haven, CT: Yale University Press, 1999), 121.
14. Jennifer Phegley, *Courtship and Marriage in Victorian England* (Santa Barbara, CA: Praeger, 2012), 110–111.
15. See Freeman, for instance, and Wolfgang Schivelbusch, *The Railway Journey: The Industrialization of Time and Space in the Nineteenth Century* (Berkeley and Los Angeles: University of California Press, 1977).
16. Samuel Richardson, *Clarissa: Or, the History of a Young Lady: Comprehending the Most Important Concerns of Private Life, and Particularly Showing the Distresses That May Attend the Misconduct Both of Parents and Children, in Relation to Marriage,* ed. Angus Ross (1747–1748; repr. New York: Penguin, 1985), 20.
17. *The Etiquette of Love, Courtship, and Marriage,* 77.

18. Ian Watt, *The Rise of the Novel: Studies in Defoe, Richardson and Fielding* (Berkeley and Los Angeles: University of California Press, 1957), 139–140.
19. Ruth Perry, *Novel Relations: The Transformation of Kinship in English Literature and Culture, 1748–1818* (Cambridge: Cambridge University Press, 2004), 231.
20. See Leslie Richardson, "Leaving Her Father's House: Astell, Locke, and Clarissa's Body Politic," *Studies in Eighteenth-Century Culture* 34 (2005): 151–171.
21. Perry, 196–197.
22. Randolph Trumbach, *The Rise of the Egalitarian Family* (New York: Academic Press, 1978), 113.
23. Anthony Giddens, *The Transformation of Intimacy: Sexuality, Love and Eroticism in Modern Societies* (Stanford, CA: Stanford University Press, 1992), 26.
24. Michel Foucault, *The History of Sexuality: Vol 1, An Introduction*, trans. Robert Hurley (New York: Vintage Books, 1990), 122–123.
25. See Katherine Binhammer, *The Seduction Narrative in Britain, 1747–1800* (Cambridge: Cambridge University Press, 2009), 110. John R. Gillis depicts pre-Victorian marriage among the rural poor as communal events in which neighbors and kinfolk remained involved at every stage. John R. Gillis, *For Better, for Worse: British Marriages, 1600 to the Present* (New York: Oxford University Press, 1985).
26. Binhammer, 137.
27. Ginger Frost, *Promises Broken: Courtship, Class, and Gender in Victorian England* (Charlottesville: University Press of Virginia, 1995), 91.
28. See Kelly Hager, *Dickens and the Rise of Divorce: The Failed Marriage Plot and the Novel Tradition* (Burlington, VT: Ashgate, 2010); Holly Furneaux, *Queer Dickens: Erotics, Families, Masculinities* (New York: Oxford University Press, 2010); Rachel Ablow, *The Marriage of Minds: Reading Sympathy in the Victorian Marriage Plot* (Stanford, CA: Stanford University Press, 2010); Elsie Michie, *The Vulgar Question of Money: Heiresses, Materialism, and the Novel of Manners from Jane Austen to Henry James* (Baltimore: Johns Hopkins University Press, 2011).
29. Hager, "Introduction," especially pp. 1–5.
30. This was the ideal. Of course, in many novels and no doubt even more often in reality, it did not happen this way. Guardians or parents might vet candidates carelessly, as in *Sense and Sensibility*, where Sir John Middleton only knows about Wickham that he has a good hunting dog. Elders might not care about the candidates' personal qualities if money and class status compensated, as is the case with Solmes in *Clarissa*. Moreover, they might consider certain factors, like age and appearance, irrelevant, though these points might be crucial to the person who had to marry him, as in Mary Delany's awful experience of enforced marriage to Alexander Pendarves. See Mary Delaney, 1700–1788, *The Autobiography and Correspondence of Mrs. Delany, vol. 1*. ed. Sarah Chauncey Woolsey (Boston: Roberts Bros., 1879).

31. Jane Austen, *Pride and Prejudice* (1813; repr. New York: Oxford University Press, 2004), 185. All future references will be to this edition and will be noted parethetically.
32. Jane Austen, letter to Anna Austen, September 9, 1814, in *Jane Austen's Letters*, ed. R. W. Chapman, 2nd ed. (London: Oxford University Press, 1952), 401.
33. Deborah Lutz writes, "The Byronic hero, particularly the Giaour and Childe Harold, roams disenchanted and always astray; he has no place in the domesticity of society." Deborah Lutz, *The Dangerous Lover: Gothic Villains, Byronism, and the Nineteenth-Century* (Columbus: Ohio State University press, 2006), 49.
34. Anthony Trollope, *Rachel Ray* (1863; repr. New York: Oxford University Press, 1988), 210.
35. See Dorice Williams Elliott, *The Angel out of the House: Philanthropy and Gender in Nineteenth-Century England* (Charlottesville: University Press of Virginia, 2002).
36. Alex Woloch, *The One vs. the Many: Minor Characters and the Space of the Protagonist in the Novel* (Princeton, NJ: Princeton University Press, 2003), 25.
37. See Talia Schaffer, "Domesticity," *The Victorian Encyclopedia*, ed. Dino Franco Felluga, Linda Hughes, and Pamela Gilbert (Oxford: Blackwells, 2015).
38. Sarah Stickney Ellis, *Women of England, Their Social Duties and Domestic Habits* (New York: D. Appleton, 1843), 28.
39. On professional, managerial domesticity, see Elizabeth Langland, *Nobody's Angels: Middle-Class Women and Domestic Ideology in Victorian Culture* (Ithaca, NY: Cornell University Press, 1995); Monica Cohen, *Professional Domesticity in the Victorian Novel: Women, Work, and Home* (Cambridge: Cambridge University Press, 1998); and Isabella Beeton, *Mrs Beeton's Book of Household Management*, ed. Nicola Humble (1861; repr. New York: Oxford World's Classics, 2008).
40. Beeton, 7.
41. See Faramerz Dabhoiwala, *The Origins of Sex: A History of the First Sexual Revolution* (New York: Oxford University Press, 2012); Ellen Jordan, *The Women's Movement and Women's Employment in Nineteenth Century Britain* (London and New York: Routledge, 1999). Mary Wollstonecraft, whom we normally associate with Enlightenment rights language, imagines a cozy cottage scene as a space where women could finally exercise her true talents and is eloquent on motherhood as the true sphere of good women, violated by the frivolous training women received. Barbara Leah Harman describes the moral ascendency preached by the "women's mission" writers of the 1840s, Sarah Stickney Ellis and Sarah Lewis. Barbara Leah Harman, *The Feminine Political Novel in Victorian England* (Charlottesville: University Press of Virginia, 1998).
42. Eve Tavor Bannet, *The Domestic Revolution: Enlightenment Feminisms and the Novel* (Baltimore: Johns Hopkins University Press, 2000), 148.
43. Bannet, 150–154.
44. Jordan, 55.

45. Barbara Caine, *Victorian Feminists* (New York: Oxford University Press, 1992), 41–42.
46. Margaret Oliphant, *Miss Marjoribanks* (1866; repr. New York: Penguin Classics, 1998), 486.
47. Oliphant, 486.
48. Clara Tuite, *Romantic Austen: Sexual Politics and the Literary Canon* (Cambridge: Cambridge University Press, 2002). See especially Chapter 3 on *Mansfield Park*.
49. Woloch, 27.
50. This is perhaps most clear in *Cometh Up As a Flower*, in which the squire Hugh remains almost wholly generic, while we burrow deeply inside Nell's mind.
51. The definitive account of this kind of extended family is Naomi Tadmor's *Family and Friends in Eighteenth-Century England: Household, Kinship, and Patronage* (Cambridge: Cambridge University Press, 2001).
52. Watt, 60; also see Stephen Greenblatt, "Fiction and Friction," *Reconstructing Individualism: Autonomy, Individuality, and the Self in Western Thought*, ed. Thomas C. Heller, Morton Sosna, and David E. Wellbery (Stanford, CA: Stanford University Press, 1986), 32. A Google n-gram chart of the word "individualism" confirms this claim. The ngram shows no usage at all before the 1840s, and very minor use through the latter half of the nineteenth century, although "individual" and "individuality" have much higher incidences, perhaps indicating that interest in personal uniqueness did not necessarily correlate with any willingness to enshrine the pursuit of that self-development into something like a philosophy.
53. R. Philip Brown, *Authentic Individualism: A Guide for Reclaiming the Best of America's Heritage* (Lanham, MD: University Press of America, 1996), 2. Brown claims the Saint-Simonians coined individualism as a negative term, although they regarded individuality as beneficial, a state that offered progress toward dignity, liberty, reason.
54. Koenraad W. Swaert, "'Individualism' in the Mid-Nineteenth Century (1826–1860)," *Journal of the History of Ideas* 23, no. 1 (January–March 1962): 78–81.
55. Regenia Gagnier, "The Law of Progress and the Ironies of Individualism in the Nineteenth Century," *New Literary History* 31, no. 2 (2000): 316.
56. Anna Vaninskaya, *William Morris and the Idea of Community: Romance, History, and Propaganda, 1880–1914* (Edinburgh: Edinburgh University Press, 2010), 1.
57. Suzanne Graver, *George Eliot and Community: A Study in Social Theory and Fictional Form* (Berkeley: University of California Press, 1984), 1.
58. Raymond Williams, *The Country and the City* (New York: Oxford University Press, 1973), 9–12.
59. Williams, 180.
60. Alan Macfarlane, *The Origins of English Individualism* (Oxford: Blackwell, 1978), 52; J. G. A. Pocock, "Review: Alan Macfarlane, *The Origins of English Individualism*," *History and Theory* 19,no. 1 (February 1980): 100, 104.

61. Jacob Burckhardt, *The Civilization of the Renaissance in Italy*, trans. S. G. C. Middlemore (1860; repr. New York: Macmillan, 1904), 129.
62. Frederic Seebohm, *The English Village Community* (1883; repr. London: Longmans, Green, 1915), 441.
63. Katie Trumpener, *Bardic Nationalism: The Romantic Novel and the British Empire* (Princeton: Princeton University Press, 1997), xii, 165.
64. See Graver, 14–15.
65. Ferdinand Tönnies, *Community and Society (Gemeinschaft und Gesellschaft)*, trans. Charles P. Loomis (New York: Harper and Row, 1957), 48.
66. Tönnies, 65. Also see Graver, 14–15.
67. Tönnies, 77–88.
68. Phil Withington and Alexandra Shepard, "Introduction: Communities in early modern England," *Communities in Early Modern England*, ed. Alexandra Shepard and Phil Withington (Manchester: Manchester University Press, 2000), 4. See also Craig Muldrew, "From a 'Light Cloak' to an 'Iron Cage': Historical Changes in the Relation between Community and Individualism," *Communities in Early Modern England*, 156–177.
69. Joshua Phillips, *English Fictions of Communal Identity, 1485–1603* (Burlington, VT: Ashgate, 2010); Natalie Zemon Davis, "Boundaries and the Sense of Self in Sixteenth-Century France," *Reconstructing Individualism*, 53–63
70. Macfarlane, 163.
71. Tony Tanner, *Jane Austen* (Cambridge, MA: Harvard University Press, 1986), 193–194.
72. Williams, 166.
73. Williams, 173.
74. Benedict Anderson, *Imagined Communities*, rev. ed. (New York: Verso, 2006).
75. Habermas has been critiqued for giving inadequate attention to the way that the public sphere excluded women and for his assumption that private and public spheres operated differently. Intellectual and economic public developments were also felt in the home, while domestic expectations shaped the public sphere. See *Feminists Read Habermas: Gendering the Subject of Discourse*, ed. Johanna Meehan (New York: Routledge, 1995); and Jürgen Habermas, *The Structural Transformation of the Public Sphere* (Cambridge, MA: MIT Press, 1991).
76. Helen Thompson notes that Habermas says that women were able to enter the literary public sphere as novel readers. However, Habermas sees the private domestic sphere primarily as a way of fine-tuning men's humanity, domesticating and pacifying him on the way to public life. Helen Thompson, *Ingenuous Subjection: Compliance and Power in the Eighteenth-Century Domestic Novel* (Philadelphia: University of Pennsylvania Press, 2005), 113–115.
77. This concept may well have a longer history; Glenn Burger has found something similar in the affective marriages of late-medieval couples, expressed through physical and moral care for each other.

78. Thompson, 9.
79. Sarah Lewis, *Women's Mission* (London: John W. Parker, 1839), 38.
80. Lewis, 21.
81. Ellis, *Women of England*, 37.
82. Ellis, *Women of England*, 36.
83. Lewis, 13, 19–20.
84. Ellis, *Women of England*, 34–36.
85. Lewis, 13.
86. Zemon Davis, 56.
87. Something like this idea would also form part of the emerging field of psychology. William James was particularly fascinated by the question of where one self ended and another began.
88. George Eliot, *Middlemarch* (1874; New York: Oxford University Press, 1996), 785.
89. Emily Brontë, *Wuthering Heights* (1847; repr. New York: Penguin, 1995) , 323.
90. Coontz, 178.
91. Jane Austen, *Sense and Sensibility*, ed. Ros Ballaster (1811; New York: Penguin Books, 1995), 23. All future references will be to this edition and will be noted parenthetically.
92. As Coontz explains, "in the seventeenth and eighteenth centuries even the most enthusiastic advocates of love matches had believed that love developed after one had selected a suitable prospective mate" (178).
93. Perry, 254.
94. Perry, 255.
95. "Mistress of a family" means that she is managing servants, not that she necessarily has children. As Naomi Tadmor has shown, the eighteenth-century usage of "family" was not constrained by biological ties. Rather, "family" often approximated "household."
96. Franco Moretti, *Atlas of the European Novel, 1800–1900* (New York: Verso, 1998), 22.
97. Moretti, 17–18.
98. Perry, 141–142.
99. Claudia Johnson, *Jane Austen: Women, Politics, and the Novel* (Chicago: University of Chicago Press, 1988), 70.
100. Moretti, 65.
101. For a vivid evocation of how the passenger transport revolution undergirded new forms of writing in the nineteenth century, with new ideas about perception and time as well as space, see Jonathan Grossman, *Charles Dickens's Networks; Public Transport and the Novel* (New York: Oxford University Press, 2012).
102. Moretti, 18.

103. A later and milder example of this type is *Emma*'s Frank Churchill, who is also handsome, flirtatious, and charming, and who also has a secret passion that renders him untrustworthy. Frank, however, is bent on honorable marriage, not seduction (although some critics have argued to the contrary).
104. Eve Kosofsky Sedgwick, "Jane Austen and the Masturbating Girl," *Critical Inquiry* 17, no. 4 (Summer 1991): 818–837.
105. This is partly because Lydia's sexual appetite—she is, apparently, the one who pursues Wickham (245)—speaks to the earlier cultural belief in women's sexual greed. Similarly, Maria Rushworth, who essentially seduces Henry Crawford, is demonized for her appetites. Maria and Lydia testify both to the continuity of this earlier idea of women's sexual hungers, and to the intense horror it inspired. In the nineteenth century, it is continent, disciplined, passionless women who are respected.
106. Darcy's parents arranged for him to marry Lady Anne de Bourgh, and Mrs. Ferrars has picked out an heiress for Edward Ferrars.
107. Mary Evans, "'Falling in Love with Love is Falling for Make-Believe': Ideologies of Romance in Post-Enlightenment Culture," *Theory Culture Society* 15, nos. 3–4 (August 1998): 266.
108. Evans, 266.
109. Evans, 266.
110. Jane Austen, *Persuasion*, ed. Gillian Beer (1818; New York: Penguin, 1998), 27.
111. Monica Cohen reads naval homes as an ideal space for exercising "professional domesticity," since ships in fiction are notable for organization, cleanliness, and good planning. She would consider the ship on which Anne sails to be a replacement for the estate rather than its competitor.
112. This name choice may also have been influenced by the fact that when Broughton wrote the novel she was living with her sister Eleanor. See Pamela Gilbert, "Introduction," *Cometh Up as a Flower* (Peterborough, ON: Broadview, 2010), 9.
113. Julia Prewitt Brown, *Jane Austen's Novels: Social Change and Literary Form* (Cambridge, MA: Harvard University Press, 1979), 62.
114. Rhoda Broughton, *Cometh Up as a Flower* (1867; Peterborough, ON: Broadview, 2010), 153–154. The footnotes in Gilbert's edition show the sources of Nell's references. All future references will be to this edition and will be noted parenthetically.
115. "Shall we be two bodiless spirits, sexless, passionless essences, passing each other without recognition in the fields of ether? God forbid that it should be so" (106).
116. Sir Hugh sports a "gray knitted waistcoat," reminiscent of Colonel Brandon's famous flannel waistcoat (260).
117. "Sir Hugh was a short man, but otherwise not ill-looking. He had a jolly countenance, not encumbered with any particular expression, a jolly laugh at anybody's service; enough brains to carry him decently through his very easy part in life," Nell explains (102).

118. Citing Tennyson's "Lancelot and Elaine" in *Idylls of the King*.
119. Gilbert, 23.
120. Anthony Trollope, *The Vicar of Bullhampton*, ed. David Skilton (Oxford: Oxford University Press, 1990), 50. All future references will be to this edition and will be noted parenthetically.
121. Both are independent women whom Frank Fenwick tries to help, but who resist his interference.
122. Michael McKeon, *The Origins of the English Novel, 1600–1740*, 15th anniv. ed. (Baltimore: Johns Hopkins University Press, 2002), 21. McKeon is describing his own theory of the novel, in which "truth" (realism) and "virtue" (character) are the two categories whose interaction spurs the development of the novel from the early modern period onwards. However, the dialectical logic of the novel's development he describes here provides an interesting model for reading the historical evolution of ideas generally in the novel, not just truth and virtue.
123. The Dashwoods and Ferrars move around constantly. The Brandon estate is not in a beloved locale, not the cherished site of many generations' ancestry, nor is it infused with sentimental attachment, for Marianne or even, apparently, for Brandon, who was the younger son and did not expect to inherit. Indeed, Brandon is more often depicted as a retired military man than as a local squire.
124. Frederic Jameson, *The Antimonies of Realism* (New York: Verso, 2015), 126.
125. See Jameson, 126, for a fascinating discussion of Tito in *Romola* as a minor character with a promotion, and Woloch's discussion of the way in which Dickens's weak main characters have to be catalyzed by a host of eccentric minor characters who nonetheless cannot be allowed to overwhelm the protagonist.
126. As Frances Power Cobbe argued, "the notion that a man's wife is his PROPERTY, in the sense in which a horse is his property . . . is the fatal root of incalculable evil and misery. Every brutal-minded man, and many a man who in other relations of life is not brutal, entertains more or less vaguely the notion that his wife is his *thing*, and is ready to ask with indignation (as we read again and again in the police reports), of any one who interferes with his treatment of her, "May I not do what I will *with my own*?" "Frances Power Cobbe, "Wife-Torture in England," repr. in *Criminals, Idiots, Women, and Minors*, ed. Susan Hamilton (Peterborough, ON: Broadview, 2004), 117.
127. George Eliot, *Daniel Deronda* (1876; New York: Oxford University Press, 2014), 115. Further references will be to this edition and will be noted parenthetically in the text.
128. Williams, 110.

CHAPTER 4

1. Anthony Trollope, *The Vicar of Bullhampton*, ed. David Skilton (1870; repr. Oxford: Oxford University Press, 1990), 94.

2. Mary Jean Corbett, *Family Likeness: Sex, Marriage, and Incest from Jane Austen to Virginia Woolf* (Ithaca, NY: Cornell University Press, 2008), 55.
3. Florence Nightingale, "Cassandra," *Florence Nightingale's Cassandra* (1860; repr. New York: Feminist Press, 1979), 47.
4. Charlotte Yonge, *Womankind*, vol. 1 (Leipzig: Bernhard Tauchnitz, 1878), 280.
5. Claudia Nelson, *Family Ties in Victorian England*, Victorian Life and Times Series, ed. Sally Mitchell (London and Westport: Praeger, 2007), 137.
6. Nelson, 100.
7. Nancy Fix Anderson, "Cousin Marriage in Victorian England," *Journal of Family History* 11, no. 3 (1986): 285–301; Adam Kuper, "Changing the Subject—about Cousin Marriage, among Other Things," *Journal of the Royal Anthropological Institute* 14 (2008): 717–735.
8. Adam Kuper, *Incest and Influence: The Private Life of Bourgeois England* (Cambridge, MA: Harvard University Press, 2009), 18.
9. Kuper, *Incest*, 40. Ellen Pollak gives a good summary of the conflicting biblical and legal regulations for endogamous marriage in chapter 1 of *Incest and the English Novel, 1684–1814* (Baltimore: Johns Hopkins University Press, 2003).
10. Nelson, 134. Diane O'Hara confirms that "as late as 1800, about 90 per cent of Lancashire villages who were of labouring or artisan status, chose brides from within 10 miles." Diana O'Hara, *Courtship and Constraint: Rethinking the Making of Marriage in Tudor England* (Manchester: Manchester University Press, 2000), 124.
11. George K. Behlmer, *Friends of the Family: The English Home and Its Guardians, 1850–1940* (Stanford, CA: Stanford University Press, 1998), 26.
12. Elizabeth Rose Gruner, "Born and Made: Sisters, Brothers, and the Deceased Wife's Sister Bill," *Signs* 24, no. 2 (Winter 1999): 428.
13. Nelson, 136–137. Also see Anderson and Kuper, *Incest*.
14. Maine believed that ancient societies were composed of small groups united by blood ties and reproducing themselves through assault and rape, and that civilization requires moving toward universal egalitarian liberal agency under contract law. Lubbock agreed that primitive marriage was characterized by violent assault, although his sense of its motivation and timing differed slightly from McLennan's. For commentary on Maine, see Kathy A. Psomiades, "He Knew He Was Right: The Sensational Tyranny of the Sexual Contract and the Problem of Liberal Politics," in *The Politics of Gender in Anthony Trollope's Novels*, ed. H. M. Marwick, Deborah Morse, and Regenia Gagnier (Aldershot, UK: Ashgate, 2009), 31–44. For more on McLennan in relation to Maine and other early anthropologists, see Corbett, 89–92; Cynthia Eller, *Gentlemen and Amazons: The Myth of Matriarchal Prehistory, 1861–1900* (Berkeley: University of California Press, 2011); Adam Kuper, *The Invention of Primitive Society: Transformations of an Illusion* (New York: Routledge, 1988); and George W. Stocking Jr, *Victorian Anthropology* (New York: Free Press, 1987). Also see Edward Burnet Tylor,

Researches into the Early History of Mankind and the Development of Civilization (London: John Murray, 1865); Lewis Henry Morgan, *Ancient Society; or, Researches in the Lines of Human Progress from Savagery through Barbarism to Civilization* (New York: Henry Holt, 1877); Friedrich Engels, *The Origin of the Family, Private Property, and the State*, trans. Ernest Untermann (1884; repr. Chicago: Charles H. Kerr and Company, 1902).

15. McLennan was not the first or the last to write about primitive marriage. He was responding to Henry Sumner Maine's *Ancient Law* (1861), and was followed by Sir John Lubbock's *The Origin of Civilisation and the Primitive Condition of Man* (1870). Other influential Victorian theorists writing about how primitive society became civilized via changes in marriage practices included Edward Burnet Tylor, Lewis Henry Morgan, and Friedrich Engels.

    For accounts of Victorian anthropology, see Stocking; Eller; Kuper, *Invention*; Peter Melville Logan, *Victorian Fetishism: Intellectuals and Primitives* (Albany, NY: SUNY Press, 2009); Henrika Kuklick, *A New History of Anthropology* (Oxford: Wiley-Blackwell, 2007), and *The Savage Within: The Social History of British Anthropology, 1885–1945* (Cambridge: Cambridge University Press, 1993).
16. John McLennan, *Primitive Marriage: An Inquiry into the Origin of the Form of Capture in Marriage Ceremonies* (Edinburgh: Adam and Charles Black, 1865), 47–48.
17. McLennan, 50.
18. McLennan, 139. Also see Lubbock, 124–125, where he enumerates the ways women weaken the group.
19. Stocking points out that although "the major sociocultural evolutionists" differed from McLennan in specific points, they all generally accepted his view of the development of human marriage. "They all tended to view marriage in terms of the control of human sexuality," and accepted the idea of primitive promiscuity (204). However, Maine saw this state as savagery and proclaimed the protection of women by contract law to be a sign of a civilized society (Maine, 163–165).
20. Engels, 59.
21. Psomiades, "He Knew He Was Right," 35. Also see Kathy A. Psomiades, "The Marriage Plot in Theory," *Novel* 43, no. 1 (Spring 2010): 53–59.
22. McLennan, 23–54.
23. However, McLennan argues that both endogamous and exogamous marriage are equally plausible points of origin, possibly equally archaic, and that endogamy can cause exogamy and vice versa (145–150).
24. This is my assessment of the consequences of McLennan's theory; McLennan himself does not explore the more theoretical results of exogamy, instead charting it as a step in a progressive historical movement toward patrilineal descent and monogamous marriage.
25. Eller, 79–83.

26. Kathy Psomiades, "Heterosexual Exchange and Other Victorian Fictions: *The Eustace Diamonds* and Victorian Anthropology," *Novel* 33, no. 1 (Fall 1999): 93–94.
27. Stocking, 201.
28. Psomiades, however, does map anthropology onto the marriage plot, arguing that primitive marriage ideas govern novels by Trollope and Oliphant in particular.
29. John McLennan, *Studies in Ancient History, Second Series* (London: Macmillan, 1896), 45. Although published in 1896, this volume is compiled from notes McLennan left behind before his death in 1881.
30. Peter Logan, "Victorian Psychology and Anthropology: In Theory," paper delivered at "Victorian Theory?" CUNY Victorian Conference, May 6, 2010.
31. Pollak, 6.
32. Cited in Sigmund Freud, *Totem and Taboo*, trans. A. A. Brill (New York: Penguin, 1938), 166.
33. Havelock Ellis, *Studies in the Psychology of Sex*, vol. 4 (Middlesex: The Echo Library, 2007), 181.
34. Freud, 164.
35. Sibyl Wolfram, *In-Laws and Out-Laws: Kinship and Marriage in England* (London: Croom Helm, 1987), 166.
36. Elsie Michie, *The Vulgar Question of Money: Heiresses, Materialism, and the Novel of Manners from Jane Austen to Henry James* (Baltimore: Johns Hopkins University Press, 2011), 12.
37. Claude Lévi-Strauss, *Elementary Structures of Kinship*, trans. James Harle Bell and John Richard von Sturmer, ed. Rodney Needham (Boston: Beacon, 1969), 43–51.
38. Lévi-Strauss, 481.
39. Gayle Rubin, "The Traffic in Women: Notes on the 'Political Economy' of Sex," *Feminist Anthropology: A Reader*, ed. Ellen Lewin (Oxford: Wiley Blackwell, 2006), 87–106.
40. Lévi-Strauss himself insisted that gender was irrelevant to his theory. In 2000, he wrote exasperatedly, "How many times will I have to repeat that it makes no difference to the theory whether it is men who exchange women or the opposite?" Cited in Marcela Coelho de Souza, "The Future of the Structural Theory of Kinship," *The Cambridge Companion to Lévi-Strauss*, ed. Boris Wiseman (Cambridge: Cambridge University Press, 2009), 93.
41. Lévi-Strauss, 480.
42. Although *North and South* and *Shirley* end with symbolic marriages between the two sides, the marriage is made possible by the fact that the woman has already learned to mediate between them. Her parents have forcibly transplanted her to the North, where she learns to appreciate (and, in turn, soften) the hardened factory owner. Thus her marriage commemorates an already established acculturation, not a primitive-marriage abduction.

43. Although the actual primitive marriage plot does not seem to work, the categories stressed in the anthropological literature do permeate Victorian fiction: savagery, male sexual aggression, female helplessness, primitive feeling. I will be using *Wuthering Heights* later in this chapter as an example of a novel with clear anthropological influence that does not necessarily extend to primitive marriage (Heathcliff thinks it does, but Catherine thinks it doesn't).
44. Primitive marriage does not seem to work in reality either. In 1877, Morgan pointed out that members of warring tribes do not in fact intermarry. Intermarriage occurs between tribes that are already peaceable; it thus cannot produce peacefulness (Wolfram, 169–170).
45. Lévi-Strauss, 479.
46. Corbett, 24.
47. For an analysis of Lévi-Strauss's socialism and political work during his years in New York while writing *The Elementary Structures of Kinship*, see Vincent Debaene, "'Like Alice Through the Looking-Glass': Claude Lévi-Strauss in New York," *French Politics, Culture, and Society* 28, no. 1 (Spring 2010): 46–57.
48. de Souza, 89.
49. Lévi-Strauss, 51.
50. Tuite points out that incest became ubiquitous in Austen criticism after the 1930s (*Romantic Austen*, 99). Among the *Mansfield Park* critics who wrestle with the specter of incest are Glenda A. Hudson, *Sibling Love and Incest in Jane Austen's Fiction* (New York: St. Martin's, 1992); James F. Kilroy, *The Nineteenth-Century English Novel: Family Ideology and Narrative Form* (New York: Palgrave Macmillan, 2007); Johanna M. Smith, "'My Only Sister Now': Incest in *Mansfield Park*," *Studies in the Novel* 19, no. 1 (Spring 1987): 1–15; Julie Shaffer, "Familial Love, Incest, and Female Desire in Late Eighteenth—and Early Nineteenth-Century British Women's Novels," *Criticism* 41, no. 1 (Winter 1999): 67–99; George Haggerty, "Fanny Price: 'Is she solemn?—Is she queer?—Is she prudish?'," *The Eighteenth Century* 53, no. 2 (Summer 2012): 175–188.
51. Smith, 1, 2.
52. Kilroy, 44.
53. Eileen Cleere, *Avuncularism: Capitalism, Patriarchy, and Nineteenth-Century English Culture* (Stanford, CA: Stanford University Press, 2004), 126, 128. Ellen Pollak also assumes that Fanny's horror at the adultery references incest (183).
54. Anderson, 286.
55. Clara Tuite, "Domestivc Retrenchment and Imperial Expansion: The Property Plots of *Mansfield Park*," *The Postcolonial Jane Austen*, ed. You-me Park and Rajeswari Sunder Rajan (London: Routledge, 2000), 102.
56. Claudia Johnson agrees with Tuite that *Mansfield Park* is about the maintenance of the country-house gentry, but she argues that the novel actually functions to expose the moral shoddiness of that class. Johnson reads *Mansfield Park* as a

"bitter parody of conservative fiction" in *Jane Austen: Women, Politics, and the Novel* (Chicago: University of Chicago Press, 1988), 96.

57. Lévi-Strauss, 479.
58. Stephen Best and Sharon Marcus, "Surface Reading: An Introduction," *Representations* 108, no. 1 (2009): 12.
59. Hudson, 9, 26–27.
60. Hudson, 25.
61. Corbett, 40.
62. Haggerty, 186.
63. *Sense and Sensibility* is the only other novel that begins a generation or two before its primary characters.
64. Jane Austen, *Mansfield Park* (1814; repr. New York: Oxford University Press, 1990), 2, 6. All future references will be to this edition and will be noted parenthetically in the text.
65. Corbett astutely asks why we should assume that men don't look for sisterhood in their wives (50–51).
66. Hudson, 2.
67. Edmund's future living gets sold to pay off Tom's debts. As Sir Thomas says, "I trust I may pity your feelings as a brother on the occasion. You have robbed Edmund for ten, twenty, thirty years, perhaps for life, of more than half the income which ought to be his" (Austen, 20).
68. Although it is not the focus of this chapter, it should not go unremarked that parenting is equally diseased. Adult authorities in *Mansfield Park* are either negligently indifferent or actively cruel to their wards. An argument could be made that sibling love reforms them too, since Lady Bertram achieves a new contentment with Fanny's sister Susan serving her, and Sir Thomas's reformation begins when "he inquired next after her family, especially William" (Austen, 160). His desire to gratify William leads him to treat Fanny better.
69. Susan Lanser, "Jane Austen's World of Sisterhood," *The Sister Bond: A Feminist View of a Timeless Connection*, ed. Toni A. H. McNaron (New York: Pergamon, 1985), 54.
70. Haggerty, 181.
71. Hudson, 7–8.
72. McLennan, *Primitive Marriage*, 47–48.
73. Even the relatively harmonious Grant menage is characterized by Mrs. Grant's anxieties about Mr. Grant's fussiness.
74. Corbett, 47.
75. E. J. Clery aptly notes that Austen's brisk conclusions, refusing to show love scenes, are "not passed over in a quiet way, but with a kind of gleeful malice, in order to cause pain to the romantically inclined reader." E. J. Clery, "Gender," *The Cambridge Companion to Jane Austen*, 2nd ed., ed. Edward Copeland and Juliet McMaster (Cambridge: Cambridge University Press, 2011), 164.

76. Yonge knew the Lefroys, Austen-Leighs, and Biggs. Sir William Heathcote, a crucial person in Yonge's life, was the son of Austen's friend Elizabeth Bigg, and Elizabeth's nephew William Bigg Wither (whose father had proposed to Austen) was the curate in charge of Otterbourne and one of Yonge's greatest friends. (Personal communication with Charlotte Mitchell, November 15, 2011.)
77. *Fraser's Magazine* 50 (1854): 490. Cited in Gavin Budge, *Charlotte M. Yonge: Religion, Feminism, and Realism in the Victorian Novel* (Bern: Peter Lang, 2007), 54–55. Budge ascribes the review to Charles Kingsley.
78. *The Clever Woman of the Family*, for instance, is indebted to *Emma*. See June Sturrock, "*Emma* in the 1860s: Austen, Yonge, Oliphant, Eliot," *Women's Writing* 17, no. 2 (2010): 324–342.
79. Margaret Mare and Alicia Percival, *Victorian Best-Seller: The World of Charlotte Yonge* (London: Harrap, 1947), 219. Also see M. H. Dodd, "Jane Austen and Charlotte Yonge," *Notes & Queries* 193, no. 22 (October 30, 1948): 476–478.
80. The link has been noted by June Sturrock, "Money, Morals, and *Mansfield Park*: The West Indies Revisited," *Persuasions* 28 (2006): 176–184; Barbara Dunlap, "Heartsease and Mansfield Park," *Journal of the Charlotte M. Yonge Fellowship* 2 (1997): 2; Barbara Dunlap, "Jane Austen and Charlotte Yonge: The Heathcote Connection," *Charlotte Yonge Fellowship Review* 6 (1997–1998); and Charlotte Mitchell, "Mansfield Park and Heartsease," unpublished paper read to the UCL English Department, 1997.
81. Sturrock, "Money," 176.
82. Some of the echoes of *Mansfield Park* are quite specific. In *Mansfield Park*, "Susan saw that much was wrong at home, and wanted to set it right. That a girl of fourteen, acting only on her own unassisted reason, should err . . ." (360). In *Heartsease*, another heroine's sister "drooped under the general disregard, saw things amiss, but was hopeless of mending them" (512). The amber cross that William gives his sister Fanny becomes, in *Heartsease*, a coral cross.
83. As editor of *The Monthly Packet* and leader of the "Goslings," Yonge made it her business to care for a younger generation of female writers, editing their work, helping them publish, and co-writing with them. See Kristine Moruzi, "'The Inferiority of Women': Complicating Charlotte Yonge's Perception of Girlhood in *The Monthly Packet*," *Antifeminism and the Victorian Novel: Rereading Nineteenth Century Women Writers*, ed. Tamara S. Wagner (Amherst: Cambria, 2009), 57–76; and Georgina O'Brien Hill, "Charlotte Yonge's Goosedom," *NCGS Journal* 8, no. 1 (Spring 2012), http://www.ncgsjournal.com/issue81/issue81.htm.
84. Mitchell. See also Gavin Budge's discussion of this maxim as it affected Yonge in *Charlotte M. Yonge*, 298.
85. Charlotte M. Yonge, *Heartsease*, 10th ed. (London: Macmillan, 1868), 40. Further references will be to this edition and will be noted parenthetically in the text.
86. Valerie Sanders, *The Brother-Sister Culture in Nineteenth Century Literature: From Austen to Woolf* (Hampshire, UK: Palgrave, 2002), 98–99.

87. John originally had two younger sisters. Both died when he was five, while they were four and two (145). His other siblings are much younger; Arthur was not born until John was nine, and Theodora four years after that, since she is nineteen at the beginning of the novel, while he is twenty-three (145, 1, 7).
88. Sanders, 99.
89. Sanders, 99.
90. Indeed, *Jane Eyre* is another source text for *Heartsease*, as *Heartsease* features an estate that is founded on West Indian money and burns to the ground. Interestingly, however, it is not the madwoman in the attic who sets the master's house ablaze, but the evil matriarch, Mrs. Nesbit, whose cynical worldliness has poisoned all family relationships and who has independent (and vast) West Indian property. The fire thus emblematizes the destructiveness of this slave-owner's influence.
91. Yonge cleaned up the husband's behavior as well. Unlike Arthur Huntingdon, Arthur Martindale keeps his depravity offstage, so that the reader does not witness most of it, and it seems to consist mainly of betting on horses, without the sexual, alcoholic, and abusive license of his predecessor.
92. Mitchell points out that a draft of *Heartsease* must have been completed by 1851, when Yonge mailed the manuscript to a friend.
93. Like Fanny, too, Violet's first wish in a new house is to write to her favorite sibling, but, tellingly, whereas Edmund helped Fanny find writing materials, in this case, it is Violet who assists John, a small example of how she will help him in more profound ways (Yonge, 13).
94. Much interesting recent work has been done on Yonge's ideas of interdependency. See Martha Stoddard Holmes, "Victorian Fictions of Interdependency: Gaskell, Craik, and Yonge," *Journal of Literary Disability* 1, no. 2 (2007): 29–40; Mia Chen, "And There Was No Helping It: Disability and Social Reproduction in Charlotte Yonge's *The Daisy Chain*," *NCGS Journal* 4, no. 2 (Summer 2008); and Tamara Silvia Wagner, "'If He Belonged to Me, I Should Not Like It At All': Managing Disability and Dependencies in Charlotte Yonge's *The Two Guardians*," *NCGS Journal* 4, no. 2 (Summer 2008).
95. Mitchell.
96. Slavery is central to *Heartsease*. It is connected to all the family's problems: the dwindling property, the daughter's "tropical" passions, the mother's "West Indian" lethargy, the great-aunt's dehumanizing control. "We all of us have, more or less, a West Indian constitution; that accounts for anything," remarks one of the sons (145).
97. See Nelson and Sanders (*Heartsease* provides the epigraph for Sanders); also Leila Silvana May, *Disorderly Sisters: Sibling Relations and Sororal Resistance in Nineteenth-Century British Literature* (Lewisburg, PA: Bucknell University Press, 2001); and Joseph A. Boone and Deborah Epstein Nord, "Brother and Sister: The

Seductions of Siblinghood in Dickens, Eliot, and Brontë," *Western Humanities Review* 46, no. 2 (Summer 1992): 164–188.

98. Austen, 43.
99. Jerome Bump, "The Family Dynamics of the Reception of Art," *Style* 31, no. 2 (Summer 1997): 106–128.
100. Leo Bersani, *A Future for Astanyax: Character and Desire in Literature* (Boston: Little, Brown, 1969): 197–229.
101. Terry Eagleton writes, "Heathcliff the adult is 'natural' man in a Hobbesian sense: an appetitive exploiter to whom no tie or tradition is sacred, a callous predator violently sundering the bonds of custom and piety." Terry Eagleton, *Myths of Power: A Marxist Study of the Brontës* (London: Macmillan, 1975), 110.
102. On Heathcliff's victimization of Isabella, see Judith E. Pike, "My Name Was Isabella Linton": Coverture, Domestic Violence, and Mrs. Heathcliff's Narrative in Wuthering Heights," *Nineteenth-Century Literature* 64, no. 3 (December 2009): 347–383.
103. Kathryn B. McGuire, "The Incest Taboo in *Wuthering Heights*: A Modern Appraisal," *American Imago* 45 (1988): 217. For other readings of Catherine and Heathcliff as incestuous, see Eagleton; Eric Solomon, "The Incest Theme in Wuthering Heights," *Nineteenth-Century Fiction* 14 (1969): 80–83; Q. D. Leavis, "A Fresh Approach to Wuthering Heights," *Lectures in America* (New York: Pantheon, 1969); James H. Kavanagh, *Emily Brontë* (New York: Basil Blackwell, 1985), 64; John Allen Stevenson, "'Heathcliff is Me!': Wuthering Heights and the Question of Likeness," *NCL* 43, no. 1 (June 1988): 74–75.
104. Corbett, 25.
105. Emily Brontë, *Wuthering Heights* (1847; repr. New York: Penguin, 1995), 81. Further references will be to this edition and will be noted parenthetically in the text.
106. Drew Lamonica, *"We Are Three Sisters": Self and Family in the Writing of the Brontës* (Columbia: University of Missouri Press, 2003), 109. John Allen Stevenson points out that the Grange and the Heights are set up for a perfectly symmetrical Lévi-Straussian exchange: each family has one daughter and one son needing a wife. But Heathcliff's advent disrupts this exchange (77).
107. Corbett, 28–29.
108. Lyn Pykett, *Emily Brontë* (Savage, MD: Barnes and Noble Books, 1989), 87–88.
109. [William Henry Smith] "Comte," *Blackwood's Edinburgh Magazine* 53, no. 329 (March 1843): 397–414. Emily read the political articles in *Blackwood's* aloud to her father, according to Winifred Gérin, *Emily Brontë* (New York: Oxford University Press, 1971), 145.
110. Patsy Stoneman, "Introduction," *Wuthering Heights* (New York: Oxford University Press, 1995), xxix.
111. Lamonica, 106.

112. Patsy Stoneman, "Catherine Earnshaw's Journey to Her Home among the Dead: Fresh Thoughts on *Wuthering Heights* and 'Epipsychidion,'" *The Review of English Studies* 47, no. 188 (1996): 521–533.
113. Lawrence Stone, *The Family, Sex, and Marriage in England, 1500–1800* (New York: Harper and Row, 1977), 4–7.
114. Maja-Lisa von Sneidern, "Wuthering Heights and the Liverpool Slave Trade," *ELH* 62, no. 1 (Spring 1995): 175.
115. Patricia Yaeger sees Nelly as a parallel case to Heathcliff, since she also hovers between foster child and servant ("Violence in the Sitting Room: *Wuthering Heights* and the Women's Novel," *Genre* 21 (1988): 227).
116. Nelly mentions "the children's room" (44) and in her feverish dying dreams; Catherine remembers when she "laid alone, for the first time," after her father died and Heathcliff was sent to the servants' quarters (125).
117. Stoneman, "Introduction," xvii.
118. Stone, 7–9.
119. Stoneman, "Introduction," xvii.
120. Stoneman, xx.
121. Lamonica, citing Cecil W. Davies, "A Reading of *Wuthering Heights*," 259.
122. von Sneidern; Christopher Heywood, "Yorkshire Slavery in Wuthering Heights," *The Review of English Studies* 38, no. 150 (May 1987): 184–198.
123. Frances Power Cobbe, "Wife-Torture in England," repr. in *Criminals, Idiots, Women, and Minors*, ed. Susan Hamilton (Peterborough, ON: Broadview, 2004), 117.
124. Lyn Pykett and Emily Rena-Dozier both read *Wuthering Heights* as a composite Gothic/realist genre. See Pykett and Emily Rena-Dozier, "Gothic Criticisms: Wuthering Heights and Nineteenth-Century Literary Criticism," *ELH* 77, no. 3 (Fall 2010): 757–775.
125. "At Wuthering Heights names are simply repeated, as if there were little difference between the generations, as if their owners kept adopting the same roles and following the same script century after century. When we add to name repetition the habit of cousins marrying cousins in a complicated genealogy, we can see why readers become as confused as Lockwood when he first enters the family. . . . Thus, as Lockwood puts it, "Time stagnates here" (32), not only in choice of names, but also in repetition of abuse and addiction" (Bump).
126. Kate Flint, "Women Writers, Women's Issues," *Cambridge Companion to the Brontës*, ed. Heather Glen (Cambridge: Cambridge University Press, 2002), 177.
127. See *Wuthering Heights*, 220, 249–250, 296–297, 300–301.
128. A writer in 1791 remarked that "the accent is invariably placed on the first syllable by all correct speakers, and as constantly removed to the second by the illiterate and vulgar," but in 1893 the *OED*'s editors remarked that in the present-day usage, "the words 'placed on' and 'removed to' should change places." Thus the accent shifted during the nineteenth century. Hareton's ambiguous

pronunciation, then, places him in the transitional era from the eighteenth to the nineteenth century, and in a transitional class as well. His first-syllable stress marks the fact that his linguistic training from gentry speakers occurred decades ago, and he has had no subsequent contact with more modern interlocutors.

129. Yonge, *Womankind*, 279, 280.

CHAPTER 5

1. This chapter actually discusses suitors with a range of physical impairments, some of which might not count as disabilities today. (In disability theory, disability is generally seen as constructed by a social or physical context that renders a particular physical or cognitive configuration problematic; i.e., in a deaf community where everyone uses sign language, being deaf is no disability, but in a realm in which hearing is expected, deafness becomes disabling.) Moreover, the modern term "disability" may conjure conditions the Victorians did not recognize or discuss. I have used the term throughout this chapter in spite of its debatable applicability because I want this discussion to be recognized within the context of disability theory. It seems to me that the idea that disabled figures participated in a social network is a vitally useful alternative to contemporary ablist assumptions that people with disabilities have neither social nor sexual lives; it provides us with a way of thinking about the kinds of connections that are positively made possible by disability (not just not precluded by disability); and by using an arguably anachronistic term in this chapter I hope to reinforce the relevance of these Victorian practices for modern understanding.
2. Paula England points out that the autonomous self is also what developmental psychology strives to achieve, and what the scientific experimenter hopes for; in science, caring for one's subjects is seen as contaminating the study. Similarly, according to Jennifer Nedelsky, American property law valorizes autonomous private ownership and associates collectivity with coercion and individualism with freedom. In short, the assumption that the self is an atomistic, rational, self-interested agent underlies quite disparate fields. See Paula England, "The Separative Self: Androcentric Bias in Neoclassical Assumptions," in *Beyond Economic Man: Feminist Theory and Economics*, ed. Marianne A. Ferber and Julie A. Nelson (Chicago: University of Chicago Press, 1993), 40–41; Jennifer Nedelsky, "Reconceiving Autonomy: Sources, Thoughts and Possibilities," *Yale Journal of Law and Feminism* 8 (1989): 12, n.12, 17.
3. David Wayne Thomas, *Cultivating Victorians: Liberal Culture and the Aesthetic* (Philadelphia: University of Pennsylvania Press, 2004), 14.
4. George Eliot, *Middlemarch*, ed. Rosemary Ashton (1871–1972; repr. New York: Penguin, 1994), 141.
5. Rochester's symbolic castration has received much critical attention, as summarized in Sandra Gilbert and Susan Gubar, *The Madwoman in the Attic* (New Haven, CT: Yale University Press, 2000), 368. See, for instance, Tamar Heller, "That Muddy, Polluted Flood of Earthly Love," *Victorian Sensations: Essays on a Scandalous Genre*,

ed. Kimberly Harrison and Richard Fantina (Columbus: Ohio State Press, 2006), 92. Similarly, Philip Wakem is called "asexual" in Patricia Menon's *Austen, Eliot, Charlotte Brontë, and the Mentor-Lover* (New York: Palgrave Macmillan, 2003), 148; and in Rosemarie Bodenheimer's *The Real Life of Mary Ann Evans: George Eliot, Her Letters and Fiction* (Ithaca, NY: Cornell University Press, 1994), 103. Comparable examples could be given for Ralph Touchett.

6. Martha Nussbaum, *Frontiers of Justice: Disability, Nationality, Species Membership* (Cambridge, MA: Harvard University Press, 2007), 101.
7. "The man here, once so arrogant/ And restless, so ambitious, for his part,/ Of dealing with statistically packed/ Disorders (from a pattern on his nail,)/ And packing such things quite another way,—/ Is now contented. From his personal loss/ He has come to hope for others when they lose,/ And wear a gladder faith in what we gain . . ./ Through bitter experience, compensation sweet." Elizabeth Barrett Browning, *Aurora Leigh* (1856; repr. Chicago: Academy Chicago Publishers, 1979), 339.
8. Fictional women who are disabled participate in a different dynamic. Their disability generally intensifies the soulful delicacy that ought to characterize the ideal woman in the first place (Bailin, Vrettos, Frawley, Keith). Since the marriage plot with which I am concerned focuses on disabled men, I do not discuss the marriageable female invalid in this chapter.
9. Disability theorists have identified specific ways that Victorian subjects understood particular kinds of disability. Martha Stoddard Holmes, Mary Anne O'Farrell, and David Bolt, for instance, focus on the special status of the blind in Victorian thought, while Jennifer Esmail has explored Victorian deafness. See Martha Stoddard Holmes, *Fictions of Affliction: Physical Disability in Victorian Culture* (Ann Arbor: University of Michigan Press, 2009); and Mary Anne O'Farrell, "Blindness Envy: Victorians in the Parlors of the Blind," *PMLA* 127, no. 3 (May 2012): 512–525. David Bolt, "The Blindman in the Classic: Feminisms, Ocularcentrism, and *Jane Eyre*," in *The Madwoman and the Blindman: Jane Eyre, Discourse, Disability*, ed. David Bolt, Julia Miele Rodas, and Elizabeth J. Donaldson (Columbus: Ohio State Press, 2012), 32–50. Jennifer Esmail, *Reading Victorian Deafness: Signs and Sounds in Victorian Literature and Culture* (Columbus: Ohio State Press, 2013).
10. Robert McRuer, "Introduction: Compulsory Able-Bodiedness and Queer/ Disabled Existence," in *Crip Theory: Cultural Signs of Queerness and Disability* (New York: New York University Press, 2006), 1–32.
11. Quayson perhaps puts it most succinctly: "Disability has always been the object of a negative comparison to what is typically construed as corporeal normality." Ato Quayson, *Aesthetic Nervousness: Disability and the Crisis of Representation* (New York: Columbia University Press, 2007), 4. Quayson's larger point, following Rosemarie Garland-Thomson, is that the exceptional body has always called for analysis, regulation, interpretation, diagnosis; it provokes a discourse. To that, this project is no exception.

12. Athena Vrettos argues that illness in the nineteenth century is associated with bodily permeability, a collective experience in which emotions, pain, and feeling could become contagious. Her interest in the communicability of feeling parallels my sense of disability as inherently shared and social. Athena Vrettos, *Somatic Fictions: Imagining Illness in Victorian Culture* (Stanford, CA: Stanford University Press, 1995).
13. One can genuinely ask whether Victorians had something akin to our category of learning disabilities (including dyslexia, ADHD, etc.), and whether we have something like their ideas of hysteria, neurasthenia, and brain fever. Mental illness, too, looked different for Victorians, as it included the idea of "moral insanity," not part of our discourse today.
14. Miriam Bailin, *The Sickroom in Victorian Fiction: The Art of Being Ill* (Cambridge: Cambridge University Press, 1994), 5. Maria Frawley concurs that the sickroom was a place where normal relations were suspended, but whereas Bailin sees this as a kind of haven, Frawley connects it with stasis and indeterminacy. See *Invalidism and Identity in Nineteenth-Century Britain* (Chicago: University of Chicago Press, 2004).
15. Charles Dickens, *Great Expectations* (1860–1961; repr. London: Penguin, 1996), 471.
16. Important reconsiderations of Rochester's disabilities can be found in *The Madwoman and the Blindman: Jane Eyre, Discourse, Disability*, ed. David Bolt, Julia Miele Rodas, and Elizabeth J. Donaldson (Columbus: Ohio State Press, 2012).
17. As Bailin puts it, "delicate, sensitive, sickly, these characters preside over the events of the novel with a moral authority and saintliness of manner for which pain is both the origin and the sign" (11). Lois Keith points out just how common such experiences are in Victorian girls' fiction in *Take Up Thy Bed and Walk: Death, Disability, and Cure in Classic Fiction for Girls* (New York: Routledge, 2001).
18. Bailin, 24.
19. On the damaging qualities of the gaze, see Rosemarie Garland Thomson, *Staring: How We Look* (New York: Oxford University Press, 2009).
20. See Rosemarie Garland Thomson's path-breaking collection, *Freakery: Cultural Spectacles of the Extraordinary Body* (New York: New York University Press, 1996). Two studies that take Garland Thomson's ideas into Victorian culture are *Victorian Freaks: The Social Context of Freakery in Britain*, ed. Marlene Tromp (Columbus: Ohio State Press, 2008); and Lillian Craton's *The Victorian Freak Show: The Significance of Disability and Physical Differences in 19th Century Fiction* (Amherst, NY: Cambria, 2009).
21. Melissa Free, "Freaks that Matter: The Dolls' Dressmaker, the Doctor's Assistant, and the Limits of Difference," *Victorian Freaks*, 259–282.
22. Bailin, 24.
23. See Bailin, 29.

24. Bailin, 19.
25. Charlotte Brontë, *Jane Eyre* (1847; repr. New York: Penguin, 1966), 297.
26. Bailin, 23.
27. Charles Dickens, *Our Mutual Friend* (1864–1865; repr. New York: Penguin, 1964), 823.
28. Bronwyn Rivers, *Women at Work in the Victorian Novel: The Question of Middle-Class Women's Employment 1840–1870* (Lewiston, NY: Edwin Mellen, 2006), 155.
29. See Kelly Hager's memorable discussion of Quilp's sexual aggression in *Dickens and the Rise of Divorce: The Failed Marriage Plot and the Novel Tradition* (Burlington, VT: Ashgate, 2010).
30. Stoddard Holmes, 39.
31. See Tobin Siebers, *Disability Theory* (Ann Arbor: University of Michigan Press, 2008), especially ch. 6, for a strong refutation of this convention. Other recent work on disability and sexuality includes William J. Peace, "Head Nurses," *Atrium* 12 (Winter 2014): 20–22.
32. Virginia Held, *The Ethics of Care: Personal, Political, and Global* (New York: Oxford University Press, 2006), 49.
33. Nel Noddings, *Caring: A Feminine Approach to Ethics and Moral Education* (Berkeley: University of California Press, 1984), 5.
34. Noddings, *Caring*, 37.
35. Eva Feder Kittay, *Love's Labor: Essays on Women, Equality, and Dependence* (New York: Routledge, 1999), 36.
36. Kittay; also Barbara Hillyer, *Feminism and Disability* (Norman: University of Oklahoma Press, 1993), ch. 3.
37. Hillyer, 194.
38. Hillyer, 216.
39. Susan Wendell, *The Rejected Body: Feminist Philosophical Reflections on Disability* (New York: Routledge, 1996), 151.
40. Nel Noddings, "A Response to Card, Hoagland, Houston," *Hypatia* 5, no. 1 (Spring 1990): 123.
41. Kittay, 68.
42. Noddings, *Caring*, 16–18.
43. Nel Noddings, *Starting at Home: Caring and Social Policy* (Berkeley: University of California Press, 2002), 13.
44. Noddings, *Starting*, 14. Rae Greiner points out that "harmony" formed part of the eighteenth-century theory of sympathy as promulgated by David Hume and Adam Smith. See *Sympathetic Realism in Nineteenth-Century British Fiction.* (Baltimore: Johns Hopkins University Press, 2012), 13.
45. Currently home health-care aides have little legal protection in the United States, partly because the law imagines them as voluntary "companions" visiting a private home. The sentimental appeal of "care-giving" thus is not enhancing their status, but

profoundly disempowering them. See Eileen Boris and Jennifer Klein, "Home-Care Workers Aren't Just 'Companions,'" *New York Times*, July 2, 2012, A15.

46. Jane Austen, letter to Anna Austen, September 9, 1814, *Jane Austen's Letters*, ed. R. W. Chapman, 2nd ed. (London: Oxford University Press, 1952), 401.
47. Brigid Lowe, *Victorian Fiction and the Insights of Sympathy: An Alternative to the Hermeneutics of Suspicion* (London: Anthem, 2007), 241.
48. Martha Stoddard Holmes, "Victorian Fictions of Interdependency: Gaskell, Craik, and Yonge," *Journal of Literary Disability* 1, no. 2 (2007): 30.
49. Of course, not every Victorian novel with a disabled character fits this story. While Lucy Snowe repeatedly gives care to others, she regards her work caring for Marie Broc, the "crétin," as grueling labor with no emotional or social benefits. Moreover, when she is the cared-for, Dr. John's tender ministrations agonize as well as please her, precisely due to their difference from an erotic encounter. Lucy demonstrates that care does not automatically create the "euphoric" relations Noddings describes.
50. Charles Dickens, *Little Dorrit* (1857; repr. New York: Penguin, 1998), 787.
51. Silvana Colella, "Gifts and Interests: *John Halifax, Gentleman* and the Purity of Business," *Victorian Literature and Culture* 35, no. 2 (2007): 397. Karen Bourrier calls him a descendant of Carlyle's Captains of Industry, an accurate connection, since John has the feudal and emotive leadership capacity Carlyle demanded in mill-owners.
52. Kiran Mascarenhas remarks, "The focalisation of a woman's desires through Phineas results in a homoerotic tension so strong that Victorian critic R. H. Hutton laments, 'During the early part of the novel it is hard to suppress the fear that Phineas Fletcher will fall hopelessly in love with John Halifax, so hard is it to remember that Phineas is of the male sex.'" Phineas and John call each other David and Jonathan, nicknames that, as Mascarenhas notes, conjure up the love that surpasses the love of women. Kiran Mascarenhas, "*John Halifax, Gentleman*: A Counter Story," *Antifeminism and the Victorian Novel: Rereading Nineteenth-Century Women Writers*, ed. Tamara Silvia Wagner (Amherst, NY: Cambria, 2009), 255–270.
53. Bailin, 5–6.
54. Colella, 404.
55. Dinah Mulock Craik, *John Halifax, Gentleman*, ed. Lynn M. Alexander (1856; repr. Peterborough, ON: Broadview, 2005), 69. Further references will be to this edition and will be noted parenthetically in the text.
56. An especially moving reading of *Persuasion* as a novel of loss and melancholy can be found in William Deresiewicz, *Jane Austen and the Romantic Poets* (New York: Columbia University Press, 2005).
57. Jane Austen, *Persuasion*, ed. Gillian Beer (1818; repr. New York: Penguin, 1998), 91–92. Future references will be to this edition and will be noted parenthetically.
58. Monica Cohen, *Professional Domesticity in the Victorian Novel: Women, Work, and Home* (Cambridge: Cambridge University Press, 1998), 15.

59. Marc Cyr, "Bad Morality, Truth, and Mrs. Smith in Persuasion," *The Eighteenth-Century Novel* 4 (2004): 203, 210. Similarly, Gloria Sibyl Gross complains that, "oblivious to her loyal girlhood chum's best interest, even more than willing to sacrifice it to her own, [Mrs. Smith] lends every support to the odious match." Gloria Sybil Gross, "Flights into Illness: Some Characters in Jane Austen," *Literature and Medicine During the Eighteenth Century*, ed. Marie Mulvey Roberts and Roy Porter (London: Routledge, 1993), 194.
60. Burney's influence on Austen is well documented. Austen references *Camilla* affectionately in *Sanditon*. Austen cited Burney's novels as examples of the best of the genre in *Northanger Abbey*, and took the title of *Pride and Prejudice* from *Cecilia*.
61. Indeed, because Eugenia is her uncle's heiress and exceptionally well educated, as well as inherently good, she is usually the one offering comfort to others.
62. John Wiltshire, *Jane Austen and the Body* (Cambridge: Cambridge University Press, 1992), 21.
63. This structure is also noted by Alistair Duckworth, *The Improvement of the Estate: A Study of Jane Austen's Novels* (Baltimore: Johns Hopkins University Press, 1971), 188.
64. Wiltshire, 168.
65. On Wentworth as a good nurse, see Wiltshire, 170–173.
66. Recent work on the Victorian novel and sympathy includes Greiner and Rachel Ablow, *The Marriage of Minds: Reading Sympathy in the Victorian Marriage Plot* (Stanford, CA: Stanford University Press, 2007). Greiner and Ablow both argue that sympathy is fundamental to the work of the Victorian novel, which is characterized by depictions of social relationships rather than objects (Greiner) and attempts to merge the reader into a quasi-marital sympathy with its characters (Ablow). I use a vocabulary of "care" rather than "sympathy" here, since I view sympathy as a primarily epistemological state and care as an activity, and I argue that it is the act of caring that constitutes communities and disabled unions. Sympathy, which may be solely a private, passive surmise about another's feelings, does not necessarily impact characters' social relationships. Meanwhile, care can be extended without sympathy, simply out of professional obligation.
67. See Tess O'Toole, "Reconfiguring the Family in *Persuasion*," *Persuasions* 15 (1993): 200–206.
68. Cohen, *Professional Domesticity*, 24.
69. Mary Midgely, cited in Lowe, 129.
70. Susan F. Feiner, "A Portrait of *Homo economicus* as a Young Man," in *The New Economic Criticism*, ed. Martha Woodmansee and Mark Osteen (New York: Routledge, 1999), 194.
71. Karen Bloom Gevirtz, *Life after Death: Widows and the English Novel, Defoe to Austen* (Newark: University of Delaware Press, 2005), 158.

72. See Peter Knox-Shaw, *Jane Austen and the Enlightenment* (Cambridge: Cambridge University Press, 2004), especially 5–8.
73. Marilyn Butler, *Jane Austen and the War of Ideas* (Oxford: Clarendon, 1975), 280–281.
74. As Wiltshire caustically remarks, "it is amusing to see critics who unquestionably accept the sailors' right to plunder French frigates getting upset at this 'nurse-accomplice' taking minor advantage of her wealthier clients" (184).
75. D. A. Miller, *The Secret of Style* (Princeton, NJ: Princeton University Press, 2003), 73.
76. Gillian Beer, "Introduction," *Persuasion* (New York: Penguin Books, 1998), xxvii.
77. Duckworth, 191, n. 8.
78. Called a "pimp" and a "villain" by Marc Cyr, she is excoriated for her manipulative qualities by Gloria Sybil Gross, William Galperin, and Lynda A. Hall. Peter Smith claims "that Mrs. Smith's charges amount to no more than prejudiced fantasy," because of "the circumstances in which this character's speeches are declaimed. The former friend of Anne's schooldays who is now an impoverished cripple languishing in a dark tenement, Mrs. Smith may speak in a voice that carries conviction, but we are surely meant to infer that her authority owes at least as much to the soothsayers and Romantic recluses of literature as it does to life." Peter Smith, "Jane Austen's *Persuasion* and the Secret Conspiracy," *Cambridge Quarterly* 24, no. 4 (1995): 281. An impoverished person, according to this theory, cannot know "life," although one might naïvely imagine that Mrs. Smith knows much more about "life" than someone as sheltered as Anne. When Marc Cyr argues that Mrs. Smith is "the villain of the piece," part of his evidence is that Mrs. Smith presumably uses the proceeds from the sale of her small handicrafts to support herself, an odd version of villainy (Cyr, 94). See Gloria Sybil Gross, "Flights into Illness: Some Characters in Jane Austen," in *Literature and Medicine during the Eighteenth Century*, ed. Marie Mulvey Roberts and Roy Porter (London: Routledge, 1993), 188–199; Lynda A. Hall, "A View from Confinement: *Persuasion*'s Resourceful Mrs. Smith," *NCGS* 7, no. 3 (Winter 2011), http://www.ncgsjournal.com/issue73/hall.htm; William H. Galperin, *The Historical Austen* (Philadelphia: University of Pennsylvania Press, 2003), 232–233.
79. Charlotte Yonge, *The Clever Woman of the Family*, ed. Clare A. Simmons (1865; repr. Peterborough, ON: Broadview, 2001), 121. Future references will be to this edition and will be noted parenthetically in the text.
80. Cohen discusses the domestic skills associated with the navy in *Persuasion* in Chapter 1 of *Professional Domesticity*.
81. Kate Lawson, "Indian Mutiny/English Mutiny: National Governance in Charlotte Yonge's *The Clever Woman of the Family*," *VLC* 42, no. 3 (September 2014): 439–455.
82. Lowe, 187.

83. Stoddard Holmes, 52.
84. Tamara Silvia Wagner, "'If He Belonged to Me, I Should Not Like It at All': Managing Disabilities and Dependencies in Charlotte Yonge's *The Two Guardians*." *Nineteenth-Century Gender Studies* 4, no. 2 (Summer 2008), http://www.ncgsjournal.com/issue42/wagner.htm.
85. Wagner, "If He Belonged to Me," http://www.ncgsjournal.com/issue42/wagner.htm.
86. Tamara Silvia Wagner, "Marriage Plots and 'Matters of More Importance': Sensationalising Self-Sacrifice in Victorian Domestic Fiction," *Antifeminism and the Victorian Novel: Rereading Nineteenth-Century Women Writers* (New York: Cambria, 2009), 147.
87. Lowe, 201.
88. Lowe, 191. No wonder that when editing her journal, *The Monthly Packet*, Yonge rejected stories in which "the whole turns exclusively on love." From Georgina Battiscombe's *Charlotte Mary Yonge: The Story of an Uneventful Life* (London: Constable, 1943), 113, cited in Lowe, 191.
89. Charlotte Yonge, *Womankind*, vol. 1 (Leipzig: Bernhard Tauchnitz, 1878), 273.
90. Yonge, *Womankind*, 279.
91. Lowe, 191.
92. See Lowe and my "Maiden Pairs: The Sororal Romance in *The Clever Woman of the Family*," in *Victorian Antifeminism*, ed. Tamara Silvia Wagner (New York: Cambria, 2009), 97–115.
93. Ermine worries about Colin's thinness, tiredness, and coughing (119, 244–245, 359, 423).
94. Stoddard Holmes, 52.
95. Recognizing this model also helps us read the novel's final scene, in which toddler cousins woo one another. "The yellow-haired, slenderly-made, delicately featured boy . . . dutifully and admirably obeyed the more distinct, though less connected, utterances of the little dark-eyed girl, eked out by pretty imperious gestures, that seemed already to enchain the little white-frocked cavalier to her service" (541). If we assume that this is a childish aping of romantic marriage, it is offputtingly precociously sexualized, but if we read it in Yonge's ethics of care system, it makes perfect sense: the two are cousins, and the attraction between them consists of the boy's sense that the girl, the stronger, can meet his needs. "Enchained" by the dual links of cousinship and caretaking, the lad is clearly destined to be the perfect partner for the girl.
96. Eileen Cleere argues that the avunculate provides an alternative model of familial and financial transmission in *Avuncularism: Capitalism, Patriarchy, and Nineteenth-Century English Culture* (Stanford, CA: Stanford University Press, 2004). For a reading of aunthood as a way of retaining an idea of female power in an era when mothers were under stress, see Ruth Perry, *Novel Relations: The Transformation of Kinship in English Literature and Culture, 1748–1818* (Cambridge: Cambridge University Press, 2004), ch. 8.

97. For important work on the role of the avunculate in queer families—and many of Yonge's families seem quite obviously queer to a modern reader—see Eve Sedgwick, "Tales of the Avunculate," *Tendencies* (Durham, NC: Duke University Press, 1993), 52–72; Denis Flannery, *On Sibling Love, Queer Attachment and American Writing* (Aldershot, UK: Ashgate, 2007). I have written about queer familial bonds in Yonge in "Maiden Pairs."
98. Alick remains permanently furious at what Bessie considers her "girlish bit of neglect after [Alick's] wound" (294), as well as Bessie's refusal to care for Mr. Clare and for her elderly husband, Lord Keith.
99. Noddings, *Caring*, 37.
100. The scene has obvious resonances with Jane Eyre's famous plea to Rochester to imagine their souls as if they had gone through the grave and stood at God's feet. In a world in which women often felt victimized by men's predatory sexuality, it is not surprising if those women imagined a world without bodies as a safer space for love, rather than trying to express desire themselves.
101. As Sharon Marcus remarks of the parallel case of lesbian partners, "the question of whether or not women in female couples actually had sex became less important than the fact that they themselves and many in their social networks perceived them as married." Sharon Marcus, *Between Women: Friendship, Desire, and Marriage in Victorian England* (Princeton, NJ: Princeton University Press, 2007), 20.
102. Kim Wheatley, "Death and Domestication in Charlotte Yonge's *The Clever Woman of the Family*," *SEL* 36, no. 4 (1996): 909.
103. Feiner, 164.
104. Feiner, 176.
105. Lowe, 198–199.
106. George Eliot, *The Mill on the Floss*, ed. A. S. Byatt (New York: Penguin, 2003). All references will be to this edition and will be noted parenthetically within the text.
107. Karen Bourrier, "Orthopedic Disability and the Nineteenth-Century Novel," *Nineteenth-Century Contexts* 36, no. 1 (February 2014): 2.
108. "George Eliot may have intended the relationship of Phillip [sic] Wakem and Tom Tulliver in *The Mill on the Floss* to repudiate Craik's sentimental portraits of Halifax and Fletcher; Robert Colby has suggested that Eliot's insistence that Tulliver was not 'moulded on the spoony type of the Industrious Apprentice' refers to the pious Halifax." Elaine Showalter, "Dinah Mulock Craik and the Tactics of Sentiment: A Case Study in Victorian Female Authorship," *Feminist Studies* 2, nos. 2–3 (1975): 18. Bourrier agrees with this judgment.
109. Mary Jean Corbett, *Family Likeness: Sex, Marriage, and Incest from Jane Austen to Virginia Woolf* (Ithaca, NY: Cornell University Press, 2008), 115.

110. Suzanne Graver explains that "the loss [of community] was often located in the near past of the last half of the eighteenth century and the early decades of the nineteenth" (1).
111. Eliot, *Middlemarch*, 211.
112. Noddings, 24.
113. For a thorough account of Eliot's ideas of sympathy, see Graver.
114. Bob Jakins and Dr. Kenn are the only non-family members who try to help, and in spite of their good will, in both cases, their assistance is limited by their financial and social constraints.
115. Iris Marion Young, "Impartiality and the Civic Public: Some Implications of Feminist Critiques of Moral and Political Theory," *Feminism as Critique: On the Politics of Gender* (Minneapolis: University of Minnesota Press, 1987), 62.
116. Noddings, *Caring*, 51.
117. Unsigned review, *Dublin University Magazine*, February 1861, lvii, 192–200, repr. in *George Eliot: The Critical Heritage*, ed. David Carroll (London: Routledge and Kegan Paul, 1971), 150.
118. Dinah Mulock, unsigned review, *Macmillan's Magazine*, April 1861, iii, 441–448, repr. in *George Eliot: The Critical Heritage*, 156.
119. Swinburne and Stephen are cited in *George Eliot: The Critical Heritage*, 164, 477–478. Swinburne originally published in *A Note on Charlotte Bronte* (1877); Stephen originally published in *Cornhill* xliii (February 1881): 152–168. Robert Polhemus praises the erotic power of the Stephen Guest section and reads Swinburne's hostility as rooted in misognyny in *Erotic Faith: Being in Love from Jane Austen to D. H. Lawrence* (Chicago: University of Chicago Press, 1990), 185–187.
120. Elaine Showalter, *A Literature of Their Own: British Women Writers from Brontë to Lessing*, rev. ed. (Princeton, NJ: Princeton University Press, 1999), 128.
121. Maggie weeps when she kisses Philip, who has "low pale face that was full of pleading, timid love—like a woman's" (350). In an evolutionary model favoring robust heterosexual pairings, this is worrisome.
122. Graver, 125.
123. Graver, 103.
124. Much has been written on the novel's evolutionary language, including Corbett, especially ch. 5; Gillian Beer, *Darwin's Plots: Evolutionary Narrative in Darwin, George Eliot, and Nineteenth-Century Fiction*, 3rd ed. (Cambridge: Cambridge University Press, 2009); George Levine, *Darwin and the Novelists: Patterns of Science in Victorian Fiction* (Chicago: University of Chicago Press, 1988); and Nancy L. Paxton, *George Eliot and Herbert Spencer: Feminism, Evolutionism, and the Reconstruction of Gender* (Princeton, NJ: Princeton University Press, 1991).
125. Graver, 27.

126. It is significant in terms of the discourse of heredity and medicalization that Eliot takes pains to point out that Philip's injury is accidental, not congenital (170). By contrast, we never learn the origin of Phineas's disability, nor is it important. In care relations, it is the type of care that matters, not the reason care is required in the first place.
127. Charlotte M. Yonge, *The Magnum Bonum, or, Mother Carey's Brood* (London: Macmillan, 1889), 298.
128. Yonge, *Magnum*, 457.
129. Henry James, *The Portrait of a Lady* (1881; repr. New York: Penguin, 2003), 63.
130. Noddings, "A Response to Card, Hoagland, Houston," *Hypatia* 5, no. 1 (Spring 1990): 123.

CHAPTER 6

1. George Eliot, *Middlemarch*, ed. Rosemary Ashton (1871–1872; repr. New York: Penguin, 1994), 43. All future references will be to this edition and will be noted parenthetically in the text.
2. Ruth Perry, *Novel Relations: The Transformation of Kinship in English Literature and Culture, 1748–1818* (Cambridge: Cambridge University Press, 2004), 197.
3. Cited in Ellen Jordan, *The Women's Movement and Women's Employment in Nineteenth Century Britain* (London and New York: Routledge, 1999), 26.
4. Amanda Vickery, "Golden Age to Separate Spheres? A Review of the Categories and Chronology of English Women's History," *The Historical Journal* 36, no. 2 (June 1993): 402–407.
5. M. Jeanne Peterson, *Family, Love, and Work in the Lives of Victorian Gentlewomen* (Bloomington: Indiana University Press, 1989), 165–166.
6. Lana Dalley and Jill Rappaport's collection, *Economic Women*, traces some of the many ways women participated in productive labor in the Victorian period, including colonial medical care, stock-market trading, novel-writing, and budgeting household allocations.
7. On philanthropic marriage plots, see Dorice Williams Elliott, *The Angel out of the House: Philanthropy and Gender in Nineteenth-Century England* (Charlottesville: University Press of Virginia, 2002), 165. For female artists in fiction, see Antonia Losano, *The Woman Painter in Victorian Literature* (Columbus: Ohio State Press, 2008). On political marriages, see Barbara Leah Harman, *The Feminine Political Novel in Victorian England* (Charlottesville: University Press of Virginia, 1998).
8. Jordan, 61–63.
9. Alan Mintz, *George Eliot and the Novel of Vocation* (Cambridge, MA: Harvard University Press, 1978), 63.
10. Lenore Davidoff and Catherine Hall, " 'The Hidden Investment': Women and the Enterprise," in *Women's Work: The English Experience 1650–1914*, ed. Pamela Sharpe (London: Arnold, 1998), 286.

11. Edward Copeland points out that genteel heroines in Regency-era fiction never even consider work: *Women Writing About Money: Women's Fiction in England, 1790–1820* (Ithaca, NY: Cornell University Press, 1995), 161.
12. In *The Vulgar Question of Money: Heiresses, Materialism, and the Novel of Manners from Jane Austen to Henry James* (Baltimore: Johns Hopkins University Press, 2011), Elsie Michie charts a similar dynamic: a vulgar rich woman functions to make her poorer rival seem soulfully pure.
13. In *Can You Forgive Her?*, the lower-class Mrs. Greenow is the only woman of the three female marriage plots who is allowed to enjoy her romantic suitor; in *The Way We Live Now*, poor Ruby Ruggles is forced to give up her romantic lover to marry her familiar swain John Crumb.
14. Trollope fears that if women are allowed to work they might not choose to marry. "That women should have their rights no man will deny. To my thinking, neither increase of work nor increase of political influence are among them. The best right a woman has is the right to a husband, and that is the right to which I would recommend every young woman here and in the States to turn her best attention." Anthony Trollope, "The Rights of Women," *North America*, vol. 1 (Philadelphia: J. B. Lippincott, 1863), 293.
15. In *The Vulgar Question of Money*, Elsie Michie discusses the bad associations accruing to female characters who sought money.
16. Copeland, 166–167.
17. Cohen, 138.
18. Sarah Stickney Ellis, *Women of England, Their Social Duties and Domestic Habits* (New York: D. Appleton, 1843), 18.
19. Elizabeth Langland, *Nobody's Angels: Middle-Class Women and Domestic Ideology in Victorian Culture* (Ithaca, NY: Cornell University Press, 1995).
20. According to Janet Todd, such emphasis on managerial talent appears in eighteenth-century conduct manuals: "The Professional Wife in Jane Austen," in *Repossessing the Romantic Past*, ed. Heather Glen, Paul Hamilton (Cambridge: Cambridge University Press, 2006), 203–225.
21. Harriet Taylor, "The Enfranchisement of Women" (London: Trübner, 1868), reprint from *The Westminster Review*, July 1851, 295–296.
22. Contributors to Josephine Butler's essay collection suggest that women ought to enter education and medicine, while Dinah Mulock Craik endorses art, literature, acting, singing, and teaching. Bodichon's specific recommendations included nursing, watch-making, accounting, teaching, lecturing, running asylums, overseeing army commissariat, organizing emigration, working for the press, doing art manufactures, and making ornaments. Barbara Leigh Smith Bodichon, *Women and Work* (New York: C. S. Francis, 1859), 17, 22–25.
23. Burton Bledstein, cited in Monica Cohen, *Professional Domesticity in the Victorian Novel: Women, Work, and Home* (Cambridge: Cambridge University

Press, 1998), 135. Also N. N. Feltes, *Modes of Production of Victorian Novels* (Chicago: University of Chicago Press, 1986), 42–43.

24. Susan E. Colón, *The Professional Ideal in the Victorian Novel: The Works of Disraeli, Trollope, Gaskell, and Eliot* (New York: Palgrave Macmillan, 2007), 14.
25. Elliott, 204.
26. Harold Perkin, *The Rise of Professional Society: England since 1880* (London: Routledge, 1989).
27. Anthony Trollope, *The Duke's Children*, ed. Hermione Lee (1880; repr. New York: Oxford University Press, 1983), 196.
28. Bronwyn Rivers, *Women at Work in the Victorian Novel: The Question of Middle-Class Women's Employment 1840–1870* (Lewiston, NY: Edwin Mellen, 2006), 3.
29. Thomas Carlyle, *Past and Present* (London: Chapman and Hall, 1845), 264.
30. Cited in Christine Alexander, "Preface," Rivers, xiii.
31. Mrs. Jellyby is the most famous antivocational figure of the period, yet, oddly, Dickens based her on Caroline Chisholm, whose work encouraging female emigration Dickens actually admired. See Clare Midgeley, *Feminism and Empire: Women Activists in Imperial Britain, 1790–1865* (New York: Routledge, 2007), 132.
32. In this respect they resemble Ellen Woods's later figure, Cornelia Carlyle, in *East Lynne* (1861).
33. See Susan Brown, "The Victorian Poetess," *The Cambridge Companion to Victorian Poetry*, ed. Joseph Bristow (Cambridge: Cambridge University Press, 200), 195; Lana Dalley, "The Least 'Angelical' Poem in the Language: Political Economy, Gender, and the Heritage of *Aurora Leigh*," *Victorian Poetry* 44, no. 4 (Winter 2006): 525–542; Marjorie Stone, "Criticism on *Aurora Leigh:* An Overview," 7–9, 13, http://ebbarchive.org/criticism/Aurora_Leigh_Criticism_Overview.pdf.
34. Jordan, *Women's Movement*, 156.
35. By advocating a "communion of labour," Jameson meant that she wanted women's work to combine with men's. She believed that men and women should continue to occupy separate spheres rather than each of them pursuing equal opportunities in shared fields.
36. Rosemary Feurer, "The Meaning of 'Sisterhood': The British Women's Movement and Protective Labor Legislation, 1870–1900," *Victorian Studies* 31, no. 2 (Winter 1988): 234.
37. Ellen Jordan, " 'Women's Work in the World': The Birth of a Discourse, London, 1857," *Nineteenth-Century Feminisms* 1 (1999): 14.
38. Jordan, " 'Women's Work," 24.
39. Elizabeth K. Helsinger, Robin Lauterbach Sheets, William Veeder, eds., *The Woman Question: Social Issues, 1837–1883, vol. 11 of The Woman Question: Society and Literature in Britain and America, 1837–1883* (New York: Garland Publishing, Inc., 1983), 111.
40. Jordan, *Women's Movement*, 163.

41. John Stuart Mill, "The Subjection of Women," *On Liberty and The Subjection of Women*, ed. Alan Ryan (1869; repr. New York: Penguin, 2006), 184–185.
42. Julia Wedgwood, "Female Suffrage, Considered Chiefly With Regard to its Indirect Results," In *Woman's Work and Woman's Culture*, ed. Josephine E. Butler (London: Macmillan, 1869), 262–263.
43. Helsinger, Sheets, and Veeder, 135.
44. Anna Jameson, *The Communion of Labour: A Second Lecture on the Social Employments of Women* (London: Longman, Brown, Green, Longmans, and Roberts, 1856), 15.
45. Jameson, 17–18.
46. Dinah Mulock Craik, *A Woman's Thoughts about Women* (New York: Rudd and Carleton, 1858), 14.
47. From "The Disputed Question," *English Woman's Journal* 1 (1858): 361–367 (quoted in Rivers, 364).
48. John Duguid Milne, *Industrial Employment of Women in the Middle and Lower Ranks*, 2nd ed. (London: Longman, Green, 1870), 27.
49. J. W. Kaye, "The Non-Existence of Women," *North British Review* 23 (1855): 536–562.
50. Kaye, 558.
51. Leigh Smith did argue that women should continue their professions after marriage, but she was in the minority. See *Women and Work*, 11.
52. Although the emphasis on rights was a new kind of rhetoric for Victorian advocacy at mid-century, this tension dates back to Mary Wollstonecraft's *Vindication of the Rights of Women*, where Wollstonecraft's insistence that women's souls and capacity for reason are equivalent to men's, coexists uneasily with her Rousseauian vision of the happy wife in the cottage, breastfeeding her children and greeting her husband at the end of a long day. Wollstonecraft simultaneously argues for women's egalitarian capacities and for her special mission.
53. Frances Power Cobbe, "The Final Cause of Woman," in Butler, *Woman's Work*, 13–14; Julia Wedgwood, "Female Suffrage, Considered Chiefly With Regard to its Indirect Results" in Butler, *Woman's Work*, 262–263, 270.
54. Bodichon, 29.
55. In an article in 1859, Parkes warned that if women have "a consciousness of aspiration for which no available medium of realisation appears" they will experience "deterioration" of the "moral force of character." Cited in Elliott, 159–160. Similarly, in *Cassandra*, Florence Nightingale wrote that women "become incapable of consecutive or strenuous work" after a lifetime of dilettantism: *Florence Nightingale's Cassandra* (1860; repr. New York: Feminist Press, 1979), 43.
56. Milne, 107. Also see Mary Taylor complaining about the "mental distress and bodily illness" of unemployed women: *The First Duty of Women: A Series of Articles Reprinted From the Victoria Magazine, 1865–1870* (London: Emily Faithfull, Victoria Press, 1870), 97. Similarly, in *Victoria Magazine* in 1877, Frances Power

Cobbe warned that "there are hundreds whose health is deteriorated by want of wholesome mental exercise. Sometimes the vacuity in the brains of girls simply leaves them dull and spiritless." "The Little Health of Ladies," *Victoria Magazine* 30 (March 1878): 414.

57. Virginia Woolf, *A Room of One's Own* (New York: Harvest Books, 1989), 70; Vickery, 384.
58. Ann Wierda Rowland, "Sentimental Fiction," *The Cambridge Companion to Fiction in the Romantic Period* (Cambridge: Cambridge University Press, 2008), 199–200; Lynn Festa, *Sentimental Figures of Empire in Eighteenth-Century Britain and France* (Baltimore: Johns Hopkins University Press, 2006), 17.
59. On sentimental fiction, see Rachel Ablow, "Victorian Feelings," *Cambridge Companion to the Victorian Novel*, ed. Deidre David (Cambridge: Cambridge University Press, 2012), 193–194. On melodrama, see Juliet John, *Dickens's Villains: Melodrama, Character, Popular Culture* (New York: Oxford University Press, 2003).
60. Ann Cvetkovich, *Mixed Feelings: Feminism, Mass Culture, and Victorian Sensationalism* (New Brunswick, NJ: Rutgers University Press, 1992). Pamela Gilbert offers a useful summary of Tompkins and other critics while contemplating sentimental fiction's applicability to Victorian fiction in "Ouida and the Canon," in *Ouida and Victorian Popular Fiction*, ed. Jane Jordan and Andrew King (Burlington, VT: Ashgate, 2013), 37–51.
61. Sarah Stickney Ellis, *The Daughters of England: Their Position in Society, Character, and Responsibilities* (London: Fisher, Son, 1842), 133.
62. Michel Foucault, *The History of Sexuality*, vol. 1, trans. Robert Hurley (New York: Vintage 1990), 32.
63. Foucault, 43.
64. In one case study of "M," Bodichon explained, a lady who spent her life doing nothing, "she became nervous, hysterically ill, and at last died of consumption" (13). Jessie Boucherett agreed that women's feeble health and nervous complaints were caused by prudishness—but not sexual prudishness, vocational prudishness, a social voice that prohibited women from exercise and work. Jessie Boucherett, *The Englishwoman's Review of Social and Industrial Questions* (London: Trübner, 1882), 7–8.
65. Bodichon, 26.
66. Bodichon, 27.
67. William A. Cohen, *Sex Scandal: The Private Parts of Victorian Fiction* (Durham, NC: Duke University Press, 1996), 3.
68. Elliott, 161.
69. Foucault, 8–9.
70. For instance, anthropologist Sir Henry Maine regarded coverture as a vestige of a barbaric earlier regime, bound to vanish as British civilization achieved fully egalitarian contract law.

71. Copeland, 161–162.
72. This dynamic of losing work begins even before the novel commences, when Mr. Weston has given up trade in order to buy an estate and marry, and the Coles have stopped their business in order to settle down and socialize with their class superiors.
73. "Jane Austen," in *St. Paul's* March 1870, 631–643. Reprinted in B. C. Southam, *Jane Austen: The Critical Heritage*, vol. 1, 1811–1870 (London: Routledge, 1979), 237.
74. "Jane Austen," 237.
75. Margaret Oliphant, "Miss Austen and Miss Mitford," *Blackwood's Edinburgh Magazine* 107 (March 1870): 294–305, reprinted in Southam, 221–229.
76. Jane Austen, *Emma*, ed. James Kinsley (1815; repr. New York: Oxford University Press, 1995), 32, 38–39. Further references will be to this edition and will be noted parenthetically within the text.
77. Claudia Johnson, *Equivocal Beings: Politics, Gender, and Sentimentality in the 1790s: Wollstonecraft, Radcliffe, Burney, Austen* (Chicago: University of Chicago Press, 1995), 192.
78. Johnson, 193.
79. Most famously, Eve Kosofsky Sedgwick, "Jane Austen and the Masturbating Girl," *Critical Inquiry* 17, no 4 (Summer 1991): 818–837. Jill Heydt-Stevenson reads Austen's humor as bawdy and body-based in *Austen's Unbecoming Conjunctions: Subversive Laughter, Embodied History* (New York: Palgrave Macmillan, 2008). Maureen M. Martin argues that Emma has to talk herself into feeling desire for Mr. Knightley in order to justify a marriage that actually appeals on political grounds: "What Does Emma Want? Sovereignty and Sexuality in Austen's *Emma*," *Nineteenth-Century Feminisms* 3 (Fall/Winter 2000): 10–24. Nicholas Preus's is perhaps the most determined attempt to sexualize Austen: He argues that sex is, in fact, " 'the secret,' or 'the enigma,' the 'mystery,' the hidden value in the novel": "Sexuality in *Emma:* A Case History," *Studies in the Novel* 23, no. 2 (1991): 199.
80. Preus, 205.
81. Sedgwick, 834.
82. D. A. Miller, *Jane Austen, or, the Secret of Style* (Princeton, NJ: Princeton University Press, 2005).
83. See June Sturrock, "*Emma* in the 1860s: Austen, Yonge, Oliphant, Eliot," *Charlotte Yonge: Rereading Domestic Religious Fiction*, ed. by Tamara S. Wagner; (London and New York: Routledge, 2012). Also Amy J. Robinson, "Margaret Oliphant's *Miss Marjoribanks*: A Victorian *Emma*," *Persuasions* 30 (2008): 67–75.
84. Oliphant's closest friend (they signed letters to each other "sister") was Geddie Macpherson, the niece, adopted daughter, and biographer of Anna Jameson. Oliphant had certainly read this biography, since she reviewed it in 1879. Elisabeth Jay, *Mrs. Oliphant: "A Fiction to Herself": A Literary Life* (Oxford: Clarendon, 1995), 18, 41. Also see Linda Peterson, *Traditions of Victorian Women's Autobiography: The Poetics and Politics of Life Writing* (Charlottesville: University of Virginia Press, 1999), 151.

85. Margaret Oliphant, "The Condition of Women," 209–230, repr. from *Blackwood's Edinburgh Magazine,* February 1858, in *Criminals, Idiots, Women, and Minors*, ed. Susan Hamilton (Peterborough, ON: Broadview, 1995), 220.
86. Margaret Oliphant, *Phoebe Junior*, ed. Elizabeth Langland (1867; repr. Peterborough, ON: Broadview, 2002), 417. Future references will be to this edition and will be noted parenthetically in the text.
87. Margaret Oliphant, *Miss Marjoribanks*, ed. Elisabeth Jay (1865; repr. New York: Penguin, 1998), 482. Future references will be to this edition and will be noted parenthetically in the text.
88. Gillian Beer, *George Eliot* (Bloomington: Indiana University Press, 1986), 156.
89. Jennifer Phegley, *Educating the Proper Woman Reader: Victorian Family Literary Magazines and the Cultural Health of the Nation* (Columbus: Ohio State Press, 2004), 153–159.
90. Beer, 165.
91. Dorothea Barrett, *Vocation and Desire; George Eliot's Heroines* (New York: Routledge, 1989), 18.
92. Barrett, 42.
93. George Eliot, "The History of *Adam Bede*," in *Adam Bede*, ed. Carol A. Martin (New York: Oxford University Press, 2008), 483–486.
94. Jennifer Stolpa, "Dinah and the Debate Over Vocation in Adam Bede," *George Eliot-George Henry Lewes Studies* 42–43 (2002): 35.
95. "Domestic life, the acknowledged foundation of all social life, has settled by a natural law the work of the man and the work of the woman. The man governs, sustains, and defends the family; the woman cherishes, regulates, and purifies it; but though distinct, the relative work is inseparable,—sometimes exchanged, sometimes shared; so that from the beginning, we have, even in the primitive household, not the *division,* but the *communion* of labour." Jameson, 4–5.
96. Stolpa, 31.
97. Eliot, "The History of *Adam Bede*," 483–486.
98. Elaine J. Lawless, "The Silencing of the Preacher Woman: The Muted Message of George Eliot's *Adam Bede*," *Women's Studies* 18, nos. 2–3 (1990): 252.
99. Eliot, *Adam Bede*, 539.
100. Eliot, *Adam Bede*, 539.
101. Barrett, 43.
102. Lawless, 264–265.
103. Beer, 161–162.
104. However, N. N. Feltes has noted that Lydgate's medical work is treated as an internal drive rather than a set of external affiliations with colleges and societies and the College of Physicians, so that vocation can be a shared drive for male and female characters in the novel. *Modes of Production of Victorian Novels* (Chicago: University of Chicago Press, 1986), 52–56.
105. Mintz, 60.

106. The dual perspective even shapes Dorothea's character in minor ways. Kent Puckett has pointed out that Dorothea's plain hairdo, odd in the context of the novel's setting in 1829, is the height of fashion for the late 1860s, when the novel was read. Dorothea therefore looks fashion-forward, not out of fashion. Kent Puckett, *Bad Form: Social Mistakes and the Nineteenth-Century Novel* (New York: Oxford University Press, 2008), 86–87.
107. Barbara Hardy, *George Eliot: A Critic's Biography* (London: Bloomsbury, 2006), 128.
108. Elliott 191, citing Thomson's *Victorian Heroines*.
109. Elliott 190, 193.
110. Karen Bloom Gevirtz, *Life after Death: Widows and the English Novel, Defoe to Austen* (Newark: University of Delaware Press, 2005), 15.
111. In *The Vulgar Question of Money*, Elsie Michie has charted the special financial and sexual power accorded the widow.
112. On Jane Senior, see Barbara Hardy, 119–128; on Barbara Bodichon see Beer, 165.
113. Barbara Hardy, 119–128.
114. *Miss Marjoribanks* was published in *Blackwood's Edinburgh Magazine* (which Eliot was reading) in 1866, and Eliot began working up her notes for *Middlemarch* in 1868. Leavis notes that Eliot's publisher, Blackwood, was enthusiastic about the new novel. The novels share many similar characters and scenes, but Leavis especially stresses the possibility that Eliot may have developed the aloof, ironic tone of Middlemarch's narration by emulating Oliphant. *Collected Essays: Vol 3, The Novel of Religious Controversy*, ed. G. Singh (Cambridge: Cambridge University Press, 1989), 145–154.
115. Catherine Judd, *Bedside Seductions: Nursing and the Victorian Imagination, 1830–1880* (New York: St. Martin's Press, 1998), 125.
116. Elliott, 211.
117. Catherine Gallagher, "Immanent Victorian," *Representations* 90, no. 1 (Spring 2005): 61–74.
118. This is a pattern throughout Eliot's fiction. In *Adam Bede*, it is the odd, dreamy, ineffective younger brother Seth who can articulate Dinah's baffled vocational wishes. In *The Mill on the Floss*, it is disabled Philip who can speak powerfully for Maggie's need for meaningful work. In *Daniel Deronda*, minor character Catherine Arrowpoint achieves a vocational marriage. It is the minor characters who can uphold and achieve work, where the heroines remain silent or martyred.
119. On Nightingale, see Elliott, 189–190; on Bodichon, see Hughes, 300.
120. Beer, 148.
121. Margaret F. King, "'Certain Learned Ladies': Trollope's *Can You Forgive Her?* and the Langham Place Circle," *VLC* 21 (1993): 307–326.
122. See Trollope, "The Rights of Women," in *North America* (1863), published fourteen months before he would begin *Can You Forgive Her?*, and "Four Lectures," delivered in 1868 and published three years after the novel. Not surprisingly, the

English Woman's Journal gave *North America* a negative review. See King, 311; Anthony Trollope, "The Rights of Women," *North America*, vol. 1 (Philadelphia: J. B. Lippincott, 1863), 283–293; Anthony Trollope, "On the Higher Education of Women," *Four Lectures*, ed. Morris L. Parrish (London: Constable, 1938); Anthony Trollope, "Notices of Books," *English Woman's Journal* 10 (September 1862–February 1863): 61–66. On his friendship with Kate Field see Jane Nardin, *He Knew She Was Right: The Independent Woman in the Novels of Anthony Trollope* (Southern Illinois University, 1989), 13–14.

123. Anthony Trollope, *Can You Forgive Her?* (1865; repr. New York: Oxford University Press, 2012), 92. Future references will be to this edition and will be noted parenthetically in the text.
124. King, 308.
125. King, 308.
126. Sharon Marcus, *Between Women: Friendship, Desire, and Marriage in Victorian England* (Princeton, NJ: Princeton University Press, 2007), 233.
127. Marcus, 234.
128. Kate Flint, introduction to *Can You Forgive Her?* (Oxford: Oxford University Press, 2012), xvi.
129. See Kathy A. Psomiades, "*He Knew He Was Right*: The Sensational Tyranny of the Sexual Contract and the Problem of Liberal Progress," *The Politics of Gender in Anthony Trollope's Novels*, ed. Margaret Markwick, Deborah Debenholme Morse, and Regenia Gagnier (Surrey: Ashgate, 2009), 31–44.
130. Christopher Herbert and Kathy Psomiades have argued that Trollope's marriage plots end with the woman's willing subservience to the man's patriarchal authority—a way of keeping traditional male rule but masking it as a voluntary, enjoyable relation, instead of tyranny. As Psomiades dryly remarks, "now the woman gets to choose who carries her off" (44). While both use *He Knew He Was Right* as their main example, it could just as easily be argued that the outrageousness of George Vavasor functions to make John Grey's despotism relatively palatable, so that Alice can "choose" him. See Psomiades and Christopher Herbert, "He Knew He Was Right, Mrs. Lynn Linton, and the Duplicities of Victorian Marriage," *Texas Studies in Language and Literature* 25, no. 3 (Fall 1983): 448–469.
131. King, 312.
132. June Sturrock, "Something to Do: Charlotte Yonge, Tractarianism and the Question of Women's Work," *Victorian Review* 18, no. 2 (Winter 1992): 40.
133. Phegley, 182.
134. Charlotte Yonge, *The Clever Woman of the Family*, ed. Clare A. Simmons (1865; repr. Peterborough, ON: Broadview, 2001), 37.
135. Sturrock, "Something," 39.
136. Sturrock, "Something," 39.
137. It is perhaps worth noting that when the New Women set out to fix the "marriage problem," they assumed that marriage inherently interfered with "a woman's

self-development" (to use the phrase Mona Caird made famous). They advocated for alternatives to marriage—free unions, divorce, single women—instead of trying to redefine marriage as a state that had historically and ideologically been perfectly compatible with women's work. 1890s activism, then, solidified and perpetuated the opposition between work and marriage initiated in the 1860s.

Bibliography

Ablow, Rachel. *The Marriage of Minds: Reading Sympathy in the Victorian Marriage Plot*. Stanford: Stanford University Press, 2010.

———. "Victorian Feelings." *Cambridge Companion to the Victorian Novel*. Edited by Deidre David, 193–210. Cambridge: Cambridge University Press, 2012.

Alexander, Christine. Preface to *Women at Work in the Victorian Novel: The Question of Middle-Class Women's Employment 1840–1870*, by Bronwyn Rivers, xiii–xv. Lewiston, NY: Edwin Mellen, 2006.

Althens, Margaret Magdalen Jasper. *The Christian Character Exemplified from the Papers of Mrs. Frederick Charles A—s, of Goodman's Fields*. Hartford, CT: Lincoln and Gleason, 1804.

Anderson, Benedict. *Imagined Communities*. Revised edition. New York: Verso, 2006.

Anderson, Nancy Fix. "Cousin Marriage in Victorian England." *Journal of Family History* 11, no. 3 (1986): 285–301.

Armstrong, Nancy. *Desire and Domestic Fiction: A Political History of the Novel*. New York: Oxford University Press, 1987.

Arthur, T. S. *Advice to Young Ladies on Their Duties and Conduct in Life*. London: J. S. Hodson, 1855.

Austen, Jane. *Emma*. Edited by James Kinsley. New York: Oxford University Press, 1995. First published 1815.

———. *Jane Austen's Letters*. Edited by R. W. Chapman. 2nd ed. London: Oxford University Press, 1952.

———. *Mansfield Park*. New York: Oxford University Press, 2008. First published 1814.

———. *Northanger Abbey, Lady Susan, The Watsons, and Sanditon*. Edited by James Kinsley. New York: Oxford University Press, 2003. First published 1818.

———. *Persuasion*. Edited by Gillian Beer. New York: Penguin, 1998. First published 1818.

———. *Pride and Prejudice*. Edited by Fiona Stafford. New York: Oxford University Press, 2004. First published 1813.

———. *Sense and Sensibility*. Edited by Ros Ballaster. New York: Penguin Books 1995. First published 1811.

Bakhtin, Mikhail. "Forms of Time and of the Chronotope in the Novel." In *Narrative Dynamics: Essays on Time, Plot, Closure, and Frames*. Edited by Brian Richardson, 15–24. Columbus: Ohio State Press, 2002.

Bailey, Joanne. "Favored or Oppressed? Married Women, Property, and 'Coverture' in England, 1660–1800." *Continuity and Change* 17, no. 3 (2002): 351–372.

Bailin, Miriam. *The Sickroom in Victorian Fiction: The Art of Being Ill*. Cambridge: Cambridge University Press, 1994.

Ballaster, Ros. *Seductive Forms: Women's Amatory Fiction from 1684 to 1740*. Oxford: Clarendon, 1992.

Bannet, Eve Tavor. *The Domestic Revolution: Enlightenment Feminisms and the Novel*. Baltimore: Johns Hopkins University Press, 2000.

Barrett Browning, Elizabeth. *Aurora Leigh*. With an introduction by Gardner B. Taplin. Chicago: Academy Chicago Publishers, 1979. First published 1856.

Barrett, Dorothea. *Vocation and Desire; George Eliot's Heroines*. New York: Routledge, 1989.

Battiscombe, Georgina. *Charlotte Mary Yonge: The Story of an Uneventful Life*. London: Constable, 1943.

Beer, Gillian. *Darwin's Plots: Evolutionary Narrative in Darwin, George Eliot, and Nineteenth-Century Fiction*. 3rd ed. Cambridge: Cambridge University Press, 2009.

———. *George Eliot*. Bloomington: Indiana University Press, 1986.

———. Introduction to *Persuasion*, by Jane Austen, xi–xxxiii. New York: Penguin Books, 1998.

Beeton, Isabella. *Mrs. Beeton's Book of Household Management*. Edited by Nicola Humble. New York: Oxford World's Classics, 2008. First published 1861.

Behlmer, George K. *Friends of the Family: The English Home and Its Guardians, 1850–1940*. Stanford, CA: Stanford University Press, 1998.

Benhabib, Seyla. *Situating the Self: Gender, Community and Postmodernism in Contemporary Ethics*. New York: Routledge, 1992.

Berman, Carolyn Vellenga. *Creole Crossings: Domestic Fiction and the Reform of Colonial Slavery*. Ithaca, NY: Cornell University Press, 2006.

Berry, Helen, and Elizabeth Foyster. *The Family in Early Modern England*. Cambridge: Cambridge University Press, 2007.

Bersani, Leo. *A Future for Astanyax: Character and Desire in Literature*. Boston: Little, Brown, 1969.

Best, Stephen, and Sharon Marcus. "Surface Reading: An Introduction." *Representations* 108, no. 1 (2009): 1–21.

Binhammer, Katherine. *The Seduction Narrative in Britain, 1747–1800*. Cambridge: Cambridge University Press, 2009.

Blewett, David. "Changing Attitudes Toward Marriage in the Time of Defoe: The Case of Moll Flanders." *Huntingdon Library Quarterly* 44, no. 2 (Spring 1981): 77–88.

Bloch, R. Howard. *Medieval Misogyny and the Invention of Western Romantic Love*. Chicago: University of Chicago Press, 1992.

Bodenheimer, Rosemarie. *The Real Life of Mary Ann Evans: George Eliot, Her Letters and Fiction*. Ithaca, NY: Cornell University Press, 1994.

Bodichon, Barbara Leigh Smith. *Women and Work*. New York: C. S. Francis, 1859. First published 1857.

Bolt, David. "The Blindman in the Classic: Feminisms, Ocularcentrism, and *Jane Eyre*." In *The Madwoman and the Blindman: Jane Eyre, Discourse, Disability*. Edited by David Bolt, Julia Miele Rodas, and Elizabeth J. Donaldson, 32–50. Columbus: Ohio State Press, 2012.

Boone, Joseph A., and Deborah Epstein Nord. "Brother and Sister: The Seductions of Siblinghood in Dickens, Eliot, and Brontë." *Western Humanities Review* 46, no. 2 (Summer 1992): 164–188.

Boone, Joseph Allen. *Tradition Counter Tradition: Love and the Form of Fiction*. Chicago: University of Chicago Press, 1987.

Boris, Eileen, and Jennifer Klein, "Home-Care Workers Aren't Just 'Companions.'" *New York Times*, July 2, 2012, A15.

Boucherett, Jessie. *The Englishwoman's Review of Social and Industrial Questions*. London: Trübner, 1882.

———. *The Measure of Manliness: Disability and Masculinity in the Mid-Victorian Novel* (Ann Arbor: University of Michigan Press, 2015).

Bourrier, Karen. "Orthopedic Disability and the Nineteenth-Century Novel." *Nineteenth-Century Contexts* 36, no. 1 (February 2014): 1–17.

Bradbrook, Frank W. *Jane Austen and Her Predecessors*. Cambridge: Cambridge University Press, 1966.

Bradley, Ian. *The Call to Seriousness: The Evangelical Impact on the Victorians*. New York: Macmillan, 1976.

Brontë, Charlotte. *Jane Eyre*. Edited by Q. D. Leavis. London: Penguin, 1966. First published 1847.

Brontë, Emily. *Wuthering Heights*. New York: Penguin, 1995. First published 1847.

Broughton, Rhoda. *Cometh Up as a Flower*. Edited by Pamela Gilbert. Peterborough: Broadview, 2010. First published 1867.

Brown, Callum. "The Salvation Economy." In *The Death of Christian Britain: Understanding Secularisation 1800–2000*. New York: Routledge, 2001.

Brown, Julia Prewitt. *Jane Austen's Novels: Social Change and Literary Form*. Cambridge, MA: Harvard University Press, 1979.

Brown, R. Philip. *Authentic Individualism: A Guide for Reclaiming the Best of America's Heritage*. Lanham, MD: University Press of America, 1996.

Brown, Susan. "The Victorian Poetess." In *The Cambridge Companion to Victorian Poetry*. Edited by Joseph Bristow, 180–202. Cambridge: Cambridge University Press, 2000.

Brownstein, Rachel. *Why Jane Austen?* New York: Columbia University Press, 2011.

Brunton, Mary. *Self-Control.* New York: Pandora, 1986.

Budge, Gavin. *Charlotte M. Yonge: Religion, Feminism, and Realism in the Victorian Novel.* Bern: Peter Lang, 2007.

Bueler, Lois E. *The Tested Woman Plot: Women's Choices, Men's Judgments, and the Shaping of Stories.* Columbus: Ohio State Press, 2001.

Bump, Jerome. "The Family Dynamics of the Reception of Art." *Style* 31, no. 2 (Summer 1997): 106–128.

Burckhardt, Jacob. *The Civilization of the Renaissance in Italy.* Trans. S.G.C. Middlemore. New York: Macmillan, 1904, first ed .1860, first English trans. 1878.

Burger, Glenn. *Conduct Becoming: Good Wives and Husbands in the Later Middle Ages.* Unpublished manuscript.

Butler, Josephine E., ed. *Woman's Work and Woman's Culture.* London: Macmillan, 1869.

Butler, Marilyn. *Jane Austen and the War of Ideas.* Oxford: Clarendon, 1975.

Caine, Barbara. *Victorian Feminists.* NewYork: Oxford University Press, 1992.

Caird, Mona. "Does Marriage Hinder a Woman's Self-Development?" In *A New Woman Reader: Fiction, Articles, and Drama of the 1890s.* Edited by Carolyn Christensen Nelson, 199–201. Peterborough: Broadview, 2000. First published in *The Lady's Realm* 5 (March 1899): 581–83.

Callaghan, Dympna. "The Ideology of Romantic Love: The Case of Romeo and Juliet." In *The Weyward Sisters: Shakespeare and Feminist*, 59–101. New York: Wi ley-Blackwell, 1994.

———. *Romeo and Juliet: Texts and Contexts.* New York: Bedford/St. Martin's, 2003.

Carlyle, Thomas. *Past and Present.* London: Chapman and Hall, 1845.

Carroll, David, ed. *George Eliot: The Critical Heritage.* London: Routledge and Kegan Paul, 1971.

Chen, Mia. "And There Was No Helping It: Disability and Social Reproduction in Charlotte Yonge's *The Daisy Chain.*" *Nineteenth-Century Gender Studies* 4, no. 2 (Summer 2008). http://www.ncgsjournal.com/issue42/chen.htm.

Clayton, Jay. "Narrative and Theories of Desire." *Critical Inquiry* 16 (Autumn 1989): 33–53.

Cleere, Eileen. *Avuncularism: Capitalism, Patriarchy, and Nineteenth-Century English Culture.* Stanford, CA: Stanford University Press, 2004.

Clery, E. J. "Gender." In *The Cambridge Companion to Jane Austen.* Edited by Edward Copeland and Juliet McMaster, 159–175. 2nd ed. Cambridge: Cambridge University Press, 2011.

Cobbe, Frances Power. "The Final Cause of Woman." *Woman's Work and Woman's Culture.* Edited by Josephine E. Butler, 1–26. London: Macmillan, 1869.

———. "The Little Health of Ladies." *Victoria Magazine* 30 (March 1878): 409–420.

———. "Wife-Torture in England." Reprinted in *Criminals, Idiots, Women, and Minors.* Edited by Susan Hamilton. Peterborough, ON: Broadview, 2004.

Coelho de Souza, Marcela. "The Future of the Structural Theory of Kinship." In *The Cambridge Companion to Lévi-Strauss*. Edited by Boris Wiseman, 80–99. Cambridge: Cambridge University Press, 2009.

Cohen, Monica. *Professional Domesticity in the Victorian Novel: Women, Work, and Home.* Cambridge: Cambridge University Press, 1998.

Cohen, William A. *Sex Scandal: The Private Parts of Victorian Fiction.* Durham, NC: Duke University Press, 1996.

Colella, Silvana. "Gifts and Interests: *John Halifax, Gentleman* and the Purity of Business." *Victorian Literature and Culture* 35, no. 2 (2007): 397–415.

Colón, Susan E. *The Professional Ideal in the Victorian Novel: The Works of Disraeli, Trollope, Gaskell, and Eliot.* New York: Palgrave Macmillan, 2007.

Coontz, Stephanie. *Marriage, A History: How Love Conquered Marriage.* New York: Penguin, 2006.

Copeland, Edward. *Women Writing about Money: Women's Fiction in England, 1790–1820.* Ithaca, NY: Cornell University Press, 1995.

Corbett, Mary Jean. *Family Likeness: Sex, Marriage, and Incest from Jane Austen to Virginia Woolf.* Ithaca, NY: Cornell University Press, 2008.

Craik, Dinah Mulock. *John Halifax, Gentleman.* Edited by Lynn M. Alexander. Peterborough, ON: Broadview, 2005. First published 1856.

———. *A Woman's Thoughts about Women.* New York: Rudd and Carleton, 1858.

Craton, Lillian. *The Victorian Freak Show: The Significance of Disability and Physical Differences in 19th Century Fiction.* Amherst, NY: Cambria, 2009.

Cvetkovich, Ann. *Mixed Feelings: Feminism, Mass Culture, and Victorian Sensationalism.* New Brunswick: Rutgers University Press, 1992.

Cyr, Marc. "Bad Morality, Truth, and Mrs. Smith in Persuasion." *The Eighteenth-Century Novel* 4 (2004): 193–216.

Dabhoiwala, Faramerz. *The Origins of Sex: A History of the First Sexual Revolution.* New York: Oxford University Press, 2012.

Dalley, Lana. "The Least 'Angelical' Poem in the Language: Political Economy, Gender, and the Heritage of *Aurora Leigh.*" *Victorian Poetry* 44, no. 4 (Winter 2006): 525–542.

Danahay, Martin. *Gender at Work in Victorian Culture: Literature, Art, and Masculinity.* Burlington, VT: Ashgate, 2005.

Davidoff, Leonore, and Catherine Hall. " 'The Hidden Investment': Women and the Enterprise." In *Women's Work: The English Experience 1650–1914.* Edited by Pamela Sharpe, 239–293. London: Arnold, 1998. Reprinted from Leonore Davidoff and Catherine Hall, *Family Fortunes: Men and Women of the English Middle Class 1780–1950.* 2nd ed. New York: Routledge, 2003.

Davidoff, Leonore. "Kinship as a Categorical Concept: A Case Study of Nineteenth-Century English Siblings." *Journal of Social History* 39, no. 2 (Winter 2005): 411–428.

———. *Thicker Than Water: Siblings and Their Relations 1780–1920*. New York: Oxford University Press, 2012.

Davis, Natalie Zemon. "Boundaries and the Sense of Self in Sixteenth-Century France." *Reconstructing Individualism: Autonomy, Individuality, and the Self in Western Thought*. Edited by Thomas C. Heller, Morton Sosna, and David E. Wellbery, 53–63. Stanford, CA: Stanford University Press, 1986.

Debaene, Vincent. "'Like Alice through the Looking-Glass': Claude Lévi-Strauss in New York." *French Politics, Culture, and Society* 28, no. 1 (Spring 2010): 46–57.

Delany, Mary. *The Autobiography and Correspondence of Mrs. Delany, vol. 1*. Edited by Sarah Chauncey Woolsey. Boston: Roberts Bros., 1879.

de Moor, Tine, and Jan Luiten van Zanden. "Girl Power: The European Marriage Market and Labour Patterns in the North Sea Region in the Late Medieval and Early Modern Period." *Economic History Review* 63, no. 1 (2010): 1–33.

Deresiewicz, William. *Jane Austen and the Romantic Poets*. New York: Columbia University Press, 2005.

de Rougemont, Denis. *Love in the Western World*. Translated by Montgomery Belgion. Revised edition. Princeton, NJ: Princeton University Press, 1982.

Dickens, Charles. *Great Expectations*. London: Penguin, 1996. First published 1860–1861.

———. *Little Dorrit*. New York: Penguin, 1998. First published 1857.

———. *Our Mutual Friend*. Edited by Adrian Poole. New York: Penguin, 1997. First published 1865.

Dodd, M. H. "Jane Austen and Charlotte Yonge." *Notes & Queries* 193, no. 22 (October 1948): 476–478.

Duckworth, Alistair. *The Improvement of the Estate: A Study of Jane Austen's Novels*. Baltimore: Johns Hopkins University Press, 1971.

Dunlap, Barbara. "*Heartsease* and *Mansfield Park*." *Journal of the Charlotte M. Yonge Fellowship* 2 (1997): 1–2.

———. "Jane Austen and Charlotte Yonge: The Heathcote Connection." *Charlotte Yonge Fellowship Review* 6 (1997–1998).

Eagleton, Terry. *Myths of Power: A Marxist Study of the Brontës*. London: Macmillan, 1975.

———. *The Rape of Clarissa: Writing, Sexuality and Class Struggle in Samuel Richardson*. Minneapolis: University of Minnesota Press, 1982.

Eaves, T. C. Duncan, and Ben D. Kimpel. *Samuel Richardson: A Biography*. Oxford: Clarendon, 1971.

Ehrenpreis, Anne Henry. "*Northanger Abbey*: Jane Austen and Charlotte Smith." *Nineteenth-Century Fiction* 25, no. 3 (December 1970): 343–348.

Eliot, George. *Adam Bede*. Edited by Carol A. Martin. New York: Oxford University Press, 2008. First published 1859.

———. *Daniel Deronda*. New York: Oxford University Press, 2014. First published 1876.

———. "The History of *Adam Bede*." In *Adam Bede*. Edited by Carol A. Martin. New York: Oxford University Press, 2008. First published 1859.

———. *Middlemarch*. Edited by Rosemary Ashton. New York: Penguin, 1994. First published 1871–1872.

———. *The Mill on the Floss*. Edited by A. S. Byatt. New York: Penguin, 2003.

Eller, Cynthia. *Gentlemen and Amazons: The Myth of Matriarchal Prehistory, 1861–1900*. Berkeley: University of California Press, 2011.

Elliott, Dorice Williams. *The Angel out of the House: Philanthropy and Gender in Nineteenth-Century England*. Charlottesville: University Press of Virginia, 2002.

Ellis, Havelock. *Studies in the Psychology of Sex*. Vol. 4. Middlesex: Echo Library, 2007.

Ellis, Sarah Stickney. *The Daughters of England: Their Position in Society, Character, and Responsibilities*. New York: D. Appleton, 1842.

———. *Women of England, Their Social Duties and Domestic Habits*. New York: D. Appleton, 1843.

Ellison, Katherine. "Introduction to the *Gentlewoman's Companion*." Emory Women Writers Project, 1999. http://womenwriters.library.emory.edu/essay.php?level=div&id=gc_complete_000.

Engels, Friedrich. *The Origin of the Family, Private Property, and the State*. Translated by Ernest Untermann. Chicago: Charles H. Kerr, 1902. First published 1884.

England, Paula. "The Separative Self: Androcentric Bias in Neoclassical Assumptions." In *Beyond Economic Man: Feminist Theory and Economics*. Edited by Marianne A. Ferber and Julie A. Nelson, 37–53. Chicago: University of Chicago Press, 1993.

Esmail, Jennifer. *Reading Victorian Deafness: Signs and Sounds in Victorian Literature and Culture*. Columbus: Ohio State Press, 2013.

The Etiquette of Love, Courtship and Marriage. London: Simpkin, Marshall, 1847.

Evans, Mary. " 'Falling in Love with Love is Falling for Make-Believe': Ideologies of Romance in Post-Enlightenment Culture." *Theory Culture Society* 15, nos. 3–4 (August 1998): 265–275.

Featherstone, Mike. "Love and Eroticism: An Introduction." *Theory Culture Society* 15, nos. 3–4 (August 1998): 1–18.

Feiner, Susan F. "A Portrait of *Homo economicus* as a Young Man." In *The New Economic Criticism*. Edited by Martha Woodmansee and Mark Osteen, 164–179. New York: Routledge, 1999.

Felski, Rita. "Context Stinks!" *New Literary History* 42, no. 4 (Autumn 2011): 573–591.

Feltes, N. N. *Modes of Production of Victorian Novels*. Chicago: University of Chicago Press, 1986.

Ferguson, Frances. "Rape and the Rise of the Novel." *Representations* 20 (Autumn 1987): 88–112.

Festa, Lynn. *Sentimental Figures of Empire in Eighteenth-Century Britain and France*. Baltimore: Johns Hopkins University Press, 2006.

Feurer, Rosemary. "The Meaning of 'Sisterhood': The British Women's Movement and Protective Labor Legislation, 1870–1900." *Victorian Studies* 31, no. 2 (Winter 1988): 233–260.

Flannery, Denis. *On Sibling Love, Queer Attachment, and American Writing.* Aldershot, UK: Ashgate, 2007.

Flint, Kate. Introduction to *Can You Forgive Her?*, by Anthony Trollope. New York: Oxford University Press, 2012.

———. "Women Writers, Women's Issues." In *Cambridge Companion to the Brontës.* Edited by Heather Glen, 170–191. Cambridge: Cambridge University Press, 2002.

Foucault, Michel. *The History of Sexuality: Vol 1, An Introduction.* Translated by Robert Hurley. New York: Vintage Books, 1990. First English edition 1978.

Frawley, Maria. *Invalidism and Identity in Nineteenth-Century Britain.* Chicago: University of Chicago Press, 2004.

Free, Melissa. "Freaks that Matter: The Dolls' Dressmaker, the Doctor's Assistant, and the Limits of Difference." In *Victorian Freaks: The Social Context of Freakery in Britain.* Edited by Marlene Tromp, 259–282. Columbus: Ohio State Press, 2008.

Freeman, Michael J. *Railways and the Victorian Imagination.* New Haven, CT: Yale University Press, 1999.

Freud, Sigmund. *Totem and Taboo.* Translated by A. A. Brill. New York: Penguin, 1938. First published 1919.

Frost, Ginger. *Promises Broken: Courtship, Class, and Gender in Victorian England.* Charlottesville: University Press of Virginia, 1995.

Fuller, Miriam Rheingold. "'Let Me Go, Mr. Thorpe; Isabella, Do Not Hold Me!': *Northanger Abbey* and the Domestic Gothic." *Persuasions* 32 (2010): 90–104.

Furneaux, Holly. *Queer Dickens: Erotics, Families, Masculinities.* New York: Oxford University Press, 2009.

Gagnier, Regenia. "The Law of Progress and the Ironies of Individualism in the Nineteenth Century." *New Literary History* 31, no. 2 (2000): 315–336.

Gallagher, Catherine. "Immanent Victorian." *Representations* 90, no. 1 (Spring 2005): 61–74.

Galperin, William H. *The Historical Austen.* Philadelphia: University of Pennsylvania Press, 2003.

Garber, Marjorie. *Vice Versa: Bisexuality and the Eroticism of Everyday Life.* New York: Simon and Schuster, 1995.

Garland Thomson, Rosemarie. *Freakery: Cultural Spectacles of the Extraordinary Body.* New York: New York University Press, 1996.

Gérin, Winifred. *Emily Brontë.* New York: Oxford University Press, 1971.

Gerson, Gal. "Liberal Feminism: Individuality and Oppositions in Wollstonecraft and Mill." *Political Studies* 50, no. 4 (2002): 794–810.

Gevirtz, Karen Bloom. *Life after Death: Widows and the English Novel, Defoe to Austen.* Newark: University of Delaware Press, 2005.

Giddens, Anthony. *The Transformation of Intimacy: Sexuality, Love and Eroticism in Modern Societies*. Stanford, CA: Stanford University Press, 1992.

Gies, Frances, and Joseph Gies. *Marriage and the Family in the Middle Ages*. New York: Harper and Row, 1987.

Gilbert, Pamela. Introduction to *Cometh Up as a Flower*, by Rhoda Broughton. Peterborough, ON: Broadview, 2010.

———. "Ouida and the Canon." In *Ouida and Victorian Popular Fiction*. Edited by Jane Jordan and Andrew King, 37–51. Burlington, VT: Ashgate, 2013.

Gilbert, Sandra, and Susan Gubar. *The Madwoman in the Attic*. New Haven, CT: Yale University Press, 2000.

Gillis, John R. *For Better, for Worse: British Marriages, 1600 to the Present*. New York: Oxford University Press, 1985.

Golightly, Jennifer. *The Family, Marriage, and Radicalism in British Women's Novels of the 1790s: Public Affection and Private Affliction*. Lewisburg, PA: Bucknell University Press, 2012.

Goodlad, Lauren. *Victorian Literature and the Victorian State: Character and Governance in a Liberal Society*. Baltimore: Johns Hopkins University Press, 2003.

Gowling, Laura. *Domestic Dangers: Women, Words, and Sex in Early Modern London*. Oxford: Clarendon, 1996.

Graver, Suzanne. *George Eliot and Community: A Study in Social Theory and Fictional Form*. Berkeley and Los Angeles: University of California Press, 1984.

Grayling, A. C. *Meditations for the Humanist: Ethics for a Secular Age*. New York: Oxford University Press, 2002.

Greenblatt, Stephen. "Fiction and Friction." In *Reconstructing Individualism: Autonomy, Individuality, and the Self in Western Thought*. Edited by Thomas C. Heller, Morton Sosna, and David E. Wellbery, 30–52. Stanford, CA: Stanford University Press, 1986.

Greiner, Rae. *Sympathetic Realism in Nineteenth-Century British Fiction*. Baltimore: Johns Hopkins University Press, 2012.

Gregory, John. *A Father's Legacy to His Daughters*. London: printed and sold by H. D. Symonds, Paternoster Row, 1793.

Green, Katherine Sobba. *The Courtship Novel 1740–1820: A Feminized Genre*. Lexington: University Press of Kentucky, 1991.

Greeson, Jennifer Rae. "The Prehistory of Possessive Individualism." *PMLA* 127, no. 4 (October 2012): 918–924.

Gross, Gloria Sibyl. "Flights into Illness: Some Characters in Jane Austen." In *Literature and Medicine During the Eighteenth Century*. Edited by Marie Mulvey Roberts and Roy Porter, 188–199. London: Routledge, 1993.

Grossman, Jonathan. *Charles Dickens's Networks; Public Transport and the Novel*. New York: Oxford University Press, 2012.

Gruner, Elizabeth Rose. "Born and Made: Sisters, Brothers, and the Deceased Wife's Sister Bill." *Signs* 24, no. 2 (Winter 1999): 423–447.

Habermas, Jürgen. *The Structural Transformation of the Public Sphere*. Cambridge, MA: MIT Press, 1991.

Hadley, Elaine. *Living Liberalism: Practical Citizenship in Mid-Victorian Britain*. Chicago: University of Chicago Press, 2010.

Hager, Kelly. *Dickens and the Rise of Divorce: The Failed Marriage Plot and the Novel Tradition*. Burlington, VT: Ashgate, 2010.

Haggerty, George. "Fanny Price: 'Is she solemn?—Is she queer?—Is she prudish?'" *The Eighteenth Century* 53, no. 2 (Summer 2012): 175–188.

Hall, Lynda A. "A View from Confinement: *Persuasion*'s Resourceful Mrs. Smith." *NCGS* 7, no. 3 (Winter 2011). http://www.ncgsjournal.com/issue73/hall.htm.

Hammerton, A. James. *Cruelty and Companionshiop: Conflict in Nineteenth-Century Married Life*. New York: Routledge, 1992.

———. "Victorian Marriage and the Law of Matrimonial Cruelty." *Victorian Studies* 33, no. 2 (1990): 269–292.

Hardy, Barbara. *George Eliot: A Critic's Biography*. London: Bloomsbury, 2006.

Harman, Barbara Leah. *The Feminine Political Novel in Victorian England*. Charlottesville: University Press of Virginia, 1998.

Harth, Erica. "The Virtue of Love: Lord Hardwicke's Marriage Act." *Cultural Critique* 9 (Spring 1988): 123–154.

Hatfield, Elaine. "Passionate and Companionate Love." In *The Psychology of Love*. Edited by Robert J. Sternberg and Michael L. Barnes, 191–217. New Haven, CT: Yale University Press 1988.

Held, Virginia. *The Ethics of Care: Personal, Political, and Global*. New York: Oxford University Press, 2006.

Heller, Tamar. "That Muddy, Polluted Flood of Earthly Love." In *Victorian Sensations: Essays on a Scandalous Genre*. Edited by Kimberly Harrison and Richard Fantina, 87–101. Columbus: Ohio State Press, 2006.

Helsinger, Elizabeth K., Robin Lauterbach Sheets, and William Veeder. *The Woman Question: Social Issues, 1837–1883, vol. 11 of The Woman Question: Society and LIterature in Britain and America, 1837–1883*. New York: Garland Publishing 1983.

Herbert, Christopher. "He Knew He Was Right, Mrs. Lynn Linton, and the Duplicities of Victorian Marriage." *Texas Studies in Language and Literature* 25, no. 3 (Fall 1983): 448–469.

Heydt-Stevenson, Jillian. *Austen's Unbecoming Conjunctions: Subversive Laughter, Embodied History*. New York: Palgrave Macmillan, 2008.

———. "Northanger Abbey, Desmond, and History." *The Wordsworth Circle* 44, nos. 2–3 (Spring–Summer 2013): 140–148.

Heywood, Christopher. "Yorkshire Slavery in Wuthering Heights." *The Review of English Studies* 38, no. 150 (May 1987): 184–198.

Hill, Georgina O'Brien. "Charlotte Yonge's Goosedom." *Nineteenth-Century Gender Studies* 8, no. 1 (Spring 2012). http://www.ncgsjournal.com/issue81/issue81.htm.

Hillyer, Barbara. *Feminism and Disability.* Norman: University of Oklahoma Press, 1993.

Hobby, Elaine. *Virtue of Necessity: English Women's Writing, 1646–1688.* London: Virago, 1988.

Houlbrooke, Ralph A. *The English Family 1450–1700.* London and New York: Longman, 1984.

Howell, Martha. "The Properties of Marriage in Late Medieval Europe: Commercial Wealth and the Creation of Modern Marriage." In *Love, Marriage, and Family Ties in the Later Middle Ages.* Edited by Isabel Davis, Miriam Müller, and Sarah Rees Jones, 17–61. Turnhout: Brepols, 2003.

Hudson, Glenda A. *Sibling Love and Incest in Jane Austen's Fiction.* New York: St. Martin's, 1992.

H. W. H. *How to Choose a Wife.* London: Partridge, Oakey, 1855.

Jalland, Pat. *Women, Marriage, and Politics 1860–1914.* Oxford: Oxford University Press, 1986.

James, Henry. *The Portrait of a Lady.* New York: Oxford University Press, 2009. First published 1881.

Jameson, Anna. *The Communion of Labour: A Second Lecture on the Social Employments of Women.* London: Logman, Brown, Green, Longmans, and Roberts, 1856. First published 1855.

Jameson, Frederic. *The Antinomies of Realism.* New York: Verso, 2015.

"Jane Austen." *St. Paul's*, March 1870, 631–643. Reprinted in *Jane Austen: The Critical Heritage vol. 1, 1811–1870.* Edited by B. C. Southam, 231–243. London: Routledge, 1979.

Jankowiak, William, ed. *Romantic Passion: A Universal Experience?* New York: Columbia University Press, 1995.

Jankowiak, William, and Thomas Paladino. "Desiring Sex, Longing for Love: A Tripartite Conundrum." In *Intimacies: Love and Sex Across Cultures.* Edited by. William Jankowiak, 1–36. New York: Columbia University Press, 2008.

Jay, Elisabeth. *Mrs Oliphant: "A Fiction to Herself": A Literary Life.* Oxford: Clarendon, 1995.

John, Juliet. *Dickens's Villains: Melodrama, Character, Popular Culture.* New York: Oxford University Press, 2001.

Johnson, Claudia. *Jane Austen: Women, Politics, and the Novel.* Chicago: University of Chicago Press, 1988.

Jones, Wendy. *Consensual Fictions: Women, Liberalism, and the English Novel.* Toronto: University of Toronto Press, 2005.

Jordan, Ellen. *The Women's Movement and Women's Employment in Nineteenth Century Britain.* London and New York: Routledge, 1999.

———. "'Women's Work in the World': The Birth of a Discourse, London, 1857." *Nineteenth-Century Feminisms* 1 (1999): 12–38.

Judd, Catherine. *Bedside Seductions: Nursing and the Victorian Imagination, 1830–1880*. New York: St. Martin's, 1998.

Justice, George. "*Northanger Abbey* as Anti-Courtship Novel?" *Persuasions* 20 (1998): 185–195.

Kavanagh, James H. *Emily Brontë*. New York: Basil Blackwell, 1985.

Kaye, J. W. "The Non-Existence of Women." *North British Review* 23 (1855): 536–562.

Keith, Lois. *Take Up Thy Bed and Walk: Death, Disability, and Cure in Classic Fiction for Girls*. New York: Routledge, 2001.

Kennard, Jean E. *Victims of Convention*. Hamden, CT: Archon Books, 1978.

Keymer, Thomas. "Shakespeare in the Novel." In *Shakespeare in the Eighteenth Century*. Edited by Fiona Ritchie and Peter Sabor, 118–140. Cambridge: Cambridge University Press, 2012.

Kilroy, James F. *The Nineteenth-Century English Novel: Family Ideology and Narrative Form*. New York: Palgrave Macmillan, 2007.

King, Margaret F. "'Certain Learned Ladies': Trollope's *Can You Forgive Her?* and the Langham Place Circle." *VLC* 21 (1993): 307–326.

Kittay, Eva Feder. *Love's Labor: Essays on Women, Equality, and Dependence*. New York: Routledge, 1999.

Knox-Shaw, Peter. *Jane Austen and the Enlightenment*. Cambridge: Cambridge University Press, 2004.

Kuklick, Henrika. *A New History of Anthropology*. Oxford: Wiley-Blackwell, 2007

———. *The Savage Within: The Social History of British Anthropology, 1885–1945*. Cambridge: Cambridge University Press, 1993.

Kuper, Adam. "Changing the Subject—about Cousin Marriage, among Other Things." *Journal of the Royal Anthropological Institute* 14 (2008): 717–735.

———. *Incest and Influence: The Private Life of Bourgeois England*. Cambridge, MA: Harvard University Press, 2009.

———. *The Invention of Primitive Society: Transformations of an Illusion*. New York: Routledge, 1988.

Lamonica, Drew. *"We Are Three Sisters": Self and Family in the Writing of the Brontës*. Columbia: University of Missouri Press, 2003.

Langland, Elizabeth. *Nobody's Angels: Middle-Class Women and Domestic Ideology in Victorian Culture*. Ithaca, NY: Cornell University Press, 1995.

Lanser, Susan. "Jane Austen's World of Sisterhood." In *The Sister Bond: A Feminist View of a Timeless Connection*. Edited by Toni A. H. McNaron, 51–67. New York: Pergamon, 1985.

Latimer, Bonnie. *Making Gender, Culture, and the Self in the Fiction of Samuel Richardson*. Burlington, VT: Ashgate, 2013.

Lawless, Elaine J. "The Silencing of the Preacher Woman: The Muted Message of George Eliot's *Adam Bede*." *Women's Studies* 18, nos. 2–3 (1990): 249–268.

Lawson, Kate. "Indian Mutiny/English Mutiny: National Governance in Charlotte Yonge's *The Clever Woman of the Family*." *VLC* 42, no. 3 (September 2014): 439–455.

Leavis, Q. D. *Collected Essays: Vol 3, The Novel of Religious Controversy*. Edited by G. Singh. Cambridge: Cambridge University Press, 1989.

———. "A Fresh Approach to Wuthering Heights." In *Lectures in America*, 85–138. New York: Pantheon, 1969.

Leites, Edmund. *The Puritan Conscience and Modern Sexuality*. New Haven, CT: Yale University Press, 1986.

Lévi-Strauss, Claude. *Elementary Structures of Kinship*. Translated by James Harle Bell and John Richard von Sturmer. Edited by Rodney Needham. Boston: Beacon, 1969.

Lemmings, David. "Marriage and the Law in the Eighteenth Century: Hardwicke's Marriage Act of 1753." *The Historical Journal* 39, no. 2 (June 1996): 339–360.

Levine, George. *Darwin and the Novelists: Patterns of Science in Victorian Fiction*. Chicago: University of Chicago Press, 1988.

Lewis, Sarah. *Women's Mission*. London: John W. Parker, 1839.

Lindholm, Charles. "Love and Structure." *Theory Culture Society* 15, nos. 3–4 (August 1998): 243–263.

Lipton, Emma. *Affections of the Mind: The Politics of Sacramental Marriage in Late Medieval English Literature*. Notre Dame, IN: University of Notre Dame Press, 2007.

Logan, Peter Melville. *Victorian Fetishism: Intellectuals and Primitives*. Albany: SUNY Press, 2009.

———. "Victorian Psychology and Anthropology: In Theory." Paper delivered at "Victorian Theory?" CUNY Victorian Conference. New York, May 6, 2010.

Losano, Antonia. *The Woman Painter in Victorian Literature*. Columbus: Ohio State Press, 2008.

Lowe, Brigid. *Victorian Fiction and the Insights of Sympathy: An Alternative to the Hermeneutics of Suspicion*. London: Anthem, 2007.

Lubbock, Sir John. *The Origin of Civilisation and the Primitive Condition of Man*. New York: D. Appleton, 1898.

Luhmann, Niklas. *Love as Passion: The Codification of Intimacy*. Translated Jeremy Gaines and Doris L. Jones. Cambridge, MA: Harvard University Press, 1986.

Lutz, Deborah. *The Dangerous Lover: Gothic Villains, Byronism, and the Nineteenth-Century*. Columbus: Ohio State University, 2006.

Macfarlane, Alan. *The Origins of English Individualism*. Oxford: Blackwell, 1978.

———. "Review of *The Family, Sex, and Marriage*." *History and Theory* 18, no. 1 (February 1979): 103–126.

Macpherson, Sandra. "Lovelace, Ltd." *ELH* 65, no. 1 (Spring 1998): 99–121.

Magee, William H. "The Happy Marriage: The Influence of Charlotte Smith on Jane Austen." *Studies in the Novel* 7, no. 1 (Spring 1975): 120–132.

Maine, Henry Sumner. *Ancient Law: Its Connection with the Early History of Society, and its Relation to Modern Ideas*. New York: Charles Scribner, 1864.

Marcus, Sharon. *Between Women: Friendship, Desire, and Marriage in Victorian England*. Princeton, NJ: Princeton University Press, 2007.

Mare, Margaret, and Alicia Percival. *Victorian Best-Seller: The World of Charlotte Yonge*. London: Harrap, 1947.

Marks, Sylvia Kasey. *Sir Charles Grandison: The Compleat Conduct Book*. Cranbury, NJ: Associated University Presses, 1986.

Marsden, Jean I. "Improving Shakespeare: From the Restoration to Garrick." *The Cambridge Companion to Shakespeare on Stage*. Edited by Stanley Wells and Sarah Stanton, 21–36. Cambridge: Cambridge University Press, 2002.

Martin, Mary Patricia. "Reading Reform in Richardson's *Clarissa*." *SEL* 37, no. 3 (Summer 1997): 595–614.

Martin, Maureen M. "What Does Emma Want? Sovereignty and Sexuality in Austen's *Emma*." *Nineteenth-Century Feminisms* 3 (Fall/Winter 2000): 10–24.

Mascarenhas, Kiran. "*John Halifax, Gentleman*: A Counter Story." In *Antifeminism and the Victorian Novel: Rereading Nineteenth-Century Women Writers*. Edited by Tamara Silvia Wagner, 255–270. Amherst, NY: Cambria, 2009.

Mascuch, Michael. *Origins of the Individualist Self: Autobiography and Self-Identity in England, 1591–1791*. Stanford, CA: Stanford University Press, 1996.

May, Leila Silvana. *Disorderly Sisters: Sibling Relations and Sororal Resistance in Nineteenth-Century British Literature*. Lewisburg, PA: Bucknell University Press, 2001.

McAleavey, Maia. *The Bigamy Plot: Sensation and Convention in the Victorian Novel*. Cambridge: Cambridge University Press, 2015.

McGuire, Kathryn B. "The Incest Taboo in *Wuthering Heights*: A Modern Appraisal." *American Imago* 45 (1988): 217–224.

McKeon, Michael. *The Origins of the English Novel, 1600–1740*. 15th anniv. ed. Baltimore: Johns Hopkins University Press, 2002.

McLennan, John. *Primitive Marriage: An Inquiry into the Origin of the Form of Capture in Marriage Ceremonies*. Edinburgh, UK: Adam and Charles Black, 1865.

———. *Studies in Ancient History, Second Series*. London: Macmillan, 1896.

Macpherson, C. B. *The Political Theory of Possessive Individualism: Hobbes to Locke*. Oxford: Clarendon, 1962.

McRuer, Robert. "Introduction: Compulsory Able-Bodiedness and Queer/Disabled Existence." In *Crip Theory: Cultural Signs of Queerness and Disability*, 1–32. New York: New York University Press, 2006.

McSheffrey, Shannon. *Marriage, Sex, and Civic Culture in Late Medieval London*. Philadelphia: University of Pennsylvania Press, 2006.

Meehan, Johanna, ed. *Feminists Read Habermas: Gendering the Subject of Discourse*. New York: Routledge, 1995.

Menon, Patricia. *Austen, Eliot, Charlotte Brontë, and the Mentor-Lover*. New York: Palgrave Macmillan, 2003.

Meyer, Susan. *Imperialism at Home: Race and Victorian Women's Fiction.* Ithaca, NY: Cornell University Press, 2006.

Michie, Elsie. *The Vulgar Question of Money: Heiresses, Materialism, and the Novel of Manners From Jane Austen to Henry James.* Baltimore: Johns Hopkins University Press, 2011.

Michie, Helena. *Victorian Honeymoons: Journey to the Conjugal.* Cambridge: Cambridge University Press, 2007.

Midgeley, Clare. *Feminism and Empire: Women Activists in Imperial Britain, 1790–1865.* New York: Routledge, 2007.

Mill, John Stuart. "The Subjection of Women." *On Liberty and The Subjection of Women.* Edited by Alan Ryan. New York: Penguin, 2006. First published 1869.

Miller, D. A. *The Secret of Style.* Princeton, NJ: Princeton University Press, 2003.

Milne, John Duguid. *Industrial Employment of Women in the Middle and Lower Ranks.* 2nd ed. London: Longman, Green, 1870.

Milton, John. *The Doctrine and Discipline of Divorce.* 1644 (second, expanded, and revised) edition owned by Rauner Library at Dartmouth College (Val. 824/M64/P8). Available at the Milton Reading Room, http://www.dartmouth.edu/~milton/reading_room/ddd/book_1/.

Mintz, Alan. *George Eliot and the Novel of Vocation.* Cambridge, MA: Harvard University Press, 1978.

Mitchell, Charlotte. "*Mansfield Park* and *Heartsease*." Unpublished paper read to the UCL English Department. London, 1997.

Moretti, Franco. *Atlas of the European Novel, 1800–1900.* New York: Verso, 1998.

Morgan, Lewis Henry. *Ancient Society; or, Researches in the Lines of Human Progress from Savagery through Barbarism to Civilization.* New York: Henry Holt, 1877.

Moruzi, Kristine, "'The Inferiority of Women': Complicating Charlotte Yonge's Perception of Girlhood in *The Monthly Packet*." In *Antifeminism and the Victorian Novel: Rereading Nineteenth Century Women Writers.* Edited by Tamara S. Wagner, 57–76. Amherst: Cambria, 2009.

Muldrew, Craig. "From a 'Light Cloak' to an 'Iron Cage': Historical Changes in the Relation between Community and Individualism." In *Communities in Early Modern England.* Edited by Alexandra Shepard and Phil Withington, 156–177. Manchester: Manchester University Press, 2000.

Nardin, Jane. *He Knew She Was Right: The Independent Woman in the Novels of Anthony Trollope.* Carbondale: Southern Illinois University Press, 1989.

Nazar, Hina. *Enlightened Sentiments: Judgment and Autonomy in the Age of Sensibility.* New York: Fordham University Press, 2012.

Nedelsky, Jennifer. "Reconceiving Autonomy: Sources, Thoughts and Possibilities." *Yale Journal of Law and Feminism* 8 (1989): 7–36.

Neely, Carol Thomas. *Broken Nuptials in Shakespeare's Plays.* New Haven, CT: Yale University Press, 1985.

Nelson, Claudia. *Family Ties in Victorian England.* Victorian Life and Times Series. Edited by Sally Mitchell. London and Westport: Praeger, 2007.

Nicholson, Linda J. *Gender and History: The Limits of Social Theory in the Age of the Family.* New York: Columbia University Press, 1986.

Nightingale, Florence. "Cassandra." In *Florence Nightingale's Cassandra,* 25–55. New York: Feminist Press, 1979. First published 1860.

Noddings, Nel. *Caring: A Feminine Approach to Ethics and Moral Education.* Berkeley: University of California Press, 1984.

Noddings, Nel. "A Response to Card, Hoagland, Houston." *Hypatia* 5, no. 1 (Spring 1990): 120–126.

———. *Starting at Home: Caring and Social Policy.* Berkeley: University of California Press, 2002.

"Notices of Books," Review of *North America*, by Anthony Trollope. *English Woman's Journal* 10 (Sept 1862–Feb 1863): 61–66.

Nussbaum, Martha. *Frontiers of Justice: Disability, Nationality, Species Membership.* Cambridge, MA: Harvard University Press, 2007.

O'Farrell, Mary Anne. "Blindness Envy: Victorians in the Parlors of the Blind." *PMLA* 127.3 (May 2012): 512–525.

O'Hara, Diana. *Courtship and Constraint: Rethinking the Making of Marriage in Tudor England.* Manchester, UK: Manchester University Press, 2000.

O'Toole, Tess. "Reconfiguring the Family in *Persuasion.*" *Persuasions* 15 (1993): 200–206.

Oliphant, Margaret. "The Condition of Women." *Blackwood's Edinburgh Magazine.* February 1858. Reprinted in *Criminals, Idiots, Women, and Minors.* Edited by Susan Hamilton, 181–201. Peterborough, ON: Broadview, 1995.

———. "Miss Austen and Miss Mitford." *Blackwood's Edinburgh Magazine* 107 (March 1870): 294–305. Reprinted in *Jane Austen: The Critical Heritage vol. 1, 1811–1870.* Edited by B. C. Southam, 221–229. London: Routledge, 1979.

———. *Miss Marjoribanks.* Edited by Elisabeth Jay. New York: Penguin, 1998. First published 1865.

———. *Phoebe Junior.* Edited by Elizabeth Langland. Peterborough, ON: Broadview, 2002. First published 1876.

Orlin, Lena Cowen. "Rewriting Stone's Renaissance." *Huntingdon Library Quarterly* 64, nos. 1–2 (2002): 189–230.

Ostry, Elaine. *Social Dreaming: Dickens and the Fairy Tale.* New York: Routledge, 2002.

Paxton, Nancy L. *George Eliot and Herbert Spencer: Feminism, Evolutionism, and the Reconstruction of Gender.* Princeton, NJ: Princeton University Press, 1991.

Peace, William J. "Head Nurses," *Atrium* 12 (Winter 2014): 20–22.

Pedersen, Frederik. *Marriage Disputes in Medieval England.* London: Hambledon, 2000.

Perkin, Harold. *The Rise of Professional Society: England Since 1880.* London: Routledge, 1989.

Perry, Ruth. "Mary Astell and the Feminist Critique of Possessive Individualism." *Eighteenth-Century Studies* 23, no. 4 (Summer 1990): 444–457.

———. *Novel Relations: The Transformation of Kinship in English Literature and Culture, 1748–1818.* Cambridge: Cambridge University Press, 2004.

Peterson, Linda, *Traditions of Victorian Women's Autobiography: The Poetics and Politics of Life Writing.* Charlottesville: University of Virginia Press, 1999.

Peterson, M. Jeanne. *Family, Love, and Work in the Lives of Victorian Gentlewomen.* Bloomington: Indiana University Press, 1989.

Phegley, Jennifer. *Courtship and Marriage in Victorian England.* Santa Barbara: Praeger, 2012.

———. *Educating the Proper Woman Reader: Victorian Family Literary Magazines and the Cultural Health of the Nation.* Columbus: Ohio State Press, 2004.

———. "Victorian Girls Gone Wild: Matrimonial Advertising and the Transformation of Courtship in the Popular Press." *Victorian Review* 39, no. 2 (Fall 2013): 129–146.

Phillips, Joshua. *English Fictions of Communal Identity, 1485–1603.* Burlington, VT: Ashgate, 2010.

Pike, Judith E. "My Name Was Isabella Linton": Coverture, Domestic Violence, and Mrs. Heathcliff's Narrative in Wuthering Heights." *Nineteenth-Century Literature* 64, no. 3 (December 2009): 347–383.

Pocock, J. G. A. "The Myth of John Locke and the Obsession with Liberalism." *John Locke: Papers Read at a Clark Library Seminar.* Los Angeles: William Andrews Clark Memorial Library, 1980.

———. "Review: Alan Macfarlane, *The Origins of English Individualism.*" *History and Theory* 19, no. 1 (February 1980): 100–105.

Polhemus, Robert. *Erotic Faith: Being in Love from Jane Austen to D. H. Lawrence.* Chicago: University of Chicago Press, 1990.

Pollak, Ellen. *Incest and the English Novel, 1684–1814.* Baltimore: Johns Hopkins University Press, 2003.

Preus, Nicholas E. "Sexuality in *Emma:* A Case History." *Studies in the Novel* 23, no. 2 (1991): 196–216.

Pritchard, Will. "Pope, Richardson, and 'Clarissa.'" *Literary Imagination* (June 20, 2012): 8–12.

Psomiades, Kathy A. "He Knew He Was Right: The Sensational Tyranny of the Sexual Contract and the Problem of Liberal Politics." In *The Politics of Gender in Anthony Trollope's Novels.* Edited by H. M. Marwick, Deborah Morse, and Regenia Gagnier, 31–44. Aldershot: Ashgate, 2009.

———. "Heterosexual Exchange and Other Victorian Fictions: *The Eustace Diamonds* and Victorian Anthropology." *Novel* 33, no. 1 (Fall 1999): 93–118.

———. "The Marriage Plot in Theory." *Novel* 43, no. 1 (Spring 2010): 53–59.

Puckett, Kent. *Bad Form: Social Mistakes and the Nineteenth-Century Novel.* New York: Oxford University Press, 2008.

Pykett, Lyn. *Emily Brontë.* Savage, MD: Barnes and Noble Books, 1989.

Quayson, Ato. *Aesthetic Nervousness: Disability and the Crisis of Representation.* New York: Columbia University Press, 2007.

Rena-Dozier, Emily. "Gothic Criticisms: Wuthering Heights and Nineteenth-Century Literary Criticism." *ELH* 77, no. 3 (Fall 2010): 757–775.

Richardson, Leslie. "Leaving Her Father's House: Astell, Locke, and Clarissa's Body Politic." *Studies in Eighteenth-Century Culture* 34 (2005): 151–171.

Richardson, Samuel. *Clarissa: Or, the History of a Young Lady: Comprehending the Most Important Concerns of Private Life, and Particularly Showing the Distresses That May Attend the Misconduct Both of Parents and Children, in Relation to Marriage*. Edited by Angus Ross. New York: Penguin, 1985. First published 1747–1748.

Rivers, Bronwyn. *Women at Work in the Victorian Novel: The Question of Middle-Class Women's Employment 1840–1870*. Lewiston, New York: Edwin Mellen, 2006.

Robinson, Amy J. "Margaret Oliphant's *Miss Marjoribanks*: A Victorian *Emma*." *Persuasions* 30 (2008): 67–75.

Rowland, Ann Wierda. "Sentimental Fiction." In *The Cambridge Companion to Fiction in the Romantic Period*, 191–206. Cambridge: Cambridge University Press, 2008.

Rubin, Gayle. "The Traffic in Women: Notes on the 'Political Economy' of Sex." *Feminist Anthropology: A Reader*. Edited by Ellen Lewin, 87–106. Oxford: Wiley Blackwell, 2006. First published 1975.

Sanders, Valerie. *The Brother-Sister Culture in Nineteenth Century Literature: From Austen to Woolf*. Hampshire, UK: Palgrave, 2002.

Savile, George, Marquis of Halifax. *The Lady's New Years Gift, or, Advice to a Daughter*. 3rd ed. London, 1688.

Schaffer, Talia. "Domesticity." *The Victorian Encyclopedia*. Edited by Dino Franco Felluga, Linda Hughes, and Pamela Gilbert. Oxford: Blackwells, 2015.

———. "Maiden Pairs: The Sororal Romance in *The Clever Woman of the Family*." *Victorian Antifeminism*. Edited by Tamara Silvia Wagner, 97–115. New York: Cambria, 2009.

———. *Novel Craft: Victorian Domestic Handicraft and Nineteenth-Century Fiction*. Oxford: Oxford University Press, 2011.

——— and Kelly Hager. Introduction to "Extending Families." *Victorian Review* 39, no. 2 (2013): 7–21.

Schivelbusch, Wolfgang. *The Railway Journey: The Industrialization of Time and Space in the Nineteenth Century*. Berkeley and Los Angeles: University of California Press, 1977.

Schotland, Sara D. "Who's That in Charge? It's Jenny Wren, 'The Person of the House.'" *Disability Studies Quarterly* 29, no. 3 (Summer 2009): n.p.

Sedgwick, Eve Kosofsky. *Between Men: English Literature and Male Homosocial Desire*. New York: Columbia University Press, 1985.

———. *The Epistemology of the Closet*. Berkeley and Los Angeles: University of California Press, 1990.

———. "Jane Austen and the Masturbating Girl." *Critical Inquiry* 17, no. 4 (Summer 1991): 818–837.

———. "Tales of the Avunculate." In *Tendencies*, 52–72. Durham, NC: Duke University Press, 1993.

Seebohm, Frederic. *The English Village Community.* London: Longmans, Green, 1915. First published 1883.

Shaffer, Julie. "Familial Love, Incest, and Female Desire in Late Eighteenth- and Early Nineteenth-Century British Women's Novels." *Criticism* 41, no. 1 (Winter 1999): 67–99.

Shanley, Mary Lydon. *Feminism, Marriage and the Law in Victorian England, 1850–1895.* Princeton, NJ: Princeton University Press, 1989.

Showalter, Elaine. "Dinah Mulock Craik and the Tactics of Sentiment: A Case Study in Victorian Female Authorship." *Feminist Studies* 2, nos. 2–3 (1975): 5–23.

———. *A Literature of Their Own: British Women Writers from Brontë to Lessing.* Revised edition. Princeton, NJ: Princeton University Press, 1999.

Siebers, Tobin. *Disability Theory.* Ann Arbor: University of Michigan Press, 2008.

Skilton, David. Introduction to *The Claverings*, by Anthony Trollope. New York: Oxford University Press, 1986.

Small, Helen. "Against Self Interest: Trollope and Realism." *Essays in Criticism* 62, no. 4 (2012): 396–416.

Smith, Charlotte. *Emmeline, or, The Orphan of the Castle.* Edited by Loraine Fletcher. Peterborough, ON: Broadview, 2003. First published 1788.

Smith, Johanna M. "'My Only Sister Now': Incest in *Mansfield Park.*" *Studies in the Novel* 19, no. 1 (Spring 1987): 1–15.

Smith, Peter. "Jane Austen's *Persuasion* and the Secret Conspiracy." *Cambridge Quarterly* 24, no. 4 (1995): 279–303.

[Smith, William Henry]. "Comte." *Blackwood's Edinburgh Magazine* 53, no. 329 (March 1843): 397–414.

Solomon, Eric. "The Incest Theme in Wuthering Heights." *Nineteenth-Century Fiction* 14 (1969): 80–83.

Solomon, Robert C. *Love: Emotion, Myth, and Metaphor.* New York: Prometheus Books, 1990.

Southam, B. C. *Jane Austen: The Critical Heritage, vol. 1, 1811–1870.* London: Routledge, 1979.

Stevenson, John Allen. "'Heathcliff is Me!': Wuthering Heights and the Question of Likeness." *NCL* 43, no. 1 (June 1988): 60–81.

Stocking, George W. Jr. *Victorian Anthropology.* New York: Free Press, 1987.

Stoddard Holmes, Martha. *Fictions of Affliction: Physical Disability in Victorian Culture.* Ann Arbor: University of Michigan Press, 2009.

———. "Victorian Fictions of Interdependency: Gaskell, Craik, and Yonge." *Journal of Literary Disability* 1, no. 2 (2007): 29–40.

Stolpa, Jennifer. "Dinah and the Debate Over Vocation in Adam Bede." *George Eliot-George Henry Lewes Studies* 42–43 (2002): 30–49.

Stone, Lawrence. *The Family, Sex, and Marriage in England, 1500–1800.* New York: Harper and Row, 1977.

———. "Love." In *The Past and Present Revisited*, 327–343. Abingdon: Routledge, 1987.

Stone, Marjorie. "Criticism on *Aurora Leigh:* An Overview." http://ebbarchive.org/criticism/Aurora_Leigh_Criticism_Overview.pdf.

Stoneman, Patsy. "Catherine Earnshaw's Journey to her Home Among the Dead: Fresh Thoughts on *Wuthering Heights* and 'Epipsychidion.'" *The Review of English Studies* 47, no. 188 (1996): 521–533.

———. Introduction to *Wuthering Heights*, by Emily Brontë. New York: Oxford University Press, 1995.

Sturrock, June. "*Emma* in the 1860s: Austen, Yonge, Oliphant, Eliot." *Women's Writing* 17, no. 2 (2010): 324–342.

———. "Money, Morals, and *Mansfield Park*: The West Indies Revisited." *Persuasions* 28 (2006): 176–184.

———. "Something to Do: Charlotte Yonge, Tractarianism and the Question of Women's Work." *Victorian Review* 18, no. 2 (Winter 1992): 28–48.

Surridge, Lisa. *Bleak Houses: Marital Violence in Victorian Fiction.* Columbus: Ohio University Press, 2005.

Swaert, Koenraad W. " 'Individualism' in the Mid-Nineteenth Century (1826–1860)." *Journal of the History of Ideas* 23, no. 1 (January–March 1962): 77–90.

Tadmor, Naomi. *Family and Friends in Eighteenth-Century England: Household, Kinship, and Patronage.* Cambridge: Cambridge University Press, 2001.

Tague, Ingrid H. "Love, Honor, and Obedience: Fashionable Women and the Discourse of Marriage in the Early Eighteenth Century." *Journal of British Studies* 40, no. 1 (January 2001): 76–106.

Tanner, Tony. *Jane Austen*. Cambridge, MA: Harvard University Press, 1986.

Taylor, Harriet. "The Enfranchisement of Women." London: Trübner, 1868. Reprint from *The Westminster Review*, July 1851.

Taylor, Mary. *The First Duty of Women: A Series of Articles Reprinted From the Victoria Magazine, 1865–1870.* London: Victoria, 1870.

Thiel, Elizabeth. *The Fantasy of Family: Nineteenth-Century Children's Literature and the Myth of the Domestic Ideal.* New York: Routledge, 2007.

Thomas, David Wayne. *Cultivating Victorians: Liberal Culture and the Aesthetic.* Philadelphia: University of Pennsylvania Press, 2004.

Thomason, Laura E. "Hester Chapone as a Living Clarissa in *Letters on Filial Obedience* and *A Matrimonial Creed.*" *Eighteenth-Century Fiction* 21, no. 3 (Spring 2009): 323–343.

———. *The Matrimonial Trap: Eighteenth-Century Women Writers Redefine Marriage.* Lewisburg, PA: Bucknell University Press, 2014.

Thompson, Helen. *Ingenuous Subjection: Compliance and Power in the Eighteenth-Century Domestic Novel.* Philadelphia: University of Pennsylvania Press, 2005.

Todd, Janet. "The Professional Wife in Jane Austen." In *Repossessing the Romantic Past.* Edited by Heather Glen and Paul Hamilton, 203–225. Cambridge: Cambridge University Press, 2006.

Todd, Margo. *Christian Humanism and the Puritan Social Order.* Cambridge: Cambridge University Press, 1987.

Tönnies, Ferdinand. *Community and Society (Gemeinschaft und Gesellschaft).* Translated by Charles P. Loomis. New York: Harper and Row, 1957.

Trollope, Anthony. *Can You Forgive Her?* New York: Oxford University Press, 2012. First published 1865.

———. *The Duke's Children.* Edited by Hermione Lee. New York: Oxford University Press World's Classics, 1983. First published 1880.

———. "On the Higher Education of Women." In *Four Lectures.* Edited by Morris L. Parrish. London: Constable, 1938.

———. *The Prime Minister.* Edited by Jennifer Uglow. New York: Oxford University Press, 1983. First published 1875–1876.

———. *Rachel Ray.* New York: Oxford University Press, 1988.

———. "The Rights of Women." *North America*, vol 1, 283–293. Philadelphia: J. B. Lippincott, 1863.

———. *The Vicar of Bullhampton.* Edited by David Skilton. Oxford: Oxford University Press, 1990. First published 1870.

Tromp, Marlene, ed. *Victorian Freaks: The Social Context of Freakery in Britain.* Columbus: Ohio State Press, 2008.

Tronto, Joan. *Moral Boundaries: A Political Argument for an Ethic of Care.* New York: Routledge, 1993.

Trumbach, Randolph. *The Rise of the Egalitarian Family.* New York: Academic Press, 1978.

Trumpener, Katie. *Bardic Nationalism: The Romantic Novel and the British Empire.* Princeton, NJ: Princeton University Press, 1997.

Tuite, Clara. "Domestivc Retrenchment and Imperial Expansion: The Property Plots of *Mansfield Park.*" In *The Postcolonial Jane Austen.* Edited by You-me Park and Rajeswari Sunder Rajan, 93–115. London: Routledge, 2000.

———. *Romantic Austen: Sexual Politics and the Literary Canon.* Cambridge: Cambridge University Press, 2002.

Tylor, Edward Burnet. *Researches into the Early History of Mankind and the Development of Civilization.* London: John Murray, 1865.

Ulrich, Laurel Thatcher. *A Midwife's Tale: The Life of Martha Ballard, Based on Her Diary 1785–1812.* New York: Vintage, 1990.

Vaninskaya, Anna. *William Morris and the Idea of Community: Romance, History, and Propaganda, 1880–1914.* Edinburgh, UK: Edinburgh University Press, 2010.

Vermilion, Mary. "Clarissa and the Marriage Act." *Eighteenth-Century Fiction* 9, no. 4 (July 1997): 395–414.

Vickery, Amanda. "Golden Age to Separate Spheres? A Review of the Categories and Chronology of English Women's History." *The Historical Journal* 36, no. 2 (June 1993): 383–414.

———. *The Gentleman's Daughter: Women's Lives in Georgian England*. New Haven, CT: Yale University Press, 1998.

von Sneidern, Maja-Lisa. "Wuthering Heights and the Liverpool Slave Trade." *ELH* 62, no. 1 (Spring 1995): 171–196.

Vranjes, Vlasta. *English Vows: Marriage Law and National Identity in the Nineteenth-Century Novel*. Unpublished manuscript.

Vrettos, Athena. *Somatic Fictions: Imagining Illness in Victorian Culture*. Stanford, CA: Stanford University Press, 1995.

Wagner, Tamara Silvia. "'If He Belonged to Me, I Should Not Like It At All': Managing Disability and Dependencies in Charlotte Yonge's *The Two Guardians*." *Nineteenth-Century Gender Studies* 4, no. 2 (Summer 2008). http://www.ncgs-journal.com/issue42/wagner.htm.

———. "Marriage Plots and 'Matters of More Importance': Sensationalising Self-Sacrifice in Victorian Domestic Fiction." *Antifeminism and the Victorian Novel: Rereading Nineteenth-Century Women Writers*. New York: Cambria, 2009, 137–154.

Waldman, Jack. *Memories, Life in the Twentieth Century in America*. Florida: privately printed, 1990.

Waldron, Mary. *Jane Austen and the Fiction of Her Time*. Cambridge: Cambridge University Press, 2004.

Wallace, Honor McKitrick. "Desire and the Female Protagonist: A Critique of Feminist Narrative Theory." *Style* 34, no. 2 (Summer 2000): 176–187.

Watt, Ian. *The Rise of the Novel: Studies in Defoe, Richardson and Fielding*. Berkeley and Los Angeles: University of California Press, 1957.

Wedgwood, Julia. "Female Suffrage, Considered Chiefly with Regard to its Indirect Results." In *Woman's Work and Woman's Culture*. Edited by Josephine E. Butler, 247–289. London: Macmillan, 1869.

Wendell, Susan. *The Rejected Body: Feminist Philosophical Reflections on Disability*. New York: Routledge, 1996.

Wheatley, Kim. "Death and Domestication in Charlotte Yonge's *The Clever Woman of the Family*." *SEL* 36, no. 4 (1996): 895–915.

Williams, Raymond. *The Country and the City*. New York: Oxford University Press, 1973.

———. "Dominant, Residual, and Emergent." In *Marxism and Literature*, 121–127. Oxford: Oxford University Press, 1977.

Wiltshire, John. *Jane Austen and the Body*. Cambridge: Cambridge University Press, 1994.

Withington, Phil, and Alexandra Shepard. "Introduction: Communities in Early Modern England." In *Communities in Early Modern England*. Edited by Alexandra Shepard and Phil Withington, 1–15. Manchester, UK: Manchester University Press, 2000.

Woloch, Alex. *The One and the Many: Minor Characters and the Space of the Protagonist in the Novel.* Princeton, NJ: Princeton University Press, 2003.

Wolfram, Sibyl. *In-Laws and Out-Laws: Kinship and Marriage in England.* London: Croom Helm, 1987.

Wollstonecraft, Mary. *A Vindication of the Rights of Women.* New York: Penguin Classics, 2004. First published 1792.

Woolf, Virginia. *A Room of One's Own.* New York: Harvest Books, 1989.

Woolley, Hannah. *The Gentlewoman's Companion; or a Guide to the Female Sex: Containing Directions of Behaviour in All Places, Companies, Relations, and Conditions, from Their Childhood to Old Age.* London, 1675.

Yaeger, Patricia. "Violence in the Sitting Room: *Wuthering Heights* and the Women's Novel." *Genre* 21 (1988): 203–229.

Yee, Nancy. "John Thorpe, Villain Ordinaire: The Modern Montoni/Schedoni." *Persuasions* 31, no 1 (Winter 2010): n.p. http://www.jasna.org.ezproxy.gc.cuny.edu/persuasions/on-line/vol31no1/yee.html.

Yonge, Charlotte. *The Clever Woman of the Family.* Edited by Clare A. Simmons. Peterborough, ON: Broadview, 2001. First published 1865.

———. *Heartsease.* London: Macmillan, 1868.

———. *The Magnum Bonum, or, Mother Carey's Brood.* London: Macmillan, 1889.

———. *Womankind.* Vol. 1. Leipzig: Bernhard Tauchnitz, 1878.

Young, Iris Marion. "Impartiality and the Civic Public: Some Implications of Feminist Critiques of Moral and Political Theory." In *Feminism as Critique: On the Politics of Gender*, 57–76. Minneapolis: University of Minnesota Press, 1987.

———. *Justice and the Politics of Difference.* Princeton, NJ: Princeton University Press, 1990.

Yousef, Nancy. *Isolated Cases: The Anxieties of Autonomy in Enlightenment Philosophy and Romantic Literature.* Ithaca, NY: Cornell University Press, 2004.

Index